BENEATH THE WIRES OF LONDON

Charlie Wyatt

Capital Transport

First published 2008

ISBN 978-1-85414-325-9

Published by Capital Transport Publishing,
P.O. Box 250, Harrow Weald, Middlesex

Printed by CS Graphics, Singapore.

www.capitaltransport.com

Front cover; Three members of Finchley depot are seen at New Southgate station on Saturday 3rd June 1961. Left to right are conductor Rookie, driver Wyatt and trolleybus 1540. Wyatt takes the weight and tension of the boom while Rookie observes the finer art of trolleyboom work. Fresh from an external lower deck repaint, 1540 is momentarily immobilised. *Hugh Taylor.*

Title page Tally Ho bus station was a focal point of work for Finchley depot staff, and on a baking hot day in the summer of 1961 all of 1503's saloon windows are open; to make himself comfortable in this heat the driver has opened both windscreens. 1503 was the only trolleybus at this time that was fitted with a Charlton style route number at the front. Typical of the Finchley cleaning staff, 1503 is gleaming. *Tony Belton*

Back cover: It is Tuesday 7th November 1961 and the last day of route 609. It was a rainy morning and having been held up by traffic, the crew of 1498 have been instructed to turn at WINDSOR TERRACE CITY ROAD; as no overhead frog is provided here, the conductor has used a bamboo pole to change the trolley arms to a dead-end set of wires. 1547's driver waits patiently before progressing to Moorgate. Both vehicles have their side and interior lights on. *Tony Belton.*

CONTENTS

AUTHOR'S NOTE

I worked for London Transport for thirty-six years. My first ten years were at
Finchley trolleybus depot where I was a conductor for four years and a driver for six.
For a mere ten weeks I was a motorbus driver there; I spent the next twenty-three
years driving at Muswell Hill bus garage. My final two years of service were as a
road official in Leaside District.

I always enjoyed and took an interest in the work and most of the conversation
there was job related. This not only applies to me but also to many others; included
in this category is Tony Belton, a road official at the same time as myself. Tony had
been following the London trolleybus scene since 1958 and it was of great interest to
him to learn that I spent a decade working on them. He introduced me to a friend of
his who he had met during the conversion programme – Hugh Taylor, who has
written a number of books and articles about the London trolleybus. Hugh suggested
that my memories could form a chapter of a book but it soon became obvious that I
had more to say than could fit into just a few pages – hence this book.

The book could not have been compiled without hundreds of hours of word
processing which has been carried out by Hugh's wife, Catherine. Hugh and I have
compiled the book on the basis of being 'on the inside'. A bonus of Catherine's input
is that she has seen it 'from the outside', and has offered many ways of explaining
things so that it is easier for the reader to understand the 'ins and outs' of trolleybus
work. Despite being in my seventies, it seems I have been a bad influence on her as
she now knows a lot of busmen's terminology. If any modern day bus worker with
this book hears a female voice call out "Stop scratching about" – she's on board!

My wife Rose has taken a great interest in the progress of the book. My three
children, Julie, Richard and Belinda have also given enthusiastic support. It is usual
for an author to dedicate a book to someone – in my instance I would like to dedicate
it to my three regular drivers (Dennis, Vic and Harry) and five usual conductors
(Tommy, Jean, Sid, Gladys and Bridie) at Finchley depot. Passage of time has meant
that most of my former trolleybus colleagues have passed away. However, I am sure
that this book will, one way or another, fall into the hands of people who are still
around and who served with me. It is likely too that it will reach relations of those
mentioned herein. If anyone wants to communicate with me, please do so by e-mail
at CharlieT9628FY@trolleybus.net. I trust that my endeavours to relay the whole
story of trolleybus work are successful, and that you enjoy my memoirs.

Andover, Hants, September 2008   Charlie Wyatt

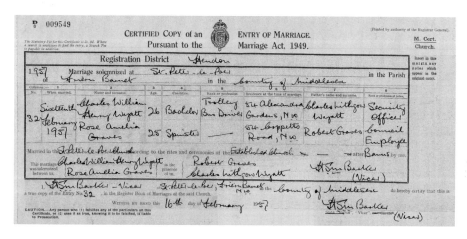

Staff mostly referred to the trolleybuses
as 'buses. On my marriage certificate
the vicar inserted my occupation
precisely as 'Trolley Bus Driver'.

COMPILER'S NOTE

I have always found it interesting to speak to staff who worked on trolleybuses, both during the conversion programme and in my time with London Transport. A long time friend, Tony Belton, introduced me to Charlie and it was immediately obvious that his recall was excellent. I found it incredible that not only could he remember that he was caught in floodwater on 9th July 1956, but that it was Monday 9th July 1956. When it was suggested that he might add to a book that I was working on, he was only too ready to agree – that his contribution might become a whole book was never thought about initially. While compiling this tome, we have become firm friends and have had a lot of fun putting it together.

I also must thank my very supportive and long-suffering wife Catherine for her input; without her contribution this book would have taken much longer to compile. A number of people have assisted our efforts. Keith Farrow has not only been a good proof-reader but has enhanced the chapters dealing with overhead wiring and associated infrastructure; he has also drawn the overhead wiring maps. Bob Williamson has provided many useful facts about tickets, and John Carwardine, using actual blinds, has made the destination, route and side blind facsimiles. Ken Blacker has checked the draft and made many useful suggestions.

Charlie and I have spent hundreds of hours together. Most of the time has been spent in conversation and it is interesting how one thing has led to another and that one memory has triggered another. Where necessary these memories have been supported by official documents of the time. On most occasions there has been little time left over at the end of a session, but on one occasion there was. I said "Let's look at a few photos that I've had blown up as enlargements". On showing him one of mine, he said "That's me", and it was. The possibility of me taking a photograph of a member of the London trolleybus staff in 1961 and then showing it to him in my house well over forty years later falls into the category of millions to one against. It is appropriate therefore that this photograph appears on the cover.

Edgware, Middlesex   Hugh Taylor

Working from Finchley depot, the individualistic 954 is seen at the Nags Head in her last months of service. Between 1st February and 25th April 1961 she was the oldest working trolleybus in the fleet. It was always a pleasure to be allocated 954 after all the J class trolleybuses had been withdrawn – it had a similar feel to them and was therefore nice to drive. In the background a 609 has worked short to the Nags Head – it now turns left from Parkhurst Road into Holloway Road. *Fred Ivey.*

Below This is the tramway pointsman's hut outside the Archway Tavern that my dad used for refreshments when he was on duty as a policeman here. On the right, a Metropolitan Electric Tramway's car is climbing Archway Road on its way to Barnet on route 19 - on the left is a conduit tram track stub. *London Transport Museum U12739.*

Opposite left Street photographers were an integral part of everyday life in Britain for many years and one of them has captured my mother pushing me in a pram in Seven Sisters Road when I was just two years old. In the background a London General Omnibus Company bus heads north while in the distance a Metropolitan Electric Tramways car is just a few yards away from the Nags Head public house at Holloway. *Street photographer.*

Opposite right My parents took me on outings to the seaside from time to time and at Clacton, when I am three, I am practising for my career in transport! The vehicle is a Reliance which is seen in the coach park there. *Charlie Wyatt senior.*

EARLY YEARS

I was born on Sunday 7th September 1930 at 35 Sussex Road, Holloway, London N7 and named Charles William Henry Wyatt. My dad's name was also Charles, it being common practice in that era for the firstborn son to be named after his father. To avoid confusion, I was (and still am) known in the immediate family circle as 'Bill'. At the time of my birth, my father was a mounted police constable and before long we moved to Ealing where he was posted for ten months. Later on, we went back to north London and lived at 19 Miranda Road, Upper Holloway as dad had been transferred to Holloway police station; then to 54 Alexander Road which was about three quarters of a mile away. At the age of two we moved to 58 Kiver Road which was a cul-de-sac, at the end of which was situated the rear exit of the London General Omnibus Company's Holloway garage. My earliest recollection of the transport scene in London was the fascination of seeing red double-decker buses emerging from this exit.

On some mornings, my mother Maisie used to wheel me in a pram to the Archway junction when my father was on point duty – traffic lights had not yet been installed there. When the time came for his meal break he would go into the London County Council Tramway's pointsman's hut to consume hot cocoa and food that my mother had brought him (there must have been an unofficial arrangement for policemen to use the hut). At the bottom of Archway Road there was a change pit for trams to transfer from conduit operation to overhead pick-up and vice-versa. While my mother was chatting with my father I would watch fascinated at the spectacle. What I particularly remember is the 'shooting the plough' part of the show which occurred on the northbound track; the conductor placed the trolley arm on the running wire and the driver moved the tram forward. The plough then glided out of its carrier beneath the tram and ended up in a parking rail, nudging into others that were already in the stub. In the reverse direction (going towards London) a plough shifter guided a plough into a position beneath the tram after which the conductor stowed the trolley arm under its retaining hook on the roof.

I can remember the trams from childhood for three other reasons. First, because from 1936 I had to regularly travel with one of my parents (usually my mother) on the number 9 or 19 tram to and from school; this was from The Winchester public house in Archway Road to The Wellington pub at Highgate. Secondly, because one of the trams (LCC number one) was painted a lovely colour, royal blue; my favourite colour was blue and therefore it always stood out. It operated on route 33 (Manor House to West Norwood) and route 35 (Highgate to Forest Hill). It was nicknamed 'Bluebird' and was regularly seen at the Archway. In 1937, a single blue letterbox was installed there – it was used only for airmail and I always associated this blue letterbox with the blue tram and, for a little while, the two could be seen there together. The third reason for remembering the trams was because I recall being taken through the Kingsway Subway on route 35 from Archway to the Embankment, there being a hollow sound to the place. This early contact with buses and trams started my interest in transport – at the early age of approximately two and a half years. They made an impression on my young mind and as I grew up I took a general interest in London's transport.

When I was about six years old my father had taken me shopping to Kentish Town one day. On the way back we got on a 27 or 137 bus, and sat right behind the driver. I was on my dad's lap; he was pointing out what the driver, in his long summer white coat, was doing. We got out at the last stop in Junction Road just before Archway where the bus terminated. Then we started to walk up Vorley Road on our way to my grandmother's home in Anatola Road. The driver had obviously noticed my interest in his bus as in Vorley Road he pulled up and asked my dad "Would your son like a ride in the cab with me?" My father lifted me into the cab and I sat on the driver's lap as the bus chugged in first gear as far as Brunswick Road (now renamed Macdonald Road). I must have travelled about two hundred yards with my hands on the steering wheel all of the time. When the bus came to a standstill the driver handed me down to my dad.

Soon after its formation on 1st July 1933, the London Passenger Transport Board decided to replace trams by trolleybuses. However, they did not make an appearance in my area until Sunday 6th March 1938 – the reason this date has stuck in my mind is that 6th March was my dad's birthday. I first saw trolleybuses the following day when my father met me from my school in North Hill, Highgate. As we were walking down Church Road towards Archway Road I vividly recall seeing one pass from right to left on its way towards North Finchley. Little did I know that many years later I would be conducting, and later driving, route 609 trolleybuses up and down the Archway Road.

Apart from going to school on the Archway Road trolleybuses, the first rides I had on them was when I was travelling with my parents to see relatives in the Putney Bridge Road area on summer evenings in 1938. We got there by using sixpenny evening tourist tickets. They cost the same for adults and children, could only be used on trams and trolleybuses, and were a bargain. We took a 517/617 or 609 from Archway Road to North Finchley where we boarded a 660 to Jubilee Clock, Harlesden; we changed there on to a 628 to Putney. On one of these excursions when we were on a 628, the trolleybus in front dewired with one of its booms going through a window of a room above a jeweller's shop in Fulham Palace Road. When we visited this place on another occasion my father pointed out to me that guard wires had now been erected between traction standards here to prevent wayward trolley arms shattering any more windows.

In September 1935 I started school, by which time we had moved to 23 Gresley Road, Upper Holloway, my nearest school being St Joseph's Infants on Highgate Hill. I was there for only a few months before transferring to Highgate Council Infants School on North Hill due to the fact that we had now moved to 18A Holmesdale Road, Highgate. We stayed there until November 1938 when we moved yet again, this time to 54 Alexandra Gardens, Muswell Hill, where for the first time we had electric lighting and running hot water – prior to this, gas had been used. The reason for these moves was to improve our standard of living and this house at Alexandra Gardens was to be the family home for many years to come. My next school was Muswell Hill Junior School as it was at the end of my road, but war broke out the following

year and most of the children from the school were evacuated to the Peterborough area. There were only a handful of us left and for a while there was no schooling at all. After a month or so the school was open for two mornings a week, then it closed down again and we were sent to Crouch End Junior School. I stayed there until most of the children started to come back from evacuation and Muswell Hill Junior School was re-opened full time for us. By this time there was an addition to the family, my brother John being born on 1st April 1941. As a youngster I didn't get regular pocket money and had to get by on what my parents and relations might give me – this could be sweets, comics or the odd penny here and there.

At the age of twelve I went back to Crouch End school again but this time to the seniors, staying there until V1 flying bombs started to fall on London. On 12th July 1944, because of these, my mother, John and myself were evacuated by Hornsey Council. We assembled at Hornsey Town Hall where there was a long line of London Transport double-decker buses waiting to take us to Euston Station where we boarded trains. The journey took all day and no-one knew where we were heading – it turned out to be Lancashire. We arrived late that night and were taken to, what seemed to me, an old mansion. The rooms were filled with evacuees and people were even sleeping on the double staircases; we slept on the big landing. The following morning we were taken to a school in the village of Edgworth and stayed there all day while people from the surrounding area came to select who they would give a home to. Somebody offered to billet my mother and John but didn't have room for me. My mother wouldn't allow us to be split up and at about half past five in the evening there were still a few small family groups left, including ours. We were taken to another village called Egerton, about four miles north of Bolton on the Blackburn Road, and housed in an empty manse where everybody made their own domestic arrangements. We were there for about a week and were then billeted with a Mr and Mrs Farnworth, Mr Farnworth being the groundsman of the village cricket club. I went to the local school and made friends with some of the Egerton children; Lancastrians are passionate about cricket so I spent many hours with bat and ball.

During the war most scholarships were suspended and, unless children had been fortunate enough to be awarded one, they left school at the age of fourteen. I attended Walmsley School in Egerton and received a leaving certificate from the Lancashire Education Committee on 29th September 1944 (three weeks after my fourteenth birthday). Almost a week later, on 5th October, we returned to London where the V2 rockets were starting to fall. Our street was badly damaged on 1st December when one landed nearby.

As I grew up, I was involved in the normal children's pastimes and was aware of the changing scene around me. I liked football, cricket and other sports which I played with friends in Highgate Woods, near to where a barrage balloon was moored. Another place where we used to congregate was 'The Grove' which was part of the Alexandra Palace grounds. During my teenage years I became interested in progressive jazz and swing music and I went around with other local fellows and girls of my age. There were six sisters who lived in Cherry Tree Cottage which was situated in the grounds of Alexandra Palace, their father working for the Alexandra Palace trustees. I didn't meet the older three as they were not in my age group, but knew the younger three quite well. One of these was Jean Blackwell who was the fifth of the six. Gradually we lost contact with each other but who would have thought that years later Jean and I would be paired up as a London trolleybus crew.

I needed to find employment and wanted an outdoor job, so went to the Juvenile Employment Agency at Hornsey Town Hall, Crouch End Broadway where it was suggested that I apply to the General Post Office (now Royal Mail) to become a walking telegraph messenger. I applied and was accepted for this position, starting work on Monday 4th December 1944 at Western District Sorting Office, Wimpole Street, London, W1. For my first year, I earned one pound, one shilling and sixpence per week less fourpence stoppages. This was considered to be a low wage and to compensate for this the GPO gave us dinner vouchers worth one shilling and three pence a day. I gave my mother a pound, leaving me with one shilling and tuppence, but she bought my season ticket for work – a monthly one used on the Underground between Highgate and Bond Street. I didn't need much money to get by, and although it sounds a pittance, one and tuppence a week was adequate. I stayed at Wimpole Street for ten months and then transferred to the Northern District Office at Upper Street, Islington in October 1945, delivering telegrams on a bicycle. In early 1946 my job was regraded to junior postman even though I was doing the same work as before. During the year I was transferred to Finchley Central and it was here that I obtained my first driving licence of any description, this being for a motorcycle. Two of us were given tuition with a Post Office instructor. He took us round many of the streets of London and into the suburbs and passed us as competent after a mere three days! (driving tests had been suspended between 1939 and 1946 because of the war) In September 1946 I became a Post Office motorcycle messenger delivering telegrams based initially at Finsbury Park, then Crouch End and finally South Tottenham post office. From this time onwards my main interest was owning a motorcycle, my first (a 1935 Coventry Eagle 150cc two stroke) being obtained in 1948.

During 1946 I attended day continuation school for young men at Golden Lane, EC1 for one day a week. This was for a year and was similar to doing ordinary school work. At the age of sixteen I took the Civil Service exam and came ninety-first out of four hundred. The first twenty were guaranteed a job as a counter clerk or a telegraphist, the next fifty or so went as post office sorters, then the next hundred were allotted a position as postmen – the rest were cleaners. My grade when I reached eighteen, would be a fully-fledged postman delivering letters and I would be allocated to Muswell Hill Sorting Office. While still acting as a motorcycle messenger I met with an unfortunate accident on 22nd April 1948. I was stationary in Tottenham High Road at the junction with Lansdowne Road, clearly signalling with my right hand that I wished to turn right. Coming the other way, a lorry overtook a moving bus and hit me full on. I was thrown backwards and ended up in the nearside gutter with my legs trapped underneath the motorcycle. My injuries were such that I was off work for a year and I spent ten months on crutches. I did not recommence work until April 1949, doing my old job of delivering telegrams on a pedal bike from the Parkhurst Road, Holloway, Post Office. By this time my wages were £3 2s 6d per week. I had been due to start my National Service in September 1948, at the mandatory age of eighteen, but this had to be deferred until I was fit. When my doctor declared that this was so, I informed the appropriate authorities and registered my choice which was the army. In due course I received my call-up papers.

I did my National Service in the Royal Signals going to Catterick Camp, Yorkshire on Thursday 1st September 1949, a week before my nineteenth birthday. I did a three month despatch rider's course at Barnard Castle, County Durham, learning to ride a motorcycle the army way. This was over all types of countryside and took nine weeks, being followed by three weeks on 15cwt Bedford trucks. Then, in March 1950, I was posted to Herford in Northern Germany with BAOR (British Army of the Rhine); I was there for eighteen months and I learnt to handle left-hand drive jeeps. All of this instruction gave me army licences to war office specification and on this basis I was able to obtain a full council driving licence without having to take a further test when I returned to civilian life. I was demobbed from Pocklington in Yorkshire in the middle of September 1951 and was then given a month's leave – this was paid leave to tide people over until they found work. My job at the GPO had been kept open for me, but a new source of employment came my way as will be related in the next chapter. While I was still on crutches, I met my wife-to-be, Rose, on 20th November 1948 (the day before her seventeenth birthday). She became my girlfriend and during my leave from Germany in June 1950 we became engaged. Rose was keen for us to get married, but first we had to save up for our wedding.

Wednesday 31st August 1949, the day before my national service commenced. Rose and I are about to go out for a last spin on my second motorcycle, a 1939 C10 250SV BSA – we're off to Dunstable for the afternoon. In those days, we just wore our ordinary clothes when we went out riding; the use of crash helmets was not compulsory then. *Charlie Wyatt senior.*

There is no picture of me in Acton Town Hall training to be a trolleybus conductor so this one in the tramway conductors' school (probably at Acton depot) is the best that can be provided. The instructor has six trainees with him; each has a punch and rack and is being told the correct way to use them. Redundant tickets are being used. The trainees are all in uniform – notice many well-polished shoes. *London Transport Museum U14568.*

LEARNING THE ROPES

One day in October 1951, myself and Ron Cook (whom I had previously worked with in the Post Office and who had finished his army service about a fortnight after me) met a former Post Office colleague, Eric Birchmore. He had been demobbed some time before us but instead of returning to his old job had taken employment as a bus conductor at Muswell Hill bus garage. Eric said "Look at my wages on the buses". His wages card showed nine pounds, one shilling. To obtain this he had worked a rest day on top of his ordinary week. Even on a flat week he was far better off than we would have been if we returned to the GPO where pay was low – only four pounds, fifteen shillings a week. Ron and I decided to apply for the buses and went to London Transport Manor House divisional office to do this. The job of bus conductor appealed to me as it was transport orientated and I was aware that being a postman didn't have the same attraction as my previous job where I was riding a motorcycle as a Post Office messenger. At this time, Britain was starting to come out of its austerity years, though bomb sites and food rationing would still be around for some time to come.

At Manor House an interviewer asked why we wanted the job. Having prepared our answers we said it was because the pay was better than the GPO, and that we wanted an outdoor occupation. Satisfied with our answers he gave us application forms for employment which we filled in. Anticipating that I might need them, I took my birth certificate and army record with me. To test our aptitude we had to sit an arithmetic test and then undergo a medical examination, passing both satisfactorily. We were offered "trolleybuses at Finchley" (which we accepted) and were given an application form for a Metropolitan Stage Carriage licence. I would have preferred to have gone to Muswell Hill as it was nearer my home, but I expect Finchley's need was greater. We had to be vouched for by two people who knew us, but who were not related. 'Taffy' Evans, a police colleague of my father and Bert Slinn, a next door neighbour, acted for me. I sent off a postal order to the value of five shillings and sixpence, this being three shillings for a three year licence and two and sixpence as a deposit for the badge. We were asked when we could start and replied that we could start straight away but would first of all have to resign from the GPO. We left the building, boarded a 679 trolleybus and travelled to Upper Street Islington where the Northern District head office was situated, and handed in our resignations. The supervisor tried to talk us out of it and said, "Do you realise it's a job for life with the Post Office?". We had made up our minds though and filled in the appropriate forms, telling him that we were leaving due to the better pay on London Transport. He said "You'll regret doing

this". I have never echoed his sentiments and I was destined to be a long serving London Transport employee. Returning to the Post Office thirty six-years later, I could see that I made the right move as a postman's job had become more arduous and the wages had not risen at the same rate as London Transport's.

Having been accepted as conductors, we were told to report to Finchley depot on what I believe was Monday 22nd October 1951. Trolleybuses were to be part of my everyday life for the next ten years. On arrival at Finchley we reported to the CDI (Chief Depot Inspector), a Mr Nicholson who welcomed us to the depot. He told us to go to Dollis Hill divisional office to collect our uniform later that day; we were given a chit to do this. When we got there we were supplied with a uniform and issued with a ticket punch backplate and strap, leather apron (for the punch), ticket rack, metal punch cleaner (for bits of ticket caught in the ticket punch slot), rule book, destination blind turning key, wooden clipboard for the waybill, cap badge and cash bag. Some of the equipment was new, some secondhand.

The next day I had to go to Acton Town Hall, in full uniform, where London Transport used an upstairs room to train new conductors; this was a mustering point for those of us in the school. It was a long way to go for those of us from the 'north side', there being recruits from Colindale, Edmonton, Finchley, Highgate, Stonebridge and Wood Green depots all learning a new job. I would have thought that there would have been somewhere nearer for this training to have taken place but at least I didn't have to traipse over to West Ham depot where training schools were also held. It was quite a distance to Acton each day from Muswell Hill so I used my BSA 500 Star Twin motorbike. There were about a dozen recruits of which most were men; however, there were two sisters who were going to Highgate and a Scottish girl who was going to Stonebridge. As she did not find it easy getting to Acton I arranged to meet her at Neasden and gave her a lift there and back each day. There were also staff from the local depots, Hammersmith and Hanwell, attending and some from Fulwell. The latter depot used TIM ticket machines which had a telephone dial on the top, so presumably those who would be based there would be given instruction on how to use them at Fulwell. We used a room overlooking Acton High Street and this was one of the few occasions when I saw trolleybuses from above.

In the room there were fare charts and blackboards. The instructors showed us how to read and understand duty schedules and crew rotas; this was done by utilising old ones from Stonebridge depot. We were also taught about the Cash

Total Sheet on which we recorded our ticket transactions (the CTS was normally known as a waybill). We were emphatically told that at the end of each day we would have to balance the number of tickets sold with the cash that we had received and then pay it in to a depot official. The instructors showed us how to use a ticket rack and punch using redundant tickets, following which we issued tickets to them. Then we took it in turns to ask each other for tickets using a fare chart for reference. As expected we made a few mistakes, such as misreading the fare charts and 'charging' our colleagues too much! We also had a lot of laughs and the instructors were patient and considerate with us. It was good fun really and we picked everything up quickly. The instructors told us all the 'ins and outs' of the job, one of which was that we should use a pencil for all paperwork entries. Mistakes were not to be erased but any wrong numeral was to be crossed through and the right number inserted. We were also given advice about report writing as there were various forms to be filled in from time to time.

After three days at Acton we were sent to our respective depots to work with conductor-instructors; they were paid a daily allowance, one shilling and sixpence a day. We were able to collect fares under their licences. I had five days 'on board' supervision and clearly remember my first day, going out with driver Bert Griffin and conductor Whale on route 609. I did the conducting with him alongside giving me guidance and everything was alright that day (the spelling alright is used in this book to give a useful distinction between it and all right). He said that he was satisfied with me and signed off my progress report favourably – this was good for morale. I worked a couple of days with Mr Abrahams on the 645s/660s. He was a very experienced trolleybus conductor and, as related later, was extremely helpful giving me tips and advice. I was working with him, probably on my second or third day, when at about midday on a journey to Canons Park on a 645, workers from Frigidaire's factory near Colindale depot turned out. The 645 was 'choc-a-bloc' till we got to Edgware, all short riders. I was upstairs trying to collect all the fares, nigh impossible for a rookie. Mr Abrahams said to the passengers, "New man here, give him a chance." However, I was just not able to deal with the situation quickly enough and he thought it best that he took over so that all the fares were collected. He put me to good use, ringing off the 'bus (we rarely used the full word 'trolleybus') until things quietened down when I took over the tickets and punch again. I was completely unfamiliar with the area that the 660 went through and didn't know where I was at all and recall Mr Abrahams pointing out, at the Jubilee Clock, the notorious Harrow Road which the 662 traversed. There were two other conductor-instructors whose names I cannot recollect, who I worked with on the 521/621 service and the 609 route and they gave me their own advice. I was a bit slow to start with but by the time I had finished my initiation, I had speeded up quite a bit.

My instructors showed me the correct way to conduct a trolleybus and everything there was to know about the issuing of tickets and cashing up. The reading and understanding of the crew rotas and schedules was again explained.

It was emphasised how important it was to be ready to pull handles to change overhead points for trolleybooms. My tutors would say "we need this frog; it's a pull and hold one, so make sure you don't let go of the handle till the poles are through the points". Alternatively they would say "this is a semi-automatic frog – pull the handle down and get back on the bus". On the first couple of occasions they would stand nearby to make sure I got it right. However, when I was busy, they did the frog pulls. They said that I needed to make myself aware of where handles had to be pulled, for if I was unprepared the trolleybus I was working on would be delayed. I had seen conductors pulling frog handles before I was on the job, so was reasonably familiar of what was required – now I knew exactly what to do. Everything about frogs is explained in another chapter.

I was shown how to change destination blinds but it was not until I had qualified as a conductor that I found out that some trolleybuses had their front blinds changed by the driver, while others had them changed by the conductor. Sometime during this induction period I was given a staff pass which entitled me to free travel, on and off duty, on Red Buses, Green Buses (but not Green Line), Trams and Trolleybuses; I never used it on the country buses or trams. It was also available on the Underground when travelling to and from work – I only occasionally used this facility.

After the on-board supervision I went back to Acton Town Hall for two and a half days. On one of them we went out on a motorbus. I recall going through the Esher and Petersham areas. We took it in turns to act as a conductor with the rest of us asking for fares for ourselves and for imaginary groups, at the same time asking for awkward permutations. Of course, each one of us came up for the same treatment from others in the group. Back at the town hall, general duties and procedures that we were to carry out were explained; this embraced lost property, the care of passengers and assisting children, the elderly and infirm. We were taught how to deal with all types of problems that might arise in a day's work but with the unexpected situations we were told to use our initiative and discretion. We were told that we could only carry one dog at a time and that it had to go upstairs with its owner. Guide dogs were allowed to travel with their owners in the lower saloon – blind people had a pass which gave them free travel. Our tutors told us to familiarise ourselves with the rule book and its instructions, and emphasised that our appearance should be such that we were presentable to the public. I was only at Acton for a short time on the last day which was Saturday 3rd November. There was an assessment and approval and then having been given a final pep talk and words of encouragement I was told that on my way home I had to go to the Public Carriage Office at Harvist Road near Kilburn. There I was issued with a conductor's trolleybus licence and badge; its number was T12315 – not a new one. I was its second or maybe third owner. It was known as a 'dead mans' badge, the inference being that its previous owner had died while in the service of London Transport. This was probably not so and was likely to have been returned by somebody who had left the job and who wanted to get the deposit back on the badge. Alternatively, it had come from someone who had retired, or a tram conductor who had returned it when the trams were replaced by motorbuses in the early 1950s. (I had to renew my conductor's licence towards the end of 1954, but when I was sent a renewal form in 1957 I let it lapse as I was driving trolleybuses then.) Leaving the Public Carriage Office I made my way to Finchley depot where a depot inspector told me what time I had to report the following Monday. From then on I would be on my own. For the next ten years I would be working beneath the wires of London.

There was often a lot of traffic in Kingsway, North Finchley as shown by the number of motor vehicles in this view; none of their drivers will argue with 1517 as it is many times bigger than their vehicle. This area is generally known as Tally Ho Corner, named after the Tally Ho! public house situated a few yards further up Ballards Lane where it meets the High Road in North Finchley. We used 'Tally Ho' and 'North Finchley' indiscriminately in our everyday trolleybus parlance.

In 1950, London Transport's trolleybus depots and bus garages were given identification codes; Finchley was allocated the letters FY. Each route had a set of running numbers embracing the vehicles scheduled on it. If more than one depot was operating on any route, then each had a different sequence. At one time, Colindale, Finchley and Stonebridge depots used the following numbers for routes 645, 660, 664 and 666: Finchley 1–18, Colindale 19–57 and Stonebridge 58–101. The running numbers were the means whereby crews identified the vehicle on which they were to work – they were invaluable to the road inspectors for regulating services. Although running numbers usually ran in sequence there were occasions when this was not so, particularly when vehicles were only operating in the peak hours or carrying out short workings. An idiosyncrasy saw some trolleybuses working on one route in the morning and another in the afternoon. For example, on Mondays to Fridays from May 1954 until March 1955, running number FY70 worked on the 660 in the morning and the 609 in the afternoon with the switch from one to the other in the depot.

Running number plates were supposed to stay on the same vehicle all day. If a trolleybus needed attention in the depot during the daytime, it would be allocated to a number that came in after the morning peak. If the work was not completed by the time it was due out in the afternoon then the plates would be put on a different vehicle. If a defective trolleybus was running into the depot for repair, the plates might taken off by an inspector in the bus station. They would be re-positioned onto the replacement when it was brought out. Inspectors would also remove them from 'dead' vehicles on the stand and re-plate them onto 'buses that were picking up from staff cuts. On many occasions a number of plates could be seen stacked in their control box at Tally Ho.

Routes 521/621 ran from North Finchley to Holborn Circus via Wood Green, Manor House, 'Nags Head' Holloway and Kings Cross. Trolleybuses working in an anti-clockwise direction around the Holborn Loop (i.e. via Grays Inn Road) displayed route 521 while those working in the other direction, via Farringdon Road, showed 621. Only between North Finchley and Wood Green were there no competing trolleybus services. With bus route 29 and trolleybus routes 629 and 641 running alongside between Wood Green and Nags Head, and then the 517/617/659 paralleling the route from there to Holborn Circus, it meant that the southern section wasn't busy all the time. On Saturday afternoons from 20th March 1955 the 521/621 was curtailed at Kings Cross, Swinton

Two Finchley depot trolleybuses are seen in Wood Green; both are running late so are not working the full length of the route. 1493 is only going as far as Kings Cross while 1511 has turned at Wood Green from the south. Having traversed Buller Road, Redvers Road and Lordship Lane, driver Len Payne places 1511's poles back onto the main line. Ominously, two trolleybus replacement vehicles can be seen on route 269. *Peter Moore.*

Street; many other trips only went as far south as Finsbury Park at these times, though this had been the case for some years prior to this. Starting on 2nd May 1956, a localised section was incorporated into the Monday to Friday schedule. These were buses that ran from North Finchley to Wood Green and back in the evening peak and were designed to cover gaps in the service that had been created by late running at the Holborn end. Starting with seven journeys it ended up with seventeen as it was found that, as time progressed, delays from Holborn were continuing until early evening. From March 1960, three morning peak journeys were added on the localised section to help with loadings. Various adjustments were made to the Monday to Friday

schedule as late as March 1961 as London Transport always wanted their services to keep up with changing passenger levels and trends. Running numbers started at FY1. An interesting feature of this route was the time spent 'on the road' by a couple of runnings. On the Monday to Friday schedule for 13th May 1959, FY7 left the depot at 12.29am and did not return until 11.56pm (a total of twenty-three hours and twenty-seven minutes). It was bettered by a single minute by FY13 on the Saturday schedule of 28th June 1958 but that running included fifty-one minutes spent in the depot. These are almost certainly fleet records.

Route 609 operated between Barnet Church and Moorgate via North Finchley, Archway, Nags Head and Islington. From

Barnet trolleybus terminus, and 1521 is the first of two 609s on the stand; both are using the inner set of wires. When the photographer opened his camera shutter at 1521 he would have had no idea whatsoever that this trolleybus would be the last to operate in London – it entered Fulwell depot in the early hours of 9th May 1962. It is now a regular performer at the East Anglia Transport Museum at Carlton Colville near Lowestoft. *Ron Kingdon.*

November 1952, Highgate depot (HT) operated a few trolley-buses on Sundays. Between North Finchley and Nags Head, the 609 operated alongside the 517/617 route and although the schedules were designed for both routes to interwork with each other, this often did not happen. In the Monday to Friday evening peak hours a few journeys ran from Moorgate to Archway Station. After about 2pm on Sundays, half the service terminated at Islington Green because Chapel Street market at Islington ceased trading at about 1pm. It was pointless running all the 609s through to Moorgate as there was little activity in the City areas on that day of the week. As on routes 521/621, there were a few journeys that only went as far as Nags Head, Holloway.

Highgate depot operated route 609 on Sundays only and tended to use L2 class trolleybuses such as 1374 as they reputedly had stronger tension on their trolley arms than others at HT – this was to enable the booms to pass safely under Barnet Bridge. Seen at the 609's northbound loading point at the Nags Head, 1374 is followed by a Routemaster on the erstwhile 611 trolleybus service. *Tony Belton.*

Opposite top Viewed from the grounds of Barnet Parish Church, 1511 leaves this Hertfordshire town on its way to Canons Park on route 645. It is extremely unlikely that anyone will be travelling the full length of the route as it is far quicker to use bus route 107. Though it is many miles away, 1511 advertises Battersea Funfair. *Ron Kingdon.*

Route 645 worked between Barnet Church and Canons Park, Stanmore Circus travelling via North Finchley, Golders Green, Cricklewood and Edgware. It was operated jointly with Colindale depot (CE), with Finchley working slightly more than half of the route's requirements. Between Barnet and North Finchley it worked alongside the 609, and between there and Cricklewood it shared the wires with the 660. From Cricklewood to Edgware there was bus route 142 and trolleybuses on the 664 and 666. As there was no service to Canons Park until about 10am on Sundays, vehicles turned at Edgware Station Road, or Colindale depot where a battery turn was made on the forecourt. Over the years there were some evening peak hour journeys from Barnet to Golders Green. The 645 had to contend with extremely heavy loadings during the peak periods as between Cricklewood and Edgware there were many factories; two that spring to mind are Frigidaire's at Colindale and Duples Coachworks in West Hendon. There were many factories on the North Circular Road so workers formed long queues at Staples Corner (the junction of the North Circular Road and Edgware Road). Conductors had to be strict when it came to preventing too many people from boarding. Not only did staff have to contend with these surges but there was also greyhound racing at Hendon Dog Track, near Staples Corner, some evenings.

Below Not only did Colindale and Finchley operate route 645, but both depots kept their vehicles in tip-top condition. This is shown to good effect by Colindale's 235 which has halted at the stop in Finchley High Road opposite the bus station. It must be a hot day as the driver has opened his offside windscreen for ventilation; he cannot do this with the nearside screen as this does not have an opening window now – these were replaced by non-opening windscreens early in their lives. It was the opinion of many, including myself, that the rear wheel spats gave a streamlined appearance to those vehicles that were fitted with them. *Fred Reynolds.*

Route 660 operated between North Finchley and Hammersmith via Golders Green, Cricklewood, Harlesden and Acton. Stonebridge depot (SE) was allocated most of the work, but by Finchley contributing in a small way it meant that the first and last few trolleybuses from and to North Finchley were operated economically. The only time that we did not work the 660 was on Christmas Day, when Stonebridge covered all journeys. On this day, the first trip from North Finchley went to Cricklewood, St Gabriels Church only and was their only scheduled turn of the year there. From North Finchley, the 660 worked alongside the 645 to Cricklewood where it linked up with the 664 (Edgware to Paddington) and Monday to Friday peak hour 666 (Edgware to Hammersmith) as far as Jubilee Clock. In May 1956 the 666 became an all day Monday to Friday service with the 664 operating on Saturdays and Sundays only. In January 1959, the 664 was withdrawn and the 666 became a daily service. Until May 1956 there were some Monday to Saturday 660 journeys that turned at Craven Park Circle from Hammersmith. There were also a few 'swingers' (vehicles going there and back) that went from North Finchley to Golders Green. They

assisted getting commuters to the Underground station in the morning and returning them in the evening; the morning ones ceased in May 1956. Only fifteen minutes running time was given to get from North Finchley to Golders Green so crews on the swingers had to leave bang on the mark and their drivers had to go 'toe down all the way' to get there on time. There were also trips that went only as far as Acton Market Place or Bromyard Avenue, Acton Vale. The amount of work on the route was gradually reduced: to five in May 1959 and then just two in March 1961 – FY101 and 102, and even then 102 spent the off-peak hours in the depot. At this time FY just had twelve trips to Hammersmith on Mondays to Fridays – there were more trolleybuses allocated at weekends though.

While working on route 660, Stonebridge's 1657 has been curtailed at North Acton and is about to pass through a facing frog; it now needs to go through a crossover, but just before it there is a kink in the wire so the driver will pass through at very slow speed. The conductress is sitting at the front of the lower saloon and waves to the photographer. *Fred Ivey.*

There was some variation to the running time on all routes except the 660 which had a constant sixty-nine minutes each way – this was peak hours, Saturday shopping times, even Christmas Day. An anomaly was that fifteen minutes was given to get from North Finchley to Golders Green while the Sunday morning staff bus which left at 4.29 was given seventeen minutes. The 645 had sixty-three minutes to get from Barnet to Canons Park both ways virtually all the time, though in weekday peak hours it was given an extra minute; this was insufficient as there were many more people, and heavier traffic at these times. Four minutes to get from 'Canons' to Edgware was virtually impossible, so it was understandable that crews due for relief at Colindale depot would leave Canons Park a couple of minutes early as they considered the eleven minutes running time inadequate.

On the 609, fifty-nine minutes was allowed to get from Barnet to Moorgate both ways on weekdays (Mondays to Saturdays). Only two minutes less was given on Sundays and Christmas Day. On the 521/621, fifty-six minutes each way was given on weekdays. On Sundays and Christmas Day, fifty two or fifty-three minutes was given for North Finchley to Holborn Circus. Schedules have anomalies. The Monday to Friday one for May 1959 only gave fifty-one minutes to get from North Finchley to Holborn at 7am, with the same time being given on leaving Holborn at 8am to get back to North Finchley – very difficult to achieve. Conversely, when there was 'nothing about' so to speak, such as on Christmas Day, the allotted time was more than was needed. One section where the running time never varied was between Wood Green and North Finchley – eighteen minutes in both directions. It could easily be done late at night but in peak hours was difficult to accomplish. All routes had short-working facilities and these are listed right.

While I was still a lad, two services came and went from Finchley depot. The 651 from Barnet to Cricklewood had only worked for three months in 1938, and the 517/617 had a short career here between 1938 and 1941. Route 666 had also been operated but only with a few journeys. While I was at Finchley we operated four services, although five route numbers (521, 609, 621, 645 and 660) were used.

A few operating practices need explaining. We used the terminology 'on the down' which meant going north to Barnet. We did not use the phrase 'on the up' although that was towards London as per mainline railway practice. Running north to south, one would expect that direction to be the 'down' track. The odd thing about all this was that the Canons Park 645 terminus was on the 'up track', and was a northern terminus as was Barnet which was shown as being on the 'down track'. One of them had to be 'up' and this was a necessary anomaly as the route was 'U' shaped. If the direction of travel on a trolleybus duty sheet showed 'D' it meant that staff took over on the 'down road'. The absence of a 'D' indicated that a trolleybus was on the 'up road' and applied to 609s going to Moorgate and to 645s towards Golders Green. 521s/621s and short working 609s/645s taken over on the stand at Tally Ho were indicated as such on the duty sheet. Any trolleybus taken out or brought back into the depot showed 'DEPOT' on the sheet.

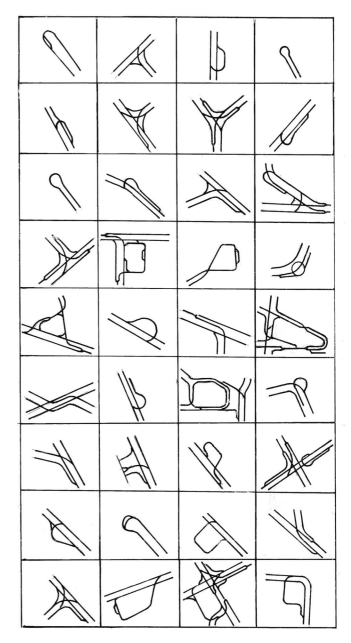

The above diagrams show the wiring layouts at termini and turns used by Finchley trolleybuses as at autumn 1956, left to right, top to bottom:
Barnet, Woodberry Grove/Ballards Lane, Golders Green, Canons Park
Edgware, Colindale Depot, Cricklewood Broadway, St Gabriels Church
Sudbury, Wembley, Stonebridge Depot, Craven Park
Jubilee Clock, College Park, Paddington, North Acton
Acton Market Place, Bromyard Avenue, Askew Arms, Shepherds Bush
Seven Stars, Paddenswick Road, Hammersmith, New Southgate
Jolly Butchers Hill, Wood Green Depot, Turnpike Lane, Manor House
East Finchley, Highgate Village, Macdonald Road, Archway
Pemberton Gardens, Finsbury Park, Nags Head, Newington Green
Drawn by Keith Farrow

Spreadover duties were worked on Mondays to Fridays. The first part of the shift was in the morning peak, the second half in the evening peak – more 'buses and crews were required at these times. The spreadovers could be up to twelve hours and forty minutes in length. It meant a long day but we got paid for the hours we weren't working, four hours sometimes. We had a good pay packet when we had a five day spreadover – if we worked a rest day as well, the rewards were very high. Spreadovers finishing by 6pm were considered to be early turns; those that concluded after that were classed as lates – they were done by about 8pm. The spreads were distributed evenly around the rota; sometimes we would only have an early finish about once a month due to the spread-overs that were classed as earlies. Living fairly close to the depot allowed me to go home if I wanted to – for those who lived further afield they had no alternative but to stay nearby. There was plenty to do – play cards or snooker in the club-room at the depot, look round the local shops or spend time in Victoria Park. In summer, staff could go to Finchley open-air swimming pool in the High Road; three regulars who availed ourselves of this facility were myself, Les Strutt and conductor Finnemore.

Included in a day's work was 'travelling time'. Two minutes was allowed to walk from the depot to Ballards Lane relief point and six minutes to take over anywhere in the Tally Ho vicinity. Included in a day's work was 'signing on' and 'signing off' time, and all time spent on the 'bus. A minimum of forty minutes was given for meal reliefs and was the only unpaid time during our working day. The maximum time in charge of a vehicle was five hours. It was six hours when including all other allowances.

Crews took over their vehicles either in the depot, in Tally Ho bus station at North Finchley or 'on the road'. The latter terminology saw 609 reliefs occurring outside Janes and Adams shop in the one-way section of Ballards Lane, North Finchley when going north, and in the High Road opposite the trolleybus station when going south. 645 reliefs were in both directions in Ballards Lane. 660s were only taken over when travelling north; it was impractical to take over going south as only three minutes running time was given from Tally Ho to the relief point at the junction of Woodberry Grove with Ballards Lane. This would have led to crews leaving early from the bus station so as not to arrive late for relief or finish.

When we took over on the stand at Tally Ho, we did so at the time a 'bus arrived there; departure time could be up to ten minutes later. We soon got to know what time we were due to leave and would not arrive until then.

The Archway Station short working point was used by 609s on Christmas Days and Monday to Friday evening peak hours; 1497 is oper-ating one of these trips which was known as an 'Archway swinger'. From Highgate Hill. we turned left into Macdonald Road, right into Vorley Road and then right again into Salisbury Road; we stood at the end of this street. Upon departure, we turned right onto Highgate Hill. My mother was born at number eight Salisbury Road in front of which 1497 is parked – she never would have thought that her firstborn would drive trolleybuses past that self-same house. *Peter Moore.*

There was only one timecard per crew as opposed to two on motorbuses. It was usually kept in the driver's cab and stayed on the vehicle from the time it left the depot until the time it returned. On trolleybuses in the 900 series and those drafted in from other depots between 1959 and 1961, it was kept on top of the contactor box. The conductor reached through the window connecting the lower saloon and the cab, and took hold of the timecard when it was needed. On the 'buses with fleet numbers in the 300s (where there wasn't a contactor box in the cab) it was propped on the top of the panel that incorporated the switches for the lights, wipers, horn etc. The driver handed it to the conductor when required.

Staff worked on one of two rotas; one comprised the 521/621 and 609 routes. While some duties might work solely on one of those services, others would be compiled in such a way that one spell was on the 521/621 with the other being on the 609. The 521s/621s were dubbed 'the twenty-ones' while the 609s were known as 'the nines'. This differed from motorbus practice whereby, apart from isolated incidences, staff only worked on one route. One terminology used at all depots was 'a rounder'. On the 521s/621s this was North Finchley – Holborn Circus – North Finchley. There were many other permutations due to the fact that one spell could be worked on the '21s, with the other on the '9s. A single duty therefore might be two Holborns and a 609 rounder.

If the mileage to be operated on a duty was three trips from Finchley to Holborn and one to Finsbury Park when working on the '21s, our day's work would be known as 'three and a park'. If a crew was about to depart for Kings Cross, they might say to the staff on the 'bus behind that they were 'going down the Cross'. A passenger overhearing a crew in a 609 saying "It's 'one and a London twice' this duty" would be totally confused. This terminology meant that on both the first half of the duty and the second, the crew had to start at North Finchley, go down to Moorgate, up to Barnet, back to Moorgate and come off at Tally Ho. This was considered to be the roughest of any duty at FY. An easy number was just three trips to Holborn. Part of a duty might be 'One and an Archway swing'; this would be Tally Ho – Moorgate – Archway – Moorgate – Barnet – Tally Ho. The 'swingers' took the short riders as far as Archway on the 609 and cleared the road for through 'buses.

The other rota, which was smaller in that there were not so many duties, covered routes 645 and 660. Most work was on the 645 as we did not run many 660s. Some duties were all 645s while others did a spell on both routes. The 645s and 660s were labelled the 'forty-fives' and 'sixties' respectively.

Monday to Friday timecard for FY81 on route 645 commencing Wednesday 13th May 1959. Duty 6 was the first to use it – at 6.12am. The underlining at 10.19 was to remind the crew to come off for their relief then – a similar mark is made for 1.23pm. Three more crews would use it until arrival in the depot at 10.36pm.

We referred to the rotas as the men's road or the boy's road with the staff on each considering themselves as working on the men's road! The crews on this rota weren't happy with a new Sunday schedule that came into operation on 11th January 1959. Until that time, the first couple of 660s had left the depot at about 6am. With reduced patronage now a factor on all central road services, southbound 660s didn't leave North Finchley till about 9am, and later starts meant later finishes. In 1952, the peak requirement at Finchley depot was 79 vehicles on Mondays to Fridays; in 1961, it had dropped to 67. Pro rata, this was typical of the reduction in services throughout the fleet during that period.

The jargon on the 645s and 660s was more mundane. If a duty was two rounders on the 660 on the first half, and North Finchley to Canons Park and back on the 645 on the second, it would be referred to as 'two Hammersmiths and a Canons'. If it was 'one and a Canons first half, Hammersmith second half' this meant that a crew was starting at North Finchley on the 645s, up to Canons Park, then Barnet, back to Canons Park and off at Tally Ho – the second half would be Hammersmith and back on the 660s. The maximum mileage on a 645/660 duty was two 660 rounders and one rounder on the 645 – very few shifts were that length though.

HAND FROGS

There were a couple of aspects of work that trolleybus staff had to deal with that their motorbus counterparts did not. One was the manhandling of trolleybooms and the other being the overhead wiring. Although drivers had to be more aware of the overhead, conductors also had to play their part and it was important that both crew members worked in tandem and were familiar with the standing instructions at all facing pointwork.

Where trolleybus services converged and diverged, overhead points enabled vehicles to go onto a correct set of wires. The points were known as 'frogs', a word derived from the amphibian which jumps about quickly. The points moved swiftly from one position to another, hence the terminology. Where routes met, the pointwork was known as a trailing frog; trolley heads joined wires from another direction. When routes parted the points were known as facing frogs. The overhead line staff described a facing frog as a turn-out, and a trailing frog was referred to as a junction. Frogs and cross-overs were known as 'special work'.

The frogs were operated by conductors who used handles or pushed buttons. The most common kind of handle was the 'pull and hold' type which resembled an old fashioned toilet

chain. The handle pulled a wire which ran up to a pulley near the top of a traction standard. The cable continued along to the pointwork and changed the frog from one position to another (the pulley and cable principle was used at all point-work, whatever the means of operating it). It was important that conductors made sure that the handle was pulled firmly down, thereby properly operating the points and ensuring that the booms would be diverted onto the correct set of wires. They then had to observe that the trolley heads passed safely through the pointwork before letting go of the handle; only then could they rejoin the vehicle. Having alighted from their vehicles, the younger conductors walked or ran to the traction standard on which the frog handle was fixed while the older ones just ambled up to them.

Some of us young conductors were a bit flash with the 'pull and hold' apparatus on the approach to the Seven Sisters Road/Green Lanes junction at Manor House. We perfected 'flying frog pulls' – operating the frog handle on the move. Routes continuing up Seven Sisters Road had frog priority with conductors on the 521/621 and 629 turning left into Green Lanes having to pull the handle. Drivers approached the points by getting in close to the kerb with their conductors leaning out from the platform and grabbing hold of the

Opposite The Pemberton Gardens/Holloway Road junction incorporated three trailing frogs, three facing frogs and three crossovers; all three crossovers and two of the trailing and facing frogs can be seen as Highgate's 1577 passes through one Sunday while working on route 609. Although drivers had 'power priority' on the 'downhill' frogs, we coasted through them. Going north, we also had the benefit of power priority on the uphill climb through all this 'special work'. Wiring to the left takes trolleybuses into Highgate depot, though by this time it is also known as Highgate bus garage and the Routemaster on route 17 behind is a resident. *Fred Ivey.*

Below A pointsman pulls the frog handle down at Jolly Butchers Hill, allowing 1548 to pass through without stopping. 1548 has probably turned at Gladstone Avenue, Wood Green as there appears to be only one passenger on board – there's probably another '21 just in front which has 'taken the road'. To give the light duty man shelter from the elements, a canvas hut is provided – it has seen better days though, as it is patched up. *Sid Hagarty.*

handle with their left hand. Keeping the handle firmly down, our left arms went back and we looked upwards and backwards to get a view of the poles going over the frog. Letting go as soon as the trolleys had taken the points, we got through without stopping. As mentioned earlier, this frog was upgraded to a semi-auto job so it was even easier for us to do this 'on the hoof'. With traffic getting progressively worse, we often approached this junction at nothing more than a dawdle and it was a piece of cake operating the handle from the platform. I readily admit to operating the handle in this manner when I was a conductor.

Where frequent frog pulls were needed, light duty men were often positioned in peak hours to pull some of the handles; these men were 'old-timers' who had been declared unfit for work. A conductor's workload was reduced in that they obviated the need for them to alight. There was no guarantee of seeing the pointsmen at any particular location – sometimes they were there, sometimes they weren't. They were to be seen at Kingsway in North Finchley pulling for 609s to Barnet, northbound at Jolly Butchers Hill pulling for 521s/621s, and at Manor House/Seven Sisters Road northbound pulling for 521s/621s/629s. Sometimes there would be one at the Agricultural Hall pulling for northbound 609s/679s and occasionally there would be one at the Nags Head in Holloway Road northbound pulling for 517s/609s/611s/617s. They were usually given a canvas hut for protection from bad weather; they were like a sentry box but there was not enough room in them to stand up, and a seat was provided. However in Kingsway, they sat on a stool in one of the side exits from the Gaumont cinema; when not operating the handle, they peered out to their left looking for trolleybuses requiring their services. They obtained a stool from the depot output and I remember seeing them carrying one along Ballards Lane. We were always grateful for their contribution as they saved us a few seconds, thereby speeding us on our way. To save them from continually stretching up, a rope was attached to some of the handles; this also assisted conductors of short stature.

Other arrangements existed here and there, and at Colindale depot one handle was fixed to a metal plate on the administration block. There was an unusual device at the top of Warlters Road, which was the street used when turning at the Nags Head. Trolleybuses on routes 627 and 653 running out of Highgate depot and going towards Tottenham Court Road turned left here and conductors pulled a cantilevered frog handle. The traction pole to which it was attached was in a garden, so the handle was on a metal extension.

The next most common sort of handle operated a semi-automatic frog. Conductors pulled down a brass handle that protruded from the bottom of a green painted box that was fixed to a traction pole which supported pointwork at a junction. On the outside of the box was a white lever that indicated the position the frog was in. It either pointed to the right or the left, and when the lever was pulled down it moved over accordingly, showing which way the frog was now set. If for some reason the white lever was pointing the wrong way, showing that the frog was set against the oncoming trolley-bus, the situation could be rectified by pushing the brass

I used this frog handle many times; it is on traction standard 215A at Edgware and was needed so that 645s could proceed to Canons Park. Despite being photographed a month after it was last used, everything is still well greased. The handle was flexible and conductors would rap it twice against the traction standard – the noise indicated to their driver that the handle was in the 'down' position and that they could proceed. *Hugh Taylor.*

In the first few minutes of Wednesday 3rd January 1962 conductress Costello pulls the semi-automatic frog handle down in Cricklewood Lane for the last service trolley-bus to pass through – Stonebridge's 1666 on route 660. The white arrow on the unit indicated that the overhead line was set for right-turning trolleybuses; by pulling the handle, the arrow moved to the left and enabled vehicles to pass directly across Cricklewood Broadway. Evidence of a heavy snowfall the previous Sunday is shown on the bus stop, the traction standard and the frog handle unit. *Hugh Taylor.*

handle upwards with the palm of the hand. A re-set skate was situated a few inches beyond the frog, either on the positive or negative wire. When a trolley head touched a skate, an electric solenoid was activated, sending the points back to their original setting. The white lever and brass handle also returned to their former positions. The noise of the returning brass handle was clearly audible. It was possible for a solenoid to burn itself out, thus making the apparatus inoperable. This could happen if it was left too long in the 'on' position and would occur if someone had mischievously pulled it during the night. These were the best type of frog handles as they speeded things up. Occasionally, a conductor would inadvertently operate a 'pull and leave' handle. Maybe they'd been working on the 609 for a couple of weeks, and were now on a 521/621 going to North Finchley. When they got to the frog for the Nags Head junction, they'd pull the handle and the Y light (mentioned below) would go on. An alert driver would see this. He'd get the conductor's attention and the handle would be pushed upwards into its original position. At the same junction if there was a long line of traffic, conductors would saunter up to the frog handle and even have to wait a couple of minutes until their vehicle reached them. If there were two 609s in a row or a 609 and a 611 running together, where both needed a frog pull, then the second conductor might say "I'll do it" and pull for both of them, enabling the leading conductor to immediately return to the first vehicle.

The third kind was akin to that mentioned in the paragraph above and was operated and functioned in the same manner. However, it had a longer handle with a brass knob at its base – the handle was attached to a box on the traction standard supporting the frogwork. There was usually a push button facility as well but having two types of equipment for the same set of points seemed superfluous – presumably the long handles were fitted retrospectively due to the unpredictability of the push buttons. The long handle types were gradually replaced by the easier-to-operate semi-automatic type, though some survived until the trolleybus conversion.

The fourth type was a push button that was fixed either to a post that was owned by London Transport, or was attached to a traction standard. There were two black buttons adjacent to each other, with conductors pressing the right or left-hand one according to the instructions in force there. This type of equipment (to all intents and purposes semi-automatic) was gradually phased out, for the buttons became unreliable as they had a tendency to spring back before trolleybuses got to the junction, resulting in dewirements. If a Y signal light indicated that its associated frog was incorrectly set, the situation could be rectified by pushing the partner button. The rule book stated that the buttons were above each other, but this was not so as can be seen in the accompanying illustration. A few push buttons were retained into the conversion era – they were known to exist at Wandsworth and Twickenham. The advantage of semi-auto frog handles and push buttons was that, having operated them, conductors were able to immediately return to their platforms.

Despite regular checking, wear and tear causes all types of equipment to fail from time to time and occasionally a

Far left Although push button frogs generally fell out of use in the 1950s, a few remained into the conversion era. Photographed on 12th May 1962 at Twickenham, this picture shows the last one ever used. *Hugh Taylor.*

Left This picture taken at Forest Gate shows the Y light signal box to good effect. *Jack Gready.*

semi-automatic frog would stop working. An official would come to the scene and advise crews to change trolleybooms by hand. If the equipment could not be rectified immediately, a temporary 'pull and hold down' handle would be fitted and a notice to that effect would be chalked onto the metal box that contained the semi-auto equipment. Alternatively, two bamboo poles would be commandeered from a couple of 'buses, and inspectors would change booms if they had taken the wrong wires. An overhead crew would be summoned to the scene to effect repairs.

The semi-automatic frogs (also known as electric frogs) were linked to a signal for the driver to look at so that he could ascertain that an 'overhead road' was set in his favour. High up, usually on the next traction standard beyond the pointwork, a green painted signal box contained what is best described as a 'Y' light. The box, which had a cover over it to give it protection from the elements, was usually on the left. However, to give better vision, some were placed on the right, on a traction standard on the other side of the road. Inside the signal box were three glass plates each of which had two white light bulbs behind them. The stalk of the Y was permanently illuminated; in its normal position one branch of it was lit. When the frog handle was pulled, this light was extinguished and the one in the other half came on, indicating the revised direction of travel. When a re-set skate was tripped, the lights in the box reverted to their original position. Seeing the illuminated lights in the Y box was a sure sign of traction supply being available. If staff were near one when the occasional power cut occurred, these lights showed that power had been restored. In bright sunshine, the Y lights weren't so obvious and were an excuse used by drivers explaining themselves to the CDI after booms had taken the wrong track, and a dewirement had damaged them.

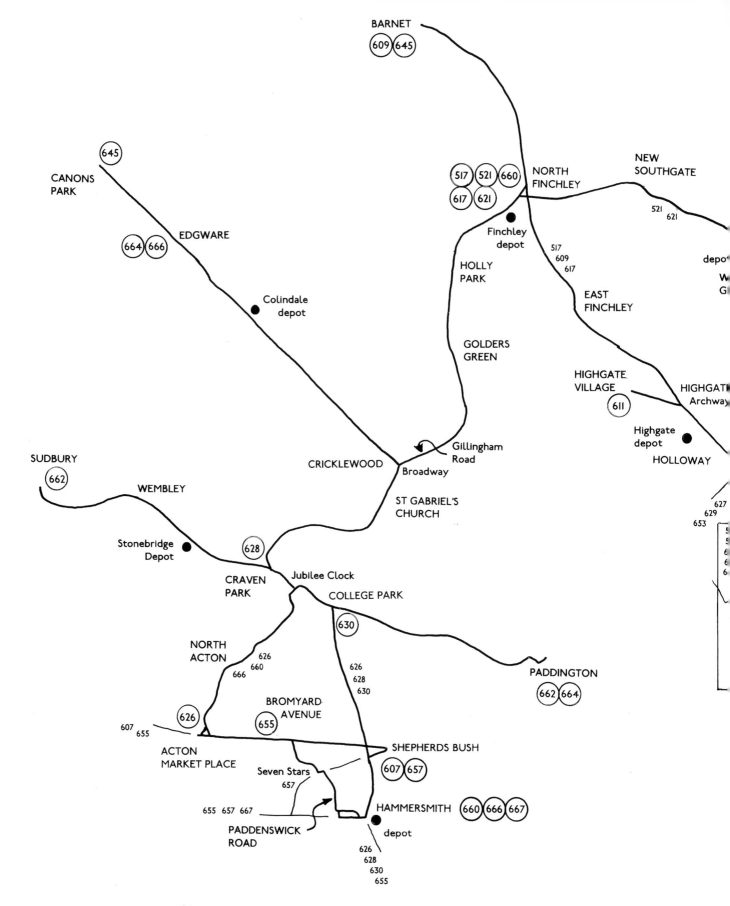

BARNET
(609)(645)

(645)
CANONS PARK

NEW SOUTHGATE

(517)(521)(660) NORTH FINCHLEY

(617)(621)

(664)(666) EDGWARE

• Finchley depot

521
621

HOLLY PARK

517
609
617

depo
W
G

Colindale depot

EAST FINCHLEY

GOLDERS GREEN

HIGHGATE VILLAGE
(611)

HIGHGAT
Archway

Highgate depot •

Gillingham Road

HIGHGATE
Archway

SUDBURY
(662)

CRICKLEWOOD

Broadway

HOLLOWAY

WEMBLEY

ST GABRIEL'S CHURCH

627
629
653

Stonebridge Depot •

(628)

Jubilee Clock

CRAVEN PARK

COLLEGE PARK

5
5
6
6
6

NORTH ACTON

(630)

626
666 660

626
628
630

PADDINGTON

(662)(664)

BROMYARD AVENUE

(626)

(655)

607 655

ACTON MARKET PLACE

SHEPHERDS BUSH

Seven Stars
657

(607)(657)

655 657 667

HAMMERSMITH
(660)(666)(667)

PADDENSWICK ROAD

• depot

626
628
630
655

26

FINCHLEY DEPOT – Driver's sphere of operations

 609   TERMINAL AND ROUTE

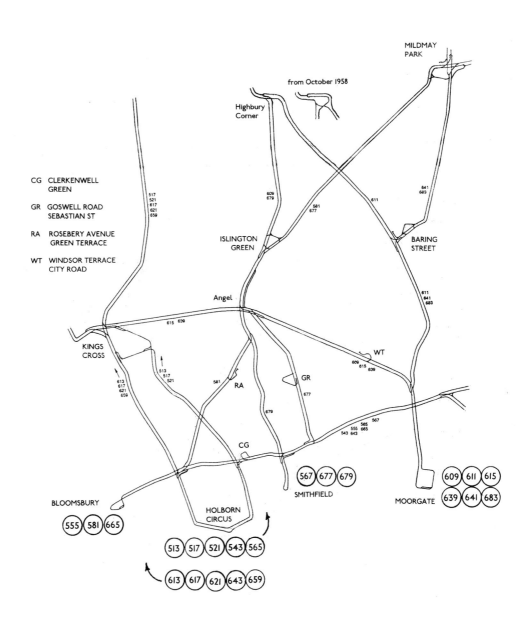

ON THE BACK

SETTLING IN AS A CONDUCTOR

I turned up at Finchley depot for an early turn on my first day's work as a fully-fledged trolleybus conductor on Monday 5th November 1951. I told a depot inspector my name and he put a tick against it on the day's worksheet. Trolleybus staff's names were listed on sheets of paper and a DI put a tick against each person's name as they arrived (motorbus staff signed themselves in on a sheet). London Transport referred to trolleybus crews' starting time as 'show-up time' and wherever this terminology is mentioned it applies to the time that crews were 'ticked-in'. Staff did not actually sign-off – they just walked away when they finished. At the same time the DI told me the name of the driver with whom I would be paired. I soon found him, and once he knew that it was my first day said "Just keep ringing the bell, do the best you can and leave the rest to me". I did not really know what to fully expect so was happy for him to take charge – as I recall, the whole duty was on the 609s. The day passed uneventfully, the tickets sold tallied with the money I had taken and I went home able to report to the rest of the family that everything had worked out well. It had not been a difficult time in contrast to some unfortunates who, having had a real caning on the 645s on their first day, walked out of the depot wondering if they had made a good career move. Over the years there were a few conductors who said "Blow this for a game of soldiers" and threw in the towel after just a few weeks. They had been unable to cope with the workload.

The first few days on my own were rather frantic. I expect that some passengers realised I was 'wet behind the ears' and took advantage of this by travelling beyond their fare stage, asking for a lower fare than that required or dodged me completely. It was alright if people asked for a specific value but if they asked for a place on the route, this slowed me up as I had to consult the fare chart. Although there was a full size one, just inside the lower saloon adjacent to the offside long seat, for quick reference I used miniature fare charts which I kept in my leather cash bag. A depot inspector had

issued the charts to me and at home I stuck them onto two pieces of stiff card and put a coat of varnish on top of the finished result. I'd got the idea from the trolleybus timecards, which were made of Bakelite, on which the times for the day were listed. They had a coat of varnish for protection from the hard wear the crews gave them. One of my fare charts had the 521/621 details on one side with the 609 on the other, while the second had the 645 on one side and 660 on the reverse. As I soon took up a rota line on the 'City' rota I did not need to use the former set for long, so kept it in my locker. I always used the charts for the 645s/660s as they were not my main routes. When there were fare increases I stuck the new miniature tables on top of the old ones and for the first few days I even had to use them when working on the 521/621 and 609 routes.

I was assigned to the 'spare' list initially, a term which applied to new members of staff who did not have a regular position on the crew rotas. Spares covered those on holiday, off sick or away for other reasons. It was a good way for novices to find out about all the routes operating from their depots as they would work all manner of duties while on the spare list. However, it meant that they experienced the inconvenience of only knowing their duties on a day-to-day basis. Some of these duties would be 'stand-by' and staff might be told that they had to show-up at 7.30am. This was colloquially known as '7.30 gate'; the gate (a terminology left over from tram days) referred to the entrance to the depot. Spares showed up at varying times during the day and would sit on a bench in the conductor's room (another name for the output). They would wait for instructions which would be: (a) complete a full duty (b) operate part of a duty after which they were to see the depot inspector for further orders or (c) go and sit in the depot canteen until they were needed. It was very rare for someone not to perform any work. Each day I had to look at the postings on the spare list to see what my following day's work would be and on one occasion when I looked to see what duty I had been allocated the next day, I saw that my name was not there. I asked depot inspector Jim Lawrence why this was so, and he said it was because I was taking up a rota line with a permanent driver, Dennis Childs, the following day, Wednesday 14th November. I now received my first permanent payroll number, having a temporary one before this. I had only been on the spare list for a few days and was never loaned to another depot, which was an option that could be activated at any time with spare staff. It was unusual for new staff to immediately take up a rota line as I was doing. That I did was due to Finchley's staff shortage at the time. As the years went by, stand-by staff became fewer and fewer.

Left Motorists in London were aware that conductors would leave their trolleybuses in order to operate overhead points. Outside Selby's store at Holloway, one of my colleagues has just let go of a semi-automatic frog handle so that 1481 can take the inside set of wires – in a couple of seconds he'll be back on board. Three-tier pavements are almost a thing of the past now but there were three places on the 609 where they could be seen in 1961: by Barnet terminus, here on the north side of Holloway Road at Holloway and adjacent to the Agricultural Hall, Islington. 1481's driver is not parked inconsiderately but has 'read the road' well as a parked car prevents him from being close to the kerb. *Tony Belton.*

My initial weeks were a time of learning and I soon found trolleybus conducting an interesting and satisfying occupation although it could be hard work at times. I really enjoyed going in and no two days were alike – it was this feature that made the job interesting rather than tedious. Apart from the night shifts and the very early turns, when the same passengers were being picked up and there was very little traffic about, there was always action and many examples are related throughout the book. Most passengers were pleasant and paid their right fare and many interesting conversations were held with them. I got to know some people particularly well –

what their jobs were, which football team they supported, where they shopped, etc. There was one elderly gent who regularly boarded at Nightingale Road (near Bounds Green) and went backwards and forwards to Wood Green. For some reason he always referred to me as 'sailor'. On the first couple of 'buses on each route there were certain people I would expect to see and if they were not where they usually should be, there was a valid reason for it – maybe they were on holiday or not going to work that day. A passenger might comment that someone was not on board and, if time allowed, I would hold the bus for a minute to see if they came.

Traffic caused delays in the run up to Christmas; a few days before the 1961 holiday, Finchley's 1458 has been turned short of its Hammersmith destination. 1458 is carrying a good load. A phrase used between crews when they had been carrying heavy loads for a long time was "been knocking on the doors for them have you?". *Tony Belton.*

My working environment for almost four years comprised the platform and the upper and lower decks of a London trolleybus; the green moquette was pleasing to the eye. Apart from 754, all of the trolleybuses that I worked on were of similar interior design. This photograph, taken on 16th April 1961 at Tally Ho bus station, is therefore typical and is of 954 whose L2 classification can be seen on the platform wall – it has a mere nine days of service left in front of it. *John Gillham.*

There were no major drawbacks to the job, though as there were no saloon heaters it could get very cold on late turns if there were no passengers on board. Similarly, it could be freezing first thing in the morning but with trolleybuses usually carrying good loads, the number of people soon warmed the place up. The regular conductors on the staff trolleybuses made sure they were well wrapped-up during the winter months. On hot summer days, with full loads on, I would sweat a bit, but by hanging off the platform the slip-stream cooled me down. There was only one downside to conducting a trolleybus. It was very unpleasant to collect fares on the top deck where most passengers were smoking. I had no alternative but to grin and bear it and it was good to get back to the platform and breathe in fresh air.

Motorbus conductors often had to carry out a balancing act as their drivers could corner at speed. Trolleybus conductors did not experience the same amount of swaying but it was still necessary at times to hold on, as a trolleybus had far greater acceleration. I counteracted this by bracing myself against the cushion of the seats with my legs. Mr Abrahams gave me good advice about rule 95. Children, women and elderly people should be prevented from alighting while a 'bus was still in motion. It was a matter for great discretion and had to be done courteously as well as firmly. He told me that although the rule book stated that conductors should not take hold of a passenger as it could give offence, it was practical to help elderly ladies on board – this assistance, of course, was also given to young ladies!

One of my training conductors gave me a tip – whatever was spent during the time on duty, use the Guvnr's money. It was known as 'living out of the bag'. All I had to do was keep a mental check of what was paid out – the money was put back before paying-in. Vic (my second regular driver) would say, "Get us a paper at Holloway tube" (he'd give me the money back later on). Items I bought out of the bag were for teas, meals and cigarettes. It saved looking for my own money, and stopped mix-ups with the cash taken from passengers.

Motorbus conductors had an easy time compared to their trolleybus counterparts for RT type buses only carried fifty-six seated passengers and five standing, while the maximum that trolleybuses could carry were seventy seated passengers with five standing. The seating capacity of a trolleybus therefore was twenty-five percent greater than an RT. Standing passengers were only permitted in peak hours, though at a conductor's discretion they could stand at other times. The rule book stated that five were allowed to stand but for some reason we allowed eight, continuing a wartime practice which was carried on in peacetime. There were never any problems moving along the gangways to collect fares, even when we had standing passengers. People knew we had a job to do and wouldn't impede us.

When taking over, I would often check that the emergency window at the rear of the upper deck was locked in the closed position. There had been instances of them falling back while a trolleybus was moving due to them not being secured after maintenance staff had been working on the roof. When upstairs, I soon got used to hearing the clatter of the trolleybooms as they passed through frogs and crossovers. Before long it became one of the everyday trolleybus noises and I became oblivious to it. What always woke me up a bit was when I was collecting fares upstairs and a dewirement occurred – there was a heavy noise from aloft and the trolleybus itself shook. Then there would be the rumbling of the bamboo pole being pulled out from beneath the vehicle as my driver used it to put the booms back on the wires. Then there would be another rumbling sound when the bamboo was replaced. To this day there is one trolleybus sound that still echoes in my head, and that is the noise of the trolleybooms hitting the bars of the retaining hooks on the roof.

Pedestrians and motorists accepted it as a fact of everyday life that trolleybus conductors would leave their vehicles to pull overhead point levers and attend to trolleybooms with a bamboo pole. Frogs, booms and bamboos were some of our everyday work implements.

Experienced conductors, particularly Mr Abrahams, were very accommodating and gave us new recruits tips as to how to best conduct a trolleybus. One piece of advice that he gave me (and which I put into practice) was very valuable. It was that when approaching frog pulls I shouldn't get marooned upstairs. This was a pitfall that many new conductors fell into because passengers wishing to alight would crowd the stairs – this prevented them getting down to the platform in order to get off and pull a frog handle. He told me that it could be very difficult trying to get past people with the result that we wouldn't be able to keep to time and there would soon be another 645 'up your staircase'. I always made sure I was on the platform in good time. Another tip Mr Abrahams gave me was that when leaving a terminus, I should start collecting the fares from downstairs passengers first, commencing with those in the long seats by the platform. Then I should work side to side, up and down the vehicle rather than collect fares from all on the right-hand side and then all on the left-hand side as some short distance riders might slip off without paying. It was best to start downstairs as these passengers were more likely to be taking short journeys. Upstairs passengers, who were probably travelling further, could be dealt with later. The most important thing he told me was the necessity to keep the trolleybus on the move – I must be quick in my fare collection duties, and ready for frog pulls. Also, apart from answering general enquiries, I shouldn't get too engrossed with passengers.

There was one problem which faced young male trolleybus conductors; girls giving them the glad eye, as related to me by fellow conductor, Jack Broadbent. In slack times or when all the fares had been collected, there were opportunities to chat with passengers. It turned out that there was a young lady who he spoke with when it was quiet for no other reason than politeness. She mentioned in the course of conversation that a few of the trolleybus crews went to her aunt Ivy's café for a quick cup of tea on their very early turns, when they were going to Barnet ('Ivy's Café' was a wooden hut near the Black Bull public house in Whetstone). If a crew fancied an early morning cuppa, and there were few or no passengers on board, they would get there three or four minutes early. Having paid for their tea, they would take the cup with them and return it on the way back. Alternatively it would be poured into their billy can to be consumed at Barnet. The young lady would board his 609 near the North Circular Road in High Road Finchley and travel to Tally Ho where she changed to a 521/621. At the time Jack didn't know that she was going to her job at a factory in New Southgate where his fiancée also worked – but he soon found out! One day, he was standing on the back platform as his trolleybus was passing a sweet shop near the factory; observing his fiancée coming out of the shop, he waved to her. However the young lady was also coming out, saw him and started waving too. His fiancée was immediately behind her and said, "Who are you waving at?" The reply was "Oh, he's my boyfriend". She was told "No he's not, HE'S MINE – I've been engaged to him for the past four years". That evening when they met, Jack was given the third degree. Eventually she believed him when he said there was nothing in it – and there wasn't.

This is where it was 'handbags at dawn'. Jack Broadbent's fiancée was coming out of the newsagent's shop behind 931 when she and a young female passenger waved at him. It was fortunate for Jack that while they were arguing about whose he was, the trolleybus he was conducting moved away from the scene! 931 is leaving the second of the two sharp curves in Station Road, New Southgate. *Don Thompson.*

Passengers tended to alight from moving trolleybuses when they were slowing down for bus stops, traffic lights, zebra crossings and the like. Most of the time this was done successfully but there were some who wanted to jump off when the vehicle was still moving at a fast speed. Many times I had to be firm and say, "Wait till the 'bus stops". Conversely, there was often someone who would attempt to board a moving trolleybus, one which had just left traffic lights or a bus stop. What these would-be passengers didn't realise was that in the 1950s, apart from a motorbike, a trolleybus had a greater acceleration than any other road vehicle. People were deceived by its quick pick-up and some were left clutching thin air as the vehicle sped away. There were instances of passengers who, having grabbed the platform handrail, were unable to lift their feet onto the platform with the result that they were whisked off their feet and dragged along the road until commonsense kicked in and they let go of the rail.

Gradually I got to know the majority of the staff at the depot by surname if not by Christian name over a short space of time. This was achieved in two ways. First, each time I worked my day off or did a bit of overtime it was usually with a driver I had not worked with before, so I needed to ask him his name and badge number which had to be inserted on the waybill. Secondly, when I was working with them, I would sit down in the depot canteen or in the refreshment hut at Tally Ho with their colleagues and would be introduced to them. Canteen talk was extremely varied; football and horse-racing were common subjects, as was the type of vegetables staff were growing on their allotments. After I had been 'on the back' for six months, the CDI called me into his office one day to say that I had passed my probationary period. I was happy to hear this as I felt I had given a good account of myself up to then.

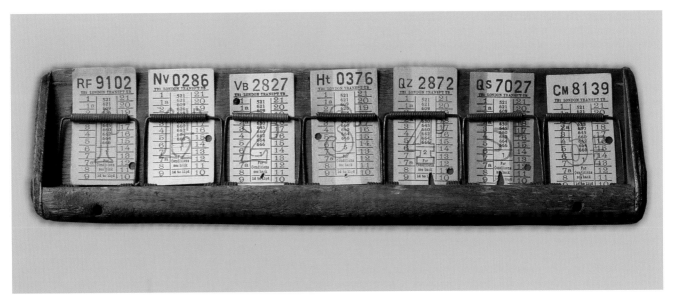

WORKING WITH PUNCH, RACK AND TICKETS

When I started, the three main pieces of equipment for conductors were ticket rack, ticket punch and cashbag. London Transport supplied us with ticket racks which had either five, seven or ten sprung clips each side. The five-a-side ones were for short routes as they only had a few fare values. The rack I was issued with had seven springs on each side and was the general issue. Conductors on Green Line routes had very big racks – ten-a-side with some being two-tiered as there was a wider fare range on these services. On the very long Green Line routes, conductors had to carry two racks. Country Bus conductors also used ten-a-side racks and my colleague, Les Strutt, somehow obtained one for his personal use. There was an element of swapping around of racks between conductors, and we used those that suited us best. I came across a five-a-side one which I found easier to use than the seven-a-side rack. Having two racks, I kept both in my locker between duties, putting both in my ticket box as soon as I started work. If I had to walk 200 yards from the depot to Tally Ho, I would sometimes put the smaller rack in my cashbag as it fitted snugly there.

For the first few months, I worked with the seven-a-side rack, and all the fare values could be accommodated with three empty spring clips. Consequently I kept two spare packs of a hundred 1½d whites and one pack of another low value ticket in the spare places, turning them round so that the backs faced towards me – this prevented me from using the wrong pack (tickets had to be issued in numerical order). Using the five-a-side rack meant that all the values could not be accommodated, but as I did not sell many of the two highest valued tickets (which tended to furl) I kept them in the seven-a-side rack where they were available when needed.

Above A ticket rack of the type used when I was conducting trolley-buses. A sample of different tickets has been placed in the holders, which were designed to hold blocks of 100 each.

Right The ticket punch.

To prevent me continually having to reach into the locker for packs of a hundred tickets, I would, at busy times, have the seven-a-side one already loaded with spare hundreds of the most frequently used values, along with the aforementioned higher value tickets. Again, the spares were turned the wrong way round and, quoting the fare range in use when I started, would probably consist of two packs of penny ha'penny whites, a hundred threepenny blues, a hundred fourpenny greens and a hundred of any other values which were running low in my five-a-side rack (sometimes I kept a spare pack of '1½d whites' in my jacket pocket for easy access). I would place the seven-a-side rack in the ticket rack holder under the stairs or put it on the ledge at the back of the nearside long seat in the lower saloon. This was not risky as members of the public wouldn't think about swiping a rack. Nearly always, I took the rack with me when I went to pull a frog handle – usually it was in my hand but sometimes I put it in my cashbag. At quiet times such as early Sunday mornings, very late at night or on the staff bus, I would leave the rack inside the vehicle when making a frog pull.

Each pack of a hundred tickets had a long staple through it. After about fifty had been issued, part of the bottom of the remaining tickets tended to get ripped by the wire as they were pulled from the bundle. It was also dangerous as the wire could go down my fingernail and the staple could scratch my hand. To prevent tickets getting damaged and to avoid hurting myself, when I was about a third of the way through each pack, I would break the wire from front to back thus pulling it out of the back of the tickets. I would then put the staple in the used ticket box.

When a ticket was taken from the pack it was done by grasping it between the thumb and forefinger, at the same time holding the rest of the pack secure by placing the middle finger over the rest of the tickets. If I did not keep the middle finger in position when taking a staple out, the tickets could fly about all over the place as I found out a couple of times. I had to grovel around on the floor, picking them up and putting them all back in order.

Issuing tickets was straightforward. I would take a ticket from the appropriate pack in the rack, insert it into the mouth of the ticket punch and push the lever down. This made a hole in the fare stage box and indicated where the ticket expired. When the ticket was clipped, the part that had been cut out dropped into a compartment inside the punch – these clippings were known as confetti. Some of the conductors who had been on the job for many years could get a ticket out of their rack, and punch it before there was time to blink. Others were able to have a fan of three in their hand and punch them in a couple of seconds. Whichever rack I was using, I kept the tickets in value order in the rack, the lowest fare being on the left-hand of one side and the highest being on the right-hand side of the other. I soon learnt which colour ticket went with which fare value. The ticket rack looked very colourful and young children were attracted to it by the colours – I could see their eyes focusing on it. Some of the kiddies opened their hands for the tickets so I gave them to them rather than their parents. After a fare increase it took a few days to adjust to the revised colours.

In the ticket boxes there was always at least one spare pack of a hundred tickets for every value. When I was down to the last ten or so in each pack, I would put a new hundred behind it. Having done this there were times when there were maybe just two left at the end of the day. As all tickets had to be taken out of the rack and placed in the ticket box at the end of the shift, I would put a rubber band (supplied in the ticket box) around the hundred and two. It was important to insert each pack of a hundred in the correct sequence but occasionally when I needed tickets quickly I picked up the wrong pack. This was termed 'making a break' and a form had to be filled in and a depot inspector informed if I had not been able to finish off that particular hundred. Occasionally I had packs of tickets that started with 0000. This signified that they were the first ones to be issued, with a configuration such as Ac0000 or Bx0000.

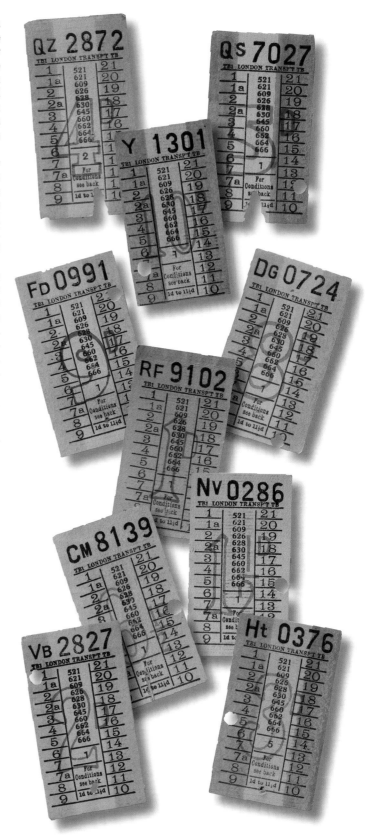

The range of trolleybus tickets in use when I began as a conductor in 1951.

Occasionally, conductors would run out of the lower value tickets on a really busy day. This could be resolved in a number of ways. If I ran out of threepenny tickets shortly before I was finishing, I would use two penny ha'pennies to make up the right amount. However, if I still had a fair amount of time to do then I would follow rule 117 and borrow some from another conductor, signing their waybill with my name, badge number and duty number. Back at the depot a form had to be filled in, detailing what I had borrowed. Initiative had to be used in these circumstances with the favoured way being to tell my driver to catch up the 'bus in front so that I could borrow tickets from its conductor. Once tickets had been obtained we would then hang back until that 'bus had got away. Another way of obtaining extra tickets would be to flag down a trolleybus going in the other direction but this was not favoured as it meant crossing the road; I borrowed tickets on the 'City' routes on a few occasions.

Conversely, I lent tickets to other conductors and recall a time when one had to borrow tickets from me when we turned short at New Southgate. He didn't have enough tickets to get him through to North Finchley, where he could get new supplies, so he took a hundred 1½d whites off me to tide him over. If I ran out of tickets when I was working on the 645s or 660s, all I had to do was to tell my driver to hang on for a couple of minutes at the top of Woodberry Grove while I nipped into the depot to obtain some more. Conductors had to borrow from their home depot so it was no good if they were at Craven Park and the nearest trolleybus was one from Hammersmith depot. In the knowledge that they were far from home, a conductor who was 'on the ball' in this area would ask their driver to look out for a Finchley 'bus. No doubt Les Strutt, who set a depot record one day when he punched nine hundred and ninety eight 1½d tickets out of a total of almost two thousand tickets on a 645 duty, had to rush into the output to get more tickets sometime during the day. He was that good a conductor that he would have kept the bell going so that the 'bus kept to time that day and would have got all his fares in despite having to get off to pull frog handles. Les, who had started before me, loved being busy and was another man who really liked the job. Like me he became a trolleybus driver, then motorbus driver and later a 'silver badge' inspector. In life, there are some people you just latch onto. Les was someone who fell into this category. He was a good friend and colleague, and shared many of his experiences with me. London trolleybuses led to marriages. Dennis Childs married an Irish conductress who came on the job, and Les Strutt met his wife-to-be at Finchley depot too. He and Diane became a husband and wife crew which was an occasional buswork occurrence.

Sometimes it was impossible to collect all of the fares from the short distance travellers who were in the upper saloon. We were advised not to take a handful of money and bang off some tickets afterwards as there could be an accusation that we had not issued a ticket. Due to the hopelessness of not being able to issue, say, twenty tickets to people piling down the stairs and thrusting money into our hands, we had no alternative, when finding that we had been given coins to say, the value of three shillings, than to knock off tickets to that

Shortage of Tickets 　**117.** If Conductors run short of tickets during a journey they must report the matter to the first Official whom they see, borrow a supply from another Conductor, and obtain a further supply from the Depot as soon as possible.

They must make the necessary entries on the cash total sheets and must subsequently report the matter on the form provided.

value. As long as we had punched or rolled off the appropriate amount it was alright, but we really had to be careful for there were some plain clothes inspectors who liked nothing better than to make something out of nothing. Some passengers, whose fares had not been taken, would leave their coins on one of the long seats adjacent to the platform. When this happened I punched off the appropriate tickets and threw them on the floor or put them in the used ticket box. In the early 1950s some journeys were so busy that it was easy to get through a pack of a hundred of the lowest value tickets on a single journey, even two hundred on a 'rounder'.

When reporting for work, I would ask for the ticket box for the relevant duty. Normally the depot inspectors knew which rota the established conductors were on so I would only have to nominate the duty number. I would say "one thirty please, Stan" if Stan Nelson was on. He would give me the relevant box. On duties where a crew were the first to take a trolleybus out of the depot, the day's timecard was on top of the box. If staff were working a duty on the rota they were not listed on, they would say "eight on the twenty-ones" (even though part of it was on the 609s) or "thirteen on the forty-fives" (which might have a trip on the 660s) and the DI would give them the ticket box and punch for the duty. Kept in large pigeon holes behind the counter, the ticket boxes were prepared by a depot assistant who had put packs of different value tickets inside. These had to be loaded in the rack as soon as possible. Those duties which were known to be 'heavy' would have many packs of the lower value fares, while those that were usually 'light' did not have so many tickets supplied. A small number of boxes were used twice a day because the lack of room in the offices meant that there weren't enough pigeon holes to accommodate all the boxes. Once a very early turn had finished, the same box would be made up for a late turn but this time without Early Morning Singles (EMS) tickets. With all this work having to be done at Finchley, which was of average size, it must have been a massive job to keep on top of things at depots as large as Highgate and West Ham. The duty number was painted in red on the end of each ticket box, but when it was used for a second time, it was chalked onto the top of it. There was not much room in the ticket boxes to carry personal items but if I was having sandwiches for my lunch, as I occasionally did, they could be accommodated inside.

The first range of tickets that I used were as follows (these had been in use since 1st October 1950):

1d salmon (child)	3d blue	6½d primrose	10d grass green
1½d white	4d green	8d yellow	11½d lilac
2d apple green (child)	5d orange	9d buff	Most values had a white central strip.

The tickets that I initially used were common to Colindale, Finchley and Stonebridge depots and were known as 'UNIVERSALS'. This was the only set used on the trolleybus system and was possible as the fare stages on all these three depots' routes interworked. All other depots had a plain T version which we used from about the middle of 1952. The change was transitional and the lower value UNIVERSAL tickets disappeared first. The higher value ones took some time to vanish as they were used less. The UNIVERSALS listed all the routes operating from CE, FY and SE depots including route 630 which had a single Stonebridge-operated journey that reached Tooting.

Following a fare increase on 2nd March 1952 some of the colours changed:

1d salmon (child)	2½d prim-rose (child)	6d brown	11d lilac
1½d apple green (child)	3d blue	8d yellow	1/- magenta
2d white	5d orange	9d green	3d blue (EMS)*

*Supplied as a T version to all depots from 1st September 1952.

Fares were raised again on 4th August 1953, with the colour range below being applicable:

1d salmon (child)	3½d prim-rose (child)	8½d yellow	1/1d lilac
2d white	5d orange	10d green	3d blue (EMS)
2½d prim-rose (child)	7d brown	1/- magenta	4d apple green (EMS)

When I started, the punch and ticket system had lost its complexities. There were no transfer tickets, Workman's Returns, through journeys to the Underground or All-day, Evening and Midday tickets. The only 'odd' ticket was a tuppenny one which was dubbed a 'Workman's ticket' and had availability similar to those which had been issued up to the end of September 1950. This facility was open to anybody, even city gents in pin-stripe suits, and was available for journeys completed by 8am on Mondays to Saturdays. The ordinary 2d apple green ticket was used – passengers had a real bargain. However, there was a procedure to be followed with Workman's tickets. If somebody was travelling from Barnet to Moorgate and had boarded at 7.30am I had to take the total fare off them at Barnet, issuing the tuppenny Workman's ticket and probably an ordinary 4d ticket that kicked in at Archway. A handwritten entry was made on the timecards as to which stop a Workman ticket was available but the schedule department didn't always get things right, as the cards sometimes showed that they could be issued on Christmas Day and Bank Holidays when this was not so. It was not in a passenger's interests to purchase a Workman's ticket after about 7.45am as it was cheaper to pay the ordinary fare. The tuppenny Workman's ticket was used for all fares up to 1/1d. Ordinary tickets were used for fares higher than this but only applied to routes 645 and 660.

From March 1952, the Workman's ticket was renamed 'Early Morning Single', and increased to 3d for any fare up to 1/1d. For fares above 1/2d, higher EMS fares applied and were met by using the 3d EMS ticket and a low valued one. From August 1953, a fare increase saw a 4d EMS ticket introduced for the higher value fares but was only used on the 645s and 660s. As I usually worked on the 'City' routes I only occasionally issued a 4d EMS. Despite this, I kept these in the rack too, adjusting the positions of the other tickets. I kept the EMS packs next to the child tickets. As soon as 8am arrived I dispensed with the EMSs, put them in my ticket box and entered the finishing number on my waybill and inserted a cash total simultaneously. At the same time I would move the other tickets up and insert spare packs of 2d whites the wrong way round. EMS tickets were also available on motorbuses from 1st October 1950 so it was an unexpected bonus for their passengers who had hitherto been denied this facility. The EMSs were withdrawn after issue on 31st December 1961. Over the years, child fares were either exactly half the adult rate or were made up to the nearest penny, e.g. the equivalent of the 1/1d fare was 7d.

There were a few inadequacies with the ticket and punch system. With some fares (both adult and child) I had to use two tickets; this was known as 'marrying'. If somebody was travelling on a 609 from Barnet to Moorgate from August 1953, I had to issue a 1/1d and a 2d ticket for the 1/3d fare. Routes 645 and 660 had even higher fares so two tickets had to be issued for a number of the lengthier journeys. If possible, fare stage numbers on common sections of route were the same. The 660 and 666 between Hammersmith and Cricklewood were, but those on the 609 and 645 between Barnet and North Finchley were not. The fare stage number for Nags Head was the same on the 521/621 as the 609.

There were some journeys that passengers did not normally make, with the prime example being a trip on route 645 from Barnet to Canons Park or vice versa; this was because it was quicker to travel by route 107. Usually it would only be people out for a Sunday afternoon ride who would participate in such a journey. Similarly, nobody in their right mind would

travel on a 645 between Henlys Corner (near Finchley) and Staples Corner at Hendon, as it was much quicker to travel on route 112. Those wishing to travel between Jubilee Clock and Hammersmith would use a 626 or 628 rather than a 660 or 666 as the former was a shorter journey. It was quicker to go from Wood Green to Holborn on a 521/621 rather than a 543/643, and those travelling between North Finchley and Holloway would normally use a 517/617 or 609 rather than a

521/621. In all these instances it was also cheaper. Those travelling between Moorgate and Nags Head or Archway had the choice of a 609 or a 611. It was the same fare on both routes but three minutes quicker by 611. However, people tended to take whatever was first in line at Moorgate, though in peak hours they would opt for a 611 rather than a 609 as the Islington 'Angel' area was often clogged up with traffic – also there were heavy passenger loadings on the 609.

Above Routes 617 and 621 operated between North Finchley and Holborn Circus via Farringdon Road; the 617 travelled via Highgate and the 621 via Finsbury Park. Highgate's 1376 and Finchley's 945 are seen outside the Gaumont Cinema, North Finchley; 945 is turning into Woodhouse Road while 1376 continues down the High Road. Locals knew it was quicker to travel on the 617 than the 621 between North Finchley and Holloway. *Don Thompson.*

Left For those wanting to travel from Moorgate to Holloway or Archway, it took a bit less time to use a 611 rather than a 609. Seen at Finsbury Square, Highgate's 1368 passes Finchley's 956. This view was taken in the earlier part of the 1950s as both vehicles have linen blinds in their front boxes.

Some passengers used pre-paid tickets as firms were able to purchase these from London Transport and issue them to their employees. There were also agreements with local education authorities who bought pre-paid tickets; these were in the same style as punch tickets and persisted into Gibson machine days. I cancelled them by tearing them in half, giving the top section to the passenger and discarding the lower part. Education vouchers were another item seen, and detailed the journey and the number of teachers and children travelling. They would state something like 'Three teachers and forty-seven children North Finchley to Old Street'. From here they went to the Geffrye Museum in Kingsland Road, getting on a 543/643 which was operated from Stamford Hill depot. Each journey had a separate voucher, so I would have handled one as would my SF counterpart. Vouchers were not always used for these trips, so when a large party boarded, one of the teachers would pay for all of them. This took a lot of the children's tickets out of my rack in one fell swoop, but the advantage was that the trolleybus was now more than two-thirds full and I wouldn't be taking too many more fares until they had disembarked. If, in punch and ticket days, forty-seven children boarded it was likely that I would have to start a fresh pack of a hundred tickets to accommodate them. Care had to be taken, for if the first ticket was numbered BC4277, then the final ticket had to be BC4323 with BC4324 being the next ticket in view. As a precaution I would count the number of tickets I was punching. If a teacher paid in cash in Gibson machine days, I would issue a very long length of paper which the children vied for.

Schoolchildren who lived more than three miles from their school used 'Scholars Term Tickets' which were available for the duration of a term. If a child was released from school early they were given a white slip which allowed them to use the term ticket before school finishing time. They were supposed to be date-stamped in ink to prevent further use and retained by conductors but some got round this and probably swapped them for marbles, comics and sweets, as some of these slips had an 'amended' look about them. Ours was not to reason why these children were showing a business acumen in the early form of a 'nice little earner' and, with a questioning look, I accepted them. At some schools, the date on which they were to be used was not entered; scholars would insert a date in pencil. A rubber would be used on another occasion, allowing the slip to be used when 'bunking off' school when they wanted to miss 'double physics'.

Now and again I would inadvertently issue a wrong ticket, say a threepenny one instead of a tuppenny one. If I could get rid of it immediately to a nearby passenger I would do so. Otherwise I would think to myself "Blow it" and I would rather lose the penny than go through all the palaver that the correct procedure entailed. This was laborious as I was supposed to withdraw the wrong ticket, obtain and verify the person's name and address, issue them with the correct ticket and then, back at the depot, fill in a 'Ticket punched in error' form (I only filled in one of these when it concerned higher values as I was not going to lose, say, a shilling). Another matter concerned passengers who needed to be charged excess fares.

These were people who were either deliberately riding beyond their stop or were genuinely unaware of the fact that they had done so. They had to be issued with an excess ticket so as to make up the fare for their whole journey – as if they had paid the full fare in the first place.

The procedure to be followed concerning passengers who had no money was to obtain their name and address, verifying this if possible, by a letter with their address on it or driving licence. Sometimes I was not able to get their particulars but that was not my problem. I had to issue them with a ticket and ask them to send the money to the Fares and Charges Officer at 55 Broadway, London, SW1. All of this was a bit of a nuisance as an unpaid fare report had to be filled in back at the depot. I only did this occasionally, for if someone was in distress I would give them a ticket and pay the fare myself. I would say "pay me another time" – sometimes they did, other times I would never see them again. If it was a regular passenger who found themselves in this situation I would do this in the knowledge that they would repay me. By acting in this way, if a plain clothes inspector was on the 'bus or a revenue inspector boarded, I would not be reported for an uncollected fare.

Occasionally someone in plain clothes would show me a silver circular medallion. These were issued to high ranking London Transport officials and they showed these rather than their staff passes. When someone presented me with one of these I would acknowledge him but would quietly think to myself "He's got nothing more than a shilling on a chain". Conductors tended to be more vigilant about their duties when they had such a person on board, though.

The waybill was a record of a conductor's daily ticket issue. It was compiled by a depot assistant who inserted the starting numbers of each value, with conductors having to ensure that the entries were correct. On the other side of the waybill, all the starting numbers had to be entered against each ticket value with their finishing numbers having to be entered at the end of each journey. When the day's work ended, the final finishing numbers were placed against the original starting numbers and by subtracting one from the other I would know the number of tickets sold at each price. By multiplying them and then adding up the totals, the amount to pay in would be known. The waybill was used for a single day's work. However, I also recall using a 'two day cash total sheet'. With these, enough tickets were supplied for what was expected to cover two days – each day's takings had to be paid in individually. Sometimes I kept my waybill on its clipboard in my cashbag, while at other times I left it in the ticket rack slot under the stairs. When a revenue inspector boarded a trolleybus to check it, he would either have to ask me for it or would take it from the slot.

There was not enough room on the waybill for the terminal points to be written in fully, so abbreviations had to suffice. I used the following for the most frequently used places:

NF	North Finchley	BAR	Barnet
MOOR	Moorgate	NH	Nags Head
CP	Canons Park	WG	Wood Green
FP	Finsbury Park	HAMM	Hammersmith
IG	Islington Green	KC	Kings Cross

At crew changeover points, conductors left an auxiliary waybill in the ticket rack slot. This served as a record of what tickets had been issued prior to them leaving the 'bus. The auxiliary waybill was completed, in punch and ticket days, by inserting the numbers of each value at the start of a conductor's final journey before being relieved, while on the Gibson machine system, its total register number at the start of that journey was filled in. If an inspector boarded the new conductor's trolleybus and said, "Waybill please, conductor" he would be handed the auxiliary waybill and the conductor's waybill. On crew changeovers, we were supposed to inspect all tickets previously issued in order to satisfy ourselves as to the limit of their availability, but in practice it was unworkable. If I had taken over a southbound 609 at Tally Ho at a busy time, I had my work cut out to get all the fares in from those who boarded there, let alone check tickets of those who had already paid. The auxiliary waybills were only used for 609s and 645s both ways at North Finchley. An auxiliary waybill was also used if passengers were transferred from one trolleybus to another.

All of London Transport's ticket punches, whether they were used on Central Buses, Country Buses or by the Tram and Trolleybus department had an identifying number. Those used on trams, trolleybuses and Country Buses were smaller than the Central bus ones and had a letter 'A' before the serial number, eg A6342. They tended to make a dull clicking sound and only a few made a ring like a Central Bus punch which had a strong rasp to it. The ticket punch clipped into a back-plate which in turn was fixed on to a small leather apron which was attached to my uniform jacket. Later on I used a punch supporting strap that rested over my left shoulder. This was better as I didn't have to keep screwing and unscrewing the ticket punch back plate on to my tunic. Some of the back-plates were fitted with a position for a cancellor to be attached. Obsolete in my time, the cancellor (also serial numbered) was a piece of equipment that carried out the same function as a punch but made a perforated mark in a Workman's ticket. I just had an ordinary back plate.

When the ticket box was given to me, the punch was on top of it (often the timecard was beneath it). The number of the punch was entered on the waybill, and enabled London Transport to know who had which punch on any particular day. Each punch was allocated to a specific duty. At the base of the punch there was a four digit register that recorded the number of times it was used. Its starting and finishing numbers were inserted on the waybill and at the end of the duty, the difference between the two had to match the number of tickets sold. Tickets were delivered to the depot by van from Effra Road, Brixton where London Transport had their own works at which they printed tickets and maintained and repaired punches.

When completing my duty I would hand in the ticket box, with the unsold tickets remaining inside, and leave the punch on top of the box. After counting the takings, a depot inspector checked the ending number on the punch after which he opened it with a special key and disposed of the ticket confetti. Then the punch went back in the box ready for use on the same duty the following day. The only time that this was not done was if there was a discrepancy; then the confetti would be counted by administrative staff. This could be instigated by a conductor if he thought there was a problem with a punch, or by London Transport if it was thought that there was some fiddling going on. When I finished my day's work I would place my cashbag and all my conducting equipment in my locker.

The punches were very reliable and I never had one that malfunctioned. The only problem that occurred was that the punch slot could get clogged up with bits of tickets, even too much for the punch cleaner. All I could do in these situations, was to tear the ticket at the appropriate fare stage until I could obtain a replacement punch. The punch register number wouldn't tally with the tickets, but that wasn't a problem as I still had to account for the number of tickets I had issued. As with many matters, a report had to be made, and the clogged up punch would be sent to Effra Road where the debris would be removed.

The combination of having to queue to pay in the day's takings and wanting to make a speedy getaway from the depot, encouraged conductors to total up before arrival and led to errors being made. Experienced staff would get their arithmetic right first time by jotting everything down on a piece of paper or, in Gibson machine days, on a piece of ticket roll. Many could do it mentally in their head, but even the most competent conductors would make errors from time to time. Mistakes were known as 'shorts and overs', and on pay day the offenders were required to make up the money or find themselves being reimbursed with a few coins. To obviate such problems, many conductors had a 'ready reckoner'. These could be obtained from a local stationer with conductor-instructors advising their trainees about where they could obtain them. Staff kept the ready reckoners, which eliminated most of the paying-in errors, in their jacket pockets. Any mistakes made on the waybill were supposed to be crossed out and the correct number inserted above. Most of us though, used a rubber. If a conductor had too many 'shorts and overs' in quick succession they would find their name on the list of miscreants who had to make a visit to the CDI. He would suggest that they make a better job of things in the future.

Paying-in problems did not apply to Bill Shaw of Colindale depot, who would not bag up any coppers or do any paperwork until he had reached the output, even if it was the last duty at night. This was to the dismay of the night depot inspector who might have to wait an hour for him to bag up all the coins, which was done meticulously one at a time. He was a very conscientious conductor and had a claim of never having made an error. On one occasion it was thought he had. He asked for the waybill to be returned so that he could personally check it – when he perused it, it was found that he had not made a mistake, a clerk had. Every depot had its characters and Bill Shaw fell into this category at Colindale. When all passengers had boarded and it was safe for him to give the bell signal he would call out in a very loud voice 'HOLD TIGHT'. His regular passengers on the 645/664/666 were used to this but for those who were not, they jumped in their seats when he made his 'broadcast'.

He was also polite and each time he finished a transaction, would say as one word "ITHANKYOU". Similarly he was thoughtful to Finchley and Stonebridge crews for when his 645 was scheduled to turn short at Tally Ho on Sunday mornings, he would drop the poles to allow others to pass. He was quite a stout man and when he did this there was a lot of huffing and puffing from his cheeks.

Occasionally, conductors took the wrong ticket box or Gibson machine box. This was easily done in the output, canteen or refreshment hut. Sometimes it would be realised before a 'bus had been taken over and boxes were exchanged but if it only came to light after it had departed, then both conductors would have to use their counterpart's equipment. With the punch and ticket system, a note was made of the starting numbers of each value ticket and at the end of the shift the finishing numbers were put alongside. With Gibson machines, the same thing could be done with the starting and finishing numbers; however, there was an alternative in that the emergency punch tickets could be used. When this happened, one of the conductors might have to wait around a bit for the other one to finish. With a bit of fumbling around between them, London Transport would get the money due to them.

A custom that had died out just before I started was 'snatching'. This practice involved spare conductors who would be given tickets and a punch in the peak hours and told to board busy 'buses and issue tickets. 'Snatchers' had to leave an auxiliary waybill on each vehicle that they boarded, so that if an inspector checked the 'bus, he wouldn't think anything was amiss when he came across two different batches of serial numbers. Many people only travelled short distances, so it was in London Transport's interests to use spare staff in this way and ease the workload of the regular conductor who might be hard pressed to collect all the fares. We had one new conductor, Johnny Pope, who on his first day's snatching thought he had to sell all the tickets in the box before he returned to the depot. He left at about 6am and when he returned many hours later, he apologised for not having sold all the tickets! When 'snatchers' were on duty, trolley staff could only work on trolleybuses and bus staff could only work on motorbuses as they had different types of tickets and conductor's licences. Snatchers were only allowed to work on their own depot's routes as, for virtually all the time that this practice functioned, each depot had its own set of tickets. This leads me on to say that throughout my trolleybus career, motorbus and trolleybus staff considered themselves to be two different firms, harking back to the times of the various tramway companies and the London General Omnibus Company.

The reader may have heard about conductors quietening passengers down by clobbering them with their ticket rack. This actually happened one evening when a revenue inspector checked one of our trolleybuses at Cricklewood Broadway. On the top deck some of the passengers were being rowdy, and the inspector, being outnumbered, came down to conductor Gilligan, who used to be an Irish policeman (Garda), and told him there was trouble upstairs. The conductor always liked to have an orderly 'bus and was a 'no-nonsense man'. Woe betide anybody who acted otherwise. He stormed upstairs and holding the tickets firmly in the rack with his hand (to prevent them flying out) whacked three offenders with it. In those days one accepted the punishment for the crime and there were no repercussions from the victims.

One of the CDIs I worked under was Bob Irons. With his hair parted down the middle, he had a foreboding appearance. If any member of staff found their name on his list saying 'See CDI' it was an even bet that he was going to get a roasting even for the slightest misdemeanour. He was a dour man, a bit of a tyrant really and only seemed happy if he could send somebody 'up the Manor' on a disciplinary hearing. This would be a visit to the divisional office at Manor House. I only crossed swords with him once. This was due to the fact that one day I paid in a shilling short, probably giving out too much change to somebody. Not having another shilling with me, I informed the depot inspector that there was a deficit; but Mr Irons got hold of me before I had the opportunity to pay it back when the 'shorts and overs' were dealt with. I had to go into his office where he questioned me about why I had paid in a shilling short. Irons said "I'll tell you where it is – it's in your pocket". It came across in such a way that I stood up and said "Are you accusing me of stealing?" I have never done London Transport out of any money and wasn't going to lose my job for the sake of such a small amount. Seeing that I was going to match him word for word, his tone then changed and he said, "What I meant was that the money is not in London Transport's pocket while it is still in yours". I flicked him his shilling and walked out. The tables were turned on Irons quite literally one day when a conductor who had been dismissed for some reason went to see him about some holiday pay that he thought he was owed. Mr Irons said he was not entitled to it and an altercation ensued resulting in the conductor turning the desk over on top of Mr Irons who ended up on the floor in the corner of the room. The police were called and a few minutes later a Black Maria police car came roaring into the depot and took the ex-conductor away. Mr Irons's office was in a right old state with boxes, files and papers everywhere. It gave us all a good laugh and evened things out a bit. Despite all the grief he gave us it was all 'cat and mouse' – manager versus staff; he had a job to do for which we respected him.

COINS OF THE REALM

I handled a lot of coins in the course of a day's work so it was absolutely necessary to use my cashbag. Being right-handed, the strap went across my left shoulder and the bag rested on my right thigh. For their fares, passengers tendered mainly copper but there was also a lot of silver. I kept coppers in the big part of my cashbag and the threepenny bits in its smaller partition, placing 'tanners' (sixpenny pieces) in the small pocket on the right-hand side of my jacket. I put large silver (shillings, florins and half crowns) into the big left-hand pocket which, along with the right-hand one, was reinforced. I did not generally keep coins in the right-hand side pocket as it got in the way of my cash bag. The only time I did was when I had too much silver in my left pocket which I then transferred to the right one. I very rarely came across small silver threepenny bits. These needed to be kept separately from the tanners as they could easily be given out by mistake, so I kept them in one of my trouser pockets. Another coin that I only came across here and there was the farthing. I got rid of these (worth a quarter of a penny) as soon as I could by giving them back in change, or paid them in at the depot. To obviate the possibility of coins jumping out of my cashbag when running for a frog pull, I held the mouth of the cashbag closed at these times. Any notes that I was given went in my wallet which I kept in my inside jacket pocket. I kept my blind changing key in my left pocket and its continual contact with the silver coins made it very shiny. Normally, there was a lot of change available but there were occasions when this was not so. I would ask the passenger to come up to me for their change when they alighted, but occasionally, in the rush, this did not happen and I was left with the coins. I always paid it in as unrefunded change but it was paid back to me sometime later if it had not been claimed.

At the top of the stairs immediately on the right, and downstairs adjacent to the top of the farechart holder, there was a coin tester. They were introduced during the war as passengers were passing off 'dud' coins to conductors. The testers were provided to help conductors identify the duds. There were a number of different sized apertures to test whether various coins were genuine or not. On one occasion I considered that I had been given a bad half-crown so I inserted it in the tester. The coin bent so I had to inform the person who had offered it to me that he would have to find me a real half-crown. I cannot recall with which coin he then paid me but this time it was genuine.

Underneath the stairs there was a locker where I kept my ticket box. The locker was opened by the blind changing key. It was not completely secure as there were a few instances of them being opened – presumably by former staff who had retained their key or by someone who, one way or another, had obtained one. If the 'bus I was working on was a J class vehicle, I would usually put my ticket box on top of the contactor box in the driver's cab, or at least place bagged up coins there for security. The C class trolleybuses did not have their contactors in the cab, so there was nowhere to put my possessions. With these 'buses I had to use the locker for my ticket box, but I would give bagged-up coins to Dennis, Vic or Harry (my three regular drivers) or whoever I was working with that day, who would keep them in their pockets. One day I inadvertently left two bagged up ten shillings worth of threepenny pieces in a 609 when I was coming off for relief at North Finchley from Barnet. A couple of minutes after it had left for Moorgate I realised my loss so boarded the next 609, told driver Jim Beckford what had happened and he flew down the road, but it was not until we got to 'The Wellington' at Highgate that we caught up with the 609 and I could retrieve the money.

Each day I was issued with three shillings and sixpence float. This was in varying amounts of small change and in a small cloth cash bag which was inside the ticket box. I would check that there was 3/6d there before starting the day's work. As soon as I had the opportunity to replace the float with money taken, I would do so. I then placed the bag back

in the box. The float was handed in when paying in at the end of the duty – a depot inspector checked it and it was returned to the box. There could be times when the firm's float was inadequate in that I didn't have enough change. I could usually get larger coins split by other passengers, but there were occasions when I had to use my own money. At some time, possibly when the change was made from the ticket and punch to the Gibson machine, conductors were allowed to keep the three and sixpence float. Somehow I retained the float bag (number 130) and cashbag, and still have both in my possession.

There were strict rules about how money could be paid in. It was alright to bag up copper (five shillings worth) and threepenny bits (ten shillings worth) in the cash bags provided, but silver coins and notes had to be counted individually by a depot inspector, acting as a cashier. All the money was placed on a metal cash tray which was pushed through a gap in a wire safety grille. He would check the money by placing the bagged up coins on a set of scales to make sure that they were the correct weight and he then dealt with the silver and notes. When he was satisfied that all was correct he would acknowledge this with an "alright" or an "okay" and push the tray back.

Usually, conductors would pay in just once a day, but a facility that was available was 'part-payment'. This meant that during their meal relief they could pay in most of the money they had taken on their first half of duty, and this enabled them to get rid of a lot of weight. It had to be in straight pounds, so no messing around with odd amounts such as four pounds three shillings and eight pence. When the duty was finished they just had to hand in the outstanding money.

GIBSON MACHINES

Mechanisation caught up with ticket issuing procedures on 28th March 1954 when our depot changed over to Gibson ticket machines. On the right hand side of the machine there were two wheels. The inner one altered the fare stage which was shown in a window, while the outer wheel changed the class of ticket (ORD for ordinary, C for child, COM for combination, EMS, etc). The large wheel on the left side selected the fare which was shown in another window. The depressing of a release button on the left enabled the handle on the right to be turned and a ticket was issued. New ticket rolls were inserted in a compartment in the top of the machine, each of which was individually numbered, e.g. 13486.

In a room in the depot, conductors had to undergo training on the new machines. There were normally three or four practising the issuing of tickets to each other for about an hour. This was carried out in the fortnight or so before the changeover; we were paid overtime for this. I preferred to use the Gibson rather than the punch and rack as it was quicker and enabled me to have both hands free. As with the punch and rack, the Gibson had its limitations and some of the higher fares required two tickets to be issued. The two nearest values were supposed to be used. If someone was taking a 1/3d journey then the procedure was to use a 8d ORD and 7d COM. Not all of the conductors did this and some used other permutations, e.g. 1/- and 3d. This was in contrast to the punch and rack system, where the procedure was to use the highest and lowest values.

The Gibson machine had four clasps onto which were fitted the four hooks of the webbing (these were the straps that were placed across the conductor's shoulder). Fixed to the webbing was a leather shield against which the Gibson machine rested; the protective shield prevented it fraying our jackets. Despite being issued with shields, some conductors didn't use them and their uniforms became very shiny. Conductors were now supplied with a fob for the webbing in which their MSC badge could be inserted. Not everybody used them; some continued to place them in the lapel of their jacket. Some conductors fitted all four webbing hooks onto the two top clasps of the machine. This lowered the Gibson machine, making things more practical – I didn't do this. The young women tended to run for their frog pulls and when they did, they held onto the Gibson machine to stop it bouncing about. Some of the young conductresses altered the webbing so that it became a belt around their waists – it enhanced their femininity. There were a few murmurings from inspectors quoting rule six, in that they had caused "damage to equipment", but a few choice comments like "If you were a woman, would you like four pound of metalwork bouncing about on your chest?" soon brought this to an end.

Working out how much needed to be paid in at the end of the duty was similar to the punch and ticket system. The starting numbers of each value (shown on a counter) had been inserted on the waybill by a counter assistant as had the total register number of the machine which was shown in a separate window. As with the punch and rack system, the finishing numbers on each trip had to be inserted on the waybill. Just as the starting numbers of each value on the punch tickets had to tally with what had been inserted on the waybill, so did the starting numbers in each window have to tally on the Gibson CTS. On both systems, any discrepancies had to be brought to the attention of a depot inspector who would alter and initial the error. At the end of the day's work the finishing numbers of each value were entered alongside the starting numbers and, by subtracting one from the other, the totals should equate with the difference on the register number counter. Multiplying the numbers of each fare value sold and then adding the totals gave the amount to pay in.

A ticket roll had enough paper for about two hundred and fifty tickets. It could run out at an inconvenient time so I often kept a spare one in my jacket. There were a few occasions when my Gibson machine packed up and I had to use the emergency punch tickets. These were kept in a flimsy wooden rack which was inside a cellophane wrapping. They were kept in the machine box and the cellophane was broken when I needed to use them. With the Gibson machines being so reliable, these trolleybus tickets could be found in Gibson boxes many years after they had ceased to be used. I cancelled the tickets by tearing them at the fare stage at which the ticket was due to expire. A waybill was provided for the emergency tickets and we were given a few minutes overtime for completing the second waybill. By adding the cash totals on the Gibson machine waybill and the emergency ticket waybill, I would know the amount to pay in. There was a ticket punch complete with rack and tickets for emergency use in the inspector's box at Tally Ho and, although some conductors used it, I did not. Later on a spare Gibson machine was available there. In a similar vein to the incident involving a ticket rack at Cricklewood Broadway mentioned earlier, one of our conductors threatened to hit a passenger with a Gibson machine at the bus stop opposite Friern Barnet Town Hall. This was due to the passenger assaulting the conductor who had to defend himself. These were only occasional incidents as there was normally mutual respect between staff and passengers. Some occasionally gave me sweets and one Christmas Day a passenger alighting at Lyonsdown Road, Barnet, gave me a bottle of beer as a present.

PEEP-HOLES AND BACKSTAMPS

My instructors demonstrated how conductors changed the front destination blinds (this is fully explained in the next paragraph). Drivers changed some blinds and when I was working with driver Bill Pratt, soon after I started, he told me on which vehicles the conductor had to change the front blind. His precise words were, "Under 920 you have to do both blinds, all the others are mine". However, there was one other trolleybus where the front blinds had to be changed by the conductor (this must have slipped Bill's mind). This was 952, which had been built earlier than 920. As soon as I took over a trolleybus, I made a mental note of its fleet number so that I knew if I had to change the front destination blind as well as the rear one. The conductor-instructors showed me how to change the rear blinds from the staircase.

To change the front destination blinds on the C class vehicles I had to go upstairs to the front of the vehicle where I had to crouch down and put the blind changing key into the turning apparatus in the blind box housing. I peered through a spy-hole where I read a miniature blind display (known as a backstamp) which was pasted onto the back of the blind. By turning my key to the correct backstamp, the right destination was shown. The front blind changing arrangements on these trolleybuses soon attracted complaints from conductors who were having to regularly stoop down. Therefore another method for doing this was incorporated into new vehicles, such as the J class trolleybuses which were coming to Finchley depot. On 905-919 and 952, conductors had to look through a peep-hole* which was in the recess above the blind box housing. We looked at the backstamp through mirrors positioned inside the housing.

However, with general wear and tear, the backstamps became faint and unreadable; the peep-hole glass also became dirty. This resulted in most conductors sitting in the front offside seat, inserting the 'male' end of the blind changing key into two keyholes, pulling out the housing, placing the key in the blind changing keyhole and turning the blinds which were now immediately in front of us. Despite having to read the wording upside down, with practice we were able to position the blinds perfectly. Sometimes there were passengers sitting in the front offside seat and I would politely ask them if they would move while I changed the blind. The blind changing keyhole was in the same position in the blind box housing on every trolleybus that needed the front destination blind changed by the conductor.

At some stage, London Transport decided that the best way for changing front destination blinds was to make them the driver's responsibility, and from 920 upwards (excluding 952) a handle was provided in the cab. It was always (and still is) embedded in my mind that all the 300s, number 754 and 905 to 919 and 952 required conductors to change the front blinds.

*Peep-hole, spy-hole and viewing window describe the oval glass panel through which the backstamp on the blind was seen.

Conductor Fuller uses his budget key to turn 1554's rear destination blind from WALTHAM CROSS to HOLLOWAY ROAD PEMBERTON GARDENS; he is doing this for the final time as it is the evening of Tuesday 25th April 1961 and 1554 will be the last trolleybus to run into Highgate depot – overnight it was transferred to Finchley where it spent its last months. Mr Fuller's Gibson ticket machine and cash bag are part of his everyday equipment – they will not be used again as he was retiring that night. *Hugh Taylor.*

Conductor Clarke opens the blind box housing of Hanwell's 738 to change the front destination blind from CLAPHAM JUNCTION to HANWELL BROADWAY. In fact this is a historic occasion as it is Tuesday 8th November 1960 and 738 is about to become the last trolleybus to leave Clapham Junction – the 6.40pm departure on route 655. Mr Clarke has elected to change the blind in this manner rather than look through the spy-hole which can be seen in the window ledge. *Hugh Taylor.*

The position for changing the side blind was awkwardly situated, for the keyhole, in which to insert the blind key, was adjacent to the top deck rear nearside seat – again this required conductors to crouch down to look into the spy-hole properly. If there was somebody sitting there when I needed access to it, I would say words to the effect of, "Excuse me mate, I've got to change the numbers", and that person would have to get up and move out of the way so that I could look through the viewing window.

Route blinds were also the conductor's responsibility. The numbers were in numerical order apart from 609, which was listed at the end as it was assigned to Finchley depot after the other routes. The front one was changed by inserting the blind winding key into the blind box housing but there was no need to pull it out as the numbers were read through the viewing window. The rear route blind was changed by looking through a peep-hole while standing on the staircase. Most members of the night staff would alter the farechart, side blind and route blinds, where necessary, when preparing the trolleybuses for their next day's work. Others would not, and having ensured that the proper farechart was displayed, conductors would have to participate in five blind-winding exercises when taking a vehicle out of the depot.

It was important when working on the 521/621 services to show the right number on the route and side blinds as some intending passengers would look for the '5' or the '6' depending which part of the Holborn Loop they wished to travel to. Most of us, as a courtesy when working 'Holborns', would make life easier for our relieving colleagues. By consulting the time-card as to whether the next trip was via Grays Inn or Farringdon, we would change the blinds accordingly. When working 'shorts' to Kings Cross, Finsbury Park or Wood Green some conductors had a lazy attitude, with the result that 521 could be seen on the front and 621 on the side and/or back. I made sure that the same number was shown all round and, to avoid confusing passengers, I wouldn't change the blinds until just before arriving at a terminus (Rule 87). Provided that all the numbers matched and the correct destination displays were being shown, front and back, a vehicle was known as being 'properly dressed'.

From time to time conductors and drivers would inadvertently forget to change their destination blinds and if an inspector noticed that this was so, he would make a twirling motion with his arm. If a driver observed a colleague coming towards him where the front destination blind hadn't been altered, he would make a similar gesture. If it was one that needed the conductor to change the front blind then the driver would tell his mate what needed to be done.

Leaving Barnet terminus, 1529 is only working as far as North Finchley on route 609; either it is running into the depot or there is no crew to take it over at Tally Ho. The side blind is poorly positioned for it shows part of a 666 display and part of a 609 one (Finchley did not operate on route 666 during the time that 1529 was at FY). The conductor has probably been unable to read the backstamp on the blind; passengers boarding at the nearside would not know whether 1529 was a 609 or a 645. The wide platform of a trolleybus is very noticeable in this view; motorbus platforms were smaller. Unusually for our depot, grease from the trolley heads drips onto the rear of the vehicle. *Ron Kingdon.*

DESTINATION BLINDS

When I commenced, the blinds were made of a linen material, having been produced at London Transport's Charlton Works. In 1952, they started to be supplied from Aldenham Works, with individual paper panels being glued onto cotton cloth. Having got to know the order of the displays on the linen destination blinds, there was a bit of confusion when the 'paper' blinds started to appear, as the displays were not in the same order. Therefore, when I was working on the 645s and 660s, I had to have a bit of a search for the appropriate display. While the linen and paper blinds were in dual use I adapted to the situation, but eventually all of the linen destination blinds were replaced and it was back to the status quo of knowing the order in which each display appeared. The very earliest paper issues did not have a PADDENSWICK ROAD display as the wiring facility had not been constructed by then. Some vehicles did not have this display right till the end of trolleybus operation at Finchley depot. HAMMERSMITH had to be shown, with conductors calling out "Paddenswick Road only". In due course, all linen side blinds were replaced too, but until 7th November 1961 a few trolleybuses could still be seen with linen route numbers.

PRIVATE
TO HIRE A BUS
APPLY 55 BROADWAY SW1
ABBEY 1234

NORTH ACTON
MARKET PLACE

CRAVEN PARK

CRICKLEWOOD
ST GABRIELS RD

HAMMERSMITH
VIA ACTON & CRICKLEWOOD

EDGWARE
STATION ROAD
VIA CRICKLEWOOD & HENDON

CANONS PARK
VIA CRICKLEWOOD

NORTH FINCHLEY

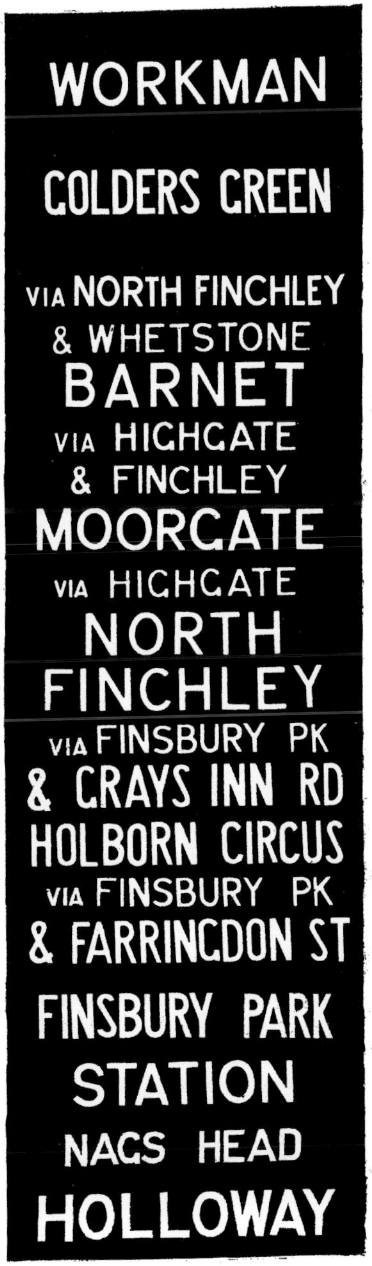

WORKMAN

GOLDERS GREEN

VIA NORTH FINCHLEY & WHETSTONE
BARNET

VIA HIGHGATE & FINCHLEY
MOORGATE

VIA HIGHGATE
NORTH FINCHLEY

VIA FINSBURY PK & GRAYS INN RD
HOLBORN CIRCUS

VIA FINSBURY PK & FARRINGDON ST

FINSBURY PARK STATION

NAGS HEAD

HOLLOWAY

HIGHGATE

ARCHWAY STN

ISLINGTON GREEN

EAST FINCHLEY STATION

WINDSOR TERRACE
CITY ROAD

KINGS CROSS

WOOD GREEN

NEW SOUTHGATE

Front/rear destination blinds produced in linen at Charlton.

PRIVATE	HAMMERSMITH	WOOD
TO HIRE A BUS OR COACH	ACTON	GREEN
APPLY: 55 BROADWAY S.W.I	CRICKLEWOOD	KINGS
ABBEY 5600	**NTH. FINCHLEY**	CROSS
HOLLY	**CRICKLEWOOD**	NEW SOUTHGATE
PARK	ST. GABRIELS CHURCH	STATION
BROMYARD AVENUE	CANONS PARK STANMORE CIRCUS	**BARNET**
ACTON VALE	CRICKLEWOOD	HIGHGATE
MARKET PLACE	NORTH FINCHLEY	NORTH FINCHLEY
NORTH	**BARNET**	**MOORGATE**
ACTON	**NORTH**	**ISLINGTON**
COLINDALE	**FINCHLEY**	**GREEN**
DEPOT	VIA HIGHGATE	**ARCHWAY**
EDGWARE	**NORTH**	**STATION**
STATION ROAD	**FINCHLEY**	WINDSOR TERRACE
HARLESDEN	VIA FINSBURY PARK	**CITY ROAD**
CRAVEN PARK	GRAYS INN ROAD	EAST FINCHLEY
GOLDERS	**HOLBORN CIRCUS**	STATION
GREEN	FINSBURY PARK	TURNPIKE LANE
PADDENSWICK	FARRINGDON RD	STATION
ROAD	**FINSBURY PARK**	
	STATION	
	NAGS HEAD	
	HOLLOWAY	

The Aldenham produced version.

46

Charlton	Aldenham
EXTRA 521 621 645 660 666 609	BOUNDS GREEN WOOD GREEN MANOR HOUSE FINSBURY PARK **521** KINGS CROSS FINSBURY PARK WOOD GREEN NEW SOUTHGATE **621** NORTH FINCHLEY GOLDERS GREEN CRICKLEWOOD HENDON **645** **660** CHURCH END TEMPLE FORTUNE GOLDERS GREEN WILLESDEN HARLESDEN ACTON **660**	BOUNDS GREEN WOOD GREEN MANOR HOUSE FINSBURY PARK **521** KINGS CROSS FINSBURY PARK WOOD GREEN NEW SOUTHGATE **621** NORTH FINCHLEY GOLDERS GREEN CRICKLEWOOD HENDON **645** CHURCH END TEMPLE FORTUNE GOLDERS GREEN **660** GOLDERS GREEN WILLESDEN HARLESDEN ACTON
EXTRA 521 621 645 660 666 609	**666** HENDON CRICKLEWOOD WILLESDEN ACTON ARCHWAY STN HOLLOWAY HIGHBURY ISLINGTON **609** HIGHBURY HIGHGATE EAST FINCHLEY WHETSTONE	**666** HENDON CRICKLEWOOD WILLESDEN ACTON ARCHWAY STN HOLLOWAY HIGHBURY ISLINGTON **609** HIGHBURY HIGHGATE EAST FINCHLEY WHETSTONE

Comparison of Charlton and Aldenham blinds for route number and nearside blind boxes.

OTHER DUTIES

The most common items of lost property were purses, wallets, shopping bags, pushchairs, spectacles and umbrellas. There was a procedure to follow for purses and wallets that were handed in by passengers. We had to open them in the finder's presence and state what was inside and then ask for their name and address. Back at the depot we had to fill in a form and obtain a receipt for anything that we handed in. With shopping bags, the depot inspectors didn't want to keep their contents on the premises and we were told to keep any perishables. Pushchairs were not popular items to find, as we had to carry them back to the depot from Tally Ho. We wouldn't push them as colleagues would take the rise out of us. Sometimes people, having realised they had left something on the 'bus, would wait for it to come back – if I was satisfied that it was their article, I would return it to them.

I had to be in full control of what was going on at all times so it was sometimes necessary for me to be vocal. The most regular phrases used were, "Any more fares?", "Hold tight", "Move down the 'bus, please", "On top only", "All change, last stop". There were times when there were too many intending passengers and I would say "Sorry, full up", or "Four only". I had to be assertive in situations like this and would put my left arm around the last passengers to board and ring the 'bus off. Although there would be a number of them still on the platform as we pulled away, my arm was the safety factor. Dogs we were only allowed to take one at a time, and if somebody wanted to board with another, I had to politely refuse them. Large items such as pushchairs and suitcases could be put under the staircase, but sometimes there would be so many large items stowed there that if anybody else attempted to bring some luggage on board, I would have to turn them away. The most unusual item that I ever carried was a third-size billiard table. The passenger boarded at the stop just before Church Lane, Finchley and wanted to go to Squires Lane which was just four stops away. I let him stand with it on the platform; otherwise he would have had difficulty carrying it.

Now and again passengers fell asleep on the 'bus. Not wanting to startle them I would give them a gentle shake. If I came across a passenger who was totally drunk and who could not be woken, I would leave them there. Eventually they would wake up but there were instances of them staying on board until the trolleybus reached a terminus or the depot where they were somehow woken and encouraged to leave.

We were not expected to call out stopping places on the route for we were often preoccupied in collecting fares or answering questions, and I only did it when asked and when time permitted. As it was, places like Agricultural Hall, the Angel Islington, Nags Head Holloway and Manor House were familiar to most, but if somebody asked me to put them off at Bounds Green, then I would call this out or go up to them and tap them on the shoulder. By being familiar with other bus and trolleybus routes in the vicinity, I was able to assist passengers wanting to get to adjacent areas.

When a trolleybus was run into the depot, there were various things that needed to be done. First, a search of the vehicle had to be made for lost property, with anything found being handed in. Secondly, if it was the vehicle's last spell of duty, all the windows had to be closed so that the seats would not get soiled when it was being washed. Finally, any defects had to be entered on a form in the output. The most common entries were windows that did not close properly, faulty lock on the conductor's locker, interior lightbulbs not working, snapped bell cord, and stiff blind winding handles. Having booked up a trolleybus for the latter fault, I might have the same vehicle a couple of days later and find that the mechanism hadn't been greased. Eventually, though, it would be dealt with.

I liked to look smart (this being a continuation of army practice) and always wore a white shirt and black tie, although I discarded the latter in the summer months. In the winter it was necessary to don a pullover. I used to regularly press my uniform trousers and I dyed my cash bag and straps black to blend in with the navy blue uniform. On some of my late shifts, Rose would accompany me. When I was a conductor she sat on one of the long seats by the platform. I always gave her a ticket so that if an inspector did board (not that one ever did) and check the 'bus, there would be no embarrassment for either of us – there was a tendency for some staff to let their friends and relatives travel free. When Rose came out with me on my late turns, when I was driving, she sat in the front nearside seat downstairs. I insisted that she had a ticket for her journey, and would square up with my conductor later. It was just not worth the chance of her having a free ride, for if a revenue inspector got on, then the three of us would be in trouble. Before we got 'hitched', I would take Rose home on my motorbike.

Not only was Cricklewood Broadway the meeting and departing point for four trolleybus routes but it was also the place where inspector 'half a minute early' Stokes ruled; woebetide any driver who arrived even two minutes early while he was on duty – the excuse of 'my watch is a bit fast' would not be tolerated. Although many of the C2s were withdrawn in the mid 1950s, one to survive until 1959 was number 231 which is turning right from Edgware Road into Chichele Road. At this moment in time, route 664 is a peak hour only service – following the 1958 bus strike it was withdrawn in early January 1959. *Michael Dryhurst.*

48

Conductors often assisted their drivers by giving hand signals and if there was time to do so I would extend my left arm to following traffic – an example of this would be turning from Islington High Street into City Road. It was also appropriate to give right hand signals at times but these were not so necessary as my driver might be doing this anyway. A place that did need a conductor to give a hand signal was at Manor House where we turned right from Green Lanes into Seven Sisters Road. This was a particularly difficult manoeuvre as we had to move from the kerb right out into the offside as there were three lanes of traffic here. Further north, an unusual driving line had to be followed at the top of Kingsway, North Finchley where 609s turned right for Barnet. Some conductors, knowing their driver's intentions, would give a left hand signal at the top of Kingsway, for we had to cross a stream of traffic coming up Ballards Lane. At Barnet, many conductors would show motorists their driver's intentions of pulling away from the stand by giving a clear signal with their right hand. When turning at New Southgate Station, where the driver was unable to give a signal as he needed both hands on the steering wheel to get a full lock on the 'bus, it was very useful for a conductor to give a hand signal there. The most conscientious conductors would signal to cyclists that a trolleybus was to turn left, and in so doing would blank them off. This was an excellent safety procedure and certainly prevented incidents occurring. Conductors who had worked with their drivers for a long time would know where their mate might give a slowing down hand signal and would do so themselves from the platform. The younger women tended not to give hand signals as it drew motorists' unwanted attention to themselves.

When theatres and cinemas turned out, big loads could be picked up at 'The Essoldo' Caledonian Road, 'The Astoria' Finsbury Park and 'The Gaumont' Wood Green. If it was a particularly good film we were sometimes unable to take all the passengers and it would be a 'three-bell load' in that drivers would not pick up anyone else until the bell was rung for someone to alight. The Gaumont at North Finchley was a popular cinema and while crews were chatting on their stand time, the trolleybus could fill up with film-goers who wanted a lift home to Friern Barnet, New Southgate and Bounds Green. A ride home by trolleybus in a convivial atmosphere was part of the night out. Trolleybus conductors had to move quickly to get all their fares in on these trips – in fact, it could be worthwhile to get in the lower deck fares before departure time. Half past ten was the usual time that people left cinemas but if there was a workshy crew on the 10.31pm 521/621 to Wood Green, they would try to get away while the inspector's back was turned. This meant that the 10.36 to Finsbury Park got them all. Most crews played the game though and took their allotted load. It is difficult now to believe that in the mid-1950s, the 521/621 was working to a five-minute headway at that time of night. Strange that the last 'bus to Holborn Circus was as early as 10.15pm. However, there were later trolleybuses to Finsbury Park and Wood Green.

To ensure passenger safety, good conductors waited until all platform movements had been made before pulling their frog handles, for many were situated at busy boarding places such as the 'Angel' Islington southbound. Drivers would expect their conductors to wait before pulling and it was a good example of what today would be called a safe working practice. Some passengers who 'knew the ropes' would board at places where they knew a conductor would pull a frog handle and get on there rather than at an official stop. One place where this happened was turning into Woodhouse Road at North Finchley, another being adjacent to the frog handle at Jolly Butchers Hill northbound.

Passengers thought they had the right to carry anything on our trolleybuses as shown by someone boarding 1669 with a carpet. This picture was taken at the first southbound stop in Woodhouse Road; by showing KINGS CROSS as its destination, it may mean that this is a Saturday afternoon as the 621 only ran that far south then (these journeys were officially designated 521, but it didn't really matter whether 521 or 621 was displayed). It would have been better if the bus stop had been positioned beyond the overhead feeder, for 1669's driver will only be able to give the vehicle a couple of notches of power before shutting off again.

PULL AND HOLDS & PULL AND LEAVES

Most of the frequently used facing frogs were semi-automatic types; however, there were four places on my routes where 'pull and hold' handles were used at busy places. (1) Jolly Butchers Hill northbound on routes 521/621, (2) the junction of City Road and Goswell Road, Islington southbound on route 609, (3) Agricultural Hall northbound on the 609 and (4) near the junction of Seven Sisters Road and Green Lanes, Manor House on routes 521/621. In some locations, 'pull and holds' were upgraded to 'pull and leaves' and this one at Manor House was one of them; in my opinion the others would also have benefited from semi-auto frogs. There were many other places on the trolleybus network (particularly in east London) where it would have been better if semi-automatic frogs had been fitted rather than 'pull and holds'. The fact that they were not was due to penny-pinching by London Transport as the 'pull and holds' were cheaper to purchase and maintain.

Though both were to be seen in great number all over the system, on my routes the 'pull and holds' outnumbered the 'pull and leaves' on a two to one basis. Although fully automatic frogs (controlled by drivers applying power on skates in the overhead, and re-set in the same fashion as the London semi-automatic type) were available, and used quite widely on provincial trolleybus systems, none existed in London.

It was a general rule that conductors had to pull frog handles or push buttons on routes that required vehicles to move onto nearside sets of wires at main junctions. Examples were the three electric frogs at Cricklewood Broadway where all conductors had to do was to walk a few feet to the equipment. There were inconsistencies to the 'pull for nearside' factor and at Tally Ho southbound, where the 609 and 645 parted, conductors on the 645 pulled for the offside for the Golders Green direction allowing the 609 a free run towards Archway. This evened things out as the 609 needed a frog pull for Barnet in nearby Kingsway.

Although at main junctions the less frequent routes normally required the frog to be operated, there were exceptions to this due to safety considerations – for example at the junction of City Road and Goswell Road Islington. Conductors on routes 609/615/639 had to 'pull and hold' for Moorgate, while the 677 had an unhindered run into Goswell Road; this was despite this route having a lower frequency than the other three routes combined. This prevented 677 conductors having to run into the roadway after their trolleybuses in the busy City Road.

An attempt was made to even out the number of frog pulls in the same vicinity. At Harlesden, 662s turned left at Craven Park and Jubilee Clock, so staff on this route would not have

Left The Angel Islington, and 1140 moves over the cobblestones in City Road. Route 677 has the overhead frog in its favour – having conductors on routes going to Moorgate pulling the frog here saves 677 conductors from having to run into the roadway after their vehicles. There are many items of special work aloft and drivers on all trolleybus routes here will be passing through slowly. *Don Thompson.*

Opposite Many Stonebridge drivers were inch-perfect at positioning their trolleybuses northbound at Craven Park so that their conductors could pull the semi-automatic frog handle from the platform – 1661 pauses there on its way to Stonebridge depot. I encountered the 628 and 662 between Craven Park and Jubilee Clock. *Brian Speller.*

required a frog pull if that principle had been applied. Evening things out saw 662s pulling at Craven Park for Sudbury but not at Jubilee Clock, as 660 and 666 conductors pulled for Hammersmith, making it one pull each. Many of the 662 drivers were artistes when it came to positioning Sudbury bound vehicles at Craven Park. Their judgement was so good that they could position their trolleybuses in such a way that they stopped just an inch or two before the frog; this enabled their conductors to just lean from the platform and pull the handle down. Road layouts also affected 'frog priority', an example being Amhurst Junction about a mile from Manor House. 653s, which had a lower frequency than the combined total on the 623/627/659/679, had right of way here as they were moving into a right-hand turn from Seven Sisters Road into Amhurst Park before actually reaching the junction.

Commonsense came into the equation with regard to the positioning of some semi-automatic frogs. Falling into this category was the one used by trolleybuses turning right from Holloway Road into Pemberton Gardens to access Highgate depot. Originally an ordinary 'pull and hold' frog, safety concerns arose as conductors were running into the roadway to reboard their trolleybuses in the busy Holloway Road, which at this point was on a downward slope. The dilemma was solved by installing a semi-automatic frog, possibly due to representations to London Transport by the TGWU. Regularly used until stage nine of the trolleybus conversion programme took place, this apparatus was only used eleven times a week thereafter – Sunday 609s running in from Barnet or North Finchley, and Monday to Saturday special 627s running in from Macdonald Road (the Archway loop). Another example of an infrequently used semi-auto frog occurred after the abandonment of route 611 where the equipment at Archway northbound was left in. Now it was only operated three times in Monday to Friday peak hours, though it got some extra action on Christmas morning 1960 as two vehicles turned there very early that day.

Frog priorities sometimes changed and, when I started, 660/666 conductors had to use push button equipment in Acton High Street to turn right into Market Place, while 607s and 655s had an unimpeded run along the Uxbridge Road towards Hanwell. In the other direction at the Askew Arms in Acton Vale, we also had to pull a semi-auto frog handle for 660s and 666s to turn right into Askew Road while the 607 had an unrestricted path to Shepherds Bush. Therefore everything was against the grain in that we had to pull twice, with both pulls being for the offside. At some stage, frog priority and equipment changed at Acton Market, with 607/655 conductors now having to hop off to pull a semi-automatic frog handle, thus evening things out. This was an unnecessary alteration as conductors on both sets of routes had no need to walk into the roadway to reboard their trolleybuses as the road was only single lane traffic at both locations; presumably London Transport had a good reason to do it though – maybe it was a TGWU request. While I am talking about 'frog matters', if a driver had over-run a frog, reversing was not advisable as a dewirement could occur – some drivers though were confident enough to do this.

Systemwide, entry into most loops and lay-bys was by a

1544's driver has had a lapse in concentration and has gone past the facing frog at Jolly Butchers Hill. His conductor is retrieving the situation and is swinging the positive boom from the Winchmore Hill wires to those for North Finchley. He is using 1544's bamboo rather than the one sloppily held against the traction standard – by being so placed it implies that problems frequently occur here. *Hugh Taylor.*

'pull and hold' frog. At a few of these places though, electric frogs were fitted and 660s and other vehicles entering Tally Ho bus station from Ballards Lane used this type of equipment. This was a good feature due to the number of trolleybuses needing to access the bus station and again it avoided conductors running into the roadway. A few of the short working points were constructed as 'dead-enders' whereby trolley arms had to be swung from one set of wires to another. These 'dead-enders' had either no facing or trailing frog or sometimes neither. North Acton, when turning from the Harlesden direction, came into the latter category, so it was important to make sure that crews were carrying a bamboo pole.

It was very important that conductors ensured, when operating all types of frogs, that any preceding trolleybus had cleared the points before operating it for themselves. In the ten years that I worked on trolleybuses, I never came across an incident where a trolleybus took the wrong road due to this, but there were two near misses that I witnessed. One day when I was driving, I was at the junction of City Road and Goswell Road and following another 609 when its conductor prematurely pulled the frog handle for Moorgate before a Smithfield-bound 677 had cleared the frog to take it down Goswell Road. Fortunately the 677 crew realised what was happening and with a lot of shouting and hollering, calamity was avoided. The other place where this occurred was at Manor House southbound, near the junction of Green Lanes and Seven Sisters Road. A 641 conductor, unthinkingly, pulled the frog handle for his 'bus to go to Moorgate before one of our 521s/621s had passed the frog. Fortunately the Finchley driver spotted the signal light change against him and attracted the Wood Green conductor's attention. Seeing his mistake he pushed the semi-auto frog handle upwards to set the correct road for the Finchley 'bus. No doubt mishaps of this nature did occur from time to time when there *would* have been a lot of shouting and hollering!

1311 has taken the 521/621 wires at Green Lanes, Manor House; either there is a problem with the frog or somebody has wrongly set it. However, 1311's driver has spotted what has happened and is getting out of his cab to rectify the situation. *Tony Belton.*

Another occasion at the same place, and somebody has erroneously pulled the semi-automatic frog handle causing 1500's trolleybooms to take the 641's wires. Fortunately the driver has noticed this and his conductor is changing the poles onto the correct ones; if he had proceeded, disaster would have followed. *Hugh Taylor.*

The folly of not watching the signal light box at Manor House is shown by a dewired 1513; the semi-automatic frog handle should not have been pulled as it has put 1513 onto wires towards Moorgate. A more alert driver would have noticed the problem; now our man is going to have to ask the car driver immediately behind him to reverse so that he can get 1513's bamboo pole out. *Peter Moore.*

When I was driving, I always ensured that any preceding trolleybus taking a different overhead road to myself had cleared the points before I proceeded. On the 521s/621s, I would sometimes follow a southbound 641 between Wood Green and Manor House. When I got there, the 641 conductor would leave the platform and pull the semi-automatic frog handle. Holding the trolleybus on the handbrake, I would wait until it had passed through the points. Once I saw the white arrow on the semi-automatic frog handle box flick back to the right-hand position, I knew that the overhead road was now set for me to turn right into Seven Sisters Road.

615s and 639s from the Hampstead direction, having reached the brow of the hill at the top of Pentonville Road, then passed through the Angel junction. A favourable downward slope allowed drivers to build up a bit of momentum as they passed through the special work there. It was necessary for their conductors to pull the frog handle at the City Road/Goswell Road junction and many of the Highgate crews devised a time-saving practice. With the vehicle still travelling at 2 to 3mph, conductors would alight, pull the handle down, see the trolleybooms pass through the points and jump back on while the vehicle was still moving – very slick. Our 609 crews also participated in this practice, but as we had just turned the corner from Islington High Street, we couldn't be as speedy as them. Occasionally I had to jog the memory of my regular conductor that they needed to pull a frog handle – they were engrossed in fare collection or chatting.

There were occasions when drivers might forget that a frog pull was required. Due to the way that the duties were compiled, it was possible to work only on the 521s/621s for a couple of weeks. Therefore when a crew arrived at Kingsway, North Finchley on their first 609 journey to Barnet after a fortnight, the driver might overlook the fact that the frog handle needed to be pulled. Having gone past the points, either driver or conductor would realise the mistake and change the poles by hand – alternatively the driver might reverse back through the frog. This was one of the few places in London where the frog handle was positioned on the offside of the vehicle – conductors could move about safely in the knowledge that other road vehicles would not be on their offside. Another 'offside pull' was situated at the bottom of Seven Sisters Road adjacent to the Nags Head where Highgate depot-bound 627s and 653s turned right into Holloway Road. Conductors had to get off their vehicles and move behind them to the offside so that they could pull the handle that was fixed to a traction standard sited within a pedestrian refuge in the middle of the road. I considered this to be an unsafe practice as it made conductors vulnerable to other road traffic, for they had to reboard when the 'bus was part way across Holloway Road. A road improvement plan was implemented in June 1956 and the standard to which the handle was fixed was removed. The frogwork was moved further back up Seven Sisters Road, with the handle now attached to a pavement-mounted traction standard. This brings to mind an incident that I saw here one rainy day where a trolleybus had dewired and the booms bent in the process. I had to overtake as the crew were having a bit of a performance trying to sort everything out.

During the winter months there were times when frogs became jammed due to ice forming in the blades of the mechanism – this happened to me early one morning at Jolly Butchers Hill where I was unable to pull the handle down. The whole contraption had iced up but we overcame the problem by changing the booms to the correct overhead road with our bamboo. Icing up usually only occurred with those frogs that were not regularly used, but on this occasion we must have been the first 'bus along for some time that frosty morning. When we got back to North Finchley we informed an inspector who organised a tower wagon crew to deal with the matter – in the meantime all other staff would have had to use their bamboo pole. 'Wear and tear' was a factor that occasionally caused a dewirement. A weak spring could cause a frog not to return to its normal position; an unsuspecting crew would pass beneath that frog and bang, the poles would come off. If it had been raining overnight, frogs that were only used irregularly had their dangers. The overtaking wire in Coleridge Road (the Finsbury Park short working loop) and the turning circles at Golders Green, Cricklewood St Gabriels Church and Gladstone Avenue at Wood Green being prime contenders. When these handles were pulled, rainwater would fall from the frog blades onto the roadway, so woe betide any unsuspecting pedestrian walking beneath!

I encountered three push button frogs – two were on the Holborn Loop. One was at the junction of Grays Inn Road and Theobalds Road on the 621, the other at the junction of Clerkenwell Road with Farringdon Road on route 521. Conductors pushed the left-hand button at both locations. The third was at Acton Market Place at its junction with Acton High Street where 660s and 666s diverged from westbound 607s and 655s. All of these had long-handled back-up equipment and, although there was the option to use either, I used the push button as it was easier. When buttons were pushed there was a distinct metal 'zonk zonk' sound and at the same time the handle would slide about six or eight inches downwards and stop with a jerk. A 'bomp' noise was heard when the re-set mechanism operated and the handle moved back up – this could be seen and heard from the platform as the trolleybus moved away. I always operated the push buttons with my right hand and, with two exceptions mentioned later, pulled handles with my left hand.

The one 'long-handled' type that I did use was at the junction of Holloway Road and Camden Road by Selby's department store in Holloway; conductors on routes 609/611/679 had to pull for Highbury. This was an awkward one to deal with as there was a three tier pavement here, and we had to watch that we did not fall over our feet. I perfected my own approach to it. I would trot up the three kerbs, get hold of the handle, put my weight on it and pull it down all in one motion. It needed a good hard yank and there was a heavy clonking noise when it operated. Conductors had to be heavy-handed when using this handle as a half-hearted effort was of no use. Being young and full of energy, I was able to do this in one movement – it was like a 'swinging pull'. This was the only long-handled variety that did not have a push button facility as well – at some stage it was changed to the newer type of semi-auto frog pull.

The drivers of these two trolleybuses have not encountered any problems at Manor House. Wood Green's 1277 passes over the setts on its way to BARING STREET NEW NORTH RD on route 641 while Finchley's 1472 is about to turn right into Seven Sisters Road on its way to HOLBORN CIRCUS on route 521. The two routes had run together from Wood Green. *Fred Ivey.*

PROBLEM FROGS

Jolly Butchers Hill. If trolley arm problems were going to happen it would be at Jolly Butchers Hill, Wood Green northbound. It was the most unpopular frog pull on our routes with the recipe for disaster having four ingredients: (1) an upward incline, (2) an immediate left turn into Bounds Green Road, (3) a frog handle set back from the overhead points, and (4) conductors anxious to catch up with their vehicles.

Difficulties occurred if drivers tried to get through the pointwork without stopping, for some wanted to keep moving slowly forward. Alternatively, they might misjudge the position of the points and go past with the result that, in both cases, the trolleybus would be through the frog before the conductor had a chance to get to the handle and pull it. Looking in his nearside driving mirror, the driver would see his conductor running for the 'bus and seeing him board, would assume that all was well when in fact it was not. The conductor would attempt to attract the driver's attention with either a rapid succession of rings on the bell, or might call out a verbal warning.

Conductors could be at fault here, but there were mitigating circumstances – their eagerness to get back on board and get their fares in. If they had picked up a full load of passengers at Wood Green, they would only have had enough time to collect a few of their fares before they needed to get out for the pull. Not wanting the 'bus to get too far away might lead them to let go of the handle too soon and could result in the poles going towards Enfield rather than North Finchley. Conductors, as far as I am aware, always saw their error and ensured that their vehicle was stopped and the situation rectified. I know from personal experience that this was a difficult place for conductors, for we often had large amounts

of copper and silver weighing us down – we would virtually hobble towards the still slowly moving trolleybus. Considerate drivers, particularly those who had been conductors themselves, were more thoughtful and once past the frog would bring the 'bus to a standstill to enable their conductors to regain the platform safely.

When the booms had taken the 'straight' rather than the 'branch', time would be lost while the bamboo pole corrected the matter. Staff could get themselves into all sorts of problems trying to get a bamboo pole out of its holder, for if there were motor vehicles immediately behind, it could be really awkward as bamboos, when fully drawn out, could end up underneath a car or lorry so these would have to be waved by to create the space. A couple of other '21s' might now be behind, and by the time everything was sorted out, there could be three trolleybuses going up Bounds Green Road together. It was neither the time or place to be without one's trusty bamboo pole. However, if they didn't have one, then all they had to do was to walk back the short distance to Wood Green depot and get one from there.

There was only one occasion when I got left behind here; my driver for the day had got twenty yards up Bounds Green Road before he realised I was not with him. I had to run and catch him up and he said a quick "sorry". Conversely I recall that on one occasion when I was driving, I was in Bounds Green Road before I realised that my conductor had not reboarded. Some drivers, play-acting and skylarking around, deliberately kept going slowly forward making their conductors run up the road. Once I found the frog wasn't working and found both of my booms on the wires to Enfield. Another time, I misjudged the position of the frog. On both occasions I had to get out of the cab and use my bamboo pole.

If a frog handle was not pulled down to its limit, a splay could occur. It happened to me a couple of times when I was a conductor, but I was able to attract my driver's attention and we used our bamboo to sort things out. It occurred to me once when I was a driver – as my conductor had caused the splay I let him do the pole-work. A few times when I was driving behind another 521/621 here, a splay happened. It looked really weird, the nearside boom going to Finchley and the offside one to Enfield – fortunately the crews realised what was happening, stopped and moved the offside boom onto the right set of wires. Another scenario was for a conductor to let go of the frog handle when the booms were actually on the frog blades – this meant that both poles came off. Things tended to be okay with my regular mate, but tended to go wrong if it was somebody who was just working with me for the day. Despite all the problems related above, there were few dewirements here – certainly I didn't experience one on the 'down road', but have to confess that I 'had 'em off' here one day on the 'up' (towards Manor House) when I came over the trailing frog a bit sharpish. All this hurriedness and impatience at Jolly Butchers Hill was counter-productive and if staff were more attentive then a lot of the delays wouldn't have occurred. It might appear that it was a hit and miss affair here, but that was not the case, as most drivers positioned their trolleybuses perfectly. We were able to stop our vehicles just before the frog; our conductors would run for the frog handle, hold it in the 'down' position, and we would be on our way.

For most of the trolleybus era, a difficult situation existed for 609 and 679 conductors whose vehicles were short working to 'Islington Green shunt' – upon departure, they had to run a long way to board their vehicle after their frog pull in Essex Road. With the withdrawal of routes 581 and 677 in April 1959, the frog mechanism was set in the favour of the aforementioned 609s/679s, thus eradicating the problem. 1518 is working a 'short' between Islington and North Finchley; RTL 980 is on route 277 to Smithfield. *Fred Ivey.*

Islington Green. An Islington Green 'short' created the most dangerous manoeuvre for Finchley conductors. Having had our stand time outside the Collins Music Hall, opposite Islington Green itself, we turned right into Essex Road where, a few yards later, conductors had to use a 'pull and hold' frog handle. 581s and 677s going towards the Angel had an unimpeded run here. This was a risky procedure for 609 conductors, as having let go of the handle, they had to get on board a moving trolleybus that was turning right and moving away from them on an upward slope. They were impeded by the incline, a lot of vehicles whizzing about, and having to get across two lanes of traffic going in opposite directions in Essex Road. Often they had to run like hell for about twenty yards to get on board, at the apex of Islington Green. Conductors never blamed their drivers for leaving them in a precarious position, for having 'power priority' on the three pieces of special work here they had to take advantage of the situation. Only on the trailing frog did drivers have to take their foot off the power pedal. The problem was removed when the 581s and 677s were withdrawn on 14th April 1959. Shortly afterwards the pointwork was altered in that we had frog priority and our conductors didn't need to pull the handle anymore. Its only use thereafter would be for any 'Archway swingers' that were running late and had to be turned at 'The Green'.

Nags Head. Another difficult place for conductors was when we terminated at Nags Head, Holloway. Here, the last passengers alighted in Holloway Road. The trolleybus then turned right into Camden Road and about fifty yards later right into Warlters Road where stand time was taken. The frog handle, for this manoeuvre, was placed on a traction standard almost at the entrance to Caledonian Road which goes off to the left from Camden Road. This meant that, when the handle was being operated, the trolleybus was moving away from the conductor and out into the main road. The conductor had to have a quick look to the right to make sure the road was clear before running to rejoin the vehicle. This was one of the two places where I had to pull the handle with my right hand. Here, it was due to it being positioned on the Caledonian Road side of the traction standard.

ROUTE 609 FROG PULLS
Route 609 needed seven frog pulls on each 'rounder' and this was due to the fact that it had to run onto seven sets of near-side wires. When we were on the 609s doing an Archway swinger, eight frog handles had to be pulled before route 611 came off – five on the way up (minus Kingsway, but plus Archway junction and Macdonald Road), three on the way back. Seemingly arduous, it was just 'part and parcel' of the job. The reason that the 609 required so many frog pulls was due to the fact that it had to run onto seven sets of nearside wires. Seven was the highest number of pulls for one full route throughout the system and was equalled by a number of other routes. However some conductors had to pull more frequently than the 609; northbound 639 conductors had to pull four frog handles in twenty minutes: at East Road, The Angel, Crowndale Road and finally Camden Town. Route 611 conductors, who often worked six journeys each day, had to

pull up to thirty frog handles during their duty – even more if they pulled for the loops at Highgate Village and Moorgate. If depot runs were included their 'frog pull tally' might reach forty. Conversely, routes 517, 627, 629, 662 and 664, all of which I came into contact with, only required one frog pull on a round journey. This applied to other routes in London as well.

FINALLY

A few of the 'pull and hold' handles were rigid in that they could not be moved from side to side, but most were moveable and enabled conductors to give two taps of the moveable handle against the traction standard. This was loud enough for drivers to hear and was the time honoured signal that indicated 'ready'. To indicate that a conductor had re-boarded, many crews developed their own call sign. Some gave a couple of foot stamps on the platform, simultaneously shouting out something like "Okay Bert". Pete Webb would always give a whistle to indicate that he was on board. Others would thump the rearmost nearside panel twice with the palm of their left hand to indicate that they were about to board; the noise was loud enough for their drivers to hear. In the daylight, drivers could see their mate get back on the 'bus by looking in the nearside mirror. It was hard to see them in the dark, so they had to visibly or audibly ensure that they were aboard.

On the flip side, there were some conductors who didn't think ahead very well. Upon leaving Tally Ho on routes 521/621, they would start collecting fares when the best thing for them to have done would have been to stand on the platform ready to pull the semi-automatic frog handle at the junction of Woodhouse Road with High Road Finchley. Consequently, the 'bus would get held-up while they rushed from the saloon, and into the roadway to get to the handle. If a traffic light sequence change was lost in the process, then the 'bus would be delayed with a possible knock-on effect of late running for some time, and picking up more passengers than would normally have been the case. Sometimes, at this junction, conductors might get some assistance from a colleague who was on board on their homeward journey and who would pull the handle for them. Alternatively, a helpful workmate who was planning to board a 521/621 in order to go home, would position themselves at the frog pull knowing that by operating the handle time would be saved. In both instances, colleagues' assistance was appreciated as it allowed conductors to get on with fare collection – it was no easy task to get in up to seventy-five fares with many of the passengers getting off at Friern Barnet Town Hall.

Notices stating 'Not to be used by unauthorised persons' were pasted onto some of the traction standards adjacent to 'pull and hold' handles. Over the years they faded and became weatherworn. Despite the notice, there was a woman in her early fifties who travelled around in the evenings for want of nothing else to do. She knew all the trolleybus routes and which ones needed auto frog pulls at the Nags Head. Sometimes she would be at the guard rails at the bottom of Seven Sisters Road just before its junction with Holloway Road, just taking the scene in. She took it upon herself to act as an unofficial frog puller and would pull the handle for

routes turning left here. She even knew that a frog pull was required for 627s/629s/653s which had been curtailed there. This was during my conducting days and I would give her a wave of acknowledgement when she pulled for me. By operating the handles she helped us save time and, to my knowledge, was never responsible for a dewirement. In truth, she was good and knew what she was doing, unlike some inspectors who occasionally pulled the wrong handles and did cause dewirements! On the subject of unauthorised persons operating frog handles, I was outside Selbys in Holloway Road one day when a man pulled the handle for a 659 in front of me when no such action was needed. Maybe he thought he was helping but he caused the 659 to dewire and we had to wait until the situation was rectified. The driver could have avoided the incident if he had looked at the Y light. Drivers were supposed to look at this light wherever a semi-auto frog was installed. I seldom did though, as the sight of my conductor pulling the handle and the white arrow changing was enough for me. I only looked at it if my view of him or her was obscured. Unauthorised frog pulling to cause mischief was rare.

There were a few occasions when I was paired with conductors on their first day by themselves. First of all I would give them words of encouragement and say I would try to help them as much as I could. I would say something like, "We've got two journeys on the 609s during the rush hour. It's going to be very busy. Apart from collecting fares, the main thing you've got to do is to remember that frog handles have got to be pulled. I'll assist you by flashing the saloon lights as we approach them. The other thing is I don't go without the bell, and try not to ring off from upstairs. Don't get trapped on the top deck as people will flood on. If you do, you won't be able to get to frog handles, and you'll have trouble with the 'bus getting overloaded if you're not on the platform. I'll take it as steadily as I can, and the likelihood is we'll run late but that doesn't matter as it is expected with new staff" (I was passing on advice given to me). Sometimes I had to remind a brand new conductor to pull a frog handle. They might not see the saloon lights flash in the summer months, so if the message didn't get across I would call out "pull the handle". Even this did not work sometimes, and without sight or sound of them I had to get out of the cab and operate the semi-auto frog myself.

An amusing series of events occurred when we only had the 645s and 660s left. We had a new conductress who thought that every handle was 'pull and leave'. Each time she operated a 'pull and hold' frog she pulled the handle down and let it go up again much to the chagrin of drivers who had to get out of their cab and re-wire their trolleybooms. Eventually, after some gentle advice, she got the hang of it – but only a few days before the trolleybuses came off.

The impression might be given that conductors had a hard time of it all, what with their fare collecting duties, frog handles to be pulled or buttons pushed, and the moving of trolleybooms from one set of wires to another. We didn't think like this – we took it all in our stride.

The Ministry of Transport did not allow trolleybuses to stand in Charterhouse Street and the police were strict that no waiting should take place there – however, if we were a bit early we had no alternative but to stop for a couple of minutes. An inspector is leaving 1440's platform – as soon as he is safely on the ground the driver will get the bell from his conductor so that the journey to Hampstead Heath on route 613 can commence; behind is an Edmonton trolleybus on route 659. *Don Lewis.*

DENNIS, VIC AND HARRY

Having worked with the GPO for some years, I was familiar with the areas in which the 521/621 and 609 services operated, particularly the London end, so was hoping to work on these routes rather than the 645 and 660 as I didn't know the districts through which they ran. Fortunately I was allocated to the 'City' routes and for the next ten years these services were to be my main working arena. I was still 'learning the ropes' when I was paired with driver Dennis Childs. Despite Highgate depot being nearer his home, he travelled all the way from Euston each day as he liked working at Finchley. He took steps to cushion my initiation and did this by taking care of the time-keeping, driving the trolleybus at a speed that allowed me to get all my fares in and being generally understanding. When necessary he would flash the saloon lights where frog handles needed to be pulled, calling out "pull this one" or "we need this frog", and I soon got used to being on the platform at the right time. No-one expected new entrants to be speedy to start with, but practice makes perfect and I gradually grew in confidence and developed my own style of working.

This is the view that Dennis Childs and I regularly saw when taking over on Tally Ho stand. At the time, linen blinds were used in all the blind boxes. 952 was numerically the last J1 class vehicle; however it had been delivered before most of the other J1s as it was fitted with a different style of body. It was constructed by Metropolitan Cammell Carriage and Wagon company rather than Weymann. *Alan Cross.*

As I have mentioned earlier, I am known as Bill in family circles, but a number of staff at the depot also referred to me as such. I'll put that down to Rose, who at the time I started on the trolleybuses, was my fiancée. Before long she sometimes accompanied me on a late turn. She came for the ride as it was something different and enabled her to see parts of London that she hadn't seen before. Rose called me Bill, so after a few weeks Dennis soon started using this name too. It snowballed partly due to my dad sometimes coming up to the depot and talking with my second driver, Vic Collins. As a result he too got into the habit of calling me Bill, as did my third driver, Harry Franks who was a distant relative of Rose. If I was working with a driver for the first time who didn't know my Christian name he would say "What do I call you" and I would reply "Charlie or Bill, whatever you like, I answer to both". Most opted for 'Charlie'. I have always responded to both names and if someone calls me on the phone these days asking if 'Charlie' is in, Rose confuses them by calling out "Bill you're wanted". When I was socialising off duty, and people asked me what job I did, I would say "I'm on the trolleys". This was a familiar terminology of the 1950s, and those asking the question knew what I meant.

There was no written rule about whether it was the driver's or conductor's responsibility to deal with trolley arms. They were also known as trolleybooms or trolley poles, but most frequently they were referred to as 'sticks'. If a driver had suffered a dewirement he would comment "had me sticks off today". Trolleyboom manipulation was something that was expected to be shared, and my first recollection of raising the poles was when Dennis and I walked through the depot one day to take a trolleybus out. He said, "Put the poles up Charlie; make sure they're on running out wires". Normally vehicles were parked with their poles up but for some reason this one had them down. I grabbed hold of a bamboo pole and pulling the booms out from under their retaining hooks, put them onto the appropriate set of wires. I had not been given any training about trolleyboomwork as nobody had ever said to me, "Come out into the yard and I'll show you how to put the poles up and pull them down". However, it was something that I had seen done before I started with London Transport, so knew what was required. I was chuffed that I was able to do this easily – you did need a good eye for it though. 'Dropping the sticks' was a piece of cake.

I worked with Dennis for fifty-one weeks when unfortunately we were parted. One day I went into the output (where crews reported for work) and overheard him say "I'm going to be split up from Bill". This was due to Finchley losing some Sunday 609 duties to Highgate depot and meant that the crew rota lost a few lines. An agreement between the Transport and General Workers Union and London Transport was that when duties were lost, those crews on and near the bottom of the rota, despite their seniority (even if it was thirty years), were positioned elsewhere on the roster, possibly displacing junior staff. Dennis and I were in one of these places with the result that he was going to be paired with a conductress who he was not keen to work with, and he came to an agreement with another driver who was on the 645/660 rota that they would change rota lines mutually. Dennis and

I had worked well together and were sad to be split up. I now found myself paired with Vic Collins, with whom I spent a very colourful year, picking up a rota line with him on 5th November 1952.

Vic was a very experienced trolleybus driver who knew the job inside out. There was nothing anyone could teach him that he didn't already know and someone had to be really clever to get one over on him. He knew which corners of the overhead he could take liberties with, and the frogs and crossovers that it was best to negotiate at the regulation five mph limit. He recognised when he had to drive at average speed to keep to schedule and when he had to get a move on and go flat out, if time was tight. When he was aware I had a full load of passengers on he would keep the trolleybus on low notches of power so that I had time to get all my fares in. However there were two occasions when he got things wrong. Once at Highbury Corner and another time at Moorgate – these are related later.

Vic's knowledge of his 'own road' is well illustrated by the following. 521s/621s alternated around the Holborn Loop and generally both arrived back at Kings Cross, on the return trip, in the correct sequence. However, this was not always so in peak hours for although 621s normally arrived at Kings Cross just about on time, 521s often did not as they had to contend with traffic around Farringdon Road. There were also overhead layouts to deal with at Clerkenwell Road, Farringdon Road and Kings Cross Road. If we were on a 621, waiting at the junction with Pentonville Road and Grays Inn Road, and Vic saw a large number of people waiting at the bus stop at the bottom of Caledonian Road, this indicated that the 521 that should have been in front of us had not gone through. He would then glance to the right to see if the 521 was there – Vic would have made a mental note of its registration number when he passed it on the loop. If it was, and he was able to beckon it past him, then the 'buses were in their right order, but if the policeman on point duty waved him through the junction, he would park short of the stop and call through to me "get the poles down, he should be in front of us". While the 'bus was still moving slowly, I would step off it, reach down and grasp hold of the grappling hook on the end of the bamboo pole. Doing it while moving meant that it came out quicker. I would pull the offside boom off the wire and place it under the nearside boom. Putting the grappling hook over the top of the nearside boom I would draw both away from the overhead at the same time. This meant that I was dealing with the tension of two springs instead of one, but as it was for only a short time I was able to do it easily. Holding both booms with my left hand I would wave the 521 past with my right arm. As soon as the 521 had passed, I would return the nearside boom onto the wire and then do the same with the other one. Doing it this way, rather than putting both booms under the retaining hooks, saved time. We would now be in the correct position in the service, but with a general sense of helping our colleagues out, Vic would park up behind the 'bus in front at bus stops so that the passenger load was spread. If traffic was light, when we were on a 621, Vic would hope to get caught in some traffic by Chancery Lane. It was a different ball game at the end of the morning peak as crews wanted to get back to Tally Ho as quickly as possible, either for a cup of tea in the refreshment hut or to go on their break. Sometimes 521s and 621s would arrive out of turn at the bottom of 'the Cally' (the nickname for Caledonian Road). As there weren't many passengers travelling out from the City at that time of day, being out of order didn't really matter.

A Ministry of Transport instruction stated that no stand time was to be taken at Charterhouse Street (Holborn Circus). Sometimes however, crews couldn't help arriving a bit early and had to wait their time there. There was nearly always an inspector on the '621 side of the road' controlling the trolley-bus services at this important London terminal point. He was not provided with an inspector's box, though there was a London Transport phone for him to use. Despite the large number of trolleybuses using the Holborn loop, an overtaking wire was never provided. Inspectors seemed reluctant to see bamboo poles used at Charterhouse Street and at times would push trolleybuses out a couple of minutes early if too many were accumulating. It didn't matter if vehicles arrived and departed out of sequence – in fact it would have been nigh on impossible for every trolleybus that traversed Charterhouse Street on any given day to depart in order. Continuing with the Holborn loop, Vic pointed out to me the turning circle at Vine Street Bridge. At this time it was only partly connected to the mainline wires and was dismantled in the mid-1950s. It had been put up as a wartime expediency – neither he nor I ever saw any vehicle using it. Vic's trolleybus knowledge was second to none and he told me about the approved battery turns at Canal Bridge in both City Road and Caledonian Road (the one in City Road was so close to Windsor Terrace that it was superfluous really). I am not aware of staff using either of the Canal Bridge battery turns. Another regulation that the MOT issued was that passenger carrying vehicles were prohibited from sounding their horns on main roads, except in emergencies, between 11.30pm and 7am.

Traffic light pads were useful as they allowed general road traffic to alter traffic light signal phases at road junctions and crossroads. The oblong rubber pads (in a metal frame in the roadway) were set back from the lights and the passing of vehicles over them kept traffic on the move by turning the lights to green more quickly when needed. They had their downside, for if a vehicle came up to the lights at the top of Woodhouse Road at its junction with Finchley High Road at a very quiet period of the day, the lights could be against them for quite a time. Vehicles from the Barnet direction would be keeping the lights on red. Fed up with this, Vic occasionally said to me "Jump on that pad" and I would go back to it and do just that. This altered the signal and I had to run to get back on board. Alternatively, and providing that we were the only vehicle waiting for the lights to change, Vic would reverse back over the pad, which made the sequence respond in our favour. These pads are now a thing of the past.

Now and again a tree lopper (a former STL bus that had had its roof removed and was painted green) would be seen cutting back tree branches at various places so that they didn't hit the trolleybuses or obstruct the overhead wires (the swish of the trolley arms did not keep the branches back). There was also a wire greaser (painted red) that Vic pointed out to me in 1952/53. I saw this strange-looking vehicle once only – it was in Finchley High Road by the swimming pool. A new type of carbon in the trolley heads was introduced in the early 1950s, making the wire greasers redundant by 1955.

I came across a couple of strange looking service vehicles from time to time; tree loppers were part of the support system and 972J is seen entering Wood Green depot – at one time it had been STL 1494. Strangely, it has National Savings advertisements on its front panels; good initia-tive by the advertising department though, as it boosts London Transport's bank account. Moving up Jolly Butchers Hill in the other direction, 1294 is on its way to Enfield on route 629. *Fred Ivey.*

Seen somewhere in London is wire greaser 114W – this strange looking vehicle had formerly been single-decker motorbus T 320. A window cleaner pedals past with his ladder slung across his left shoulder. *Alan Cross.*

608/3
(5,000M. 10-57-X-Stock).

LONDON TRANSPORT EXECUTIVE

5/-
COPPER

NAME _____

BADGE NO. _____   DATE _____

LOCATION _____

One of the bags that Vic found useful for another purpose.

This view was familiar to all London trolleybus crews. The window between the cab and saloon is in the 'down' position, allowing drivers and conductors to converse; also seen is the cab mirror which enables drivers to look through the vehicle. *Alan Cross.*

Rule 44 said that vehicles should not be left unattended. With some spells of duty being about five hours in length, the rule was ignored when the call of nature had to be answered. To meet staff's needs, London Transport made arrangements with some public houses for staff to use their toilets for which a small annual payment was made. The Red Lion at Barnet and The Cricketers at North Finchley are two places that spring to mind. We used the facilities at The Cricketers as, surprisingly, there were none in the refreshment hut at Tally Ho. We got to know where toilets were situated on each route. They tended to be nearer the City but not at Holborn or Moorgate. We might stop at the urinal just over the canal bridge at Moreland Street on the City Road coming back from Moorgate, or at the one just prior to the big railway bridge in Holloway Road, that carried the main line from Kings Cross to Edinburgh, on the way there. The only available WC on the 521/621 was opposite Guilford Street in Grays Inn Road.

It was Vic who enabled me to find out about the strength of the blue London Transport thick paper bag for copper coins! He suffered from a weak bladder, and many a time during darkness would say to me "Give us a copper bag". These were watertight and when he had finished with it, he would throw it out of the cab door window. Another use for them was also demonstrated by Vic as he used them as cups when he wanted water from the drinking fountain at the end of the horse trough near Barnet terminus. I was regularly having to replenish my stock of copper bags when working with him – good job London Transport didn't limit the number we could use!

London Transport allowed their staff to obtain refreshments *en route* and nominated various cafés as there were no refreshment facilities at most termini. Canons Park, Holborn and Moorgate had none. It was different at North Finchley as staff on journeys that terminated there could get a cup of tea in the refreshment hut. Having approval to obtain refreshments meant that tram and trolleybus staff were able to have them on the move or at a stand. Staff who participated in this were generally the older men who had their own tea cans. On the really early turns on the 609, they would leave their billy can at Don's Café in Holloway Road at the Archway on the way to Moorgate. The conductor would nip in quickly and leave a few coins in or alongside the can, the passengers not minding the brief delay. When the crew came back on the return journey, there would be hot tea for them. Another place where this happened was at the Forum Café at Edgware. Having pulled and released the frog handle for Canons Park, a conductor would take the tea can to the café on the other side of the dual carriageway and would pick it up on the way back. I only ever got a cuppa in this way if I was working with one of the older conductors for the day – of course I would chip in my few pence. At Barnet, the stand was opposite the Terminus Café which was regularly used by the trolleybus staff. Better than this though was an arrangement that Vic had with his cousin Tilly, our canteen manageress. When we were on very early turns she would have tea and toast ready for us at her house opposite Barnet terminus. By having refreshments ready for us, she had the guarantee of travelling on the 'bus with us to get to work on time. Stopping off on route brings to mind that sometimes a crew member would stop off at a tobacconist to buy some cigarettes. One Colindale conductress was in the habit of buying her groceries from a shop *en route*. She would leave the trolleybus, and her driver and passengers had to wait for her return.

Rapport between passengers and platform staff (drivers and conductors) was very good during trolleybus days as exemplified by the following. One evening, we pulled up at Harringay Stadium when a crowd from the dog track was coming out – we filled up completely and carried on to Manor House. Nobody wanted to get off there so we could not take any more passengers. Vic pulled into the centre of the road so that he could turn right into Seven Sisters Road towards Finsbury Park. While we were stationary, three yobbos, who had been waiting at the stop, attempted to board – I could not allow this as we were full. They verbally abused me and one of them who was eating an apple, threw it at me hitting me on the left shoulder. The jolt dislodged my MSC badge which dropped onto the platform; luckily it did not fall into the road. It was then that a young passenger on the offside long seat in the lower saloon said "Leave this to us mate, we'll sort them out for you" at which he and his two friends jumped off to chase the yobs away. The next thing I saw was the six of them running along the middle of the road at Manor House, my 'assistants' pursuing the yobs down Green Lanes towards Newington Green. That was the last I saw of them, as we turned into Seven Sisters Road. I never found out about the outcome of the pursuit and I often wondered if my helpers, who lost their ride, caught the troublemakers. There was only

one other occasion when I needed assistance – this was when we were only going as far as Islington Green on the 609. I got out to pull the frog handle and two male passengers got nasty as they wanted to go on to Moorgate. My driver for the day, Bill Blagdon, got out of the cab to assist and back me up and eventually they walked away. Behavioural problems were rare and I would only refuse a passenger if they were paralytically drunk. Sometimes I had to cajole difficult passengers into paying their fare. Other problems encountered 'on the back' were youths who threw snowballs onto the platform during winter and, at or near November 5th each year, hurled fireworks onto the platform. There was nothing much I could do about these incidents and I had to be alert to the situation and keep away from that area.

It was standard practice at busy times for drivers to go slowly in order to allow their conductors to collect all the fares. It was no good taking on a full load at Archway southbound and drivers hacking it, for many who had boarded there would get off at the Nags Head; even the best of conductors wouldn't be able to get all the fares in during that short run. When all the fares had been collected, they would go to the window between the cab and saloon and say "got them all in" and the driver could then get a move on. One day when Vic was allowing me time to get my fares in and we were creeping up Green Lanes approaching Manor House, there was a mother and child occupying the front nearside seat. The child said "why is the bus going so slowly, Mummy?" I was next to them issuing tickets and heard Vic call out loudly, "So I can give the conductor time to collect all the fares". There was no reply from mother or child – they heard him through the open cab/saloon window and his booming voice wrapped the situation up. When crews talked to each other between the cab and saloon, most of the conversation was job related – who were the lazy staff, conductors going driving, a new member of staff, an unusual face on the route (off the 645/660 rota). Vic and I talked about all manner of things and he told me that he had previously worked at Holloway depot, had been in the navy in the First World War and had lived in Canada for a while. I wasn't interested in football but might speak about dog racing as I liked a flutter.

Vic would get irritated by schoolchildren upstairs at the front of the 'bus who banged their feet on the floor. This caused a racket in the cab and he dealt with it by hitting the timecard against the wooden roof of the cab. This had the desired effect but the timecards became scuffed by all this, and they left indentations in the cab roof. One driver got so upset with them one day that he got out of his cab, went upstairs and gave them a real telling off. Something else that annoyed not just Vic but all drivers, were the persistent bell ringers. These were people who thought that they had gone past their stop when they hadn't, with another excuse being that they did not hear the bell ring – in fact, with a weak bell that was so. Loud bells could be very annoying to certain drivers who, to stop the bell ringing in their ears, would deaden the sound by stuffing newspaper into the back of the mechanism. This meant that when the bell was rung there was just a dull thud. As the bell was hardly audible, it meant that some passengers assumed that it wasn't working. They would then repeatedly keep pressing the bell or pulling the cord much to the annoyance of the driver, making his actions counter-productive. Whenever I took over a vehicle and became aware of newspaper in the bell, I would remove the obstruction. The signal made by passengers upstairs wishing to alight was for them to press a button which gave a buzzing noise in the cab. Drivers could not tamper with this device, and there was nothing that they could do with repeated buzzing.

In the summer, if it was really hot, Vic would take his boots off and drive the trolleybus in stockinged feet; he would sometimes take his jacket and detachable shirt collar off as well. He was never pulled up for driving in his shirt and braces, but officials might have had something to say if they knew that he didn't have his boots on either. However, Vic always had an answer for everything and so if he had been pulled up he would have probably told a questioning inspector "nothing in the rule book saying I have to drive with my boots on."

One day Vic had a problem with a trolleybus that resulted in us having to call for roadside assistance. We had just left the northbound stop at East Finchley Station when the 'bus came to a halt. Each time an attempt was made to pull away, instead of being able to take up the second and third notches smoothly on the power pedal, the breaker knife switches blew, preventing the vehicle from moving. The trolleybus was awkwardly situated with its back half under the bridge (still with the booms in the troughing) and the front half out in the open. It had stopped just before the loop into the station fore-court but fortunately no vehicles needed to have their poles swung onto the dead-end wires which existed there at this time. Badly parked, it was difficult for other trolleybuses to overtake. 'On the spot' attention was required and would be achieved by using a telephone that was available to trolleybus crews – it could not be accessed by motorbus staff. These phones enabled staff to call for assistance for dewirements, punctures or any kind of failure. Vic lowered the booms and, deciding that it was best to stay with the vehicle, handed me a key that opened up a compartment that was fitted to the top of some of the feeder pillars. I walked back about fifty yards to the conveniently sited section box outside the White Lion pub. Inside the compartment was a telephone which automatically connected to 'Northern trolleybus control' at Hackney depot (despite this establishment being renamed Clapton in 1950, the original terminology remained). ('Southern trolleybus control' was at Oval station). I picked up the phone and told the person at the other end what the problem was, the fleet number of the trolleybus and our loca-tion. They arranged for a repair wagon and crew to come out to us. They soon arrived, proving the value of London Transport's internal phone system. On getting away, Vic said "Hang onto that key, we might need it again". However, I never needed to use the 'trolleybus telephone' again. These keys were supposed to be kept in a case at the back of the cab of each trolleybus but it was rare to see one there. They were normally to be found in drivers' pockets as they wanted to have one to hand. The key that Vic gave me is still in my possession to this day as he never asked for it back.

This is the inside of a feeder pillar; seen in Isleworth depot, the bottom section shows the line switches for the overhead. For staff use, the top part had contained a telephone; as the pillar is within the depot confines it has been removed (this one had been used on the tram system at Lambeth Baths). *Hugh Taylor.*

Vic would always leave Moorgate a few minutes late on the 'last boat'. This terminology was only used by trolleybus staff (never by their motorbus equivalents) and was a colloqui-alism for the last trolleybus on each route at night. Vic reckoned that it gave people a chance to get the last 'bus if they were running behind time, and he would make up the time on the way back to the depot. He liked to let a trolleybus out and knew how to handle one at speed. On occasions like this, when he virtually had the 'juice' to himself, he went like a rocket. I will now relate one of the two occasions when he got things wrong. We had left Moorgate about eight minutes late and were haring back to North Finchley. As we crossed the junction of Upper Street with Canonbury Lane, Vic found that the power was off, but initially didn't know why. We were still moving on momentum, but gradually slowing down. We

Trolleybuses were sometimes left parked inconsiderately at the top of the bus station. Although 1451 and 1540 are just within its confines, 1496 is still partly in Ballards Lane. Something's wrong with 1540's negative trolley boom – it looks as if it has jumped off the wire; before it can get going again a member of staff will have to rectify the situation. *Chris Orchard.*

knew the poles hadn't come off, as there hadn't been any crashing or banging from above. "The neon light's out – the power's off" Vic said. There was a slight downward gradient here, so Vic put the 'bus into battery mode, released the handbrake and with the assistance of the gradient, we drifted downhill. Seconds later we could see the reason why we had no power for two tower wagons were positioned at Highbury Corner where some staff were working on the overhead line. The night gang had quite rightly assumed that the last 609 had passed through and said "you shouldn't be here, you should have gone through by now". I asked them to turn the juice back on again and they threw a switch in a section box. It was then hell for leather back to the depot which we just about reached on time. Next night, we left eight minutes late again – but with no hold-ups this time.

The bus station could get congested and there could be problems getting through when we were running into the depot. The reason for it being so full would have been 'buses parked out of service for one reason or another – usually due to staff shortage or by crews coming off late on their first part of duty, and unable to take over their second 'bus on time. Similarly, if running into the depot on a 521/621 and there were some 660s standing in Ballards Lane unable to enter the bus station, Vic would go in as if we were terminating there. I'd hook the poles down, he'd battery down the slope, I'd get 'em up again and we'd be in the depot in double-quick time. If Vic saw that there was a line of 521s/621s blocking entry to the bus station, he would get me to pull the frog handle in Kingsway, and get in from Ballards Lane – as if we were running into the depot. I have just mentioned that

Apart from those running in from Barnet, all trolleybuses needing to access Finchley depot needed to pass through the bus station. More often than not there would be a 660 on the stand and its crew in the refreshment hut; they could be by-passed either by placing its poles on a span wire or beneath its retaining hooks – the crew would later materialise and the booms be hoisted onto the wires. Here, though, 1515's driver has indicated to 1619's crew that he wants its poles dropped and the Stonebridge driver is obliging. Once 1515 has passed by, 1619 will be re-poled. All of this will not happen much longer for, on the strangely numbered traction standard 02, a 'Buses for Trolleybuses' poster can be seen. *Ron Kingdon.*

the congested bus station prevented 660s from getting in – trolleybuses to Barnet had to hang on for a couple of minutes or so until everything had sorted itself out.

Vic had his own way of working and I was happy to fit in with him. He always wanted to get off quickly to go home as he lived in Summers Lane, which was about half a mile from the depot. If we were coming off in the bus station on a 521/621 he would assess the situation to see where he could park up. Having got the lie of the land he would often call out "Get 'em down". I would get hold of the bamboo from its holder beneath the 'bus or grab hold of one that was hanging

on a traction standard, and drop the poles. I would then shove our bamboo, grappling hook first, into the lower saloon as it would have been impossible to have got it back under the 'bus at the speed Vic was doing things – if it was not 'our' bamboo, I would return it to a nearby traction standard. There was no stopping Vic; he was going to park up come what may and all I had time to do, while he was running the trolleybus down the slope on battery or gravity, was to get the poles down. Having parked the 'bus, Vic would be out of the cab and away like a jack rabbit. As he hurried away, he might say "see you later".

There is not a photograph of Vic Collins 'downing the wires' at Moorgate, but this picture taken on the last evening of trolleybuses there (7th November 1961) illustrates the kind of thing that happened that day. Wood Green's 1294 is already on the outer wire but 1669's driver has not realised this and passes the 641. The result was that 1669's booms clouted 1294's with the 609 dewiring. 1669 is being rewired – all of this was within sight of an inspector who turned a blind eye to the situation. 1669 was the highest numbered trolleybus ever allocated to Finchley depot; 1294 and 1669 have only a few more hours of life in them as both were withdrawn from service that night. *Hugh Taylor.*

Experience taught us to be canny and if we knew that we could turn something to our advantage then we would. Let's say that Vic and I were on FY46 on route 609 at the Nags Head on our way back to North Finchley for our break, and saw our second 'bus, say FY58, running about twenty minutes late. If it was still showing MOORGATE we'd know that it was a dead cert that it would come back late for us to take over on time at Tally Ho. We would agree that there was no need for Vic to rush back and we would turn up about ten minutes after its scheduled arrival time. We wouldn't make it any more than that as 58's crew may make up a few minutes coming back. Similarly, if we were on 'Holborns' and saw our second 'bus running late at Finsbury Park and still showing HOLBORN CIRCUS, we could be confident it would come back late as 'buses tended not to be turned after they'd left Wood Green. We'd stay in the refreshment hut at Tally Ho and, from time to time, look out to see when it arrived.

My most memorable dewirement as a conductor was when Vic 'downed' the wires at Moorgate, this being the second time that he got things wrong. It was about 6.30, at the end of the evening peak, with the City having gone quiet and with virtually nobody about. We had arrived late so it was going to be an 'in and out job' (forgoing the stand time) as we were on relief back at North Finchley. Vic said that we'd need to leave before a 641 that was parked on the inside set of wires, and this was to be achieved by using the outside loop. I got off to pull the frog handle but I reckon Vic thought I was a potential four-minute-miler for he was through the frog before I had a chance to get anywhere near the handle. I sprinted and caught the 'bus up hoping that I could tell Vic to stop but it was too late and all I could do was watch the sequence of events unfold. He had gone straight round the square on the inside set of wires, passing the stationary 641; our poles collided with the 641's poles which strangely enough stayed on the wires. On impact ours came off and unfortunately one of the running wires broke. As the live wire came down, it hit a Rolls-Royce car that was parked in front of the

641, causing showers of sparks to fall over its roof. When the traction wire hit the ground it snaked under the front valance of the 641 and there were orange sparks jumping about all over the place. Quite nonchalently, as if it was an everyday occurrence, the 641 driver immediately got out of his cab, put on rubber gloves that he had removed from his emergency box, and pulled the traction wire, that was draped in front and underneath his 641, into the side of the road. In situations like this the procedure was to 'short' the wire against some metal. A traction standard is ideal so this is presumably what he did. Having secured the fallen wire, he would have contacted 'Control' as the damage would have to be repaired. I got our bamboo pole out and gave it to Vic who re-wired our booms. Seeing there was no inspector about (they took their breaks after the evening peak) Vic said, "Come on, let's go" – and we did. The overhead electrical arrangements allowed power to be fed in when there was a wire break – this allowed Vic to move. He told me to keep quiet about the matter and we went back to Tally Ho as if nothing had happened. I didn't see him on his break, as he went home, and he didn't discuss the matter with me until about two hours later when we were on a 621 having a couple of minutes break at Charterhouse Street. On Holborns, if we had a couple of minutes to kill, we were inclined to get out and stretch our legs, which we were doing on this occasion. Vic had become a bit concerned about the episode and said "I'd better report what happened at Moorgate earlier." Vic used the unattended inspector's phone and got on the blower to 'Control'. When we got back to the depot, Vic filled in a dewirement form but I didn't hear any more about the matter. He must have come up with some cock and bull story as to why he'd delayed reporting it. I never knew what he told the CDI about the incident. Despite it being well over fifty years since this happened, it is one of my most vivid trolleybus recollections, and I can still picture the Wood Green driver pulling the flashing and sparking wire away from his 641, and the traction wire's electric sparks bouncing off the Rolls-Royce.

Harry Franks was a 'steady old plodder' and looked older than he was; here he manoeuvres 336 around the Gladstone Avenue loop at Wood Green in the summer of 1959 – the year is known by the 'Boy and the Bridge' adverts. 336 is on FY23 which made four turns here; his conductor will have to change the front blind to NORTH FINCHLEY soon as the main boarding point is only a few yards away. Trolleybuses turning at Wood Green from the north were designated 621s rather than 521s. *Fred Ivey.*

After working with Vic for about a year, he decided to go on the 645/660 rota and I was then paired with Harry Franks, a really nice bloke and, as I've said before, a distant relative. These two factors led to him soon inviting me to his house for breakfast when we were on early turns rather than going to the depot canteen for our break. Therefore, on most Monday to Saturday mornings, I would rush into 'Gunns' (an old fashioned grocers shop with sawdust on the floor) and buy eggs and a tin of Chef brand 'sausages and beans' for our

breakfast, splitting the cost between us. After a while, the old boy who worked there got to know what I was going to buy and just said "Usual is it?". The shop was conveniently opposite Tally Ho bus station and as soon as I'd bought the food we would be on a 521/621 down to Friern Barnet where we went to Harry's house in Goldsmith Road.

Harry and I had to be shrewd about getting a lift to Friern Barnet. If we could get off a bit sharpish, we could have longer at his house. This could be achieved by arriving at

Tally Ho a couple of minutes early on say FY23. To prevent me performing a juggling act with my ticket equipment and the food, Harry would say "Give us your box Bill, you go and get the grub". He would ask the crew of FY22 to hang on for a minute or so while I did this. Leaving Gunns, I would beckon its driver forward and would pull the frog handle at the corner of Woodhouse Road and board there. When on 22, I might say to its crew, "Watch out for us this week, we're going down to Harry's for breakfast". Harry had laid the table before he left the house in the morning in readiness for our meal break. All we had to do was switch the kettle on and cook the food – we had to do it ourselves as his wife was out at work. If we were on a short break of about forty-five minutes, it was a bit hectic as that only left us with about twenty minutes from the time of our arrival to the time we had to leave. During that short time, we had to cook and consume our breakfast.

It was important for us to get back to North Finchley to take over our second 'bus on time, so we had to be at the Town Hall stop with a few minutes to spare just in case the 'bus we were hoping to board came up a bit early. The approach of a trolleybus was signalled by the dancing of the wires. Sometimes I would board here when travelling to work, and on a cold frosty morning, would hear a shrilling sound travelling along the wires, indicating that a trolleybus was on its way. Sounds from the overhead could be heard from a fair distance; in this case from Friern Barnet hospital gates, about a quarter of a mile away. Often, the 'bus that came up was the one (say FY10) that we were going to take over at Tally Ho. If it was a Monday, I'd say to the crew, "You on it all week?". If they replied in the affirmative, I'd tell them "Look out for us as we'll be riding up with you". Being astute, we would look out each day to see if 10 was on the road. If we didn't see it (hadn't been running due to staff shortage) we wouldn't go to Harry's. Similarly, if we'd been told to take our second 'bus out of the depot (wasn't running for some reason), we didn't go to his house for breakfast – the canteen had to suffice. If we had gone to his house, and then to the depot, there might have been a bit of a panic if FY10 had not been prepared for us.

Harry and I always made sure that we left enough time to get back to Tally Ho but there was the odd occasion when we did get back late, through no fault of our own – possibly the 'bus we were planning to board being curtailed at New Southgate. We would have to dodge any inspectors who might be hovering; it was only Inspector Bill Cole who once had to have a word with us. We were always more anxious to get back if we were taking over a 'live' 609 going to Barnet or Moorgate but there was not that urgency if we were on 521s/621s as they were taken over in the bus station. On the few occasions when we did get back a tad late there was no inconvenience to the service, and there were no times when another 'bus had to go in front of us. We were sometimes relieved that having turned up a couple of minutes late, the 609 we were meant to take over came up late anyway. If I had a lot of coins to pay in then Harry went home by himself and I had a meal in the canteen. Usually, it was only bad weather and late turns that kept us at North Finchley for our grub.

DRIVING DAYS BECKON

I had learnt to drive in the army and like many of my young conductor colleagues wanted to go driving. I had to bide my time as London Transport's ruling in the mid-1950s was that staff wanting to attain this grade had to be twenty-five years of age. However, there was a concession that allowed conductors to apply for it on their twenty-fourth birthday – they couldn't start tuition though until they were twenty-five. I decided to avail myself of this opportunity and on 7th September 1954 went to see Mr Irons, informing him that I wanted to become a trolleybus driver (when I did, my driving seniority would start from my application date). He gave me the appropriate paperwork, which I filled in there and then, and told me to see him nearer the time about applying for a driver's licence. Immediately afterwards I went into the canteen and told Bill Bennett, one of the driving instructors, that I had just put in for driving. He replied, "You might come out with me" (which I did for a week). London Transport was going to give me the opportunity to achieve my driving ambition and it was to be at no cost to myself. By working 'on the back', I had an advantage over men with no trolleybus experience because I was forever peering into the cab and generally picked things up. I took an interest in the driver's job and observed what was required. My regular drivers told me a lot about overhead features and at some of the big junctions I made it my business to know what needed to be done. I soon found out that the power pedal was operated with the left foot, and the brake pedal with the right. I was aware of the different battery/trolley changeover positions on the Cs and Js and knew where spare fuses were kept. I also knew that there was more to driving a trolleybus than to driving a motorbus. I was looking forward to the driving course and it was to be a challenge to be able to master the controls of one. It was a unique type of vehicle. There was nothing else like it on the road and it was very different to anything else I had driven before.

Shortly before I started the trolleybus driving course I was working with driver Johnny Waite for a couple of days – maybe Harry Franks was on holiday. Knowing that I was going driving in a few days time he suddenly said, "Come on, you have a go at the wheel" (we were chatting through the cab/saloon window at the time). It was late at night with no passengers on board (I'd already taken off my conducting equipment when he said this). I quickly nipped round to the front and clambered into the cab and onto the driving seat. Johnny had moved over to the left and was sitting on the battery box so this meant that it was a J type trolleybus. He watched over me and didn't have to give me any advice, he just let me get on with it. I drove between The Triumph pub in Woodhouse Road and North Finchley, about half a mile, but for safety's sake I didn't go higher than third notch. As he thought that I had done well on the first occasion, he said to me the following night, "This is where you take over". And I did …. again on a J type and over the same distance. On both occasions we reverted to our normal roles just before High Road, North Finchley. I felt comfortable having my first drive of a trolleybus but of course it was against all the rules and regulations of London Transport.

The training simulator in Stonebridge depot was an elaborate affair. Novice drivers were faced with fixtures that included a diagram which showed how contactors, the regenerative brake, the rehostatic brake and air brake worked. An open display shows contactors; next to the driver's seat is a reverser key. As it is only pretend, a handbrake is not provided. *London Transport Museum U26765.*

TROLLEYBUS DRIVER TRAINING

In August 1955, my CDI gave me an application form for a trolleybus driver's licence. I needed two character references and, as relatives were not allowed to do this, a friend of my dad, PC 'Taffy' Evans, and a neighbour, Bert Slinn, who had both vouched for me when I applied for a conductor's licence, were happy to sign the form for me. I sent a postal order for five shillings and sixpence (three shillings for a licence and two and sixpence deposit for a badge) to the Public Carriage Office in anticipation that I would pass my test. The CDI arranged for me to have a medical at Manor House, which I passed. There was no such thing as a provisional trolleybus driver's licence; the application form and the displaying of L plates on a trolleybus throughout the course sufficed.

I was instructed to report for trolleybus driver training at Finchley depot at 8am on Monday 12th September 1955 – full credit to London Transport for organising this to start just five days after my twenty-fifth birthday. There were three of us in the school that commenced that day – fellow conductor Johnny McGrath, who had formerly been in the Ulster Constabulary, and a conductor from Stonebridge depot called Bill who had previously been a milkman. Instructor Bill Bennett had a trolleybus ready for us, parked inside the depot with its poles down. He had put L plate signs inside the vehicle as it was statutory for all learner drivers to display these – one was fixed in the front windscreen, the other in the rear window. Bill Bennett moved the trolleybus onto the forecourt where we were each told to climb into the cab and familiarise ourselves with the layout. He soon discovered that we had taken it upon ourselves to find out about the controls but was aware that we didn't know about the touch and feel of the pedals, and the position of the switches. He also explained the different type of braking available to us but we only got the hang of these when we were out on the road.

Before long, he asked if we were all confident and ready to give it a go – we answered in the affirmative and were ready for the off. Instructor Bill drove the 'bus to Stonebridge depot as we were to visit the small training centre there. It was in a wooden hut which was situated on the right, a few yards inside the depot boundary. We were introduced to senior Instructor, Mr Marjoram, who was immaculately attired and who was in charge of training here; at home, after a day's training one day, I told my parents his name. They both knew him, my mother from her schooldays and my father from his days on point duty at Archway. They made the connection because of his unusual name. During the training course they coincidentally met up at Finchley depot when my parents were picking me up after a day's tuition. They had a good old chin-wag, immediately recognising each other despite the passage of years.

The training hut wasn't a state of the art structure but was adequate for the purpose it was designed for. Inside, trolleybus electrical circuitry diagrams were displayed on blackboards, and Mr Marjoram explained how electricity was fed from the sub-station into the overhead line and that the current was passed via the trolley head, down cables in the booms and through the bodywork to the chassis-mounted traction motor. In turn this drove the vehicle. There was a driving simulator that was used for testing novices' aptitude, and enabled trainees to familiarise themselves with the functions of the foot brake and power pedals. Not every budding trolleybus driver had a go on the simulator, and our school was one of those that didn't have the opportunity to use it (it has never been ascertained why some men used the simulator and others didn't). Leaving the hut, we were given an initial feel of driving a trolleybus by being let loose, under supervision, on the wiring circuit especially constructed here for familiarising new trolleybus drivers. Having had a few laps we went out onto the main road and into the traffic conditions of the day.

Most trainees attended 'Stonebridge School' where a number of trolleybuses from various depots would be parked on the forecourt when Mr Marjoram was in session. There'd be vehicles from as far afield as Carshalton, Finchley and West Ham, though Ilford staff did not bring over their South African type trolleybuses and would borrow a standard one from Bow or West Ham. Bexleyheath staff, who were isolated from the rest of the system, were not able to attend and had to make do with their own special training circuit within their depot confines.

Our first couple of days of training were carried out in the quieter parts of our area but Bill Bennett soon had us spending a fair amount of time on the 'nine and twenty-one roads' which were in congested areas such as Holborn, Manor House, Moorgate and Wood Green. This was useful as we would be meeting heavy traffic once we, hopefully, had passed our tests. The unusual system of left foot drive did not cause me any problems, despite being used to driving motor vehicles with my right foot. It should be borne in mind that a trolleybus has two foot pedals only – power and brake. Each had a metal P or B embossed on them; over the years they became shiny with use but the letters didn't wear out.

We met in the Finchley depot canteen at about 7.30am for a cup of tea each morning. Although convenient for Johnny and myself, it meant that trainee Bill had to travel quite a way each day. As we arrived at different times we paid for our own tea, but when we were out and about we took it in turns to pay – when we had a meal we paid for ourselves. Refreshments were looked forward to and on one occasion we drove along the Uxbridge Road to Hanwell depot where we had our break. The Stonebridge learner trolleybus also made its way here from time to time, so maybe the instructors considered it to be a good canteen. However, it may have been for another reason as some learner trolleybuses could be seen well away from their usual stomping grounds due to the fact that some instructors used the trolleybus system as their own mail and visiting service. They were able to justify this (to themselves) in that there was no extra cost incurred as the same amount of power was being used wherever they went. For our tea breaks and meal reliefs we visited Colindale and Stonebridge depots as well as using our own facilities at Finchley. Going to Stonebridge for refreshments enabled trainee Bill to pick up his pay packet on Fridays. While mentioning pay, we were less well off during the driver training course than if we had carried out our conducting duties. We were paid the standard rate for the day and lost spreadover and weekend enhancements that would otherwise have been paid. At the time we were on a six-day week so had to come in on Saturdays. We didn't train right up till 4pm on this day as the instructors wanted an early weekend finish! Conductors were allowed to work 'on the back' during the period of the driving course. I worked two of my Sundays off over the three week training period, but it only partly made up for my lost earnings.

It was policy never to have more than three learners to each 'bus as it was necessary for each individual to have an adequate amount of driving time each day – we had four sessions of about thirty minutes each. When the staff shortage really started to bite, sometimes there was just one trainee per 'bus. We had to turn up in full uniform, including our white cap and our conductor's badge on display. This was London Transport's dress code of the time and was compulsory throughout the course. However, we were allowed to take our caps off on the 'bus. Direct entry drivers had to have a driving licence and tended to have two weeks training. Conductors learning to be drivers had three weeks training as it was assumed that most did not have a driving licence. It was also a TGWU agreement that conductors had this length of training.

At this point the difference between motorbus and trolleybus driving instructors should be explained. Those who worked on buses were employed as permanent instructors, while on the trolleybus side, instructors were experienced drivers who were prepared to 'act up' when necessary. When doing this they were paid a supplementary amount of money for their extra responsibilities. Bill Bennett and Fred Chapman were Finchley's regular instructors but, as learner 'buses were not required all the time, they could be seen 'on the road'. As a conductor I worked with both of them. Trolleybus driving instructors did not always wear their instructor's light blue badges, which made them look the part. Some opted to show their everyday red trolleybus badge on their caps – this meant that they were not continually changing the badges around. To be seen in the refreshment hut at Tally Ho was Ilford depot's John Baird having a trolleybus driving school in session. He wore his instructor's badge all the time. He was obviously considered to be a good tutor for regardless of his depot closing in August 1959, he was assigned to train new trolleybus staff for many months after this. Despite the fact that he was now officially a motorbus driver, he was even training new Highgate men in 1961. Instructors were wise to the tricks that a few conductors learning to drive would resort to. Some of those in one of Highgate's schools made out that they weren't good enough by deliberately dewiring when all the time they were progressing well. They did this so as to prolong the course, wanting to have extra time in the training 'bus rather than drive passengers around. Such miscreants were persuaded to change their ways by a few choice words! In our case this did not apply as we just wanted to get on with it.

After a week, 'Sandy' a driver from Colindale depot, took over from Bill Bennett who was either on holiday or was required elsewhere, for instructors went where they were told. With Sandy, we did most of our training in the Acton, Canons Park, Hammersmith and Willesden areas as he was a 'Colindale man'. We found that Bill and Sandy were very good instructors and were patient, cheerful, approachable men. Both had a wealth of experience with many useful tips to pass on to us as they had driven trolleybuses for many years. Sandy said that we all gave a smooth ride and picked up trolleybus driving very easily. The fact that I already had road sense put me in good stead.

While one of us was in the cab, the other two sat downstairs on the long seats near the platform and I still think of the days when I was sitting on the offside seat with Johnny McGrath opposite me. We sometimes made ourselves comfortable by putting our legs up on the seats! Most of the day's conversation was about picking up the art of trolleybus driving, the instructors responding to our questions appropriately. Although learner 'buses were not supposed to pick up members of staff in case they distracted the trainees, if one of our colleagues was trying to get a lift up to North Finchley from Friern Barnet or Golders Green, we would let them board with the instructor's say-so. We always made sure that we carried a bamboo pole on our daily wanderings. We kept it in its rightful position beneath the 'bus rather than the slapdash method of keeping it in the lower saloon where any of us could trip over it. We took it in turns to raise and lower booms and pull frogs, but there was no cutting of corners such as 'flying frog pulls' at Manor House!

Some matters had to be learnt quickly. The operation and role of the circuit breaker was one, it being important that we got the hang of this early on for, as novices, we were likely to initially try to give the 'bus too much power (the circuit breaker prevented too much electricity being fed into the motor). Without being big-headed, there wasn't much 'blowing of breakers' as we picked things up well. When we did blow them we just knocked back the switches in the roof of the cab. Also to be mastered was how the regenerative and rheostatic braking systems worked, but our instructors advised us not to get used to using the regen brake, the reason for this being explained in a later chapter.

An advantage that trainee motorbus drivers had over novice trolleybus drivers was that they could have their first feel of driving a large vehicle in a quiet backwater at low

speed. Trolleybus driver-trainees did not have the same opportunity and had to get up to service speed straightaway so as not to delay the services. This was one of the most heavily emphasised features of the training course and Sandy was always on about it – I remember being told this near Willesden Bus Garage. While we found our feet there was an element of 'upping and downing' of trolleybooms to let one or two service 'buses go past. We were told that we were to be particularly aware of the nearside of the trolleybus, to give clear and precise hand signals and to be safely forceful. Our instructors communicated to us by bell and worked to normal procedures in that they would ring it once for stop and twice to start. Sandy tied some string around the bell cord so he wouldn't have to get out of his seat and stand up each time he wanted to ring it. At the start each day, Bill or Sandy would say something like, "We'll have a trip to Hammersmith and back now" or "let's go up to Barnet" or "Canons Park today and we'll nip into Colindale depot on the way back as I've got to see someone there". Training under the wires was considered to be route-learning. This was completely different to the motorbus side where new men did their route-learning after they had passed their PSV tests.

At the start of the course, Bill explained the duties that were to be carried out at each terminus. The handbrake was to be fully applied and, if we were leaving the vehicle, both circuit breakers were to be tripped. We were told that when we changed drivers we should keep a sharp look-out for any overtaking vehicle before opening the cab door and getting out. When taking over a 'bus we should walk round to the front of it from the nearside, meaning that we were only in the road for a short time. This was good advice which I generally put into practice in my driving days – I say 'generally', as there were times when it was more practical to walk to the cab from the rear offside. Before leaving a trolleybus on the inclines at Edgware terminus and Islington Green shunt we were to turn the steering wheel so that the front driving wheels pointed towards the kerb.

We didn't traverse all the short working points. We went into the regularly used ones at Finsbury Park and Islington Green, and even the infrequently used North Acton circle. However, New Southgate, Windsor Terrace and St Gabriels Church were given a miss. Using a facility like Finsbury Park enabled us to do a driver change as it was convenient, although there were times when we did this on the roadway when traffic was quiet. Bill Bennett emphatically told us the correct way to hold the steering wheel. This was to have our hands in the 'ten to two' position, and always push and pull. However, once I had passed my test, I drove in the way I was most comfortable with, and participated in over-arm steering when necessary.

It was stressed that we must be alert to the overhead, as road positioning was often different to that of other road vehicles. Two places where we were told to take particular care and caution were the Woodhouse Road bends just south of North Finchley, and when passing under Barnet bridge southbound. Sandy told us that we were to closely examine all the overhead junctions as we would need to be familiar with them once we had passed our tests. As it was, I knew most of these as I had observed them during my four years conducting – my drivers had often told me how to approach 'special work' on our routes.

After we had completed a few days training we returned to 'Stonebridge School' for further instruction. On the right-hand side of the hut there were damaged pieces of overhead equipment such as frogs, crossings and section breakers. Mr Marjoram said that they were in this condition because drivers had drawn power on them when they should not have done – he strongly advised us against adopting such slipshod practices. We were shown different types of frogs, sections of overhead and a re-set skate. It was on the second visit to Stonebridge that we practised reversing and battery manoeuvring, and driving over wooden fire ramps that stood a few inches high; this enabled fire hoses to go under them. The ramps were used to simulate situations when fire appliances were using hoses that had to cross the public highway. This was a good exercise as I had to use these in service in Holloway one day. Mr Marjoram also gave us a demonstration of how a trolleybus was lifted by an emergency team. He showed us the emergency box, the contents of which are explained in a later chapter. He stressed that if we needed to move traction wires we should use the rubber gloves that were to be found inside the box.

Sandy kept drumming two points into us, one mental and one practical. Mentally, we should not be hesitant; after all we were driving the largest vehicles to be seen in everyday use in London. Therefore it was important that we were confident and decisive in making our moves and that as soon as we left a stop, we should get out of the kerb and into mainstream traffic. Practically, that as we pulled into a bus stop we should 'feather' the air brake and at the very last second ease our foot back off the pedal, thus giving a very gentle stop. There were times when Sandy was wily, for having stopped the trolleybus at a bus stop he would sometimes give the starting signal when he saw a line of traffic approaching us from behind. He did this to test our reaction but at the same time would say, "Watch your mirror, driver, watch your mirror. Wave them on."

All told, Bill and Sandy gave us similar instructions and would regularly call out, "Check your nearside", "Watch the kerb", "Section insulator ahead", "Get a move on, we've got a couple of 'buses behind", "Watch your speed", "We're coming to a bend, look at the overhead", "Road positioning, road positioning" and so on. There were many overhead junctions that we had to become familiar with and we were told to look at what was required to get us through each one. As the course progressed we gained in confidence, experience and knowledge and towards the end of the training, Sandy needed to advise us only occasionally. There was one piece of advice that Sandy gave us which I put into practice throughout my trolleybus driving career. As we were continually pulling up at bus stops, we should at the very last moment give the 'bus a little bit of right-hand lock so that the front wheels pointed out from the kerb. He would call out, "Get that lock on, then you won't have to put pressure on the steering wheel as you move off. When you do, take up first notch and she'll come out from the kerb". This brought the 'bus out easily into the centre of the road, enabling us to hand signal at the same time. This eased our path back into the traffic and prevented too much tugging and heaving on the steering wheel.

London Transport had some trolleybuses that could be quickly adapted for driver training duties. 317 and 905 were those used for this purpose at Finchley. By having a C class and a J class available, we were able to familiarise ourselves with the different type of battery/trolley changeover switches that were used. Although a trolleybus has enough room in the cab for two people, instructors worked from the saloon as the window behind the driver was taken out. This was done by the 'inside staff' inserting a trolleybus blind winding key into locks around the frame and removing the window, which was kept somewhere in the depot – probably the coachmaker's shop. Initially, the instructors stood right behind us just in case they needed to grab the handbrake in an emergency; however they never needed to do this with us. Most of the time they sat on the front or next to front nearside seat enabling them to see the view in the offside driver's mirror. Another benefit was that the absence of the window made it easier for us to hear our instructor's words.

The depot engineers were told each night if learner trolleybuses were needed the following day and if so, would set one aside. Sometimes it was necessary to use one in service for a journey beforehand and this was signified by finding tickets on the floor when we went out to the 'bus, which was always parked inside the depot. We normally left just after 8am and although finishing time was supposed to be 4.30pm, we were normally back by 4pm, meaning that after the window had been replaced, the 'bus could be used in the evening peak.

As far as I know, there was only one school at a time at Finchley, though the larger depots sometimes ran two concurrently. By having two training trolleybuses available, it meant that if one was being repaired or going through routine maintenance or away for overhaul, then the other could be used. On the rare occasions when both were unavailable then another trolleybus had to be commandeered. This happened to us one day. Sandy reckoned that our ability was high enough to make do without a training 'bus with a removable window. He called his instructions while standing by the saloon nearside front window. Any 'bus could be called upon and though we didn't use it, our unique 954 was used in this capacity on one occasion. In situations such as this, if an instructor did not think his trainees were competent enough to use an ordinary 'bus then a training trolleybus would be borrowed from another depot. There were times when Highgate used one of ours. After 317 and 905 were withdrawn in November 1959, Finchley used 1500 and 1517 which had come over from East End depots. 905 always sticks in my mind as the learner 'bus so I expect that was the vehicle that I did most of my training on.

Each day, instructors had to complete assessment forms as to how their trainees were getting on. Mr Marjoram would peruse these and as he had a close working relationship with the instructors, would ask for a frank opinion of each trainee's ability just before a progress check took place. Mr Marjoram attended these in person. He was one of a number of Senior Instructors that were employed throughout the trolleybus system, each keeping to their own area. When he took us out on our progress check we went to the congested

A summer Saturday in 1961 sees 1500 on learner duties – rather than go into Tally Ho bus station, the instructor has told his trainee to park in the middle of Kingsway. The instructor changes the trolley arms from one set of wires to another – this will enable them to finish a few minutes early for the weekend. Occasionally, the regular crews cut corners and rather than go through the bus station would perform this manoeuvre too! *Hugh Taylor.*

Holloway and City areas as he wanted to see what we were made of. I reckon part of the reason that we came this way was because he lived near Archway so it was handy for him to be dropped off there. When he had me up the front, he rang the bell and stopped me at Ducketts Common, saying, "Be decisive, forceful and get going" and then rang me off. I suppose his presence made me cautious. He told me that I should not be hesitant and should push myself out into the middle of the roadway if necessary. We all passed the check and continued to practise for our new trade.

The driving course took eighteen working days and towards the end of it Sandy said that he was satisfied with our ability and that we were 'up for test' on Tuesday 4th October. When we met that morning, Sandy let us have a late breakfast as he deemed it wise to forgo our meal relief that day, choosing to spend the maximum amount of time on last minute practising. He gave us words of encouragement and said that if we drove as we had been doing during the course, then we would all pass first time. All instructors hoped for a high pass rate as this reflected their teaching ability and we

When the newer trolleybuses came over from the East End, 1500 and 1517 were the two vehicles used for regular driver training. On the day that this picture was taken, the instructor wants to get his novices into the thick of the traffic, and an ideal place for this is central London; 1517 turns from Seven Sisters Road into Holloway Road. The Nags Head public house is on the right. *Michael Dryhurst.*

said that we hoped we could do him credit. He emphasised that each time we got out of the cab, when we were changing drivers during the tests, we must knock the circuit breakers out and have the handbrake fully on as we had done up to now. He told us that we were to wear our caps for the test, and that it would be best if we wore them all day long so that there wouldn't be any last minute hitch locating them – of course we complied. Sandy had found out who the examiner was and that we were to pick him up in Acton. Intuition told him that the test would take place between there and Hammersmith. On the morning of the test we were running up and down between Acton Market and Hammersmith so that we would get used to the route that he reckoned we were going to be examined on. We also traversed Bromyard Avenue loop a couple of times enabling us to be in the thick of traffic in Acton itself. Sandy's hunch paid off as related below.

London Transport had their own driving examiners, these being men approved by the Ministry of Transport to carry out the testing of potential motorbus and trolleybus drivers. Some were permanent examiners while others were Divisional Mechanical Inspectors (DMIs) who combined this with their responsibilities of following up allegations against drivers and vehicles. The examiners did want men to pass their test but wanted a perfect or near-perfect drive. If a trainee was to even let a 'bus roll back an inch, or to commit the most cardinal of sins and take the rear nearside road wheels over a kerb, it was instant failure. Most trainees passed first time, and did so by their own efforts, but for those who did not, they were often given a few days extra training. If they failed at the second attempt, OUT. However, some of the unsuccessful candidates might be given a second chance a few months later.

Some examiners (like the one who would test our school) were based at Chiswick Works and would meet the would-be trolleybus drivers as near as possible to there. Having run the 'bus to Craven Park to turn, we picked our man up at a pre-arranged meeting place in Horn Lane, Acton at the appointed time that afternoon. The three of us had a degree of apprehension for the ordeal in front of us. Boarding the trolleybus the examiner said words to the effect of "Good afternoon. Obey the starting and stopping signals I give you. We'll have a drive down to Hammersmith and see how we get on from there". Some examiners insisted that, when a trainee was on his test, the others in the group go upstairs so they wouldn't know what to expect when it was their turn. However, our examiner let us sit downstairs while he was on board. Johnny was in the cab when the examiner boarded so he was 'up first'. He drove to Paddenswick Road, after which Bill took over; he drove into Hammersmith and back to Acton Vale where I climbed into the cab. It was very congested at Acton. In the Market Place there was only just enough room for me to squeeze through as there was a long meat lorry delivering its cargo. I made it OK, keeping the trolleybus going all the time. It must have confirmed to the examiner that I had the right measure of confidence for the job. Back in Horn Lane, he told me to pull up and called out, "Round here lad". Entering the saloon, the examiner told me that I had passed my test, as had Bill and Johnny. We had all only had a short run so he must have thought that we had coped well. The examiners had been drivers themselves and could soon tell whether a man was confident or proficient enough to handle a large passenger carrying vehicle in everyday service. The booms had been dropped by now so that he could give us a short pep talk and wish us well – he then left 905.

The examiner gave each of us a pink slip stating that we were entitled to have a group H licence. The local licensing authority issued me with a revised licence incorporating group H which commenced on 5th October 1955 (in later years it became group 8). At the time, and for a number of years afterwards, council driving licences had to be renewed yearly and my initial one is illustrated below. Group 8 stated 'trolley vehicle' and there were some drivers at the depot who only had these licences, not driving anything else. My Metropolitan Stage Carriage driver's licence and badge were sent to the depot. I was issued with badge number T9628, another 'dead man's' badge. My MSC licence commenced on 6th October 1955. I had to renew it in October 1958 and October 1961. This allowed me to drive London trolleybuses until 5th October 1964, more than two years after they had come off the road. However, I had a 'trolley vehicle' category on my driving licence for many years after that, as it did not disappear from the statute book for another twenty years or so.

We were pleased with ourselves and Sandy congratulated us. The 'bus had to be driven back to Finchley so 'Stonebridge Bill' took it as far as Craven Park where he got off; Johnny and myself split the rest of the mileage between us. It had been a good result for Sandy with all of us passing at the first attempt and, to cap it all, we covered the whole course without any of us dewiring. A notable achievement. We were each given an 'ABSTRACT OF LAWS' and a booklet titled 'SPECIAL INSTRUCTIONS TO TROLLEYBUS DRIVERS'.

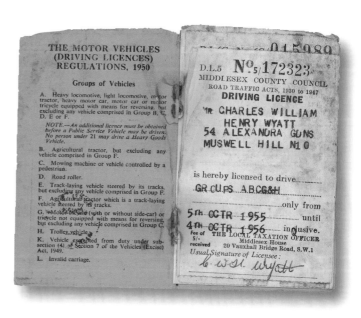

Sandy had done me proud and I wanted to acknowledge his help in a tangible way. Anticipating that I would pass, I had bought forty Players cigarettes and put them in my locker. When we were having a celebratory cup of tea in the canteen, I gave them to him wrapped in a brown paper envelope so they were not on show. When I got home the family was pleased to know that I had achieved my goal and passed at the first attempt. Next day I came down to earth with a bit of a bump as I was back conducting.

London Transport could keep any conductor who had passed out as a driver in his former position for six months – such staff were known as 'composite'. There were many instances of men alternating between driving and conducting on successive days although this was not required of me. I was unable to take up a driving position immediately as the depot needed to balance the number of drivers and conductors available for duty. I did not ask when I would be taking up a permanent driver position and let events take their course. Even if there was driving overtime available, the depot inspectors wouldn't pencil me in for any. I could only do overtime as a conductor as could those driving one day and conducting the next. It seemed silly to me but it was the way things were done. It wasn't till six weeks later that I took up my first driving duty, having been informed a week in advance of the date when I would be changing grade from trolleybus conductor to trolleybus driver. I remember coming home one evening and telling my parents of the date that I would start driving – a late turn too. My dad, who was wiping up the dishes at the time, questioned me as to whether I was going to get a refresher course having not driven a trolleybus for six weeks. I answered "No". He replied "Do you mean to say that you're expected to go out and drive a full trolleybus on a dark night for your first time when you haven't touched one for six weeks?". I said that I was.

I was working with Harry Franks on my final day as a conductor. I recall that last journey for a specific reason. A mother and two children boarded halfway along Woodhouse Road. It was quite common that no more passengers would be picked up after that. Certain that these would be the last tickets I would issue, I related this to the lady. As we passed the Gaumont cinema in Kingsway she offered the tickets to me, saying that it would be best if I retained them for a keepsake. I did for a time but at some stage I lost them.

I was naturally apprehensive about things as I hadn't driven a trolleybus for six weeks and the whole shift would be in the dark. However, everything worked out alright on my first day, and once 'up front' it was just a matter of gaining confidence in my new job. I had to have a few curtailments when I ran late, but I soon became confident and able to keep to schedule. The trolleybus cab was to be my domain for the next six years.

LICENSING
Throughout the land, motorbus drivers and conductors were required by law to hold a Public Service Vehicle licence which was valid for three years at a time – the fee was three shillings. Simultaneously, a numbered badge was issued – the number was in black on a white background. The edge of the badge was red for drivers and green for conductors. A deposit of two shillings and sixpence had to be paid for the badge and this was returned if it was surrendered at the end of a person's service with London Transport.

Outside London, trolleybus drivers and conductors did not need to wear a badge as it was not a legal requirement. Trolleybuses were not classified as public service vehicles and came instead under Light Railway legislation. However, drivers had a 'trolley vehicle' category inserted on their council driving licence. With operators that used both trolleybuses and motorbuses, staff tended to be 'composite', working on both modes of transport. This meant that those working on trolleybuses could be seen with a PSV badge. The situation was uniquely different in London, and all trolleybus drivers and conductors held a Metropolitan Stage Carriage Licence. With it went a badge in the same form as a PSV one; it was grey-blue for drivers, orange for conductors. The badges and licences were issued by the Public Carriage Office at Penton Street near Islington. The fee and deposit was the same as for the PSV licence and badge. Because they were exposed to sunlight, many of the early issue badges faded – they were so well worn that they were virtually unreadable. Some drivers were given a brand new badge which led to some ribbing from other staff. Comments like "Is the paint dry yet" were commonplace – this was because new badges had a shiny surface.

Some drivers who had formerly been tram men had interesting licences. Having passed their trolleybus driving test, their tram driving licence was endorsed 'ALSO LICENSED TO DRIVE TROLLEYBUSES' on the reverse. When the time came for renewal, it was the tram licence that was being renewed (the tram and trolleybus licence used the same T badge). This meant that some of the former Metropolitan Electric Tramways men, who had not driven trams since 1938, were relicensed to drive them for many years after that. In fact those whose licences came up for renewal in early 1952 could drive London trams until 1955 (the last London trams were withdrawn in July 1952!). After that, the anomaly ceased, and thereafter they were licensed for the first time as 'pure' trolleybus drivers.

A letter was sent to drivers and conductors shortly before their MSC licence expired. Three shillings had to be sent to the Public Carriage Office for the new licence, along with a renewal form which the CDI signed. When it was returned from the PCO, it had to be shown to a depot inspector so that London Transport knew a valid licence was held. Although the PCO wrote to many staff for the return of their badges once the trolleybuses had finished, I was not asked to return either of mine.

I kept my conductor's MSC badge in the lapel of my jacket, but when I became a driver I bought a leather holder from 'Marks and Sparks', the Highgate entrepreneur. I cut the exterior of the holder away so that my badge was fully visible. The holder was then placed around an LT griffin badge in the lapel at the top of my jacket.

To sum up, trolleybus drivers developed their own style of driving – this depended on confidence, stature and a willingness to get on with the job.

The J class trolleybuses had opening nearside windscreens, and this has allowed the learner plate to be positioned between the upper and lower part of 905's screen. 905 has just left Tally Ho bus station – this is the vehicle I remember doing most of my learning on. *Michael Dryhurst.*

IN THE DRIVING SEAT

Despite there being a six week gap between the time I passed my test, and taking up service as a driver, I quickly picked up the 'ins and outs' of my new job. Soon I was able to manoeuvre a trolleybus around the streets confidently and with comparative ease. I had become familiar with a trolleybus on the driving course, but there is no better way of learning how to cope with one than through day to day experiences – I soon got the feel of the pedals and the vehicle. Not only did I become accustomed to coping with the length and width of a trolleybus but I soon became familiar with the positions of all the cab equipment – for example, the order of the bank of switches that operated the lights and the wipers. I had been told in training that the safety and comfort of passengers was my prime consideration; time-keeping, though important, was secondary.

I did not refer to the trolleybuses by their class specifications – I had my own terminologies. I called the C3s the 'three hundreds', the Js the 'nine hundreds' and the later vehicles 'fourteen hundreds', 'fifteen hundreds' and 'sixteen hundreds'. However, the 'odd' vehicles (219, 754, 954, 993B and 1587A) I referred to by their fleet numbers. One feature from my conducting days was to my advantage: I immediately knew which trolleybuses needed the front destination blind changed by the driver and those that did not.

No matter which class of trolleybus I drove, all had a wide and spacious cab where there was ample room to manoeuvre. At the end of each journey I could stretch my legs without getting out of the vehicle. The roomiest were the 300s for I could stand in the well of the cab, though I had to bend my head a little when moving about – there was also plenty of space in the 900s. The reason for the luxurious amount of room in the 300s and 900s was that the contactors were chassis-mounted; this also meant that the sound of them notching up was barely audible. In the 1400s, 1500s and 1600s (the classification of these vehicles was either L3, M1, N1 or N2) the contactors were situated in the cab, so I could hear them clicking as the speed picked up. Although less roomy than the older trolleybuses, the newer ones were still much better than the cramped motorbus cab.

There were a few trolleybuses that weren't comfortable to drive, I made a mental note of their numbers – they were slow to pick up speed and were a bit slack. Many were really good and I got to know the numbers of the better and faster ones. In fact, some were very smooth running and could really shift. While I might consider 923 as really good, 924 might be sluggish and, although still safe to drive, wouldn't feel right. I had to accept that I was going to have the ropey ones from time to time.

When I worked with Dennis, Vic and Harry, I often looked through the window that separated the cab from the saloon, to see what they were doing. This enabled me to get an idea of what was needed to drive a trolleybus and put me in good stead for my training course. However, this is L3 1473, a class of vehicle I drove in my later years. From left to right are the battery/trolley throwover switch, the Westinghouse air brake signal, the unit that showed the brake cylinder air gauge*, speedometer and brake reservoir air gauge. Also seen are the steering wheel and the bank of switches that controlled the lights and wipers; this panel also incorporated the horn. The cab seat has seen better days; attached to the steering column is the heater unit. The power and brake pedal, shiny through use, are embossed with the appropriate letters. *Alan Cross.*

*There was a moveable flap over this window – it was for engineers' use but we often had it uncovered.

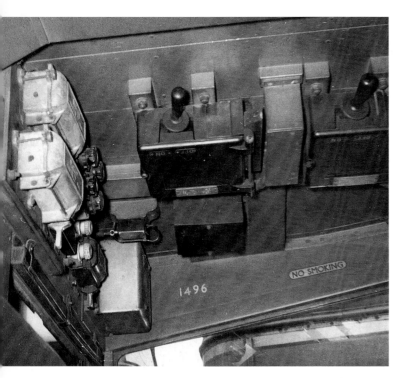

1496 is parked up, withdrawn from service, in Fulwell depot. This view shows the circuit breakers in the OFF position; the triggers for the control switch and motor generator set can be seen next to the fuses. Some trolleybuses had the emergency box fitted adjacent to the position of the cab fleet number while others, like 1496, had them placed lower down in the cab area. *Hugh Taylor.*

CIRCUIT BREAKERS

Two circuit breakers were fitted to the cab of each trolleybus; they were painted black and easily reached. The C class vehicles were originally built to half-cab design so the breakers were positioned in the right-hand side of the cab roof. On the J class trolleybuses and those built later, they were to the left of the driver's head. The function of the breaker knife switches was to prevent current from flowing too rapidly into the traction motor. If it did, one or both of the switches would jump forwards (that is towards the front of the 'bus), at the same time moving from the 'ON' to the 'OFF' position. Simultaneously the power supply to the traction motor was cut off. When the breakers tripped I knew all about it for there would be a loud bang and the 'bus could also jerk violently. Some passengers would be visibly startled by this and even veteran trolleybus drivers could get a bit of a fright when it happened. The breakers were easily re-set, being achieved by pulling the switches back to their original position. Breakers tended to blow if I tried to notch up too quickly. This tended to happen when pulling away from stationary, so it was best not to hurry, just take that extra second or two which in the long run was beneficial. General wear and tear could affect the calibration of the breakers, and it was possible for them to blow quite easily. If that was so I would have to be gentle with it and book the fault up on the defect sheet as

'breakers keep blowing'. The defect sheets were kept in a recess in the cab door.

The breakers were supposed to be placed in the OFF position whenever drivers left the cab – this was something that I did most of the time. Now and again when taking over on Tally Ho stand, I would find that only one or neither of them had been switched out by the previous man. We didn't knock them out when we had driver changes on the road, and I didn't do this when I turned at New Southgate or Windsor Terrace where trolleybooms had to be changed to a dead-end set of wires. I didn't knock them out if I had a dewirement as I'd want to get going as soon as my poles were back on the wires. There was scarcely a time when I took a trolleybus out of the depot when the breakers were not in the OFF position as the shunters did this when they parked the 'buses up. Checking that circuit breakers were in the correct position became routine – it was par for the course to see that they were properly set.

The motors of the C3s tended to object to too much juice being fed into them, so I had to be very careful with these 80 horse-power motored vehicles. Two places where the circuit breakers could blow on them come to mind. I could have my foot right down on the power pedal between North Finchley and Squires Lane when they'd both go. This might also occur in Regents Park Road near Holly Park, when coming down the incline from Finchley Church End. The motor was being overloaded – I was trying to make these lower horse-powered vehicles do too much. If the breakers blew when I was shifting on a C3, I could only get up to two-thirds speed again when I reset the switches, and would only gradually be able to get onto top notch for fear of them going again. An impediment on the 'three hundreds' was that the breakers would sometimes blow just as I was about to shut off power and coast. When this happened, I just re-set the breakers and continued coasting.

I preferred the J class of trolleybus to any others as they didn't have any weak spots. The most favourable thing about them was that their breakers seldom blew when building up on the power notches. This was because they had powerful 95 horse-power traction motors. I knew I could confidently and quickly build up speed on them, and once I had reached third notch I could put my foot down to the floor and all the other notches would pick up without there being much chance of them blowing. On the rare occasion that they blew on a high notch on a 'nine hundred', I pushed the switches back in and got back onto the notch I had previously been on.

The Ls, Ms and Ns were temperamental 'buses. Giving them just a couple of notches of power could be too quick for the breakers and they'd blow. There was also a tendency for the first notch to kick in if I just rested my foot on the power pedal. However, the first three notches came in very quickly without much pressure being placed on the pedal, but I had to be delicate with it so as to give a smooth take-off from stationary. They tended to jerk when working up the notches and to drive them properly was a technique I acquired. On the plus side, these 95hp motored trolleybuses tended not to blow their breakers when on top notch and I soon got used to them, but give me a nine hundred any day.

As a rule, our 300s were on the 645s and 660s. We worked these routes with Colindale and Stonebridge depots who, in the main, had only vehicles with 80 horse-power motors too; by not allocating the 95 hp motored J1s/J2s to these routes, our depot did not have an advantage over theirs. There were occasions when Js were on the 660s, though it was rare to see one on the 645. The 900s were usually allocated to the 'City' routes, though as FY had plenty of C class vehicles, it was common to see them on the 521/621 and 609. Although they were only four foot longer, London trolleybuses looked massive compared to their motorbus counterparts; this view clearly shows their impressive styling and how handsome the trolleybuses fitted with rear wheel spats looked. Finchley's 322 halts at the compulsory bus stop at Edgware on its journey from Canons Park to Barnet on the 645. *London Trolleybus Preservation Society.*

Crew changes 'on the up' in Finchley High Road. Both trolleybuses belonged to Finchley depot for a long time but are now coming to the end of their lives in this late 1950s view (both were withdrawn in November 1959). On this dismal day 934, which is on its way to Moorgate on route 609, has its interior and exterior lights switched on. 317 waits for its conductor to board so that it can proceed to Canons Park on route 645. *Fred Ivey.*

Golders Green turning circle was regularly used by 660s so this view of 1506 waiting there on the 645 is not typical; it has probably taken up late for some reason and the crew are enjoying some layover time. Behind, Enfield garage's RT1195 on route 102 waits for its next trip to CHINGFORD ROYAL FOREST HOTEL. I drove on both of these routes in my time with London Transport. *Fred Ivey.*

BRAKES

There are two pedals for a trolleybus driver to operate. The one on the right is the brake, the one on the left is for power. I never found using the left foot for acceleration a hindrance; it seemed so natural to me even though I was used to driving motor vehicles which had right foot acceleration. The braking efficiency of a trolleybus was very good indeed.

A London trolleybus was fitted with four types of brakes and I soon got used to its rather complex braking system – experience taught me how to correctly handle them. One worked on a regenerative principle, but to me it was totally unsuitable for frontline trolleybus work. Using the power pedal as a brake seemed unsafe, particularly if an emergency arose. Although my instructors told me how to use the regen, they strongly discouraged trainees from using it. They considered it to be a flawed system and that it gave a bad ride. However, it is worth explaining how the regen worked. If the power pedal was drawn back slowly (as it was supposed to be) like letting in the clutch of a car, the regenerative brake was activated. This caused the 'bus to slow down with a jerk and gave passengers a rough ride. The art therefore was to come off the power pedal quickly so that the speed was not checked. This brake would not stop a trolleybus, only slow it down and I was reluctant to operate it. In fact I only used it inadvertently.

When initially depressed, the brake pedal activated the rheostatic electrical brake. This would not only slow the vehicle, but would bring it to a halt if the vehicle was only doing between 1–5 mph. To stop from a higher speed, the rheostatic brake would not be noticed as the air brake was the main form of braking. It should be borne in mind that the weight of the load being carried should always be considered. A handbrake was used for parking.

EVERYTHING COMES WITH EXPERIENCE

Wherever there was general traffic snarl-up, I could only give a trolleybus one or two notches or two of power; then it would be a notch or two of electric brake. This was repeated until the road started to clear. The hot contactors and resistors overheating gave an electrical burning smell in the cab. However, there was no alternative but to keep going slowly. As soon as I had cleared the offending area, and with the rheostatic brake now not being used, the resistors cooled down as they now had a good air flow to them. On my training course I had been told not to drive on the lower notches longer than necessary.

Coasting was an important part of trolleybus driving and by lifting my left foot regularly away from the power pedal, this mode was obtained, When a trolleybus is coasting, the motor continues to rotate but not operate. Very often I would build my speed up to about twenty to twenty-five miles per hour and then let the vehicle coast – it would only slow down gradually, and experience told me when more power was needed. When picking up speed after coasting, it sometimes meant going onto top notch, straight through to the floor of the cab. At other times I picked up the notch that matched the road speed. If, after coasting, full power was reapplied at a slow speed, the motor would be overloaded, the breakers

would blow, and the passengers would be jolted by a sudden deceleration as the 'bus checked itself. The correct throw of the pedal became automatically built into me – it became second nature to use the appropriate notch when applying more power. Driving a trolleybus properly was an art to be perfected and only came with practice. Coasting took up about forty percent of driving time – this is completely different to a motor bus where the accelerator is used virtually all the time it is in motion. There were two circumstances for coasting: (1) under overhead junctions and crossovers where adverse electrical polarity occurred and (2) when enough speed was built up for the vehicle to coast on its own momentum, downhill or on the flat.

To enable readers to understand the concept of coasting, I will describe 'a rounder' on the 609. Jean and I are waiting at the relief point 'on the down' in Ballards Lane: 917 comes up to the stop and we take up our respective positions having had a brief conversation with our counterparts as we change over. I get the bell signal and we're away and for the first half mile, through Finchley shopping centre, it is congested so progress is slow – I can only use the first three or four notches of the power pedal. Passing the Swan and Pyramids public house, better time is made and I am able to use the full range of notches, holding the top one for a short time and then releasing it quickly to avoid the regenerative brake cutting in. The trolleybus then coasts and without an engine or gearbox to slow it, 917 freewheels along. Only fifteen minutes running time is given between Tally Ho and Barnet Church so it's a good job that Jean is quick on the bell as this allows minimum dwell time at each stop. We've probably lost two or three minutes already but as the route along the Great North Road is ideal for making up time, I can stay on top notch past the county boundary and come to a halt at the compulsory stop at Station Road. I approach the Northern Line railway bridge at the foot of Barnet Hill at about 10mph, but with a touch of footbrake slow 917 down to the regulation 5mph speed limit beneath it – this allows the trolley booms to pass safely through the troughing (sometime in the 1950s a tube train came off the track and rested perilously close to the embankment here). Rarely is there anybody to pick up at the stops on Barnet Hill, so again it is full power and I come to a halt at the penultimate stop before the terminus. The trolleybus signal light allows me up to the stand, and as I approach it, the point inspector pulls the frog handle down – there's a 645 already there and we're due out before it. I have to coast through the facing frog to access the loop. Having had two or three minutes stand time, the inspector blows his whistle, Jean gives two rings of the bell and has changed both destination blinds to show MOORGATE – off we go.

I take up first notch and release the handbrake at the same time. 917 moves out from the kerb immediately as I had put the road wheels on full right hand lock on arrival; this practice alleviates the necessity to pull hard on the steering wheel. I also give a hand signal so that other drivers know my intentions – to perform a U turn. Once I've got 917 on the move, I momentarily take my foot off the power pedal as the electrical insulation is against me on the trailing frog. Once past it, I get on to second and third notch as I come out of the

turn – then I shut off power and coast to the first stop which is about fifty yards down from the top of the hill. There are always a number of passengers to pick up here, but once we're away, and with a traffic free road in front of me, I build up to fifth notch and then release the pedal quickly. I then 'ride' the brake pedal with my right foot as the trolleybus coasts down the hill – covering the brake is strongly emphasised in the training school. 917 slows as I approach Barnet bridge again, and I hold pressure on the brake pedal – as I mention elsewhere, this causes the booms to pivot and rise, thereby decreasing the likelihood of a dewirement. On leaving Station Road, I build up power and then coast a bit; then on to top notch up the rise which is known as Prickler's Hill. I then power and coast through Whetstone and on to North Finchley as far as road and passenger traffic allows.

917 is at Barnet terminus; when 609s arrived, there was often a 645 parked up. 645s tended to have more stand time than 609s so the frog needed to be operated in order for them to access the loop. Inspectors were often positioned by the frog where they would pull the handle, thus indicating who would be first away. In my opinion the J class trolleybuses were the best to drive – and I was paid for enjoying myself as well. *John L Smith.*

Trolleybooms dipped to pass beneath Barnet Bridge. 1507 is on its way to Moorgate but its rear destination blind is poorly set as it shows a bit of the 'Barnet' display and a bit of the 'Moorgate' one. It was necessary to use three short traction standards here – one on the lefthand side is fixed into grassland. *Ron Kingdon.*

The 609 and 645 part ways here; the 609 has power priority against it on all the special work at Tally Ho, so I let 917 coast through the three frogs and the crossover. For the next three-quarters of a mile it's a fast stretch of road, ideal for making up a couple of minutes, especially if I don't need to pull up for the request stop half way down. Crossing over the Summers Lane/Granville Road Junction, I come off power and coast downhill to the Squires Lane stop, just before the North Circular Road. There are a lot of passengers aboard now and Jean needs all the help she can get collecting the fares, so I assist by driving slowly for the time being. I now start to climb a short hill – up Finchley High Road as far as Oak Lane; then there's a short flat stretch to St Pancras and Islington cemetery gates, following which there's a steep climb up to Church Lane with power all the way – then it's power and coast until I reach East Finchley. If I wish, I can pass under the trailing frog here on power, as trolleybuses coming out of the station loop have to coast through. Passing beneath the railway bridge I start to climb up to Highgate station – after that it's all downhill so I coast down to Archway Junction; power priority is in my favour here where I join the 611. I'm now in Holloway Road and am soon confronted by the Pemberton Gardens junction – again the special work insulation is in my favour but as it's on a downward gradient I just let 917 glide through.

Apart from a single manoeuvre at Ilford Broadway, where eight items of special work were traversed, six was the highest number of pieces of equipment that had to be negotiated when moving across any junction in London; one place where this occurred was at the Nags Head, on the 609 going to Moorgate. It is a complex overhead layout with a lot of special work aloft; drivers on all routes had to know where they can take power and where they can't. I'm there now so I have to carry out a juggling act with my left foot and remember that it is power on the first junction, with the order then being 'dead', 'power', 'dead', 'dead' and 'power'. So far, no frog handles have had to be pulled. From now on though, there's a lot of running about for Jean as seven handles have to be pulled on each 609 'rounder' (if the frogs have to be operated for the loops at Barnet and Moorgate it's nine). I stop outside Selby's store where the first frog is encountered; Jean climbs the three-tier pavement and pulls the semi-automatic frog handle down – this only takes a few seconds. I have power in my favour so any driver going down the Cally has to coast here. It's a level road now so it's a mixture of power and coast as I keep 917 moving as best I can to cope with traffic and serve bus stops. Passing slowly under Holloway Road station bridge, I come to Highbury and Islington station where I coast through the facing frog – no need to pull here as that's the 611's conductor's job. I power through the crossover and move into Upper Street. I keep 917 moving until we get to Islington Green where I coast through all but one of the five special work items.

It's always busy approaching the Angel and the traffic's a bit slow. Jean jumps off to operate the semi-automatic frog which is near the trolleybus sub-station in the High Street; her actions divert my trolleys onto the running wires that turn left into City Road (the 581 and 679 'have the road'

here). I have power in my favour through this facing frog, and also the trailing frog that brings 615s and 639s into City Road. We've picked up a lot of passengers at the Angel, but Jean stays on the platform, not bothering to collect any fares as she needs to operate a 'pull and hold down' frog around the corner in City Road (at its junction with Goswell Road). We've got to be quick here, so Jean quickly jumps off and runs for the frog handle; having completed this task she chases after 917 and jumps on board. I'm only going slowly and coast through the pointwork (609 conductors had to pull two frog handles within about two hundred yards here). It's now power and coast as far as St Mark's hospital, then it's power over the canal bridge and coast under the Windsor Terrace crossover at slow speed.

As we're nearing the end of the journey now, people are alighting, not boarding. Reaching East Road junction, I coast under the crossover but power through the trailing frog which has brought the 611/641/683 into view. I'm now at Old Street where there is a two-way crossover. Although not universal throughout the system, it was usual practice at this arrangement of crossovers for drivers to have power on the first one and to coast over the second; these crossovers tended to be at traffic lights and helped us get away from a standing start (this was case at all four crossings here). If the lights are not against me I would just come off the power pedal and let 917 drift through on its own momentum. For those at ground level there was a distinct clattering from above as the trolley heads quickly passed through these crossovers. It's then a mix of power and coast along the City Road, slowing right down as I turn left into Finsbury Square; this is a sharp left turn so it is over-arm steering. Then it's a right turn around the square where I stop on the far side for passengers to alight. There are a lot of trolleybuses here already and as they go to the boarding point, we all move ourselves up. Not worth getting out of the cab to stretch my legs, as I'd soon need to get back in again to move the 'bus up Eventually I get to the stand, having applied two notches of power to drift round the bottom corner of the square. While we're waiting, a couple of 'buses on other routes pass us on the overtaking wire (drivers doing this have a dead section on the facing and trailing frogs) – inspectors had beckoned them round. Jean puts up BARNET on the blinds and sits on the front nearside seat and chats to me through the open cab/saloon window.

Opposite The parting of the ways at Angel Islington sees Finchley's 932 on route 609 turn left into City Road while Edmonton's 1230 heads down St John Street on its way to Smithfield on route 679. The lack of traffic indicates that this picture was taken on a Sunday; this would have meant that trolleybus drivers turning right from City Road into the High Street would be able to make the manoeuvre easily. At busy times and with a slight uphill incline, it needed a good deal of skill not to get stuck on a 'dead' piece of overhead here. *Don Thompson.*

More often than not, trolleybuses banked up on the eastern side of Finsbury Square; the alighting point was outside Finsbury Square House where four vehicles are parked. 1439 is on the 615, with the driver yet to change the destination blind for his next trip. *Don Lewis.*

A route I came across at Moorgate was the 683; over the years, its times of operation were reduced and it was withdrawn before the trolleybus conversion programme started. The driver is showing STAMFORD HILL AMHURST PARK, so 1202 is running into Stamford Hill depot. *Michael Dryhurst.*

It's imperative to leave Moorgate bang on time and Jean raps the bell cord for me to move; we're finished for the day when we get back to Tally Ho, so there's to be no hanging around. If it's the lunch time rush there'll be plenty of people wanting a 609, and by the time we're at Old Street there are a fair number on board. It's power and coast through the crossovers here, and when I arrive at East Road, Jean gets off to pull the semi-auto frog handle down (she's certainly getting plenty of exercise today!). Frog handles were often conveniently positioned at compulsory stops (as was the case here) and this was a good operating practice – electrical priority enables me to pass through with my foot on the power pedal. By the time we leave Moorfield's Eye Hospital, 917 is almost full, and this time I can't assist Jean by keeping the speed down as that would delay us; she'll have to move fast to collect all the fares. Few people need to board or alight as I move up City Road and, having passed under the Windsor Terrace trailing frog on power, I am able to get 917 up to a good speed until we get to the Angel. 615/639 conductors have to pull the frog handle at the top of City Road.

Six items of overhead equipment need to be negotiated at the Angel. This is a difficult manoeuvre to make as an uphill right turn is required; to successfully do this day in, day out required a great deal of skill. I have to remember that the sequence is 'power' on the first two special work items, then a 'dead', followed by 'power', 'power', 'power' which takes me into Islington High Street. If I found myself 'stuck on the dead' here I would call through to my conductor to see me safely back a few yards. This was achieved by just rolling back, or using reverse battery mode (this was something I had picked up working with Vic Collins). However, if I was forced to stop just before a dead section, I would give the bus a quick flick on the power notches in the hope that that would get me through. It was essential that the correct driving angle was taken as I worked through junctions and I have to consider the whole road and overhead layout including the positioning of any traffic islands – precision played a factor as I had to make sure that the rear wheels did not mount them.

A lot of people board and alight at Liverpool Road as people have been purchasing their wares at Chapel Street market. When we get to the 'pull and hold down' frog at Agricultural Hall (another three tier pavement job, and where the 581 and 677 bear right into Essex Road), Jean alights and does the necessary. I have power priority at the three frogs here, and take them at a steady speed. Then it's power and coast through Upper Street until I get to the 611 trailing frog at Highbury Corner which I pass through on power. I then continue along Holloway Road, moving as traffic conditions allow – however, it's definitely a slow speed under Holloway Station Road bridge again. I'm coming up to the Nags Head now, but before that the routes from Caledonian Road connect with the 609 at the bottom of Camden Road – I coast through the crossover but am able to power through the trailing frog. Jean operates the semi-automatic frog handle just before the bus stop – this enables me to proceed straight across the junction. I take power on all of the special work here apart from the crossover used by routes 627/629/653 which are making

for Manor House. Throughout this trip I've been following trolleybuses and others have been trailing me; when I know there's a couple in front I let them go as otherwise I'll be drawing their power and slow the whole show down. A likely place for this to occur is between Nags Head and Archway – 517s/611s/617s, or trolleybuses running into Highgate depot. I'd call through to Jean and say, "I'll hang on for a minute at the next stop and let them get away". I continue towards North Finchley and before long approach Pemberton Gardens junction again. I'm climbing now and power priority is in my favour throughout – therefore I can pass through without having to lift my foot off the power pedal.

At Archway Junction, I have power through the facing frog and crossover, and I keep my foot flat down as we climb the incline and pass under Suicide Bridge (Archway Bridge). I slow through the troughing at East Finchley station and with power in my favour on the special work, my speed is not impeded. I keep going and use power and coasting mode appropriately. As I approach North Finchley, I pass under the final section breaker of this 'rounder' – throughout the run I have been taking my foot off the power pedal as I go through each one. I now turn from Finchley High Road into Kingsway and pull up on the offside of this one-way street – I'm now alongside the Gaumont Cinema. Good; a light duty pointsman is there and he operates the 'pull and hold down' frog handle to divert my trolley booms onto the running wires to Barnet; when he wasn't there conductors had to do it and then run after the 'bus. Going back to my earlier reference, this was the second place where I pulled a handle with my right hand – this was due to the standard to which it was attached being on the offside of the trolleybus. Although I am turning right into Ballards Lane, I first have to drift over left to be beneath the Barnet-bound running wires. Having done this, I slow at the facing frog that enables 660 trolleybuses to enter the bus station. The 609 has had power priority on all the special work here so far, but now it is in favour of trolleybuses entering the bus station. There's just another sixty yards to the relief point where the next crew are waiting for us.

I first encountered the 609 trolleybus route on 7th March 1938, its second day of operation. I was with the route on its last day, which was 7th November 1961. The 609 was the only route that for the whole of its journey served the old Great North Road, even though long sections of it were given other names. These were Barnet Hill, High Road Whetstone, High Road North Finchley, High Road East Finchley, Archway Road, Holloway Road, Upper Street and City Road (eventually it reached the Bank and London Bridge). 'Great North Road' name plates can still be seen today on two stretches: from the junction of Archway Road/Aylmer Road to East Finchley station and from the county boundary through to Barnet and beyond. As an aside, New North Road, which trolleybus route 611 used, was part of the revised way north. A chance photograph captures me powering 314 through Archway junction. 1367, on route 611, has followed me from Highbury Corner; now we're on separate wires its driver can get a move on to his terminus at Highgate Village. 314 is fitted with experimental ventilator scoops below the centre band. *Fred Ivey.*

CAB EQUIPMENT

In the cab of each trolleybus (just above the front wind-screen, to the right) there was an orange neon light in the 'Trolley Dewirement Indicator'. It played an important part in trolleybus driving and showed that power was available. The light could be extinguished for a number of reasons. The 'juice' going off, or a dewirement were two possibilities, but it also went out if the poles were being swung from one set of wires to another, or if booms were being lowered. As my eyes were always fixed on the road ahead I wasn't constantly looking at the neon light. However, I often glanced at it and usually kept my eye on it at crossovers, junctions and section insulators where the neon light would momentarily blink. I never had a trolleybus where the neon light wasn't working – it was one of the items that was inspected when a 'bus received one of its regular checkovers. Most provincial operators used dewirement buzzers and the omission of them on London trolleybuses was strange since an audible signal is invaluable as it allows the driver to keep his eye on the road at all times.

A heater was fixed to the front of the steering column. It was turned on and off by a switch in the bulkhead to the left of the driver; an element within the unit provided the warmth. The heater only just took the chill off the air and I thought it was wrongly positioned and could never get my legs and feet warm on cold winter days – they were like blocks of ice. The outer casing of the heater unit got very hot and if touched, could burn my bare hands. I often put my hands near it to warm up, even if I was wearing leather gloves. To combat the cold, I sometimes wore a scarf. On the other side of the coin, if a trolleybus had been parked out of service on Tally Ho stand for quite a while on a hot day, the steering wheel got very hot and had to be handled lightly until it cooled down. On the same theme, I had to squint when the sun was shining directly in my face, as sun visors were not fitted to trolleybuses.

Behind the driver's seat was a leather blind. During the hours of darkness it was supposed to be unbuttoned so that it dropped down and covered the window behind the driver. This prevented the saloon lights shining onto the windscreen, and gave better vision ahead. A square was cut into the blind so that drivers were able to look into the saloon. The blind was supposed to be fastened in the 'up' position in daylight. If it wasn't, an official might instruct it to be lifted. A few drivers had the attitude that it didn't matter whether it was up or down, and having it down enabled them to have a cigarette. Getting told off for not returning a blind to its rightful position was nothing and was just one of the minor indiscretions which were part of everyday trolleybus life. We were supposed to furl the blind up neatly when arriving at the depot at night. I usually did this a couple of stops before I got there. Some drivers didn't do this and many times I had to furl it up in the morning. In the winter time there was a tendency for the blinds to be left in the 'down' position when they arrived at the depot, as it would still be dark when the 'bus went out first thing in the morning. There was also a leather blind at the back of the cab on the nearside, but it was nearly always in the 'up' position.

The emergency box, in the driver's cab, held a number of items. One of these was a saw, so that if anybody got trapped beneath a 'bus, it could be used to cut the lifeguard rails at either side of it. There was a pair of thick rubber gloves so that fallen traction wires could be moved to a safe position – maybe to the gutter and away from the public who would be warned to keep clear. A feeder pillar key was provided along with spare fuses. On one occasion, the lights on a trolleybus I was driving went out – a fuse had blown. Following instructions given on the training course, I took a fuse out of the box, undid a big porcelain screw and inserted a new fuse into a compartment in the bulkhead behind me – it did the trick. Tightening up the porcelain screw, I booked the fact on the defect sheet that I had used a spare fuse – this would ensure that another one would be placed in the emergency box later on. Two spanners were supposed to be in the box; these were for attending to trolley heads – I never saw them on any of our 'buses. Attached to the inside of the cab door was a fire extinguisher. I have only one recollection of one being used. Driver Chris Golder saw a car on fire at East Finchley one day, and quick-thinkingly got out of the cab and used it to quell the flames.

The motor generator set controlled the electrics, boosted the battery and made the lights work. When the MG set was operating, the saloon and destination blind lights came on and enabled the backstamp on the blinds to be easily seen. This led to some drivers leaving the MG on permanently. The MG set could become noisy but I got used to it – in fact I would use the phrase 'I'd hear it but I wouldn't hear it'. At night, if the trolleybooms were down and all the interior lights on (say on Tally Ho stand), the MG set could not charge the batteries – in fact they were being drained of power. The MG set was always on at night-time and when there was poor light. When re-poling, and in the knowledge that the MG was on, there was not a stirring of activity when the first boom was placed on the overhead, but as soon as the second one was hoisted onto the running wires everything perked up. I could tell if a vehicle's batteries weren't up to much by the MG set; the interior lights would be noticeably dimmer. This could be rectified by switching the lights out if circumstances dictated.

WINDOWS AND MIRRORS

On hot days I was able to make trolleybus driving very pleasant by opening the top part of the windscreens about an inch or two (on the C class 'buses, only the offside screen opened). By doing this, very good ventilation was obtained. The top section was opened by unscrewing two round screws either side of it and then pushing the glass forward. The windscreen frames had ridges in them and the windscreen catch was placed in the ridge required. Drivers had to be alert with open screens, for there were occasions when they forgot that they were open and broke against another 'bus or a large vehicle in front. Trolleybuses were so sound that there were rarely any water leaks in the cabs or saloons. However, over the years the jolting that the 'buses had received caused the top and bottom screens to become misaligned and not close properly. To stop draughts some drivers put newspaper between the two screens. Cab ventilators were fitted but were not very good; in fact they sometimes created draughts in the winter. Another place where draughts occurred was through the gaps where the pedals and handbrake came through the cab floor.

Motorbuses had two driving mirrors. Trolleybuses had three, for in addition to those on either side of the cab (which I considered were much too small) another was fitted in the driving cab. This gave drivers a view into the lower saloon enabling them to see the platform. However, if there were standing passengers, it lost its effectiveness. This mirror was otherwise an excellent safety feature, especially if the trolleybus was rung off by the conductor using the upstairs buzzer. When this occurred, I would glance into the cab mirror, and the nearside one, to see that everything was clear. With drivers being of different stature, there was a lot of adjustment of mirrors to suit each man.

The windscreen wiper could have been better. It was usually too slow but I just had to live with it. Wipers packed up very occasionally – all I could do then was to peer through the screen and drive slowly and get the 'bus changed over as soon as possible. It only became a problem when it snowed, as the wiper just cleared a small patch of it away from the screen. At these times initiative had to be used. I would take hold of the timecard, get out of the cab and clear both screens with it. It would do for a time, but as the screen kept clogging up, I would repeatedly have to scrape it off as I did not want the snow to obliterate my view. Sometimes my conductor would do this, as it saved me continually getting out of my cab (when I was a conductor I did this for my drivers). It was not possible for the destination and route number apertures to be cleared of snow but some crews used a finger to write the route number on the front panel. Some even cleared snow away from the registration number.

Two high numbered vehicles were allocated to Finchley depot in the mid-1950s, these were 1655 and 1656. The bus station is full, preventing 1656 from entering – it therefore has no alternative but to wait in Ballards Lane. Trolleybus driving in the summer could be made very comfortable by opening both front windscreens. *LTPS.*

TRACTION BATTERIES

The trolleybuses I drove were fitted with traction batteries which enabled them to move without the aid of overhead wires. A good set would propel a vehicle for a few hundred yards at about 2-3mph. Rule 64 stated that the efficiency of the battery should be tested before leaving the depot – I often complied with this edict. If they were low and only gave minimal movement I would ask an engineer to find another 'bus, for I never knew when the battery might be needed. Batteries were normally only used in the depot, or at times when drivers got marooned on a 'dead' section of overhead.

An item of equipment that was known as a reverser key was kept on each trolleybus. Its main function was to obtain forward and reverse positions. It was pushed towards the front of the vehicle for straight ahead and pushed backwards for reverse. The key was also used to switch from trolley to battery mode – again this could be forward or reverse. In electrical terms, trams had 'series' and 'parallel' positions for building up speed. Oddly, London Transport used this terminology for their trolleybuses; series was battery position while parallel was for trolley operation.

On the Cs, Js and 954, the reverser key was in a casing on the left-hand side of the driver. To obtain battery mode the key was put in its neutral upright position, taken out of its casing and inserted in a changeover switch which was to the drivers left. It was in a vertical column on the C class vehicles and adjacent to the driver's seat; on the J class 'buses it was also to the left but on a horizontal stand to the rear of the nearside of the cab. A turn of the hand and the switch moved from 'TROLLEY' to 'BATTERY'. The reverser key was then taken out of the stand and put back in the 'neutral' position: forward or reverse was then selected. To move in battery mode, it was necessary to depress the battery button which was situated on the cab floor. This was done with the left foot (I used the heel of my shoe). Having completed the battery work, drivers would then go through the same procedure but in reverse before they could get back to trolley mode. It was a bit of a performance using the battery when a driver got trapped on a 'dead' piece of overhead. The lesson was 'don't stop on the dead'.

Different arrangements applied with reverser keys on the L3s. Forward and reverse were obtained by using a lever that was inserted into what resembled a gear hand-change gate of an old type of motorcycle. The lever was low down to the driver's left. There was a neutral middle position; for forward mode the lever was pushed into the lower gate position – for reverse it was brought back into the higher gate. To obtain battery operation, the reverser key, which was like an open-ended spanner, was taken out of its normal position in a spindle fixing near the floor, and placed in a change-over unit that was situated at the front of the cab. Again a turn of the hand changed the mode from trolley to battery. The key was then put back into its 'neutral' position, after which forward or reverse was selected. Then the battery button was used. To go back to trolley operation the same procedure was gone through but in reverse. An interlock on all trolleybuses prevented any two actions being carried out together. When the reverser key was in neutral position, the power pedal was

locked. Between February 1960 and April 1961, only 954 had, what was to me, a normal reverser key. With the allocation of some of Highgate's trolleybuses in the 1539–1669 range in April 1961, this type of key became familiar again.

Rule 79 stated that if the battery had been used, then once back on the wires the MG set should be turned on so that it would be recharged. It also stated that after use, the matter should be noted on the vehicle's defect sheet. Both of these items were carried out only if the batteries had been used for a considerable distance. When the batteries were being used the circuit breakers, control switch (the reverser key) and MG set (if it had been on) were to be placed in the 'off' position. I don't think any of us did this as no 'juice' could be obtained while we were using the batteries.

In all the time I worked on trolleys I never had one where the batteries were absolutely flat, precluding any movement. Although there were instances of passengers getting out of a trolleybus that had flat batteries and pushing them onto a live section of overhead, I never experienced this.

RESPONSIBLE DRIVING

There were various items that drivers and conductors were supposed to check before taking a trolleybus out of the depot (the only time it was done was when there was a work to rule). Many of these items were given scant regard – the trolley poles would obviously be on the wires and the trolley dewirement indicator would be aglow. Sometimes I would have a quick look over a vehicle. One of the things I'd look for was to see that the lights were working; I often checked the emergency box to make sure that all the equipment was there. What I always did (whether in the depot or taking over on the road) was to ensure that I had a comfortable driving position for my height, reach and closeness to the steering column. This was important, so I wouldn't just get into the cab and go. I would wind the driving seat up quite high and adjust it accordingly; occasionally I would have to lower it, and maybe move it backwards or forwards. This ensured that I was in full control of the vehicle. I then knocked out one of the circuit breakers (this prevented any power being taken) and pressed the power pedal right down to its fullest extent so I was able to obtain the full range of the pedal without overstretching my left leg.

Whenever I took over a trolleybus, I wanted to know that the braking system was in full working order. I did this by pressing the brake pedal down a few times to make sure that the compressor was in A1 condition. There was no knowing when the compressor would cut in – sometimes it would start when a 'bus was moving, at other times when stationary. The cutting in and out of the compressor was very noticeable, and the pumping of air into the system was one of the sounds that was part of everyday trolleybus life. Continual pumping of the brake pedal expelled air out of the reservoir. If used frequently, the Westinghouse red metal air brake warning flag (immediately in view at the front of the cab) would gradually rise. It stopped with a thud against the end of the black-painted unit – the metal flag had the word STOP vertically cut out of it. When the flag rose, l would stop and wait for the compressor to replenish the tank. The flag slowly dropped as the air pressure built up. The working range of the air system was between 65 and 85 lbs per square inch, and if everything was okay, the needle on the air gauge indicated that. The compressor cut out between 85 and 95 lbs. If the pressure fell below 50 lb per square inch or exceeded 120 lb (when the release valve was sticking) the vehicle was to be parked at the nearest convenient place, taken out of service and the matter reported to the depot or a road official. Similarly, if the flag regularly lifted, this was a serious problem and the vehicle would be taken out of service. I would glance at the air gauge needle from time to time as I had been encouraged to do this on the driving course.

When taking over 'on the road', I had to trust that the previous driver was happy with the brakes. A few words were often exchanged so the driver being relieved might say: "This 'bus has heavy steering" or "It's got fierce brakes" (they'd have just been re-lined). Alternatively he might say "It goes really well" or "Got light steering this one".

Bearing in mind that trolleybuses were not fitted with winking traffic indicators, the importance of giving hand signals, clearly, correctly and in good time cannot be overestimated. It was another factor that was emphasised on the driving course. When I was slowing down or stopping I would extend my right arm outwards and with the palm of my hand turned, move my arm slowly up and down. This gave a clear indication of my intentions to following vehicles. If I considered it safe to be overtaken, I would extend my right arm and move it backwards and forwards, indicating that it was safe for following vehicles to pass me. When I was pulling out from a stop I would indicate with my right hand that this was so and would allow one, maybe two vehicles to go in front of me by waving them on. This I considered to be a fair balance between authoritative and considerate driving. When I was about to turn right I held my right arm in a rigid horizontal position. This was not always easy as it meant that only my left arm was free for the steering wheel. I was supposed to rotate my right arm in an anti-clockwise position when I was turning left – this was seldom done. There was one terminus that was difficult to leave – Barnet Church. I usually had the front wheels on right-hand lock so that as soon as I was ready to depart I had my right hand free to give the appropriate hand signal. This indicated that I was turning across any traffic that had reached the top of the hill. The only other instances of staff using hand signals is when they were complying with rule 22. This stated that drivers, and any conductors who were on the platform, should signal with waves of their left hand that their vehicle was full.

Most police constables knew which trolleybus routes went right, left or straight on at road junctions they controlled. There was a 'copper' at Kings Cross where vehicles turned right from Pentonville Road into Caledonian Road. If he wanted me to pass behind him he'd wave his arm down by his side, then behind his back. A brand new policeman might be at a loss and I would try and help him out by pointing out the direction I wanted to go. To make them more conspicuous, police on point duty at busy locations wore white armlets.

I wanted to give passengers a comfortable ride and this was achieved in a number of ways. On the training course I had been told of the importance of the use of the handbrake. Therefore I *always* used it at bus stops, traffic lights and in heavy traffic. Holding the handbrake tension hard on, I would press the power pedal lightly to obtain first notch; once I felt it take I would release the handbrake trigger. This buffered the jerk and prevented the trolleybus from jumping forward. I didn't consider this to be irksome. To have acted otherwise would have meant that the trolleybus would start with a jolt. After a few yards I would obtain second and then third notch. After a slight pause, I would press the power pedal more firmly and fourth and fifth notch would be obtained without any jerking. When road conditions allowed, I was able to get up to top notch. Trolleybuses had good and smooth acceleration and just glided away.

It was important that passengers' comfort was maintained when slowing down. I would gradually reduce the speed so that the trolleybus gently slowed and at the last second, ease off the foot brake – this gave a very smooth stop. Feathering the brake all day gave conductors and passengers a good ride; I would not hold a trolleybus on the foot-brake alone.

BELL SIGNALS
One bell to stop, two to start, three for full up, with a rapid succession of bells meaning stop immediately. These were the time honoured communication signals between conductor and driver. A few crews had their own starting arrangements, and conductors would tap a coin a couple of times against the window behind the driver – this indicated that it was okay to move off. Conductors were supposed to ring the 'bus off from the platform but some, when upstairs at the front, would stamp their feet to signal to the driver to move off. Alternatively they would tap their blind changing key or ticket rack against the blind box housing. I didn't participate in this, but did ring my driver off from the buzzer at the top of the stairs as approved by rule 24. I could see the platform from the staircase mirror even though I didn't have a full view of all intending passengers – it was a point of using commonsense for if I went back to the platform at every stop then the 'bus would be delayed. While travelling as a passenger I would hear or observe certain conductors stamping their feet from upstairs as a signal to their drivers. To all intents and purposes that just said 'I'm upstairs'. With crews that did work this way, drivers would look carefully in their cab and nearside mirrors to make sure there was nobody boarding or alighting. If a conductor rang me off in this manner, I wouldn't move until I got the bell or buzzer and they soon got the message. I would have a quiet word and say, "I only move off when I get the proper signal". None of them took umbrage at this as it was the correct way of working. No doubt, some said to their colleagues, "When you're working with Charlie Wyatt, he only works to the bell". There was a tendency amongst trolleybus staff that if there were no passengers waiting at a compulsory stop, the conductor would give a double ring of the bell or shout out "No-one here, keep going". I'm not saying that I came to a halt at every 'white' stop, but would slow up and if my conductor gave the bell to continue when we were trying to pick up a bit of lost time, then I would carry on.

Coming to Finchley depot in February 1957 was 993B which was a trolleybus that had been rebodied by East Lancashire Coachbuilders; it is seen just below Wood Green depot on route 621. HOLBORN CIRCUS is not fully shown – this was because Highgate (its former owner) had masked the front and rear destination blind boxes to accommodate reduced depth blind displays. Our staff have not removed the masking. *Alan Cross.*

EVERY ONE AN AEC

London Transport operated three types of trolleybus – AEC, BUT (British United Traction) and Leyland. The BUTs were confined to Fulwell, Hanwell and Isleworth depots with the AECs and Leylands being spread around the fleet. For engineering purposes most depots only operated one type for any length of time; this was a good working practice as it meant that AEC depots only kept spares for AECs and Leyland depots only kept parts for Leylands. This system meant that at most depots, drivers kept to one make of trolleybus. Those driving Leylands believed that they had a better braking system than the AECs, while those with AECs thought that Leylands had fiercer brakes. By segregating the two as far as possible, confusion was avoided. Finchley was never stocked with Leylands, though there were occasions when a Wood Green one was used to replace a failed Finchley AEC – this enabled the crew to return to Tally Ho. During my time at Finchley there was never a Leyland trolleybus at the depot, so every one was an AEC.

When I arrived at Finchley, the allocation was made up of some C3s, an experimental trolleybus (number 754), all the J1s and some J2s. Between 1954 and 1956, N2s 1655 and 1656 were on the books and C2 219 was there for a while in 1958. Prototype 954 arrived from Highgate in 1957, the same time that 993B also came from HT. 993B had been rebodied by East Lancashire Coachbuilders after its original one had been destroyed during the war – it stayed until November 1959 when it returned from whence it came. 1587A had been rebodied by Weymanns in the war, and came to us in November 1958. Constructed heavily in wood, there was a wooden sound when the cab door was closed – it was withdrawn in November 1959. Many chassisless L3s arrived in 1959/60, replacing the Cs and Js. In April 1961 some unit-constructed M1s, a solitary N1 (1575) and some N2s were transferred in from Highgate depot. Apart from 754, all our trolleybuses were to the standard seventy-seat configuration; thirty seats downstairs, forty upstairs.

When a trolleybus came back from overhaul there was a smell of new paint, and everything was clean and sparkling. However, looks are sometimes deceptive and there was a stiffness about them – the steering wheel was noticeably heavy. With the tightened up feel, I had to put more pressure on the power pedal until the trolleybus had loosened itself up – this would only be for a few days though.

Motorbuses leak fluids, particularly oil. Problems arose at bus stands where continual drips caused a build-up of oils and fuel. To combat this, London Transport staff regularly put down sand at these locations. This was not a problem on trolleybuses and *I never* saw sand on a trolleybus stand.

Following the 1958 bus strike there was, in January 1959,

Although most of the Weymann rebodied trolleybuses were in a poor state by the mid-1950s, a few managed to hang on until 1959. Outlasting all the others was 1587A which spent its last year at Finchley depot. Here it turns from Finchley High Road into Woodhouse Road while working on route 521 to Holborn Circus; the driver has made a poor job of changing his destination blind. In the background 907 heads for Canons Park on the 645 and another trolleybus is about to leave the bus station. *Fred Ivey.*

a general reduction in service levels. This included trolleybuses, and four of our Js were transferred to other depots. 1449, 1452 and 1489 moved in from Poplar in part replacement – they just turned up one day as did 1473 in September. Bill Bennett or Fred Chapman showed us how to use the reverser key, battery/trolley change-over switch and main operating lever on these L3s. The training was no more than equipment familiarisation. It was only when our native trolleybuses were replaced wholesale by L3s from Poplar and West Ham in November 1959 and February 1960 that we got used to them (the TGWU had informed us beforehand of the impending change of class of trolleybus).

The front lower deck saloon window of a standard trolleybus had an opening section. This could be lowered and enabled drivers and conductors to converse at quiet times. Some crews kept it open all the time but it could distract drivers from watching the road and prevent them from giving their full attention to the overhead. At busy times and when it was raining, it was better to keep this window closed as this prevented the windscreen from misting up through condensation created by passengers' breath. If the windscreen did mist up, I would wipe it with my hand. An advantage of having this window closed meant that any warmth in the cab was retained and if for any reason the conductor and driver didn't get on then the window would remain closed anyway.

754 is on Tally Ho stand waiting the time for its next trip. This view clearly shows the closed up front door which was sealed early in its career; despite this, an EXIT ONLY sign continued to be shown. Finchley drivers considered 754 to be the fastest trolleybus in the depot. *London Trolleybus Preservation Society.*

London Transport had a few experimental trolleybuses and I worked on one of them. This was number 754, which was their first trolleybus of chassisless design. It was constructed 'in house' at Charlton Works and was unique in being the only one built with a front exit. 754 was used as an experiment in passenger flow, spending its working life at Finchley depot. It was built to half-cab design with a double seat facing inwards looking towards the driver – it retained these features until withdrawal. The fact that passengers looked directly at drivers did not affect our men who did not make any adverse comments about the half-width cab. At termini, conductors would sit on the seat that faced the driver and speak directly to them as its glass partition only reached half-way across the cab. Although the front exit was used when it was new, it was permanently locked in my days at FY

although I do not recall how this was done. When I, as a conductor, first came into contact with 754, it had blue moquette and paintwork upstairs and ordinary décor downstairs. When it came back from overhaul in January 1953, it had been upholstered throughout in standard trolleybus moquette with appropriate paintwork. Classified X4, it was two and a half inches lower than a normal height trolleybus and had seats for only sixty-eight – it had thirty-eight seats upstairs instead of forty. It weighed in at several hundred-weight less than a standard vehicle, with its lighter weight being the main reason for it being a fast 'bus, the fastest in the depot in fact. It was very popular with crews as it kept on catching up others in front! To counteract this, 754's drivers would sometimes leave a terminus a bit late.

One Sunday morning when I was a conductor and in the

754 on its way to Moorgate on route 609 is seen at the Nags Head junction; the driver has placed his cap in the area open to passengers at the front nearside of the vehicle. Behind is 989 which may have followed 754 much of the way from North Finchley. *Bus of Yesteryear.*

canteen with driver Les Strutt, he said that he would be driving 754 that afternoon. Les was a keen trolleybusman and considered it to be the best trolleybus in the depot – very fast and smooth running. Trolleybus speedometers only recorded as high as 35mph, so for a long time Les had wondered what speed he could get it up to! While we were nattering, it transpired that I would be finishing work shortly before he took over 754. Between us we came up with the idea of a speed trial! The two participants were to be my Star Twin BSA motorcycle, which I used to get to and from work, and trolleybus 754. When the time came, we positioned the vehicles accordingly with Les in front and me behind. He was on route 609 and heading south on just about our fastest section of track, this being between Tally Ho and Squires Lane just before the North Circular Road. No passengers

were picked up after he left North Finchley so he was able to go hell for leather; I clocked him doing 45mph. This was soon relayed back to the chaps at the depot and there were comments like, "You were lucky you didn't get nicked". If the police had been around they couldn't have done him for speeding because trolleybuses were not classed as motor vehicles. One of the 653 drivers at Highgate was timed at almost 50mph by the police somewhere on the stretch between Nags Head and Tottenham Court Road. When they caught up with him they said that they were going to 'do' him. The driver nonchalantly said, "You can't touch me, I'm Light Railway" – and he was right (tram drivers though, could get done for speeding under tramway legislation). 754 was withdrawn in March 1955 and lay gathering dust in the depot for just over a year before it went for scrap.

Wanting to explore the chassisless concept further, London Transport ordered a prototype trolleybus to this design. Numbered 954 it was delivered in 1938 and was classified L2. As I have already stated it came to FY in 1957 – to me though it was just one of the 900s. It had its lower cream band stretched right round the front of it because the windscreen was placed higher than usual. Less obvious were the cab ventilators which were placed in the central cream band above the windscreen. 'Nine-five-four' was so recognisable and distinguishable from any other trolleybus, I immediately knew when it was approaching. When we lost our C and J class vehicles in the winter of 1959/60 it was retained, as chassisless trolleybuses were not being withdrawn at the time. I was always pleased to have 954 during this period as it was similar to drive as my favourites, the Js. Between stages nine and ten of the trolleybus conversion programme, 954 was the oldest trolleybus in the fleet and it stayed with us until 25th April 1961 when it 'bit the dust'.

Vic Collins's trolleybus knowledge was vast and one day he pointed out 1379 to me. This was an experimental trolleybus which was allocated to Highgate depot. It was known to their staff as the 'Tunnel bus' and was to have been a forerunner of a batch of trolleybuses that were to run through the Kingsway tram subway, but which did not materialise. 1379 had a straight back end and looked really odd. It was predominantly used on the 627s and 653s, but I have seen it on the 517s/617s at Tally Ho and on the 615s/639s at Moorgate. It could have been used on the 513s/613s, and even on the 611s as it was fitted with coasting and run-back brakes. Vic also pointed out number 62, another Highgate 'bus. This was the 1934 prototype for the fleet – I didn't see much of it as it was withdrawn in 1952. Between Manor House and Nags Head, 62, 754, 954 and 1379 could be regularly seen and there may have been times when all four were together on this section. Another vehicle I saw was Hanwell's 1671 on the 607 in Acton Vale, and at Hammersmith on the 655. It had a four-wheel front drive which made it look peculiar. Finchley staff could have passed experimental trolleybuses 61 and 63 (from Isleworth depot) at Seven Stars junction and West Ham's 1670 in the City, meaning that they would have seen all of London Transport's experimental trolleybuses. Only Finchley crews were able to do this.

L2 954 belonged to Highgate depot for a long time and also crosses Nags Head junction; it is working on route 627, and is followed by Edmonton's 1074. Over the road, another Edmonton trolleybus heads for Ponders End – the destination blind display indicates that it belongs to EM rather than Highgate or Wood Green which also operated on route 627. On the day that this picture was taken it has been raining – the combination of wet cobblestones and tram lines made conditions very slippery. *Bus of Yesteryear.*

Above left X5 class 1379 was a very distinctive trolleybus due to it being constructed for operation through the Kingsway subway. It was usually seen on routes 627 and 653, but on 13th December 1952 it has been allocated to the 615. It stands in Finsbury Square, Moorgate, with two other trolleybuses in front. *Lyndon Rowe.*

Above right A trolleybus I came across now and again was 1671 – it is seen at Hammersmith working on route 655. It was a four-wheel front drive vehicle and, as can be seen, the driver's foot step is between the two front offside wheels. 1671 has a Lancastrian registration number. *John Gillham.*

Below The prototype trolleybus for the fleet, and on Highgate's strength for many years, was number 62. Most London trolleybuses had matching fleet and registration numbers but, as can be seen, this did not apply to 62 . It is seen outside the Holloway Arcade in Parkhurst Road (near the Nags Head) while working on route 653. *Clarence Carter.*

With Finchley having such a wide operating area our staff rubbed shoulders with a wider spectrum of vehicles than at any other depot. Q1s were passed in Acton Vale on route 607, at Hammersmith where we looped round with them on the 667, and at Seven Stars Junction where we crossed them on route 657. Vic also told me that trolleybuses (J3s and L1s) on the 611 had a special braking system, a coasting brake for going down Highgate Hill and a run-back brake when ascending it. Other types I came across were the short-wheelbase trolleybuses (B2s and B3s) working on the Hampstead routes. They were noticeably shorter in length than ours and were all withdrawn by 1952. Our staff could even have seen the occasional 'Diddler' (the original 1931 trolleybuses) at Hammersmith terminus. This brings to mind that some of these antiquated vehicles were dumped in Finchley depot for some of 1951/52 before they were towed away for scrap.

During the course of a day, it was possible to see trolley-buses going to as far flung places as Barking Broadway and Hampton Court. I would cross the 567 route at Old Street when I was on a 609 on my own duty and if I did some over-time on route 660 I ran alongside the 667 at Hammersmith. Due to our wide operating area we came into contact with more trolleybus services than any other depot. They were: 513, 517, 543, 555, 565, 567, 581, 607, 611, 613, 615, 617, 625, 626, 627, 628, 629, 639, 641, 643, 649A, 653, 655, 657, 659, 662, 664, 665, 666, 667, 677, 679 and 683; we also came into visual contact with routes 623 and 630. This meant that I saw forty different trolleybus route numbers during my service with London Transport: the other five were my own routes (521, 609, 621, 645 and 660). Some of the older staff could claim forty-one routes as they had worked on the 651. In the same vein, we came into contact with more depots' routes than any other, for we rubbed shoulders with those from Clapton, Colindale, Edmonton, Fulwell, Hammersmith, Hanwell, Highgate, Isleworth, Lea Bridge, Poplar, Stamford Hill, Stonebridge, Walthamstow, West Ham and Wood Green.

Left Eight foot wide Q1s were the standard fare on route 657 for most of the time that I worked on the 660. However, for the last few months that I saw the 657, they had some of Wood Green's cast-offs; trolleybuses I had been rubbing shoulders with in north London now crossed my path in west London. In the last phase of Q1 operation, 1807 passes through Seven Stars junction on its way to Isleworth depot; it seems that dewirements occur here regularly as a bamboo pole hangs from a traction standard. *Sid Hagarty.*

Below Although this picture was taken before I started with London Transport, it illustrates the short-type trolleybuses I came across. These were classified B2 of which 131 was the penultimate member; these vehicles seated only sixty and were sufficient for the trade offered on the Hampstead routes. 131 on route 639 is waiting to pick up passengers on the south side of Finsbury Square; 1359 on route 611 is tucked in right behind. *Alan Cross.*

Bottom For my first few months of service there were a few delapidated trolleybuses parked in Finchley depot; these were some of the original vehicles used by London United Tramways – they passed to London Transport in 1933. All had been withdrawn from service by 1948 but a few were retained as training vehicles; when this reprieve was over they were driven to FY and left there until the scrapman collected them in 1952. Here, three 'Diddlers' can be seen: an unidentifiable one, 54 and 48 – all still have their Fulwell blinds in place. *Alan Cross.*

Above An unusual allocation to Colindale depot was 1543B – as 1543, its body had been badly damaged in the war and although allocated to Highgate depot in the post-war years, it spent a couple of months at Colindale in 1956. Bearing in mind that CE operated low numbered vehicles, it would have been better to have supplied them with another C class trolleybus, but its allocation was one of the idiosyncrasies that occurred. It must have been very strange, at the time, for Colindale staff to have operated such a high numbered vehicle, and led to their drivers having to change the front destination blind for the first time. 1543B passes the bottom of Tally Ho bus station while the temporary arrangements for terminating vehicles are in force. *Len Anderson.*

Left I saw route 581 at three places – Rosebery Avenue, Theobalds Road and Islington, where 1352 passes through the Angel junction on its way to Bloomsbury. In the other direction a 677 travels towards West India Docks. Many cars of the era can be seen. *London Trolleybus Preservation Society.*

I mention in the text the far flung corners of the trolleybus network to which I saw trolleybuses operating and the large number of depots that I came into contact with; Old Street was where I met many other trolleybus services. 1253 is working on route 555; this vehicle now resides in the London Transport Museum at Covent Garden. Other routes I saw here were the 565/567/665 group which, in essence, were one service. One of Poplar's L3s is on the 567 heading for, what was to me, faraway Barking; many of PR's trolleybuses came to FY in due course, so I may have driven this one. *Denis Battams.*

I came across route 625 at Wood Green where Walthamstow's 383 turns from Lordship Lane into the High Road; its next trip will be to Woodford. The mid-1950s service cuts saw the withdrawal of many of the lower numbered vehicles; many of the victims came from Colindale and Stonebridge. To replace them, some were drafted in from other depots with 383 going to Colindale. In the background is an RF on route 233. *Don Thompson.*

Craven Park circle was the northern terminus of route 628; it was also used as a short working point for other routes as shown by a 660 behind. 192 has only one boom on the wire; presumably its crew have 'dipped their sticks' to allow 446 to start its journey to Clapham Junction. As on all standard trolleybuses, a fog lamp is fitted to 446; these were used when fog descended and in trolleybus days this occurred often. *Tony Wright.*

1325 is at Acton Market Place on peak hour route 626; it is 18th July 1960, the penultimate day of operation for both the vehicle and the route. The driver has saved himself a turn of the blind handle and shows DEPOT HAMMERSMITH rather than HAMMERSMITH DEPOT which is the next full display up – he is a good judge of destination blind backstamps. A man hitches up his trousers at the zebra crossing. *Jack Gready.*

TOMMY, JEAN, SID, GLADYS AND BRIDIE

I had five regular conductors during my time driving at Finchley, and only parted when circumstances dictated. They were all 'salt of the earth' types and I considered that we pulled our weight, used our own 'know-how' when necessary and apart from the odd hiccup, enabled our passengers to get to and from their destinations when they wanted to. In fact I would say that my three regular drivers and five usual conductors were all close colleagues.

I was initially paired with Tommy Walker; we were only together for five months because he 'went driving' (conductor upgraded to driver). On Christmas Eve 1955 he invited me to have a meal at his house and to see the Christmas presents he had bought for his children. He introduced me to his wife Ruby who later became a conductress at the depot. He only worked for London Transport for a few years as he left the job to join the GPO. My next conductor was a woman, though I now need to back-track almost a year. About four months before I took up driving duties, I was conducting a 609 at North Finchley when an old friend, Jean Blackwell, boarded. She had lived near me in Muswell Hill, and was one of the crowd I had hung around with in Alexandra Palace grounds about ten years previously. Having taken her fare and given her a ticket, she told me that she had married and was now Jean Westbrook and living in North Finchley. She worked for Simms Motor Units, the same company that Rose worked for. It was good to see her again, and having related to each other what we had been doing since the Alexandra Palace days, she left the trolleybus.

At some stage Jean decided to change her job and become a bus conductress. Of all places, where was she assigned? Finchley trolleybus depot. I was very surprised, therefore, to pass her in the depot one day. She was initially on the spare list (and worked with me a few times) but was then given a service with me from the end of March 1956. This was at neither her or my request – it was pure coincidence (incidentally her sister Cathy was a trolleybus conductress at Stamford Hill depot). Having known Jean in my youth, I knew her better than my other conductors. She was pleasant to work with, always smiling, polite to passengers and would never complain about the number of people being carried. With me this was often a full load, as I didn't participate in the practice of a driver 'nursing' his conductress – giving her an easy time by close-poling other 'buses. Jean had names for two of our trolleybuses. If we took over 927 she would say "We've got the snow bus today" – this was the vehicle we had when it was snowing heavily one day. She dubbed 963 the 'flood bus' as this was the trolleybus we were on in Harringay when it got immobilised by floodwater. Jean and I were a regular crew until September 1958, when she left to start a family.

My next conductor was Sid Game whose brother Ernie was a driver on the 645/660s. Sid's main talking points were his garden and allotment. I worked with him for fifteen months after which he transferred onto the 645s/660s. Next was Gladys who was new to the job, so to a degree I taught her the ropes. She had been demobbed from the Auxiliary Territorial Service and lived at Highgate with her flatmate who had one of the new mini-vans when they first came out. She would pick Gladys up from the depot on late turns and they would often give me a lift home – her mate delighted in giving a rough ride and many times threw Gladys and me together in the back of the van! Gladys only stayed for nine months. My last conductress at Finchley was Bridie Morrin, a very nice Irish lady from Co. Donegal. She had a younger sister at the depot, it being a common feature on London Transport for there to be family connections. I only parted from her because I transferred to Muswell Hill garage in early 1962. In the 1980s, Finchley and Muswell Hill jointly worked route 43 and I would sometimes see her at London Bridge.

Trolleybuses are renowned for their hill climbing capabilities and 313 on route 645 effortlessly ascends Barnet Hill in this fading evening sunshine view during the summer of 1955. The three RT type motorbuses, the first of which is a 'top box' RT on route 84 to St Albans, are being left behind. A traction standard on the right points towards High Barnet station while on the left a number of hoardings add colour. *Ray DeGroote.*

READING TWO ROADS

Motorbus driving and trolleybus driving in London were two completely different experiences. Although the practicalities of driving a large passenger carrying vehicle were much the same when it came to width and length, it was there that the similarities ended. The greatest distinction between the two forms of transport was that the motorbus driver only had the carriageway to deal with while the trolleybusman had two roads to read, one below and one above. The road above was the overhead wiring, which had to be treated properly.

There was only one downside to driving trolleybuses. We were unable to overtake others, but just accepted the fact that the overhead line, with this restriction, was part of the set-up. If it really was necessary to overtake another trolleybus to get on schedule or to get in the right order in the service, I would flash my headlights at the driver of the one in front. I'd hope that he'd see my lights in his offside driving mirror, understand my signal, slow down and 'dip his sticks'. Alternatively I would open my front windscreen and call to the conductor that I wanted their poles dropped. Another way of doing this was to signal the conductor and mime that I wanted this done.

With trolleybus routes criss-crossing each other throughout London, drivers at each depot needed to know how to negotiate each overhead junction, the features of each having to be memorised. It was particularly important that they knew if power priority was in their favour or not at these places, as there was no hard and fast rule about which overhead road had the priority. There had to be good co-ordination between brain and foot. Drivers also had to be aware of the position of the section insulators (most were made of wood but some were of a Bakelite type material). They were also known as 'breakers' or 'feeders'. All this meant that it was imperative that drivers took their job seriously, and experience enabled them to do this. For new men it could be a fraught time, but they would soon grasp what was required and become proficient at their work. There was no difference between reading the overhead road at night or day, as drivers became familiar with the routes on which they worked.

From time to time there were aberrations in the form of trolley arms losing contact with the traction wires, and unfamiliarity with overhead layouts could lead to problems. I recollect the Nags Head junction lighting up like Blackpool illuminations on several occasions when drivers took power in the wrong places. Another time a driver at Tally Ho took power on three pieces of special work where he shouldn't have done – the overhead illuminated the place like nobody's business due to the heavy arcing and flashing. Even more spectacular was another man doing the same thing at Cricklewood Broadway where the overhead lit up the darkness as if it were daytime. A wooden running bar was burning up like a child's large sparkler and bits of burnt wood were falling down onto the roadway bouncing and fizzing about all over the place. Now and again a driver would adopt a couldn't care less attitude and would take power over a junction; but in the main, drivers drove professionally.

A Colindale trolleybus enters the depot at dusk on the final day it is open – 2nd January 1962. The driver should have taken his foot off the power pedal as he enters, but he's not bothered today. This photograph shows how brightly the overhead could light up when misused. *Roy Makewell.*

Roadworks are in progress in Whetstone and part of the carriageway is inaccessible. Having just passed a section insulator, 1513 uses the middle of the road. To allow easy movement for southbound vehicles, the bus stop flag by Woodside Grove has been covered and is temporarily out of use. The ends of 1513's booms are painted white, a practice adopted by a number of depots. *Don Thompson.*

FEEDERS

It was a statutory requirement that the overhead line was split into electrical sections no longer than 880 yards, and so feeder pillars were positioned at approximately half-mile intervals. At some locations, there was a large box that fed both the 'up' and 'down' roads. At other places there was a small box on both sides of the road, each feeding one set of wires. Heavy cables led from the cabinets to adjacent traction standards, running almost to the top of them where they ran out to section insulators on the positive and negative wires. It was impossible to tell, just by looking, what the function of each section insulator was. They could be acting as feeders, or as merely a bridge to link adjacent sections according to how the switches were set in the adjacent feeder pillar. There were also many instances of feeders, and their associated pillars, positioned between the legal half-mile interval. In fact of the twelve sections between Cricklewood and Canons Park, all but two were fed mid-section. If there was a problem in one section then the overhead staff would come along, open up the section box with a special key and switch the affected section out. This allowed juice to be fed in from an adjacent section. Overhead line voltage was nominally six hundred volts.

The positioning of feeders was indicated by a white band around traction standards on both sides of the road. I soon got to know by heart where the feeders were. It was necessary not to draw power when passing beneath one so I had to momentarily come off the power pedal wherever they were situated. Experience enabled me to be almost inch perfect in this regard. However, if I was coasting on the approach to one, I just glided through. Once past a breaker I could pick up the same notch and speed as before. Failing to observe the rule of not taking power at section insulators caused a big electric flash. Driving like this damaged the runner bar and made an uneven surface which led to dewirements occurring. It was a personal discipline that I did not stop on or just before an overhead feeder. Due to the proximity of feeders, two bus stops on the 609 were unsuitably positioned, so I took steps to avoid arcing. One of them was on the level, at Drayton Park bus stop in Holloway Road, so I always pulled up a couple of feet past it so as to clear the insulator. The other one was at the top of City Road just south of the Angel on the way to Moorgate. Here, the stop was sited on a downward incline so I obviated any problems by drifting past it. As I did so I looked at the neon light in the dewirement indicator and as soon as I saw it blink off and then on, I knew I had passed the feeder. If, for some reason, I misjudged things or a vehicle stopped me from positioning myself where I wanted to here, I would release the handbrake and let the 'bus pass under the feeder as I moved downhill on gravity.

There were stretches of road where there were inclines and hills. If a trolleybus was fully loaded, there would be the temptation for drivers to keep their left foot on the power pedal when passing beneath the section insulators. This was not necessary as it only required a momentary lift-off of the power pedal. It was only the few 'couldn't care less' staff who would power through an insulator when moving uphill.

With routes operating to frequent headways, trolleybuses

There were two places on route 609 where I had to drift past a feeder where a bus stop was also positioned; one was at the first southbound stop in City Road, just after the Angel. 1468's driver is also aware of the necessity to do this for if he had not done so, there would have been arcing from the overhead when he applied power. It looks as if there hasn't been a motorbus or a trolleybus along for some time as a lot of people are boarding 1468. *Clarence Carter.*

could easily bunch in the evening peaks. The section between Archway and North Finchley used by routes 517/617 and 609 was typical of this and is a good one to illustrate. The upward inclines and the convoys of trolleybuses all trying to share the power available on any half-mile section on this stretch caused 'low juice' to be experienced. It was noticeable to all drivers in the procession but particularly so to the man in the leading 'bus. If I was driving the first of a group of trolleybuses, I would only be able to travel at about a third of the speed required despite having the power pedal pressed down as far as it would go. The 'bus wouldn't do any more than about 10mph. The interior lights would dim slightly, though it wouldn't stop passengers from reading their newspapers. Once into the next section I would feel the vehicle pick up speed. When I felt this surge I knew I had to make as much use of the full power I was now receiving so that I could pull away from those behind. All of this could be repeated section after section with the worst place being after leaving Squires Lane bus stop where the incline was more pronounced. Therefore, I was always anxious to see the white band on the traction standard which denoted the next injection of power into the overhead which was approximately halfway between Squires Lane and Granville Road, two stops before North Finchley. Once the 517s/617s had ceased at the end of January 1961 things became easier, as only the 609s were left. Scenarios like this were less noticeable on a level road.

KEEPING THEM ON THE WIRES

For Finchley drivers there were a number of locations that were prone to dewirements, the most notorious being the long sweeping left-hand bend by Woodhouse School in Woodhouse Road, Finchley, when travelling south on the 521/621. Keeping directly beneath the overhead was the correct way to drive here. Equally effective was to position the trolleybus as near to the crown of the road as possible with the offside wheels hugging the centre of the roadway. This meant that the 'bus was slightly outside of the curve in the overhead wires, allowing the booms to cling strongly to the running wires. The wrong approach was to 'cut the curve' whereby the nearside wheels were close to the kerb. This had the effect of making the booms travel a greater distance along the wires than the 'bus was travelling along the roadway, causing them to race and whip around faster than necessary. This increased the likelihood of the booms leaving the overhead. It was unwise to travel at speed here but most of us have gone round this bend quicker than we should have done, and on occasions lost our poles. A number of dewirements here were dramatic with poles going all over the place; some trolleybuses ended up with bent booms and scuffed insulating tape. If a driver came a cropper here, then the crew of the next northbound 'bus would probably be asked to relay the information to the Tally Ho inspector, saying something like, "FY8 has bent poles by Woodhouse School and needs assistance". Another place that could be a bit tricky was at the slight curve in Friern Barnet Road when approaching the Town Hall bus stop on the way to North Finchley. I have known a trolleybus come round the bend here far too fast, with the dewirement causing feet of insulating tape to be pulled off a boom. Under the tape, at the end of the boom, there was a leather sheath with eyelets through which a gaiter was laced to secure it – the worst dewirements could even cause the sheath to tear.

Driving a trolleybus around a right-hand bend was no more of a problem than going around a left-hand one, as long as drivers kept as close to the nearside kerb as possible. There were not many sharp right-hand bends on the City routes but there was one at the curve just south of the canal bridge in Caledonian Road on the way to Holborn. Here, I would slow the 'bus down and hug the nearside kerb. The trolley arms would now be on the outside of the vehicle and in the correct position under the overhead.

Once I had a few month's trolleybus driving behind me, I got to know which curves in the overhead I had to treat with particular caution and where I should keep my eye on the speed. I would not normally build up on the power notches until I had left a curve but there were locations where the overhead allowed me to go round them without slowing down. One of these places was in Bounds Green Road (in both directions on routes 521/621) between the North Circular Road and Warwick Road; another was southbound at Lyonsdown Road on route 609. Driving like this saved a few seconds – handy if I was finishing my duty. A location where I couldn't be complacent was on the bends below New Southgate going towards Holborn – commonsense and experience told me to take them slowly. Going the other way was never a problem as I was climbing and my speed was naturally impeded.

There were some places where the overhead allowed me to drive at a fast speed. If I didn't have to stop at Summers Lane I would say that the section from Tally Ho to Squires Lane on the 609 was the fastest. In fact when Highgate garage started working RMs on the 17s (and later on the 609s on Sundays) we had no trouble keeping up with them despite the expectation that they would move faster than us. Other fast stretches on my routes were (i) Lyonsdown Road to Station Road New Barnet both ways, (ii) the Woodman public house to the Wellington public house in Archway Road northbound, (iii) from Manor House to Finsbury Park southbound, and (iv) City Road southbound towards Moorgate, but being careful when crossing over the Canal Bridge. There were some places on the 645/660 where a good speed could be obtained: (i) between Dollis Hill Lane and Staples Corner northbound, (ii) coming down the hill at Temple Fortune towards the North Circular Road northbound, and (iii) from East End Road in Regents Park Road down to Henlys Corner southbound.

When it was necessary to use the other side of the road in order to pass a broken down vehicle or roadworks, I never had any problems if the manoeuvre was taken cautiously as I knew the limit to which the booms could stretch. However, a dewirement could be caused if this was done too quickly. In my conducting days, a lot of congestion occurred when the tram lines were being removed in Holloway Road and Upper Street Islington. Trolleybuses had to use the wrong side of the road at various places while the workforce moved along taking the lines up. The booms became outstretched but by travelling slowly, they moved safely along the wires.

Watching from the pavement it looked as if the booms were making to-ing and fro-ing movements; this was not so and was an optical illusion. Trolley arms were a little bit unpredictable; we could go round the same curve at the same speed, and nine hundred and ninety-nine times out of a thousand, the poles wouldn't come off. Then they would jump off on the last occasion for no reason. There were a few occasions when Dennis, Vic and Harry had a dewirement. It was normally me who replaced the poles on the basis that I was nearer the bamboo than they were.

Bamboo Trolley Poles   454

The attention of trolleybus staff is drawn to the danger of injury to pedestrians and staff, when passing behind a trolleybus, due to the bamboo trolley pole projecting beyond the end of its container.

Staff are reminded of the importance of ensuring that, the pole when pushed fully home, is held by the retaining clip in the container and that, where fitted, the spring cover is closed.

Staff are also requested to exercise care in the use of these poles as damage is frequently caused by insufficient care in handling and by allowing them to fall to the ground.

When the tram lines were being pulled up during the big changeover to trolleybuses in the 1930s, spare staff would be instructed to go to a certain location where, with bamboo poles, they would swing trolley arms from one set of wires to those in the opposite direction. This was possible as a trolleybus motor had a magnetic field which was created by windings taking current from the overhead supply. This meant that, when trolleybooms were moved from one set of wires to those going in the other direction, not only did the armature current reverse, but the magnetic field reversed too, allowing the motor to operate normally. The notion that using the overhead in this way would cause a trolleybus to operate in reverse was a misconception. Using overhead in the opposite direction to the way that we were going enabled major obstructions to be by-passed.

One of the places that Finchley drivers had the greatest respect for was Barnet bridge where the Northern Line crossed Barnet Hill. Going to Barnet we could drive under it at a reasonable speed, say 10mph. Negotiating the bridge southbound was a different matter for dewirements were likely to occur there if the bus's speed was not reduced sufficiently when coming to the bottom of Barnet Hill – I dealt with this by braking slightly so that the speed was checked just before I got there. I would be down to maybe 5mph so that the 'bus coasted through the troughing under the bridge. The slight braking gave stronger contact between the booms and the gradually lowering wires; I approached many of the easier junctions in the same way. The delicate braking slowed and lifted the booms to give a pivoting action on the roof.

Knowing that I wanted to go driving, Vic Collins gave me tips about the job and quoted which bridges could be driven under faster than others – the one at Noel Park, just south of Wood Green was one where the speed could be more than the regulation 5mph. He also told me that those at North Acton and in Cricklewood Lane had to be approached very cautiously due to the dips in the road beneath them. Vic also told me where I should and shouldn't take power on particular pieces of overhead. His advice was freely given and gratefully received.

DEWIREMENTS

When a dewirement occurred I knew all about it. There was a thudding noise from above and a singing and swishing from the overhead. The vibration of flailing trolleybooms could be felt in the cab and the neon light in the dewirement indicator was extinguished. The first thing I did, having 'lost them', was to get out of the cab and look up, hoping that no damage to the overhead or trolley gear had occurred. Usually nothing was amiss. When dewirements occurred at junctions, there was a tendency for booms to scrape under the frogs and crossovers. I have seen the aftermath of dewired booms hitting traction standards and breaking street lights – glass on the roadway and a trolleybus parked up nearby waiting for a breakdown wagon to turn up. The braking system was not affected by a dewirement as it was independent of the power supply. There was always sufficient air in the air tank to stop a trolleybus when this occurred.

A dewirement could be caused by another trolleybus having its poles off and causing the overhead to shake. On two occasions at Manor House, three trolleybuses including my own were dewired by a 627, 653, 659 or 679 heading northbound crossing through the main junction too fast. Another time, when I was at the northbound stop at the main loading point in Wood Green, a London-bound 629 or 641 came through the Lordship Lane/High Road junction too fast. Both its trolley arms dewired, flew up into the air and the booms bounced about all over the place, causing the whole overhead junction to shake and vibrate violently. This caused my poles to come off together with those of two other Wood Green trolleybuses going the other way. I got out of my cab and noticed, surprisingly, that there was no damage to the culprit's poles or the overhead. We all put our poles back on the wires and got on our way as if nothing had happened. The miscreant was rather fortunate in getting away with it. It was inconceivable for a trolleybus driver to think of going through a junction at such a speed so I assume that his attention was elsewhere. I can understand this, for although I gave the job my full attention, I have driven from Barnet to Moorgate virtually in automatic. I'd get to Finsbury Square at Moorgate and think to myself, "Can't remember going through Archway". At the Nags Head I sometimes had to think about whether I was going to North Finchley via Wood Green or Archway – I never took the wrong road here, though. However, on one occasion I over-ran the northbound 609 frog at the Nags Head; it was set for 'buses turning right towards Finsbury Park – having realised my error I stopped and changed the booms onto the right set of wires. This is an example of the job never being monotonous on trolleybuses.

One day I was stationary at Whitehall Park bus stop on Archway Road travelling northbound when a 617, manned by a brother and sister crew from Highgate depot, passed me at full belt. His booms were knocked off when they collided with mine which stayed on. How he didn't see me I don't know, so I presume that he thought that my vehicle was a motorbus.

Drivers damaging booms or overhead was a favourite topic to talk about in the depot or canteen. One day the message was relayed that following a dewirement in Whetstone, a driver had put his poles up on the set of wires going the other way. He had continued for quite a distance until he realised his mistake and averted a mishap. In the same vein, I have seen a driver mistakenly put the negative trolley on a parallel span wire and the positive one on the negative running wire. He then got in the cab and wondered why the trolleybus wouldn't go. When he got out again and looked at the situation he soon realised his error and corrected it.

Speaking for all of us, it wasn't so bad if booms were bent following a dewirement as it only involved one 'bus (though it might mean a dressing down from the CDI) but it was serious if there was damage to the running wires as this could affect many trolleybus services. All dewirements were supposed to be reported on a special form. Drivers didn't like filling these in and if they could get away without reporting one, they would. If there was no damage, why fill one in? If an official saw a dewirement and no harm was done, he probably raised his eyebrows or made no comment – they didn't insist that a report was made.

Dewirements could occur without apparent reason; my first experience of one as a driver was on Boxing Day 1955. I had just pulled away from the northbound stop at Turnpike Lane Station and was passing across the junction of Wood Green High Road with Turnpike Lane when I suddenly didn't feel anything on the power pedal. My conductor, Tommy Walker, looked out of the back of the 'bus and said, "One of the poles has come off". He got our bamboo pole out and put the boom back on the wire. To this day I have never understood why it happened. In like manner, I had just pulled away from the northbound stop under the bridge at East Finchley Station one evening and my nearside boom came off – again for no apparent reason. The trolley head became wedged between the girders and the wall of the bridge and a number of pigeons flew out from a crevice. I couldn't get the boom down, so my conductor nabbed a bamboo from another 'bus and we literally had to lever it out with two bamboos. We did this successfully without any damage to the boom but the pigeons weren't very happy as we had disturbed their perches!

There were other times when my poles came off for no reason, the most notable occurring one day at dusk when I was on my way to Moorgate. Both booms came off the wires as I approached the section insulator just before Windsor Terrace in City Road. This was unexpected as I was moving at normal speed. Although there was no damage to my booms, the dewirement caused the positive running wire to snap – some of it was hanging down. I got my bamboo pole out and put the poles under their retaining hooks while my conductor transferred our passengers onto the next vehicle that came along. As services had to be maintained on routes 609/615/639, it was necessary for me to stay on the scene and guide other trolleybuses through. I flagged each one down as it approached and informed its driver that I'd be lowering their offside boom as they neared the break in the wire. Each driver either passed through on battery or gave his vehicle a couple of notches of power and coasted past. When they opted for the latter, I held each boom in mid-air while the 'bus traversed the offending section. I put it back on the wire as soon as it had passed the section insulator. I asked the driver of the first trolleybus I dealt with to inform an official at Moorgate about the situation so that the required assistance could be drummed up. Keeping the bamboo pole in the gutter between each 'bus, I must have dealt with about a dozen vehicles. Help soon arrived in the form of a tower wagon. For it to have arrived so quickly meant that it must have come from Islington sub-station where one was often judiciously parked. It took a while for its staff to insert a splicing ear (this joined the broken sections of wire). Now the 'up' track was completely impeded and I had to lower both booms of vehicles that came down the City Road – they passed by on battery. Once the repair had been made, I carried on to Moorgate but had to make out a dewirement report on return to the depot. For years afterwards I would see the splice and think to myself that I was the reason for it being there.

On another occasion the positive running wire had come away from one of the hangers at Ducketts Common, near Turnpike Lane. A 641 was parked up nearby with its poles

Top In Edgware High Street, the positive overhead wire has come adrift because of a dewirement. Once a tower wagon arrives, its crew will put the wire back into the twin-line hanger; 645s will then be able to pass freely again. *Hugh Taylor.*

Centre and above A piece of overhead is missing at Edgware: the first driver on the scene has taken his trolleybus out of service and assists others to get by. 1664's positive boom is being held away from the gap while it is batteried past the obstruction. An overhead linesman called to the scene observes the situation. *Hugh Taylor.*

down. I don't know whether the driver of this 'bus had dewired and caused the damage, or whether its crew were first on the scene. It was a training course instruction that staff who were the first to come across an overhead problem would park up, report the incident and assist other trolleybuses to get by. As each one came along, its driver would give it a few notches of power to get him across the fault while, at the same time, the 641 conductor dipped its right-hand boom. Although the overhead line staff regularly checked the overhead, fittings worked themselves loose, with globe insulators in crossovers being a favourite to come adrift.

One morning, on the down track on route 609, I went around the bend at Lyonsdown Road (the Hertfordshire/Middlesex county boundary) no faster than on other occasions but both booms careered off the running wires with one of them bending in the process. It hadn't hit a traction standard, as they did from time to time, but had come up against the well-tensioned overhead. It was only with a bit of brute force that I was able to get it under its retaining hook. Although I had a trolleybus telephone key in my pocket, there was no section box nearby, so I asked the following crew to report the matter to the inspector at Barnet. A while later a breakdown crew came out, repaired the booms and got me going again. I filled in a dewirement form back at the depot and a few days later had to see the CDI. He didn't make an issue of it as we agreed that the cause was due to slack tension on the booms.

An appendix in the rulebook said that if, after a dewirement, there was any apparent damage to the overhead equipment, it should be reported to an official. A few drivers, in the hope of getting away with it and to avoid filling in a dewirement report, would take a chance and not report damage if there was no inspector or other crew in the vicinity. If they were later questioned about any incident they would say something like, "Everything was fine when I went through" and the finger could not be pointed at them. There was a kickback to this for although there may not have been any obvious damage, a trolley head might have been knocked out of true with the result that an innocent member of staff would later find himself regularly dewiring despite driving properly.

A prime example of 'clearing off' occurred one night to the driver of the last but one 521/621 who wanted to get back to the depot early so that he could get a ride home. He came tearing through Friern Barnet at a speed far in excess of what the curve in the wires would allow, with the result that both trolley arms came off the wires near the Town Hall. At the speed he was doing both the positive and negative traction wires came out of their spacer bars. The running wires were not broken but were hanging lower than they should have. Amazingly, the booms were not damaged and there was little scuffing to the insulating tape, no more than could be normally seen. Quick-thinkingly he put his poles back up and continued on his way. At the depot he parked up, with the thought that nobody would be any the wiser, but curiosity and the need to shift the blame from himself got the better of him and he waited in the shadows for the last 'bus to come in from Wood Green. When it did, he asked its driver if he

had 'had his sticks off' in Friern Barnet, which of course he had. Both men went into the output and told the depot inspector that they were victims of an unreported dewirement, and the culprit avoided a visit to the CDI.

One driver who was very unfortunate was Noel Byrne from Stonebridge depot. He was one of the last men to pass out as a driver there (September 1961) and pulled some of the overhead down when he was leaving the depot on his very first trip by himself. Sometimes damage was exaggerated and when it was reported in the canteen that somebody had 'pulled the lot down' at Manor House it was a far cry from what actually happened. There was a lot of overhead strung aloft there and one single 'bus couldn't have brought everything down to the ground. Although I didn't see what happened, it was probably no more than damage to a crossover, and a couple of broken spacer bars at Manor House.

Continuing the 'other depot' theme, Highgate only had a residual fleet of trolleybuses between February and April 1961. These were used weekdays on route 627 and Sundays on the 609. With most of the crews now working on motorbuses, it could be difficult to persuade staff to work a 'trolley job' but if for some reason a member of staff reported late for work they might be offered a trolleybus duty or none at all. Not wanting to lose a day's pay they would take the trolleybus out, but it could prove more trouble than it was worth, as exemplified one Saturday morning when a conductor and driver, both of whom were to all intents and purposes motorbus staff, were paired up on a 627 duty. All went well until they reached Manor House where some routes, including the 627, continued along Seven Sisters Road towards Tottenham, while others turned left up Green Lanes heading for Wood Green. The Highgate driver must have forgotten that he was on a trolleybus until it was too late and hit the frog in Seven Sisters Road at a colossal speed. Both booms came off the wires and buckled so much that they could not be put back on the overhead. They were in such a state that they could not even be placed under the retaining hooks so the conductor put one under the other and held onto both of them with a bamboo pole while the driver batteried the trolleybus over the main junction and parked it outside the divisional offices. It was as well for the driver that it was a Saturday when no London Transport big-wigs were on the premises. In due course a repair wagon would have come out and straightened the booms, but with the vehicle losing mileage it had not been a wise move putting this driver to work on a trolleybus.

One thing to avoid was to dewire in driving rain, particularly if the trolley head had turned. Rewiring at these times was never relished as it meant that staff had to face a deluge of rain, causing them to squint. Drivers would not expect their conductors to do this in these circumstances. Raising poles in a torrential downpour was not recommended but sometimes there was no alternative when 'livening' up a 'dead' trolleybus on the stand at Tally Ho.

It might appear that we had our poles off more often than we had them on. Of course this was not so and we would go hundreds of miles without a dewirement. Even the most experienced drivers, though, 'had 'em off' from time to time.

1466 has dewired when passing the facing frog that splits routes 609 and 645 at North Finchley. It is impossible to tell whether the driver has passed through too quickly or if the frog had erroneously been set for a 645. Conductor Morley is about to re-wire 1466; once this is done the vehicle can get on its way. The signal box light at the junction of Woodhouse Road and Finchley High Road is in favour of 609s. *Chris Orchard.*

1472 has dewired at the crossover in Kingsway, North Finchley; the driver is retrieving the errant nearside boom. It is not easy as his left foot is off the ground, so a bit of a stretch for him. Another 609 and a Green Line coach wait behind. Four Finchley trolleybuses were fitted with sliding ventilators in both saloons rather than the standard drop down ones – 1471, 1472, 1528 and 1529. *Chris Orchard.*

St Gabriels Church loop was difficult to negotiate. Attention had to be given to the road space as it was a tight place to get round without reversing. I had to use full lock on the steering wheel, with the front nearside of the 'bus almost touching the pillar box in Chichele Road as I came out of the loop. The manoeuvre was carried out very cautiously, though I could take power on the crossover and trailing frog. On the right is a stench pipe – these gave ventilation for sewers. 921 heads for Hammersmith on route 660. *Don Thompson.*

POWER PRIORITY

The biggest and most intricate overhead layout I had to deal with was the complex Nags Head layout at Holloway where eleven trolleybus routes, all on frequent headways, passed through. At this location, Holloway Road met with Parkhurst Road and Seven Sisters Road, so was a busy intersection with a lot of traffic passing through for much of the day. The drill to cross this junction differed according to the route I was on. The most complex manoeuvre to make was turning from Holloway Road into Seven Sisters Road on the 521s/621s, so is the most apt to describe. Although the frog in Holloway Road was set for me, I had to coast through it as the dead section was on my running wires. Power priority was in my favour on the three overhead crossovers in the main junction which eased matters if I had to make a standing start from the traffic lights, or was impeded by traffic or pedestrians walking in front of me. As it was, I usually had to wait for traffic passing the other way to clear, so power priority was of great assistance here. The only time I was able to make this manoeuvre without stopping would be on Sunday mornings when, if the lights were in my favour, I would be able to build up a bit of speed and drift through much of the junction. I would never rest my foot on the power pedal and wouldn't get into Seven Sisters Road until I was reasonably sure that I had a clear run into it as the penultimate piece of special work to negotiate, outside Abbots, had to be coasted through because power priority was against me.

Help was not always given on inclines. New Southgate loop was an example of this. When turning here, a crossover had to be negotiated on the incline and with power priority against us, was a challenging manoeuvre. Oddly, priority was given to 'buses travelling towards London which were moving downhill, and didn't need assistance. Two other idiosyncrasies come to mind. At Islington Green, where 609s shunted downhill into the loop, power priority was given to 'buses making this manoeuvre rather than those continuing on the flat through to Moorgate. At Macdonald Road, (the first of three roads used for the Archway short-working) trolleybuses had power priority to enter this street when it would have been better for 611s going up Highgate Hill to have had this facility.

Although many of the loops were of the same configuration, some had different electrical arrangements, all of which had to be memorised. When negotiating the short-working circles at Golders Green Station and St Gabriels Church, there was no power priority on the facing frog, the trailing frog or the crossover, while at Bromyard Avenue, power could be taken on the facing frog, the crossover but not on the trailing frog.

Very occasionally power priority changed. In 1958 a roundabout was constructed at Highbury Corner and whereas I'd had to coast through the crossover going towards London until then, the revision meant that I now went through on power. In the reverse direction I could go through the trailing frog on power rather than coast. I think we just found out about this rather than being given information.

WATCH OUT FOR THE DEAD

One piece of equipment that I had to observe particularly was an item that was officially known as a 'jumper', but which drivers referred to as a 'bridge'. When I came across a 'bridge' (at frogs and crossovers), I knew I had to coast through. It carried the juice on 'my road' above the special work I was crossing onto my next live section of overhead. If there was no bridge it meant that I could pass through on power. When it came to entering and leaving loops and passing junctions at depots, trolleybuses on mainline wires generally had power priority. Initially I didn't know the intricacies of all the short-working points and would only find out about what was required when I first turned there – I had to hope for the best until I got the hang of things – 'hit and miss' really. The following paragraphs detail how complex the situation was.

When moving north out of London, there were several main roads where gradients were encountered. When trolley-buses came on the scene, as much assistance as possible was given to vehicles that encountered junctions on upward

The overhead at the Theobalds Road/Clerkenwell Road/Grays Inn Road junction meant that drivers on all but two of the services that passed through had a challenging time – the 543 and 565 only had a facing and trailing frog to contend with. When I was driving a 521 to Holborn, I had power in my favour on the first crossover but I didn't use this facility as I had to coast through the long metal runner bar that embraced the two crossovers in view. I was able to go through the trailing frog on power. Thirteen trolleybus routes passed through this junction – more than anywhere else in London. Seen with many other road vehicles of the era, Stamford Hill's 1213 turns from Clerkenwell Road into Grays Inn Road. *Jack Gready.*

1520's driver has momentarily taken his foot off the power pedal as he passes under the feeder just south of Wood Green depot; he can pass through the facing frog on power. WN drivers had to be craftsmen here, for they had to position their vehicles just beyond the feeder but not too near the facing frog. Once the frog handle was pulled, they needed to get up enough momentum to coast through it and into the depot – all on an upward gradient too. 1520's conductor is on the platform, ready for his frog pull at Jolly Butchers Hill. London Transport loved rainy days; more people used their vehicles at these times, thereby increasing the takings.
Terry Cooper.

slopes, with the electrical circuitry usually being arranged in their favour. I will quote three examples on my routes. The first two were at Highgate and were in quick succession for northbound 609s: (i) at Pemberton Gardens which was the approach to Highgate depot, (ii) Archway Junction where northbound 609s crossed southbound 611s. Having power priority in our favour at these places was of great value when trying to keep to schedule at busy times.

The third was at Wood Green; when arranging the overhead layout outside the depot, those responsible for this were caught between the devil and the deep blue sea. Either drivers continuing northwards or those going into the depot would have to take their foot off the power pedal while moving uphill. It was deemed more important for trolleybuses on the main line to have power priority as they would be carrying passengers whereas those going into the depot would be empty. Drivers entering the depot had to coast through the 'pull and hold' frog, requiring their professionalism to be sorely tested as they tried to avoid getting stuck 'on the dead'. A few yards further north, and still moving uphill, the requirements of 521s/621s were considered more important than 625s/629s/641s at St Michael's Church, so power priority was given to Finchley 'buses where conductors had to operate a frog handle.

A power failure in Caledonian Road brings trolleybus services to a halt. The leading vehicle is Finchley's 310; if the crew are due to finish at North Finchley they won't be happy, though if they've still got a wedge of work to do, then they're going to be curtailed somewhere. Although some crews are stretching their legs, most are still in their vehicles. *Fred Ivey.*

'THE JUICE IS OFF'

When the power went off, it would do so unexpectedly. My first reaction on seeing the neon light extinguished, was that the booms had left the wires. I would open the cab door and look upwards to see if that was so. If the booms were still connected to the overhead the most likely explanation was that the power was off and this would be confirmed by other trolleybuses in the vicinity gliding to a halt. I would call through to my conductor and say, "The juice is off – we'll be stuck here for a while". Power failures could occur due to electrical faults in the supply system, and occasionally due to the sub-station being overloaded by the pure volume of trolleybuses all trying to take power at the same time.

If the juice went off when I was notching up, I would suddenly not feel anything on the power pedal – there'd be no response from it. If it went off when I was coasting I wouldn't know anything about it unless I noticed that the neon light had gone out. If the current went off when I was stationary I would not be able to draw any power when I wanted to move away. When a power failure occurred there was no electric brake. This meant that drivers lost the first part of the braking system (the rheostatic brake) and would go straight through on to the air brake to give normal stopping. The electrical circuitry was designed in such a way that if the interior and exterior lighting was on when the juice went off, it was not extinguished. The batteries lit the vehicle, preventing the trolleybus being thrown into darkness.

When the juice was off I didn't know how long it would be for. All I could do was wait for it to come on again. When the juice was restored I'd hear the humming of the motor generator set as it started up and see the neon light come on again. There could be a problem when the power went off – when it did, the compressor stopped working and meant that the air in the brake cylinder could leak out and cause the air pressure to drop. This would cause the Westinghouse low air pressure flag to rise. If this happened, then when the juice came on again I had to wait a minute or two while the

compressor pumped up enough air for the flag to drop. I would add that air could leak out of the air cylinder of a 'bus that had been parked overnight. This was soon restored once the booms were on the wires and the compressor was replenishing the air in the brake cylinder.

A disadvantage levelled against trolleybuses was that they were subject to frequent power failures and this was bandied about by the management when it was announced that the trolleybus system was to be scrapped. In my experience, this was not so and power failures only occurred occasionally – even then the 'juice' was only off for about three or four minutes. Such problems tended to happen in the peaks when more trolleybuses were on the road putting a greater strain on the power supply. Rule 35 stated that when a power failure occurred, vehicles should be batteried into the side of the road and be positioned so as to cause as little inconvenience as possible to other road users. Furthermore, that if it happened during the hours of darkness, the lighting switch should be placed in the emergency position to reduce the load on the battery (the emergency switch was situated under the staircase and operated by the conductor). With these brief delays, we could often make up lost time by forgoing stand time or just getting on with it. Lazy crews would seize an opportunity such as this to obtain a curtailment. I was involved in two lengthy power failures – one was in Acton Vale and is mentioned in a later chapter. The other occurred sometime in the late 1950s when there was a spate of them three evenings running in Holloway Road. The worst was outside Holloway Road Underground station during the peak hour when it went off for about twenty minutes. Eventually inspectors appeared and when the power was restored, they turned vehicles short of their destinations to get back on schedule. They made sure that we departed singly rather than in convoy; as otherwise the power would have gone off again. Sub-station staff soon knew where and when there were power failures, and would move quickly to get power restored.

HAZARDS & HITCHES

Trolleybuses were very reliable, with electrical and mechanical faults being few and far between. Occasionally, contactors missed a sequence – they would jump from notch two to notch four; passengers would get jolted every time a driver notched up. We couldn't carry on like this and the 'bus would have to be changed over. Another problem could be 'noisy trolleys' (carbon inserts in the trolley heads wearing down). A driver may not have become aware of this until he had left Moorgate; when he got to Archway he would ask an inspector to phone the depot engineers for a substitute 'bus to be brought out at Tally Ho. They wouldn't consider this a safety issue and as there wasn't a lot of time to get things organised, the driver would be told that the change-over would take place on the return from Barnet. The engineers had two options: (1) place the 'sub' in the bus station and when the crew got there, usher the passengers over to it: (2) make a right-hand battery turn by the Tally Ho pub, about sixty yards further along Ballards Lane, and park it poles down opposite the bus station. Either way, the delay would be minimal and the trolleybus would be on time at East Finchley.

If on arrival at Moorgate on a 609 a driver thought that the brakes were not as good as they should be, but still considered that it was safe to drive the vehicle back to North Finchley, then a substitute 'bus would definitely be there for him. Sometimes I would be waiting to take over a 609 and find one parked in the roadway with its poles down and without any running number plates. An inspector would say, "The 'bus is being changed over, this will be yours."

On the few occasions that there was a complete failure, drivers would call for assistance; before long a breakdown wagon would turn up. If its crew thought the problem could be easily fixed, they would sort it out there and then, and the trolleybus would soon be back in service. If a fault rendered a trolleybus unserviceable, but it was capable of getting back to the depot under its own power following a temporary repair, then the driver would take the vehicle back to the depot 'light'. Very infrequently, a major fault occurred and if the problem couldn't be sorted out on the spot, a service vehicle would tow the vehicle back to its depot.

One day a Barnet bound 609 became defective as it turned from Kingsway into Ballards Lane at North Finchley. Having stowed the trolley arms, Les Strutt, myself, a policeman, an inspector and a couple of other members of the trolleybus staff came to the rescue. We pushed the 609 for about seventy yards and parked safely in the side of the road.

I only occasionally experienced a 'spongy' footbrake – a weak one where I had to apply more pressure than usual to get good braking efficiency. This was probably due to an air leak in the system. I could not carry on in service like this and would arrange for the vehicle to be substituted at Tally Ho. If at any time a footbrake was not up to service standard and therefore unsafe, drivers would report the matter to an official at the earliest opportunity. They would contact the depot staff who would give instructions for the 'bus to be taken out of service immediately. A two-man crew, from the depot, would arrive and the 'buses would be changed over. They would drive the defective one back to the depot for attention. Our engineering staff regularly took trolleybuses out for brake tests to ensure that they were up to scratch so it was unusual for one to have a weak footbrake.

The maintenance at FY was very good with drivers rarely having to book the same vehicle up for a recurring problem. The most common faults were heavy steering and weak handbrake; sometimes the driver's blind furl would jam or tear. The defect sheets were looked at daily so that any problems were rectified. If there was no fault on a vehicle, the sheet was signed off as 'Nil'. The cleaners made a big effort to keep our trolleybuses in a presentable condition; only on the filthiest of days did vehicles look grubby. On the subject of cleanliness, the inside of a trolleybus depot was completely different to a motorbus garage; there was no oil or water over the floor nor any smoke or deafening noise to contend with.

Now and again I would take over a trolleybus on Tally Ho stand and discover that it had a weak handbrake. The lever would come right back, far more than normal – there was barely enough adhesion to hold the 'bus stationary. As soon as it started to load up, it would inch slowly forward on the slight slope. This meant that the vehicle had to be changed

Opposite The frogs were regularly oiled, inspected and maintained by the overhead line staff – where necessary they also did repair work. The crew of tower wagon 414P are working on the overhead at the bottom of Finchley bus station. 926 can easily get past but before any vehicles using the other set of wires can proceed, the wagon will have to be moved away from the immediate area (it looks as if 931 is out of service on the stand). If a tower wagon crew was working on the overhead we would sometimes be delayed for a short time; when they finished they would swing the platform out of the way and beckon us on. However, if trolleybuses started to bank up, we would pass by on battery. *London Trolleybus Preservation Society.*

over there and then. I had only one experience of a poor hand-brake while in service: I had taken over a 521 or 621 at Tally Ho, and had gone all the way to Holborn without a problem. On the return journey when coming down the hill from Manor House towards Harringay, with a heavy load on, I found that the handbrake was not as good as it should be. At the traffic lights at Endymion Road, the 'bus was still moving forward as it could not be held on the handbrake alone – I had to use the footbrake as well. I didn't really want to take the 'bus out of service and reckoned that by taking things carefully I could get it back to Tally Ho, which I did. I saw an inspector at Wood Green and arranged for a substitute to be brought out for me at North Finchley. At times like this, drivers had the final say. They could carry on at their own discretion and nurse it back to Tally Ho; alternatively they could pull it out of service.

I never suffered a puncture, but they occasionally occurred. A driver would battery his vehicle into the side of the road, get the 'sticks' down, rest the bamboo pole against the back of the 'bus and wait for assistance to arrive. A breakdown wagon would come out, its crew would change the wheel, the driver and conductor would get their backsides off the down-stairs long seats and the 'bus would be on its way.

When a trolleybus failed a long way from home – be it Hammersmith, Holborn, Moorgate – and its crew due for relief at Tally Ho (and no chance of it or them returning for some considerable time), arrangements were made for a 'special sub' to be brought out for the next crew. There were a couple of items that would be missing. First, there wouldn't be any running numbers so the 'sub' would run with nothing at all, or have the numbers chalked onto the paintwork. Secondly, there wouldn't be a timecard as that was on the original vehicle. This wasn't a problem for regular crews, as they knew the number of minutes between timing points. If they were unsure of departure times, an inspector would tell them the time they were to leave each terminus. Unfortunately there were some crews who would take advantage of situations like this – they would waste time and obtain a curtailment, increasing the number of route miles lost. A trolleybus without a timecard could be a problem for new staff. An inspector would jot down on a piece of paper arrival and departure times for each terminus – this would get them by. Although depot inspectors tried to steer clear of pairing up a brand new driver with a brand new conductor, it was sometimes unavoidable. Putting two rookies together could hold the whole show up and inspectors would probably have to curtail them two or three times in a day so as to avoid trolleybus services being delayed.

Backing up trolleybus operation were Leyland Cub and Albion breakdown tenders – other support vehicles were AEC tower wagons. The Finchley tower wagon was out and about most days, and sometimes our linesmen would assist those from other depots. While they were patrolling the routes assigned to them they inspected and, if necessary, repaired any fault they saw. Trolleybuses would bank up for a couple of minutes until they had finished. They would also carry out routine maintenance – tapping and adjusting fittings, and checking frogs and crossovers. They also had to ensure that the overhead remained at the correct tension – for this they used a special tool which was known as a 'come-along'. When they were tightening up, the overhead would noticeably vibrate and any slackness would disappear. Contacted by telephone, the linesmen responded quickly to call-outs. They would speed to the location concerned and deal with broken runner bars, broken span wires, and in Vic Collins's case, a broken traction wire.

It was important for all staff, whether they worked on motorbuses or trolleybuses, to be quick thinking when life threatening situations arose. In my conducting days when we reached Wood Green one day on our way to North Finchley, a passenger had a fit on the top deck. This was brought to my attention by another passenger and when I went upstairs I saw that an unfortunate individual was foaming at the mouth. It was rather alarming and he needed medical attention. Straightaway I went across to the point inspector and asked him to call an ambulance. I pulled our poles down to allow a free path to following trolleybuses and transferred the passengers to the next 521/621. The man was taken to hospital and I got the inspector at Wood Green to make a note of the incident; we reported the matter back at the depot. We were either late finishing that day or had to be curtailed on a later journey.

One day I was doing an 'Archway short' on the 609 and was passing the entrance to the Underground station at the bottom of Highgate Hill when a man rushed between two parked vehicles and straight into the nearside of the driver's cab. He bounced off and was shaken up, but was not injured in any way. I took his name and address and reported the incident but there was no comeback on the matter.

One weekday afternoon when I was driving and working with Tommy Walker I pulled up at the stop outside Pentonville prison in Caledonian Road on the way to Holborn. Suddenly, there was an almighty whack – a 517 had ran into the back of me. The impact was so great that I was jerked backwards and banged my head on the window behind me. Tommy had seen what was going to happen and ran to the front of the vehicle. Apart from a few bumps we were both alright, but that could not be said of the staircase, which was badly splintered and bent – the back window was also broken. Fortunately I had the handbrake on so there wasn't much movement of my vehicle. There were only two passengers on board and they were both downstairs and neither of them was injured. The 'bus was still capable of being driven so having wound up PRIVATE on both destination blinds, we carried on to Kings Cross, the first available turning point, and ran it back light to the depot. The front of the 517 was badly damaged, but was able to be driven back to Highgate depot. Its driver said that his attention was taken by a lorry pulling out of Brewery Road and he thought that there might be a collision between them. He had been looking in his offside mirror to see that he had cleared the lorry, and wasn't aware that I had pulled up at the bus stop. This happened just a few weeks after I started driving trolleybuses.

When I was working with Vic on a trip from North Finchley to Holborn Circus one day, a mother with two young girls boarded at the 'Ranelagh' pub (the stop before Bounds Green

1471 had a whack up the back in December 1960 – a lorry probably ran into it and stoved the rear in. It was immediately withdrawn and sold to Cohen's who picked it up later in the month and took it to Colindale scrapyard where it is seen. This reduced the 'sliding ventilator' trolleybuses at FY to three. Despite the extensive damage, 1471's rear window has not broken. The trolleybus that ran into the back of me in Caledonian Road caused nearly as much damage; 'my vehicle' was deemed worthy of repair though. *Fred Ivey.*

Station). One child was a four year old with the other one being younger. The mother sat on the nearside long seat with the little 'un, while the older girl knelt on the offside one looking out of the window. I rang the 'bus off and started collecting fares. As the mother had her arms full I did not approach her straightaway as I wanted to give her time to get her money out. I was at the front of the lower saloon as we approached Bounds Green station when there was a scream from the mother who shouted that her child was falling into the roadway. I didn't actually see what had happened, but when my attention was drawn to the situation all I could see was the child, face-down sliding feet-first off the rear of the platform into the gutter. I hit the bell cord bang, bang, bang and Vic pulled up quickly. I alighted to see the child on the roadway. I picked her up and took her back the few yards to the 'bus, and was relieved to see that she was just shaken up and unscathed, apart from a few grazes. As the incident occurred opposite Bounds Green Cottage Hospital, I, with the mother in attendance, carried the child over there where she was checked over and given the okay. In our own interests, the police were called and took particulars. In the meantime, seeing there was going to be a delay, Vic got the poles down and transferred the passengers to the next 'bus. When we had finished with the incident we made our way to Wood Green, where an inspector was informed of the situation. He turned us short of our intended destination and when we got back to the depot we made out a report about

the matter. I remember writing that the incident happened about two hundred yards after they had boarded, and quoted the adjacent traction standard number. Some weeks later I was called in to see the CDI and was told that the woman had put in a claim saying that the 'bus had been rung off too quickly and had started with a tremendous jolt, causing her child to fall onto the roadway. This was untrue. I had estimated that the incident had happened approximately two hundred yards after they had boarded and when London Transport measured things up they found that it was one hundred and eighty seven yards. The claim was thrown out but nobody seemed to know how the child came to land in the roadway. I expect that she had got off the seat by herself, lost her balance and fallen. A far cry from the mother's idea that we had been responsible for the child's tri-directional fall (from the seat onto the gangway, then onto the platform and into the roadway). It was fortunate that I had made a note of the trolley standard number for it obviously had a bearing on the claim being dismissed.

Sometimes, advance warning was given about operations that would affect London Transport's road services and forward planning was possible. When road closures took place, motorbuses would be diverted away from their normal routeing but this was not an option always open to trolleybuses and alternative arrangements had to be made. These would be put into operation on the appointed day, such as Sunday 8th March 1959, when major work was carried out on the bridge that carried the North London railway line over the Caledonian Road. This road was closed to all traffic apart from trolleybuses, but as the 'juice' was unavoidably cut off, we could not proceed in the normal manner. A number of service vehicles were specially brought in for the day so that trolleybuses could be towed northbound through the un-energised section – passengers were allowed to stay on board during the tow, this being a rare event. Southbound we were able to battery through aided by gravity. A tower wagon was in attendance in case it was needed and the whole operation was supervised by inspectors. The front valance was taken off each 'bus and put inside the vehicle, with each supposed to be replaced at the end of the tow; they were not put back on a few 'buses which ran around looking very scruffy indeed. The railway engineers completed their work in the allotted time and a normal service was operating the next day.

One Sunday afternoon when driving a 521, I had to stop at the traffic lights at the junction of Grays Inn Road and High Holborn. There was a film crew on the opposite corner with all their lights and equipment and they appeared to be having a rest from filming. I noticed that Alfie Bass was amongst them. He looked across the road to my stationary trolleybus and walked across to the cab, extended his arm and offered me a bite of the apple he was eating at the time. I declined the offer. Other actors I've seen in my London Transport career are Harry Fowler, Richard Todd and Ian Carmichael. Another notable individual was politician Michael Foot. The time I saw Harry Fowler was in the 1960s when I was driving an RT bus on route 134 in Charing Cross Road. I was stationary in heavy traffic at the time and he squeezed between me and the vehicle in front. In doing so he placed his hand on the hot radiator of the bus. He burnt his hand, looked up at me, gave a yell and continued on his way.

Something that drivers did occasionally, through force of habit, was to go north rather than south when leaving the depot. It was easily done for if we had been going to Barnet on our first trip every day Monday to Friday, and on the Saturday were supposed to go to Moorgate, we could automatically find ourselves going in the wrong direction. If we realised quickly enough we would pull down the booms and change onto battery and turn through the slipway in front of the Tally Ho public house. Here there was a slight gradient which helped us to regain the proper direction. If it didn't register immediately that we were going the wrong way we would have to go through to Barnet. We could not turn in a side street as it would make matters worse if the battery was low and we became stranded.

When drivers made the mistake of arriving at Barnet rather than Moorgate an inspector might welcome them as he could make use of the 'bus to cover a gap in the service. It depended on who the inspector was and whether he would report such a mistake. If he decided that he wouldn't, he would write on his day's summary that the 'bus had been extended to Barnet and subsequently curtailed at Islington Green or Nags Head for service requirements. I went to Barnet instead of Moorgate on at least one occasion and I expect the Barnet inspector probably thought that Wyatt didn't know his right from his left that morning.

I was only involved in a diversion once – even that, though, was not in the true sense of the word. There was a hold-up in Grays Inn Road, so instead of travelling round the Holborn loop in an anti-clockwise direction, I had to go via Farringdon Road. In essence I was a 521 that was made a 621. Drivers could inadvertently go round the Holborn Loop the wrong way; maybe they had made two trips in the anti-clockwise direction and assumed that the third had to be negotiated likewise. When this happened and they got to Charterhouse Street, an inspector might come up to them and ask what was going on – it was only then that they would realise their mistake. Inspectors would never make a meal of it as they knew that something like this was nothing more than a genuine error. Sometimes we might be asked to go round the loop the opposite way to that scheduled in order to cover a gap in the service.

There were occasions when I took the wrong trolleybus, e.g. FY23 instead of FY24 from the stand at Tally Ho. I wouldn't realise this until either I or my conductor had a look at the timecard, possibly not until Wood Green. Having found I had taken the wrong vehicle, I could work out what my time was by my knowledge of the service frequency, and would conceal my error by removing the running number plates. In the meantime, the other crew would twig what had happened, and would take 24. I would see its crew around the Holborn Loop or he might even catch me up – we would exchange timecards and plates wherever we met (inspectors would be none the wiser). If I hadn't been able to change the relevant items, then when I got back to North Finchley I would explain the situation to an official, give him the timecard and running plates, and let him sort it out. When conductors took over a 521/621 at Tally Ho they didn't know initially whether they were working as a 521 or a 621. As soon as their driver knew the configuration he would call from the cab "We're doing a five" or "We're doing a six". They would then know whether to show 521 or 621 on the route and side blinds.

I made sure at the North Finchley relief points that I did not breach rule 44 which stated that 'vehicles in service must not be left unattended' – the police got upset about 'buses being left at the roadside. If a crew member didn't turn up here, the passengers had to be transferred to another 'bus, the trolley poles dropped and the vehicle taken into the depot. If it was the conductor who hadn't materialised, the driver would run it in. If it was the driver, then an inspector or another driver would do the honours – a sense of orderliness now prevailed.

The reverse was so at Craven Park and it was common to see crewless Stonebridge trolleybuses parked all over the place. Highgate vehicles were forever 'dumped' in Warlters Road (used for trolleybuses short working at Nags Head) though in fairness at least they were out of the way. Often when I turned there, trolleybuses on other routes would be seen, so there was an element of boom lowering and raising to allow others to pass – particularly 627s/653s working from Highgate depot towards Tottenham Court Road as there was no direct wiring link from Holloway Road into Parkhurst Road at Nags Head junction itself.

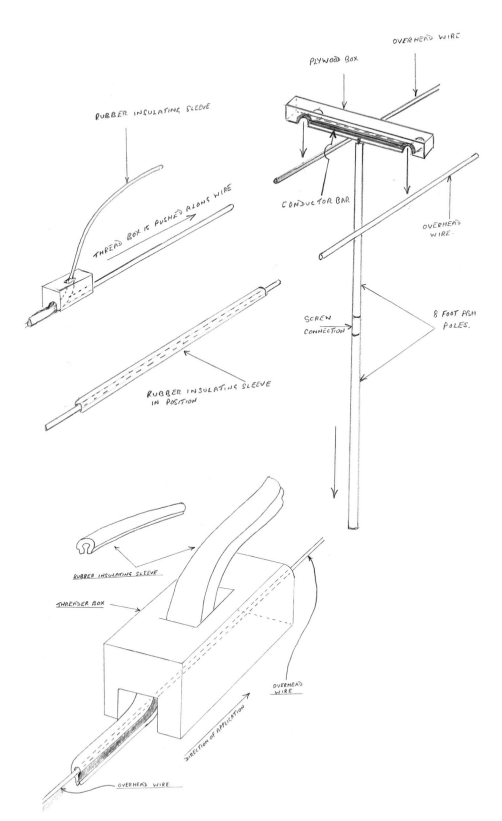

RUBBER INSULATING SLEEVE

PLYWOOD BOX

OVERHEAD WIRE

THREAD BOX IS PUSHED ALONG WIRE

CONDUCTOR BAR

OVERHEAD WIRE

RUBBER INSULATING SLEEVE IN POSITION

SCREW CONNECTION

8 FOOT ASH POLES.

RUBBER INSULATING SLEEVE

THREADER BOX

OVERHEAD WIRE

DIRECTION OF APPLICATION

OVERHEAD WIRE

My brother John was a sub-officer in the London Fire Brigade, and told me about a trolleybus overhead wire short-circuiting device. Kept in the lockers of fire engines, they were used when fires occurred adjacent to trolleybus services. The device was in the shape of a letter T and was made of ash. The device was in two parts and each pole was eight feet in length – it was assembled at the location of the fire and screwed together. At the top of the pole was a plywood box. The pole was pushed up between the positive and negative traction wires and turned so that it rested on both. This short-circuited the overhead and enabled firemen to work in safety on their ladders. As a precaution against firemen receiving an electric shock, a secondary unit was placed on one of the traction wires, shown in detail bottom left. One day, I was close to a fire when working on a trolleybus; T poles were not needed as the fire was in a store set back from the road. This was in Holloway Road between Camden Road and Parkhurst Road, on my northbound approach to Nags Head. There was smoke everywhere, but traffic was able to continue as the firemen brought out their wooden fire ramps to protect their hoses. The trolleybus lifted and rolled, but the ramps easily took the weight of the vehicle. *John Wyatt.*

Some of the young conductresses who joined the Finchley trolleybus staff in 1960/61 liked to have a go at raising and lowering trolley booms. 1452 has been parked, out of service, adjacent to the Gaumont cinema; the driver has battered the vehicle over to the nearside to allow passengers to board. Having re-wired the nearside boom, this young lady is now putting the positive one back on the overhead; the tension on the booms was so strong that sometimes the girls were bent backwards with the effort. Staff had to be careful when manipulating trolley arms on the Queen's highway, for at times we could be on the crown of the road when dealing with them. *Hugh Taylor.*

ARMS, HEADS AND BAMBOO POLES

Now and again I would take over a trolleybus and notice one or both of the booms not quite straight. Alternatively there might be ragged insulating tape, indicating that a dewirement had recently occurred. If a 'bus was left for me like this, I would inform an official and ask him to observe it. I recall pointing out to inspector Charlie Atkins at Tally Ho one day that a boom looked a bit bent. He said, "That'll be alright till you get back" – and it was. If I did take over a 'bus with a bent boom I would book the fact up on the vehicle's defect sheet. I would never leave a trolleybus with a bent boom for somebody else, but if I'd 'had them off' and the boom was a bit bent, with the 'bus still serviceable, I would get it back to North Finchley. In the meantime I would ask an official to arrange for a substitute to be brought out at Tally Ho. At the depot, I would fill in a dewirement report as there was no point in trying to get away with things; it could always be traced back to me.

If there was one thing that a Finchley trolleybus driver didn't want, it was to go in front of Mr Irons to explain a dewirement. First of all, he would greet the miscreant with a false smile – he would be beaming all over his face but it was all put on and he suddenly became serious. It was like going in front of the Gestapo, for he would lay down the law and say to an offender something like, "What speed were you doing?" Though they would reply, "Ten miles an hour", he knew it would be more like twenty or twenty-five. He was an astute man and could not be fooled on any matter and most drivers would come out of his office with some type of reprimand. They might have been told "Bend your booms and have the breakdown wagon come out, and you'll be up at Manor House explaining yourself to the District Superintendent".

The relationship between the maintenance staff and drivers at Finchley was good, so rather than report a dewirement, some drivers would give one of the inside staff a couple of shillings to straighten a bent boom. This was achieved by using a 'Jim Crow' implement. This tool was fastened onto a trolleyboom, and by continually screwing the clamp of the Jim Crow over the bent parts of the boom, it was straightened. It was in the interest of any driver who could make it back to the depot with a bent boom to make a financial investment in this way as otherwise it was deemed as 'damage to vehicle' and a driver could lose his safe driving record. It also saved making up a feeble excuse for the CDI. The maintenance staff would turn a blind eye and re-tape booms that had scuffed insulating tape as they wanted Finchley depot's good image to be maintained. When a trolleybus was seen with torn tape, its driver would be ribbed with words such as "See you've got the flags flying today".

Generally speaking, trolleys slipped out of their retaining hooks easily but sometimes I had to give a bit of a tug to get them out. Although I had to use more strength on booms with strong tension, and which were heavy to handle, I considered that weighty booms were good booms as they gave stronger adhesion to the overhead. Continual use caused booms to slacken off and one day I had to change a 'bus over before I left the depot as I considered the tension on them was too slack. If I came across a 'bus in service that had weak booms, and which I thought would be an impediment before long, I would report the matter. This was done by writing 'slack tension on booms' on the vehicle's defect sheet – they would be adjusted in the depot later. When I had to pull down outstretched booms it was my strength against the strength and sway of the booms.

Drivers could be unlucky and be lumbered with a 'bus where the tensioning of a boom was weak and would find that it would regularly dewire. Either they would reach the end of their tether and take it out of service, or it would dewire once too often and bend the boom. If this occurred and the CDI was later told, when the driver was interviewed, that trouble had been experienced with the boom previously, he wouldn't be impressed with him for allowing a defective vehicle to continue in service.

The carbons in the trolley heads were supposed to be checked every night. Occasionally they were overlooked and, if they wore down, there would be a high pitched screeching noise. It became so infuriating that sometimes fitters had to come out and change the carbons at North Finchley. Or, they might be instructed to run the 'bus into the depot and get another one. If the situation wasn't too bad I would keep the vehicle running and book it up as 'low carbons'.

Trolley heads were firmly bolted onto trolleybooms and were designed in such a way that if one was to come off, it would still be attached to the boom by its safety rope. This didn't always happen as, following a dewirement, the rope sometimes broke. This could result in a head becoming detached from a boom and either falling to the ground, getting caught in a span wire or resting in the point-work of a frog; if heads got caught in a facing or trailing frog, other trolleybuses had to pass by on battery. Sometimes, heads fell to the roadway, with these incidents being known as 'heads to ground'. Their descent was sometimes stopped by a car roof; when this happened, a letter to the claims department would follow. Occasionally, dewired trolleybooms, flying around, broke the windows of trolleybuses going in the other direction – it was not unknown for a trolley base to be almost wrenched from the roof of a 'bus.

1514 has dewired in Wood Green High Road; its offside trolley head has caught in a span wire and detached itself from the vehicle. An overhead repair crew are retrieving the head and will put it or another one back on the boom. While they are at it, they are applying new insulating tape to the nearside boom, which was scuffed during the incident. *Hugh Taylor.*

I never experienced a 'head to ground' incident. I can do one better than that as I had a whole boom pulled from the roof of a trolleybus. One afternoon as I was turning into Caledonian Road from Camden Road at Holloway, I was intending to pass a stationary RT bus on route 14 at the request stop there. As I was about to do so both booms dewired. They must have come off when I passed through the Warlters Road facing frog. I was driving at the correct speed through the frog, so I suspect that it had not returned to its correct position after its previous use (this could happen unexpectedly anywhere). The head on the offside boom caught in a span wire, but the head did not leave the boom, it stayed firmly bolted to it. This caused the boom to be pulled completely out of the trolley base and it was hanging down from a span wire. It just cleared the roadway, with the cables draping down the side of the trolleybus. For a whole boom to come out of a vehicle implies that there was something not quite right with it. I informed a point inspector at the Nags Head and he phoned for assistance. I had been able to get the good boom under the retaining hook but the other one looked a strange spectacle, held in the overhead by the span wire with the boom's cabling still attached to the trolleybus. Although I was stranded in the middle of the road, other vehicles were able to pass me on the inside. This included trolleybuses, as the running wires were not impeded. A breakdown wagon turned up and released the boom from the overhead. Another boom would need to be fitted back at the depot so there was no alternative but to tow the vehicle in. My conductor and I made our own way back to the depot on a service 'bus, where I filled in a dewirement report. When I saw the CDI about the matter, I told him of my suspicions and he agreed that the dewirement was not down to me. This was only the second time I had required a breakdown crew.

When he was a conductor, Les Strutt was teamed up with Jim Wright. They were heading north on route 609 one day when both poles came off at the Green Man by the North Circular Road. Jim found this inexplicable as the overhead there was on straight track. One of the heads actually detached itself from the boom and landed in somebody's front garden, so either Jim or Les opened the gate, went in and retrieved it. When the breakdown wagon arrived, they put the original trolley head in the work area of the wagon, fitted a new one and got the 609 on its way. Front gardens were popular places for trolley heads to land; a crew of a Colindale 'bus were not able to find theirs following a dewirement near Childs Hill. A breakdown crew attended the scene and fitted another one. Sometime later a member of the public turned up at our depot with a trolley head that he had found when he was digging his garden. Another trolleybus dewired on the approach to a bridge, with the head flying into the air and landing in the truck of a coal train passing above – the trolley head was never seen again. One day, some small boys wedged a tin can in a frog handle mechanism, then hid round the corner and waited for the fun and games to occur, which it did when a trolleybus came to grief and lost a trolley head. The crew saw the tin can still in position and the boys running away. They wrote these facts on the dewirement form, which exonerated the driver from blame.

Sometimes a 521/621 would be parked at the very front right-hand side of the bus station at Tally Ho for one reason or another. To return it to service we'd have to move it as far as we could to the left where we picked passengers up. The 'bus wouldn't be directly under the wires and the skewed trolley heads needed to be turned so that their carbon inserts could be easily hoisted onto the overhead. The trolley heads swivelled – they had to, just as booms pivoted on their bases. There were three ways of dealing with turned trolley heads. One, and my preferred way, was to bang the head up against the running wire causing the head to swivel into the correct position. Otherwise, I would rest the top of the boom across the running wire and turn the head with the grappling hook, so that it was directly beneath the trolley wire. Alternatively, I could turn the trolley head with the top of a bamboo while the booms were under the retaining hooks – this meant that once under the wires, the carbon skids were directly under the overhead

Trolley booms could become crossed – only when 'buses were being parked up though. A driver or conductor might have to stow booms on Tally Ho stand just before he was finished, and in his eagerness to get away, could place the nearside boom under the offside retaining hook. Then he'd wonder why he couldn't get the offside boom under the other hook – they were crossed on the roof. Most staff would give some extra pull on the bamboo and get it under the wrong hook. It didn't really matter, although the next man would find himself with a bit of a puzzle.

In the twenty-first century it might seem archaic, even clumsy, that fifty years ago many of London Transport's road operating staff used an eighteen foot bamboo pole as an everyday item of equipment. Without one, though, trolley-buses could be stranded so it was in staff's interests to ensure they were always carrying a pole. When taking over it was a good idea to check that one was stowed in its rightful position in its holder beneath the 'bus. This was not always feasible, for in the depot it wasn't always possible to see if a bamboo was there as vehicles were often closely parked one behind the other. Similarly, staff weren't always able to check when taking over on the stand at Tally Ho, due to the proximity of other 'buses, or in Ballards Lane where speedy crew change-overs were required. If I was aware that I wasn't carrying a bamboo I would have an uneasy feeling about things and would keep an eye out for one that was hanging from a traction standard or that had been discarded and left in the gutter by crews who, following a dewirement, had been unable to replace it due to the closeness of following traffic. I have retrieved a number of bamboos these ways, for the last thing a trolleybus driver wanted was to dewire with a full load of passengers and find no bamboo below – and that has happened to me! I was stranded and unable to do anything about it, I could not go searching, so had to wait for one to come to me. When a trolleybus with a bamboo turned up I would ask its driver if I could borrow his; he might insist on its return but on the other hand he would let me keep it if he was pressed for time. If I stopped to help someone who had dewired and who had no bamboo, I would often re-wire the other 'bus myself; that way I would keep my pole.

It is the last day of trolleybuses at Moorgate but this has not deterred 1263's driver from 'throwing his poles' there. The booms have gone so high in the air that the driver of the following 641 needs to come to his aid with a second bamboo. A man with a handcart looks on, probably unaware that it is the 641's last day. *Peter Moore.*

Sometimes, with a dewirement, trolley arms went up so high in the air, or far away from the traction wires, that a man on his own wasn't able to retrieve it A second bamboo would have to be procured from another trolleybus – either one coming the other way, or one following the stranded vehicle. Two crew members, each armed with a pole, now got to work to retrieve the situation. The grappling hook of the first bamboo would be placed as high up the trolley arm as possible; it would then be pulled down as low as possible and held there. The man with the second bamboo would then place his grappling hook on the boom and, while the first man released his grip would, hopefully, be able to rewire the 'bus. However, the second man may not have been able to rewire the 'bus at this attempt, so the first man would put his grappling hook around the end of the boom and the 'bus would be re-wired. Following a dewirement, one driver solved his predicament by seeking help from a local builder. He found his longest ladder, which he placed against the side of the 'bus. He clambered up it and by using the bamboo pole handed to him by the driver, got the trolley arms back on the wires.

I recall an incident of a trolleyboom swinging into an almost unreachable position at Highbury Corner – I was one of two 609s running together from Moorgate. I was going to Barnet, following an 'Archway short' when for no apparent reason one of its booms slipped off the wires. I was so close to the 609, that its driver was unable to get his bamboo out, so he went to the back of my 'bus and got mine out. There was not enough room between the two 'buses for him to get at the dewired boom, and the bamboo was of little use as the boom had gone up so high. To solve the problem he moved his 'bus up a few yards on its batteries which had the effect of dragging the boom down a bit so that it was resting under a span wire – this also gave him room to manoeuvre between the two vehicles. Despite being a tall man, he still had to stand on tiptoe on the platform to get the boom down and back on the overhead. Another way to correct such a situation was for a crew member to have one or both feet on the platform, one hand on a handrail and the other hand holding the bamboo pole. This was very hard to do because of the weight of the trolleyboom – it eventually was sorted though.

This is the 'Marie Celeste' of the trolleybus world. The photographer arrived at the Nags Head and to all intents and purposes saw an abandoned 1177; the nearside boom had slipped off the overhead when turning from Seven Sisters Road into Holloway Road. With no bamboo pole stowed beneath it, 1177's crew are searching for one in the vicinity; once they found one they went on their way – only to Islington Green though, as 1177 is running behind time. Staff could never be reported for not carrying a bamboo because there was nothing in the rule book saying that they should check to see that they had one. *Hugh Taylor.*

Staff could get caught out thinking that they didn't have a bamboo pole when they did have one all the time. In the depot, a crew member might have noticed that a grappling hook was not protruding from its holder beneath the 'bus. Grabbing hold of the nearest one available, they may have inadvertently taken one of the short ones that were used there (these had been full length bamboos which had had a few feet cut off the end to ease manipulation in the depots where booms would not go any higher than the troughing. The bottom of a full-length bamboo tended to drag against the floor when lowering booms in the depot). The short pole would have been shoved 'up the pipe' beneath the vehicle. As some of these holders had wider tubes than others the whole pole, grappling hook and all, would disappear inside. At a later date, another crew on the same 'bus, would, on seeing that a grappling hook was not protruding from the holder, think that one was not 'up the shoot'. They would obtain a full length one and attempt to push it up the holder, but find that it would only go so far. The crew would eventually twig what had happened, turn the full length bamboo round the other way, and with its grappling hook pull the short pole, by its hook, out of the tube. The short pole would then be discarded and the full length one inserted ready for action. Short bamboos were of little use when rectifying a dewirement on the road, so when landed with one we'd acquire a proper length one at the first opportunity. The short ones were dispensed with – maybe they would find their way back to the depot; maybe not.

Now and again we would find ourselves with another kind of duff bamboo – one that was splintered, usually near the top. Instead of gaining an upright position when we tried to raise it, we would find that it would bend right over above the splintering. With a deft flick of the hand though, like an angler, we could raise the pole into an upright position. Alternatively we could slide the top of the bamboo against the back of the 'bus which enabled it to straighten. We would use these only if there was no alternative, for really they had reached the end of their days. However, they gave us the opportunity to get our own back on one of our colleagues – on the stand at Tally Ho we would swipe their bamboo and give them the useless one. One thing that was never done, when getting one over on another member of staff, was to take their bamboo and leave them without one. It might be needed in an emergency, such as a trolleybus becoming electrically live; therefore the borrowing of bamboos was only done with another crew's consent. However, it was okay to take one out of a 'dead' trolleybus on the stand at Tally Ho as the next man should check anyway.

As I have already said, bamboo poles were eighteen feet in length. They were about two inches wide at the base but nearer the top some were thinner. The butt end was reinforced with insulating tape; bamboos were often banged down on the roadway, so the tape protected the base of the pole. Bamboos tended to last very well but were prone to breakage and damage. Splintering was the most common defect, although if they were repairable, the depot staff would bind insulating tape around the affected areas, thus prolonging their lives. A few drivers would only manipulate a

Staff could get caught out if they were told to turn at New Southgate where no facing frog was fitted. They may not have received this instruction until Wood Green, leaving them little time to find a spare bamboo if they didn't have one. All they could do then was to wait at New Southgate until a 'bus that had one turned up, hoping to persuade that crew that their need was greater. This has not happened on this occasion and trolley-bus etiquette pertains; 1452 is having its poles moved off the main line so that 1498 can get on its way to North Finchley. 1498's driver might have opened his windscreen and said to 1452's conductor something like "Dip your sticks and swing 'em across later so I can get a move on". Crews would always oblige as they might find themselves in the same situation. *Tony Belton.*

bamboo with gloves on. This was due to getting splinters in their hands from a split pole. Bamboo poles could be lethal things and some staff contracted dermatitis through dealing with a splintered bamboo.

There never seemed to be enough bamboos to go round. To meet the shortage, the depot foreman was often requisitioning new ones which would arrive from Charlton Works by lorry. When Charlton closed they came from Fulwell Works. Sometimes I had a brand new bamboo pole. It was robust, bright and shiny and noticeable for its cleanness and pristine condition. In fact right up until a few weeks before the changeover to motorbuses, brand new bamboos were still being delivered. They were in great contrast to some that had been around for a long time and were shabby. I would have thought that good bamboos could have been retrieved from scrap 'buses that were being broken up behind Colindale depot but as new ones were already in the main stores, it was these that were sent. I once saw the staff of a service vehicle placing bamboos around the bus station at Tally Ho – I expect our foreman had told its crew to position them there.

Occasionally a grappling hook would work itself loose from the bamboo, the bolts holding the two together having rusted away. Parting company, the hook would shoot up in the air as if it had been fired from a catapult, landing in the roadway or on the pavement. This happened to me on the stand at Tally Ho and I was just left with a piece of bamboo and no hook. Taken by surprise I stumbled backwards with the trolleyboom waving about in the air. I disposed of the old one as it was no good anymore to anyone and went for a replacement.

A bamboo pole was needed at the places where 'dead-enders' existed as trolley arms had to be swung from one set of wires to another. The dead-enders had either no facing or trailing frog. In a few places on the system there was a circle of wires that were not attached to the main line – however, they were electrically fed from them. At North Acton, when turning from the Harlesden direction, trolleybooms had to be swung on entry and exit to the turning circle, so it was important to make sure that when turning there, crews were carrying a bamboo pole.

Windsor Terrace was another place where trolley arms had to be swung onto a set of dead-end wires. The instruction to curtail there was normally given at Barnet or North Finchley, and if upon checking for a bamboo we found there wasn't one underneath, we had plenty of time to obtain one. If the instruction hadn't been given until Archway, there was little opportunity to get hold of one and on arrival at 'The Terrace' we might find that we were 'up the creek without a paddle'. However, there were so many trolleybuses going up and down the City Road we'd usually get hold of one quickly. Despite Windsor Terrace being used frequently as a short-working point, very rarely was a bamboo pole seen hanging up there. Odd really, as they tended to be positioned at places where staff needed easy access to one. Even at a trolleybus nerve centre like Wood Green there was not always one to hand.

At some locations, where it was considered that bamboos would be regularly required, an arm was fixed near to the top of some traction standards on which the grappling hook of a bamboo pole could be placed. The bottom of the bamboo was kept in position by a clasp on the standard. An almost circular ring was fixed near the top of traction standards that held a number of span wires, and bamboos were sometimes hooked onto them too. Bamboos were often seen hanging from standards at prime dewirement spots – this gave crews easy access to one. Sometimes I'd see one, sometimes I wouldn't, and there were many places where bamboos were to be seen hanging and then vanishing. Vic would sometimes call out to me "There's a pole over there Bill. We haven't got one, grab it will you". They were also available at locations where it was thought one might be needed for general use: Barnet, Hammersmith, Islington Green, Moorgate, Nags Head, North Acton, Paddenswick Road and Tally Ho. Really, they could be seen hanging from 'any old traction standard'. For some weeks one was hooked onto a standard at the junction of High Street and Station Road, Edgware. Presumably a trolleybus had dewired and the crew were unable to replace the bamboo beneath the vehicle and had hung it on the most convenient pole. When it was windy this pole swayed around as there was no clasp on the standard that it was attached to. Eventually it disappeared, being taken by someone who needed it.

At Golders Green, bamboos were propped against the Underground railway arches. These were used by inspectors putting vehicles which were out of running order back in their right place. There were other locations where bamboos could be commandeered – leaning against the operating block at Colindale Depot or against a wall outside Willesden bus garage. When bamboos at Nags Head were taken by crews who needed one, an inspector would arrange for replacements. This was achieved by some being put in the lower saloon of a trolleybus in Highgate depot and the vehicle being driven down to the Nags Head by a member of their inside staff.

All of the men (even the 'old boys') had no trouble in dealing with trolleybooms; they would just grab a bamboo and place the poles straight up on the wires. We became adept at putting them up quickly. Hold the trolley arm directly beneath the overhead and when the head was about four inches away from it, bang it on – viewed from a distance the overhead, despite its tightness, would noticeably lift. Lowering trolleybooms was a piece of cake; it was done in two ways. Most of the time we would walk left or right with the bamboo. When space was restricted we used it hand over hand, scarcely moving in the process. Conductresses were not expected to carry out trolleyboom work. It was an accepted practice for drivers who were teamed with them to chivalrously carry out this heavy work. However, in the latter days, some of the young clippies had a go at upping and downing trolleybooms; in fact they relished the task. Although they were wrestling with the tension of the trolleybooms, they were able to raise poles successfully even though they would noticeably lean backwards. When lowering trolley arms the girls who indulged in this practice were a lot slower than the men. We welcomed their participation as it saved us time. One dark morning when I dewired at East Road/City Road junction by taking an obstruction too wide, my conductress for the day, Mary Finn, saved me some time. Aware that the poles had left the wires, she called out "I'll get them", and did the honours by rewiring the booms. She was a dab hand at this kind of thing.

When re-wiring a trolleybus, staff were encouraged for safety reasons to place the nearside (negative) boom back first. In practice though, the positive trolley arm was usually replaced first as this was normally easier. The normal way of raising trolleybooms was to face forwards so that everything was in front of us but Colindale driver Joe Gowland, when he was placing poles on the overhead, did it the opposite way round so that he could see traffic coming towards him. I expect that he had probably had a bit of a close shave with a motorist at some stage. It looked cack-handed but he always got them up without any problems. Putting booms up under direct sunlight was very difficult; the problem was dealt with in one of two ways. The first option was to raise each boom with my right arm and shield my eyes from the sun with my left hand. The alternative was to turn around with my back to the sun and re-pole in the Joe Gowland fashion.

Often, 521s/621s were parked out of service at Tally Ho, booms down with a bamboo pole propped against the back. Being professional trolleybusmen, staff ensured that the bamboo rested between the two booms so that it couldn't fall sideways. Sometimes, the bamboo was slid across the plat-form and inside the lower deck – not only did this save us getting it out from underneath, but it also indicated to potential passengers that the 'bus was out of service.

Sometimes a bamboo would be seen resting in the spinney at Canons Park terminus. This gave staff easy access to a pole if one was quickly needed, such as if one trolleybus needed to jump another there. This would be for scheduling purposes or for Colindale staff going back to the depot earlier than they should! Only eleven minutes running time was given from Canons Park to Colindale depot and it was not unreasonable for crews to nick a few minutes in this way if the vehicle was finishing at CE. Continuing with the theme of pinching a few minutes, crews on some 664s/666s running into Colindale depot from Edgware terminus would jump another 'bus by changing their poles from the siding wires to those coming down from Canons Park. This enabled them to get back to CE a few minutes early. One morning, a 666 crew were instructed to run their 'bus in due to a staff cut; this will be called CE24. On the stand was CE23, so CE24's driver signalled to the conductor of CE23 to pull his poles down. CE23's conductor was pulling the nearside boom down when CE24 went straight past him, resulting in CE24 dewiring as it hit CE23's offside pole. CE23's conductor had the bamboo pole snatched from his grasp by all the swinging trolley-booms, his bamboo shooting up in the air and landing in the roadway. Why CE24's driver had done this, I don't know and can only assume that he was misled into thinking that the first pole being drawn away from the wire was in fact the second one. By the time the four booms had been placed back on the wires, the time that was to have been saved was lost, although CE24 was actually in front of CE23. This was a sloppy bit of trolleybus work but spectator-wise it was good entertainment to the onlookers with four crew members trying to restore order to the chaos.

On one occasion at Tally Ho, I pulled out a bamboo and caught it under the front valance of the 'bus behind, a bit of twiddling with the grappling hook freed it. It was always wise to look behind when withdrawing a bamboo pole as it could trip up and injure pedestrians – there were instances of this happening. When new, vehicles were fitted with a flap at the

end of the pole holder to prevent bamboos from protruding, but through the passage of time the flaps came off, not to be replaced. This led to bamboos not being fully pushed up the holder and occasionally I would be following another trolleybus when I would see that one was sticking out from beneath it. When this happened I would endeavour to attract the conductor's attention by pointing to the bamboo – this wasn't always successful though. On one occasion, at Tally Ho, I tripped over a pole that was sticking out of its holder having not been pushed right in when it was previously used; I stumbled but recovered my footing and shoved it back into its rightful position. Some men didn't know their own strength and when they pulled a bamboo out of its holder, not only would it come out in one go but might also pass them by a few feet. Normally, two three or four pulls were needed to draw one out.

The caution with which bamboo poles should be treated is illustrated by an incident that occurred when I was following a 613 at the Kings Cross end of Grays Inn Road. I was on a 621 and we were both going to turn left into Swinton Street to traverse the Holborn Loop in a clockwise direction. The conductor of the 613 had pulled the frog handle and returned to the 'bus. The 613 was then delayed for a minute by other road traffic; also held up was a cyclist who stopped between me and the 613. The cyclist hadn't noticed that about two feet of bamboo pole was sticking out from the holder beneath the 613 and that his bicycle spokes were caught in the grappling hook of the bamboo. It had not been replaced properly on the last occasion it had been used. When the 613 turned left, the bike pulled the bamboo completely out of the holder with the cyclist looking on in sheer bewilderment. The crew hadn't heard it being pulled out – maybe they were deep in conversation. An inspector came rushing across to the cyclist and good humouredly said, "What's your game, stealing 18 feet of London Transport's property!". The bamboo was disentangled from the bike and the inspector put it in the gutter on the other side of Grays Inn Road and waited for the 613 to return. On the Holborn routes, the vehicle followed in was normally the one followed out, and when we came back to the top of Swinton Street the inspector flagged down the driver of the 613. Although I did not hear the exchange of words between the inspector and the crew it would have been along the lines of "Have you lost anything?". Being unaware of anything untoward they'd have replied "No". Producing the bamboo pole, the inspector would have said " What about this then!". The bamboo was replaced and the crew would have been reminded that they should ensure that bamboo poles were put away securely in future. The inspector did not get his book out so there was no report. There would be a time in the future when the inspector would need a favour off the crew concerned and this incident would be stored in his memory and the debt called in later.

A bamboo pole is placed through the back handrail of 1528 and into the lower saloon – this prevents passengers from boarding this 'dead' trolleybus at the bottom of Tally Ho bus station. By already showing FINSBURY PARK STATION, this indicates that a last minute staff cut has occurred.

1521's route number matches the numerals of its registration plate; it has just turned left from Jolly Butchers Hill into Bounds Green Road at Wood Green. On the 'up' track and 'down' track, recording skates can be seen – 1521 is about to pass under the northbound one. *Fred Ivey.*

ACCOUTREMENTS

TRACTION STANDARDS

The running wires, from which trolley heads picked up electricity to power the traction motor, were attached to twin line hangers which in turn were fixed to span wires. The spans stretched across the road and were attached to steel traction standards. These were in three sections of gradually reducing diameter, welded together to produce a pole of tapering appearance, each was about an inch or so narrower at the top than the bottom. The vast majority were eight and a half inches in diameter at the top and thirty-one feet in length. At junctions, where more substantial support was required to support the weight of the heavy overhead fittings, more standards were used. These were often larger, heavier poles up to forty feet in height and about twelve inches in diameter (all measurements refer to the top of the pole). Standards were normally positioned opposite each other at forty yard intervals (the legal maximum), but on curves in the road they were often closer together. It was necessary in some places to use bracket arms instead of span wires – some stretched right across the road while others, some to a bowstring design, only reached part way. At Finchley Central and New Southgate, extra long span wires were used as standards could not be positioned on the railway bridges there. Occasionally a span wire would snap – through old age or errant trolley arms. This wouldn't delay the service as drivers could proceed with caution. The matter would soon be reported and a tower wagon crew despatched to rectify the matter.

By law, London Transport were allowed to position traction standards wherever they wished to on the pavement. No fee was paid to local councils for this – wayleaves were only paid where standards were placed on private land, e.g. front gardens and railway property. For identification purposes, each had a white number painted onto it. The hollow standards had a circular concrete haunch at the base. This was to stop water seeping into the ground and corroding the six feet of pole beneath. To prevent rainwater entering from above, the standards were capped with a finial. I vividly recall, as a youngster, seeing finials lying in a heap on the ground, by the Winchester pub in the Archway Road in 1938 when the trolleybus overhead was being erected. A few days later they had been placed on the top of the standards. It looked really strange – green traction standards with shiny copper finials on top of them. The finials were soon painted green. The bottom couple of feet of each standard was painted black – possibly as an antidote to the corrosive effects of dogs living alongside trolleybus routes! Rosettes (wall attachments) were fixed at places where traction poles could not be positioned.

The last day that trolleybuses could be seen at Moorgate was Tuesday 7th November 1961; it was not a foggy evening so the fairy lights here were not really required. Probably, just for the sense of occasion, an inspector has turned them on. *Hugh Taylor.*

Some were fitted to an insurance company's building on the left turn into Finsbury Square at Moorgate. They could also be seen at fire stations, Underground stations and in trolleybus depots.

Many councils used traction standards for street lighting. With the trolleybuses coming off, alternatives were required, and most put up new lighting standards in their place. These became unintended targets as there were cases of trolleybooms dewiring and hitting the lamp fittings, causing the glass to shatter. If possible, staff would re-wire and drive off! Council officials were none the wiser, though they probably had their suspicions. Throughout the trolleybus era there were many instances of trolleybooms dewiring and striking traction standards. This was metal against metal, and trolleybooms always came off second best.

FAIRY LIGHTS

Fairy lights were a line of light bulbs positioned between two sets of wires where it was considered wise to give drivers a clear indication of the position of the overhead. They were a good guide in foggy weather and were to be seen at a number of places on our routes. The lights were turned on by either a tower wagon crew or inspectors – a ladder was used to reach the switch boxes which were positioned on traction standards. The same staff turned them off. Traffic circulars of the late 1930s stated that conductors of the last 'buses should switch them off. This never happened in my days and I can't see how it could as the boxes that held the switches were higher than arm's length.

GUARD WIRES

Since early trolleybus times there had been numerous instances of dewired trolley arms going through upstairs windows of shops and department stores; London Transport had to pay out for new panes of glass that were broken by wayward trolleybooms. To obviate this, guard wires were strung loosely between traction standards at strategic locations. In essence, they were restraining wires and were effective in arresting wayward trolleybooms. Made from span wire they were strung in horizontal and vertical form. One retailer to suffer frequent damage was Abbots which was the first shop on the left-hand side of Seven Sisters Road opposite the Nags Head at Holloway. As I regularly passed these mesh guard wires at this location, I noticed that they became ragged as drivers sometimes still crossed the junction too quickly on their northbound trips.

RECORDING SKATES

These devices operated 'traffic interval impulse and recording clocks' whose function was to monitor the frequency of trolleybuses. The skates were positioned slightly above the traction wires at various locations throughout the system. Places on Finchley's routes where one was positioned in one direction only were near the bottom of Archway Road, Green Lanes Manor House and outside Colindale depot. Locations where they were fitted in both directions were at Ballards Lane Finchley, Rosemont Avenue Finchley, Golders Green and opposite St Michael's Church Wood Green. Two of the Finchley skates recorded in our depot output – where the other two did has not been ascertained. Each time a trolley head hit one of the skates a loud 'bump' was heard, an impulse was activated and a mark was stamped on a circular paper disc. The discs were changed early each morning and sent off to the appropriate department to check the regularity of the services. If there were equal gaps between the marks on the disc then a good service was being provided; in the peak hour the marks became a black smudgy line. If there were long gaps between the marks, the service was 'up the wall'. The skates at Golders Green recorded not only in the Finchley Road entrance of the Underground station but also in viewing chambers in the hall of London Transport's headquarters at 55 Broadway. The Manor House and Archway devices also recorded there.

SPIKES

Routes 521/621 passed Friern Hospital (formerly known as Colney Hatch Lunatic Asylum) in Friern Barnet Road. In tram times, the Metropolitan Electric Tramways had been directed to place spikes on collars on the northbound traction standards immediately outside the institution. When the trolleybuses came along the new traction standards were also fitted with these accoutrements; these were officially known as anti-climb guards but we referred to them as 'lunatic spikes'. It is commonly thought that the spikes were installed to prevent patients climbing over the wall, clambering onto the traction standards and then sliding down to freedom. This is a fallacy, for the standards were in their ordinary position, close to the kerb and could not be reached from the wall. The standards' *raison d'être* was to prevent ordinary people from shinning up them and peering into the grounds to see the 'unfortunates' – hence the 'anti-climb guard' terminology. Perhaps there should have been some spikes on the perimeter wall as very early one frosty morning, driver Terry Harwood and conductor Ken Graves saw one of the patients climb over the wall, jump down and make good his escape along Friern Barnet Road. He was barefoot and only wearing a nightshirt when he absconded. Terry and Ken mentioned this incident to other staff who for quite a while afterwards asked whether they'd see 'Frosty' again.

TWO HORIZONTAL LIGHTS

The combined frequencies of routes 609 and 645 meant that there were many occasions when three trolleybuses were scheduled to be at Barnet terminus at the same time. However, only two were allowed on the stand together and, as this was not visible from the previous bus stop (by the Red Lion public house), protection had to be given to prevent any more vehicles gaining the stand. It was accomplished in the following manner. A signal box was attached to a traction standard adjacent to the Red Lion, and when a trolleybus passed a skate on the overhead positive wire there, the top of two vertical white lights in the box lit up. If a second 'bus passed the skate when another one was on the stand the lower one was illuminated. This indicated that the stand was full and that no drivers should proceed past the Red Lion. Further movement could only be accomplished when the lower light in the signal box was extinguished. This was achieved by the trolley head of the first vehicle leaving touching a skate on the positive wire as it started to descend Barnet Hill. The skate sent an impulse to the signal box – the lower light went out, indicating that a trolleybus could proceed to the stand. However, it was not foolproof and occasionally drivers did not observe the light if they were finishing their day's work – knowing the stand was full they could use the overtaking loop and get back early. Other drivers missing the light would have to go slowly up to the terminus but, as it was almost impossible to have three trolleybuses on the stand, the inspector on duty would send the first 'bus out a couple of minutes early, telling the crew to wait at the bus stop on the other side of the road until departure time.

TROUGHING

At most places where trolleybuses passed beneath railway bridges, the overhead wires were held in wooden channels beneath the bridge. The channels were known as 'troughing' and were a safety feature as electric wires could not be fitted to the metalwork of bridges. The traction wires were held in place by metal ears. When we passed through troughing, there was a roar and an echo which could be heard in the cab. At East Finchley station there were two bridges but as they were at different heights, the northbound one was fitted with troughing while the southbound one was not. The longest piece of troughing to be negotiated was that under the bridge at Finsbury Park. This was always taken cautiously.

Many lines of troughing could be seen in Finchley depot. Running the length of the building, most were for parking

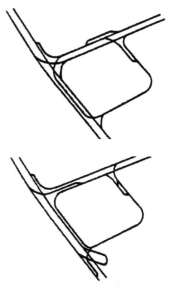

purposes only, and we had to swing our poles onto running-out wires to take up service. In the very early mornings when I was the only trolleybus moving in the depot, there would be a dull woody echoing sound as the trolleys clanked through the troughing. During the early morning run-out one day, a trolleybus dewired when it left the depot – the most likely cause was that the driver had forgotten he was on a dead-end road. Even though they had just slipped off, the booms were in an almost irretrievable position. A few 'buses could not get out until we had shunted a number of others backwards and forwards. Many of us were late leaving.

Above The Wood Green overhead layout as it was in 1953 and a layout that pertained from 1956.

Above Left The original arrangements for trolleybuses on the Lordship Lane services to terminate at Wood Green saw them turn in a clockwise direction. During that time, 1110 waits in Redvers Road while working on route 649A to Liverpool Street. To all intents and purposes 1110's driver should move up a bit as there are three vehicles behind him; in fact the last one is still partly in Lordship Lane – with its cab door open, maybe its driver is going to ask 1110's man to move up. However, the Stamford Hill driver knows his overhead, and positions 1110 in front of the trailing frog in case a trolleybus wishes to by-pass him. *Geoff Rixon.*

Centre Taken from the top deck of trolleybus 1458, this photograph shows the 'lunatic spike' attached to traction pole 59 outside Friern Barnet Mental Hospital. *Hugh Taylor.*

Left Redvers Road is being used in anti-clockwise fashion in this view taken on 3rd June 1961; on Saturday afternoons, route 643 worked only as far south as Shoreditch. By this time the blind in 1307's rear destination box was the only one in the Stamford Hill fleet that gave GT EASTERN STREET as a description for this short-working point; all the others showed SHOREDITCH. *Hugh Taylor.*

WIRING ALTERATIONS

When I started on the job, any trolleybuses short working on routes 521/621 at Wood Green from the Finchley direction had to turn left from Jolly Butchers Hill into Lordship Lane and then right into Redvers Road, where stand time was taken. When it was time to leave, they turned right into Buller Road and then right again onto the High Road where trolleybooms were swung onto the down track. This enabled 'buses to pick up passengers at the main boarding point. Sometime in the mid-fifties, London Transport wanted to do away with the right-hand turn made by 543s/625s/643s/649As moving from Wood Green High Road into Lordship Lane, and this was achieved by using Redvers Road in the opposite direction. The revision meant that these 521s/621s continued down the High Road where trolleybooms were moved onto a newly-positioned set of wires which formed part of the terminal arrangements for the Lordship Lane services. They then turned left into Buller Road and left again into Redvers Road where a frog handle was pulled to take them onto a set of wires that led into Lordship Lane. Another handle was operated a bit further on which enabled them to make a right turn up Jolly Butchers Hill. What had previously been a clockwise manoeuvre around Buller Road and Redvers Road was now an anti-clockwise movement.

Until 1st May 1956 most of the scheduled 521s/621s that turned at Wood Green from Finchley were late night journeys. Passengers waiting at the boarding point in the High Road just saw the back of them disappearing up the hill past the depot. These problems ceased from the following day when Wood Green 'turnbacks' were scheduled to turn around a traffic island at the top of Gladstone Avenue during the evening peaks. There were three duties that did four consecutive 'Wood Green shorts' as part of a day's work. Depending on what the service was like at the Holborn end, conductors could get either a real 'caning' or take just a few fares. The Gladstone Avenue circle had been constructed and used as a temporary measure when the Wood Green wiring was being remodelled in 1954. After its brief use, it became disused – now it was re-activated. Although this loop looked difficult to negotiate, most of our trolleybuses had relatively light steering and a good turning lock, and having power priority on the three crossovers, it was an easy manoeuvre to make. Before the wiring changes at Wood Green, passengers waiting in the High Road had the odd sight of seeing 521s/621s going south to Holborn Circus, while on the other side there were 543s/643s heading north to Holborn Circus.

1956 saw other changes to the overhead at Wood Green and a set of wires was erected that restored the facility for trolleybuses to turn from the Manor House direction – some battery manoeuvring had been needed for this since the 1954 changes. What it meant though was that a facing frog, three crossovers and a trailing frog had to be negotiated in quick succession, none of which had power priority. I never had to carry out this manoeuvre, but it must have been a nightmare for any Finchley driver who had to do this – 521s/621s were only curtailed at this point occasionally so there was little chance of getting across the pointwork without drawing power somewhere. To compound the situation, the two 'pull and hold' frogs in Redvers Road did not have power priority. Apparently there was no other manoeuvre in London where seven consecutive movements had to be made over dead sections of overhead. Conductors operated a frog handle in the High Road that took trolleybuses into Buller Road. In Redvers Road a frog handle had to be pulled to take trolleybooms onto an overtaking loop; another had to be operated at the top of this street so that 'buses could get into Lordship Lane. After a few yards they turned left into the High Road where trolleybooms were swung onto the outside set of wires. With three frog pulls and a trolley swing, this was not a popular manoeuvre with conductors.

When trolleybuses were introduced to Wood Green in 1938, vehicles entering the depot from the north could get in directly via the overhead. Though scheduled to go down to Wood Green itself and set down passengers before going back up the hill and running in, this rarely happened as it meant travelling via Lordship Lane, Redvers Road and Buller Road. Two frog pulls and a trolley swing needed to be carried out, and to avoid all this performance, most crews ran straight into the depot. This led to the frog and associated pointwork outside the depot soon being taken out with the hope that the 'buses would now go down into the High Road. The Wood Green staff had other ideas and, having pulled their poles down on Jolly Butchers Hill, freewheeled into the depot by a combination of battery and gravity power. The crews had outmanoeuvred London Transport who now gave up the battle and scheduled the 'buses to run straight in. The Wood Green staff didn't hang about getting their poles down and moving into the depot, and there was only a short delay if as many as three vehicles simultaneously wanted to get in. Trolleybuses making this manoeuvre had to wait for traffic coming up the hill to clear. Often it would not give way and many times I eased up on my northbound trip to let a 629 or 641 go in. Going the other way, we would often pick up Wood Green staff at their relief point in the High Road as this saved them walking uphill to the depot. They usually put their hand up as they were about to board – this indicated that they wanted a lift up the road. Knowing that they wanted to alight at the depot entrance we would ease up to let them off. Sometimes they gave us a couple of bells to let us know that they wanted to leave. When they left, some would give the side panel of the trolleybus a couple of raps to signify that they were off the vehicle.

There were two cases of temporary overhead being put up in the second half of 1956. While sewer works took place at Barnet, the overtaking loop was modified to take all movements. It led into the original wiring as vehicles started to descend the hill. Although it looked a tight manoeuvre, no problems were experienced – it was essential that vehicles left in the right order, so boom lowering was employed on the stand. Also, two sets of wires were put up in Nether Street, North Finchley while the roadway of the bus station was dug up in order to take out buried tramlines. Although it got a bit cluttered at times no major problems were experienced. When the roadworks were completed, and before we returned to the station, the overhead wiring there was upgraded to give more manoeuvrability than before.

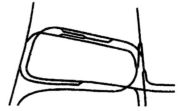

The overhead layouts before and after the road was resurfaced in Tally Ho bus station in 1956.

Tram tracks are being removed from Tally Ho bus station in 1956. They were last used in 1938, and had been covered over since then. Before trolleybuses return, a new wiring layout will be put in – for the moment, the previous one is still aloft. In the adjacent Nether Street, trolleybuses use the temporary terminus. In the left foreground, scotches are provided – drivers only used these occasionally. *Len Anderson.*

The temporary stand in Nether Street caused no operating problems. 660s (and depot-bound vehicles) used one set of wires while the 517, 521, 617 and 621 used the other. The two identifiable vehicles belong to Finchley depot. 320 is on the 660 with the conductor yet to alter the front blind – 909's has already been changed by the conductor to show ISLINGTON GREEN. *Don Thompson.*

Above While sewer works took place at Barnet in 1956, temporary wiring was in use. What had been the overtaking wire was extended into a tighter turning circle used by all vehicles – as can be seen it was within the original layout. For the duration of the work, the facing frog was set for the new inner circle; the other wire was not used at this time. Despite being tighter, it was still easy to get round in one turn. Conductor Eric Cannon is on the platform as 959 leaves for Moorgate on route 609. *Len Anderson.*

Left Near the top of Barnet Hill and adjacent to the Red Lion pub, the signal light box, which is fixed to traction standard 303A, shows that Barnet trolleybus stand is not full. This means that 1519 can proceed; in a few seconds time, 1519's positive trolley boom will touch the activating skate for the 'Barnet light'. The driver has already changed his destination blind for the return journey south. *Brian Pask.*

Opposite 'The Barnet light' apparatus was installed upon completion of the sewer works at Barnet. Prior to this, when three trolleybuses had been on the stand together the road became cluttered, impeding traffic entering Wood Street. The Barnet light eradicated the problem. Leaving the terminus is Finchley's 315 whose offside trolley boom will soon touch the skate that will extinguish the light further down the hill. *Heinz Zinram/London Transport Museum.*

136

The driver of Colindale's 232 is wisely keeping to the crown of the road as he passes through Whetstone after a snowfall. Wheel grip problems could arise in untouched snow and his actions will mean that 232 will be able to keep moving on its trip to Canons Park on route 645. *Don Thompson.*

FLOOD, FOG AND FREEZE

It had been raining heavily all night long when I turned up for early turn on Monday 9th July 1956. I had travelled to work on my motorcycle and had a problem crossing the North Circular Road at the junction with Finchley High Road due to flooding. However Jean, my clippie, and I were able to leave the depot on time on our trip to Holborn Circus. By the time we reached Wood Green, the High Road was badly flooded and through the window of Wheatland's furniture store I could see some chairs and light furniture bobbing up and down in the floodwater. Turnpike Lane was also awash and Green Lanes was flooded at Harringay near the junction with St Ann's Road where, by Allison Road, there was a car that had been abandoned on the northbound side of the road. I was driving 963 and was keeping to the crown of the road. A 641 going in the opposite direction came towards me like a destroyer, throwing up a big bow wave as it passed between 963 and the car (the 641 driver was definitely not observing the 5mph speed limit upon flooded roads). The water knocked out some of 963's electrics, bringing it to a halt. I could not get any response from the power pedal so changed over to battery, parked the 'bus in the kerb and pulled the poles down. It was still raining with the water level continuing to rise – eventually it was lapping over the platform meaning that passengers could not alight without getting very wet. Wood Green inspector Albert Billet, dressed appropriately in heavy raincoat and Wellington boots, soon turned up and took charge of the situation. He stopped an RT bus on route 29, boarded the immobilised 963, carried all of my passengers off piggy-back style, and put them onto it. There was nothing I could do, so from about 7.30am until 1pm we had to wait with another ten stranded trolleybuses (Finchley and Wood Green vehicles). I know there were eleven of us as I counted them on my treks to a nearby café to get refreshments for Jean and myself. Les Strutt and his wife-to-be, Diana, were also marooned. The 'buses were out of action between St Ann's Road and the bridge by Harringay Arena – some trolleybuses were not affected by the flood-water and were able to carry on. Despite the water level receding later in the morning, the eleven 'buses were still immobile, so we had to wait for breakdown wagons to arrive. Priority was given to towing in 'buses on the 645 and 660, so those of us in the Harringay area had to wait our turn. We were not allowed to leave our vehicles unattended, so it was not until the wagons turned up that we were able to make our way back to the depot. Jean paid in a mere eleven shillings for we had only worked from Finchley to Harringay.

Rule 78 stated that a one hundred yard interval between each vehicle should be maintained on flooded roads – this was impractical, and we carried on as normal. The same rule said that trolleybuses should not be driven through floods when the level of water was higher than the bottom edge of the lifeguard slat – this part of the rule was observed.

Drivers had to be very careful when snowy or icy conditions prevailed for, unlike a motorbus, there were no gears to help control a trolleybus on descending hills. When the snow froze, they could only be driven at walking pace. It was easy to get into a slide and in my conducting days, I remember a northbound 609 turning full circle on the downward gradient of High Road Finchley at the 'Green Man' by the North Circular Road. We were the second of four 'buses that came to a halt. It was deemed wise to wait as there was a lot of traffic coming the other way. However, 'Ginger' Tuttlebury, the fourth in line, wanted to have a go at it. Three of us pulled our poles down and he went past us. He got into an uncontrollable slide, with the back end coming towards the kerb with the vehicle revolving clockwise – it ended up turning 360 degrees. He was sliding on the crown of road, with booms swinging around in all directions – how on earth the wires didn't come down I'll never know. He had lost the steering, but amazingly did not hit any other vehicle and ended up in the same direction in which he wanted to go! Putting trolleybooms onto running wires when there was snow underfoot was always a problem, and on many occasions when doing this at Tally Ho, I slipped and slid all over the place. We had the same problem here when we attempted to re-wire his 'bus – eventually we got them up and he made it away. A short time later when there was less traffic coming the other way, we re-wired our 'buses and eventually reached North Finchley safely. There were some places that were very difficult to ascend and descend in snowy weather – Barnet Hill, Childs Hill, ascending Bounds Green Road from the North Circular Road, and Cemetery Hill in High Road East Finchley. In snow, some conductors sensibly used Wellington boots, and Mike Norris, a friend of mine at FY, often wore them at these times. This was sensible, as conductors had to plough through deep water and slush many times when operating frog handles during the course of a day.

One of the most difficult driving days I experienced was due to snow and ice. I was on an early turn on the '21s and had been able to complete the first half of the duty without losing any mileage – two trips to Holborn and back. When Jean and I came out of the canteen at Tally Ho after our meal relief, 927 was waiting for us on the stand – this enabled us to leave on time. We were only a few minutes down at Holborn and departed for North Finchley straightaway. The snow hadn't let up, but because of traffic on the way back, most of it was turning to slush. We reached Wood Green still only a few minutes late. There were no problems ascending Jolly Butchers Hill, but on turning into Bounds Green Road, conditions deteriorated for the snow was much more compacted and in places turning to ice. Now I was finding trouble pulling away from stops. I was giving 927 first notch and then second notch but all I was getting was the wheels spinning on the icy roadway; zzz zzz zzz was the noise they made. They were not biting the road surface. I was not meeting with much success, so on ascertaining from Jean that the road was clear behind, I put 927 into reverse and moved back about twelve inches. I then put it in forward mode and attempted to pull away again. This was successful, as with a bit of momentum I was able to get over the ice that was causing the trouble. It was all trial and error, and getting away was a problem that repeated itself on a number of occasions on this trip. Using reverse a few times was the answer. When I had to stop for passengers to board and alight, I didn't pull into the kerb as the snow was deeper there and I would have got stuck. I called through to the saloon and told Jean to inform passengers that I wouldn't be stopping at the top of the incline by New Southgate Station (as I wanted to keep the 'bus going) but would halt around the corner in Friern Barnet Road. On leaving this stop, I saw another '21 about three hundred yards ahead of me. When he reached the long sweeping curve in Woodhouse Road by Woodhouse School, he almost came to a standstill because his wheels were spinning on the icy road. Suddenly four teenagers appeared from nowhere; armed with sacks and a couple of planks of wood, they assisted the driver by thrusting them under the rear wheels which gave them adhesion. I was relieved to see him moving along as I was still having problems of my own – wheel spin. Eventually I got 927 past Woodhouse School and reached Tally Ho. We were about twenty five minutes late finishing so were paid overtime for our troubles.

In adverse weather conditions (snow or rain), a trolleybus might become 'live'; this was due to static current, and a passenger could get a mild electric shock. They would feel a tingling sensation in their hands when touching a grab or hand rail – these seemed to be the main objects from which people got a shock. I remember receiving a shock from a handrail when we were at Tally Ho; I took the 'bus out of service for rectification. If a trolleybus became 'live' on the road, passengers would be transferred to another one and the faulty vehicle would be taken out of service.

Fog could be a problem for trolleybus drivers as they could inadvertently stray from beneath the running wires. It was the worst time to have a dewirement and it was more than likely that both poles would come off. It could be a right old performance trying to locate the booms, for crews had no idea where they were and they just had to poke around with their bamboo until they found them. There was one particular foggy night in 1952 when the 'bus I was working on drifted away from the overhead. My driver for the day, Johnny Bull, lost the kerb line at the junction of the North Circular Road and Station Road, New Southgate. Only one of the booms came off but this really was a problem and it took us ages trying to locate it with our bamboo pole. Eventually when we

did get hold of the trolley arm it was try, try, try again until we eventually found the overhead wire.

Another episode in fog occurred nearby and is best described as the 'fishing party' incident. I was driving along Bounds Green Road and came across a string of trolleybuses that were making their way back to Finchley. Initially I thought it was a general hold-up in fog but before long I found out that the front one had dewired with both booms coming off and there wasn't a bamboo pole between the lot of us. Jean became very cold because of all the waiting around, so I suggested that she get into the cab which was warmer – she opened the window between the saloon and cab, clambered in and sat on one of the ledges there. Eventually two bamboos were obtained from trolleybuses coming the other way and the staff of the dewired 'bus were fishing around for the booms for ages. By the time that everything had been sorted out we were all so late that it didn't really matter. We were all past caring as we knew that we would all receive a hefty overtime docket.

When drivers dewired in fog it was more than likely that they had driven too far to the right. Therefore, the booms would be on the nearside of the 'bus. Having batteried nearer to the kerb, they would start searching on that side first, and if they were lucky they would feel the bamboo strike against one of the booms and would then get it under a retaining hook which was the best place for it. If it had been replaced on the wires it could have impeded the search for the other one. The trouble was that they didn't know if they had the positive or negative boom under the hook and when they got the second boom down, hopefully quite easily, they might find that the booms were crossed on the roof. Eventually, it would be ascertained which was which. The really interesting part came when re-wiring. Staff would get into the middle of the road and raise the positive boom first and poke around until they got a blue flash – then it would be prod, prod, prod until they got it on the wire. The second boom would be easier to rewire as they'd just have to nudge it against the boom they had already put up and then move it a couple of feet until it was on the wire. In my opinion, the best way to resolve matters once the booms were 'roofed' would be to poke around with the bamboo between the positive and negative wires until it could be felt bashing against both wires. The position of the overhead was now ascertained, and the poles could be put back up. Fog was only a problem if it was very thick, so at places such as the bottom of Barnet Hill and by New Southgate gasworks where it would hang in the hollows, we just had to be cautious.

When dense fog materialised during the daytime and early evening, 'fogmen' were positioned to pilot trolleybuses across difficult crossings and junctions. The rule book stated "The points where these men are to be expected will be published from time to time". However, I never saw one of these notices. Staff carrying out this task were either light duty men or inspectors. I recall, as a conductor, seeing fogmen at the Nags Head. No chance of drivers knowing where, and where not, to take power here – hope for the best and if there was arcing on the special work then so be it. Outside of those hours, or if no fogman was around, conductors would assist. I helped my driver across The Angel junction one day as it was impossible for him to see how to be in the correct position under the wires when turning from City Road into Islington High Street. The post-war fogs made visibility so poor that even the vehicle's fog lamp was ineffective. Therefore, it was sometimes necessary for conductors to use flares and to walk in front of their trolleybuses to guide their drivers. The flares were handed out by inspectors who kept them in a bin next to their box; they were made from paraffin wax and were supplied by Brocks Fireworks. The wax wore down and staff had to be careful so as to avoid their hands being burnt; they lasted for two or three hours and were left in the depot when finished with.

There was a really bad smog in 1952 – it lasted for a week. I had to use flares one day and walk in front of my driver, Vic Collins. We left Holborn in daylight, about 3pm – it was creep, creep, creep all the way to North Finchley. It took ages to get back; not many people boarded my 'bus as it was quicker to walk. However, I ensured that those who did ride paid a fare as from time to time I got back on. Drivers had to plod along on first notch, which was not good for the trolleybuses as it meant the resistors got very hot. Ron Cook and I were the first two 'buses of our batch back – well after 7pm. Then everybody ran them in as crews were ordered back into the shed. A lot of us then went to the Moss Hall Tavern in Ballards Lane, close to the depot. When we were about to leave, a suggestion was made that some of us go to the house of one of our conductresses for supper – so to Peggy Scriviner's house we went, where we had baked beans and sprats. It was the only food she had in the house. Three of us ended up in her double bed all night, with her and her flatmate Kathy (who was a clippie at the depot) sleeping in another room. Kathy was a character in her own right and if she mislaid the webbing for her Gibson ticket machine, used pieces of string. It was all a bit of a lark really, three London trolleybusmen (Dennis, Ron and myself) all sleeping in the same bed. What with all the fooling about, none of us got much sleep. Peggy lived at Friern Barnet and as the next day was Friday we had to go to the depot on a 521/621 to collect our wages. The explanation we gave to driver Fred Nottage, who was on the 'bus in his civvies also going to get his money, as to why we had spent the night together, was met with a disbelieving look – but the whole episode was totally innocent.

When I was working with Charlie Bonner one day, it became extremely foggy and when we got to Acton Market Place on our way to Hammersmith he said "I've had enough, we're going no further". Drivers had to use their discretion about whether to continue in dense fog. He told me to pull the poles down in King Street and he went to a mobile snack bar and bought sausage and onion sandwiches and cups of tea for the pair of us. We consumed them on the 'bus. We got back to North Finchley very late but as it was only our first spell of duty this did not concern us.

During the 1952 smog, driver 'Lofty' Nash and conductor Phillips ('Big Phil'), had taken a very long time getting from North Finchley to Islington Green. When they got there, they took the 609 into the loop, dropped its poles and went into the Blue Hall cinema where they watched a full film, hoping in the meantime that the fog would clear. After the film was over they returned to the vehicle, upped the poles and headed back to Finchley. Vehicles were taking such a long time to carry out their trips that inspectors didn't know who was where and what instructions crews were working to. Any crew could have done what they wanted to really but this one really had had enough and wanted a break. They made no secret about it and it was the talk of the depot for a day or two.

On very frosty mornings, the first trolleybuses on each route were fitted with 'iron' shoes in the trolley heads. The shoes were made of gun metal and cut ice that had formed on the traction wires overnight. There was an adverse consequence in that they scraped the overhead, so it was essential that they were changed over for ordinary carbon skids before too long. The first trolleybuses to Barnet, Cricklewood, Holborn and Moorgate were fitted with iron skids (the sections to Canons Park and Hammersmith were covered, but by other depots). When our trolleybuses returned to Tally Ho after their first journey, a breakdown wagon would be waiting for them. The change would be speedily effected by placing a set of ladders against the rear of the 'bus, climbing up them and changing the skids. Sometimes it was carried out by the men opening the rear emergency window and standing on the window ledge. When the change had been completed we would be relieved, as the skids caused a lot of arcing and flashing as well as creating a screeching noise. Even though 'skid trolleybuses' had been through on frosty mornings, it was still spectacular for the next few 'buses as there was still a lot of flashing, sparking and noise coming from the frost-covered overhead.

A trolleybus depot on a winter's morning. There were no heaters in the parking areas and with the depot doors open, the trolleybuses at the front were likely to have frosted-up windscreens. I scraped the ice off with the timecard – this enabled me to see clearly. Then I would get into a freezing cold cab, set all the controls into the 'on' position and be away. All for nine pounds, six shillings a week in 1956.

During hot weather, the copper traction wires could expand and become slack. I could see the wires looping downwards between twin-line hangers. When this happened it was best to keep directly underneath the traction wires. Experience told me that I should ease off on the power pedal at these times as to go too fast, even on straight wires, could cause a dewirement. If another trolleybus was in front and I saw its booms oscillating, I would hold back in case its booms shot off the wires. After the hot spell, the wires would revert to their usual tension. Extreme cold did not seem to affect the overhead and I am not aware of traction wires becoming brittle or taut at these times.

When they had a few minutes to spare, trolleybus crews weren't always in the refreshment hut at Tally Ho bus station; here some of my colleagues are deep in conversation alongside 1514. Fourth from the left is driver Covington. Doubtless, the crews will later breach rule fourteen which stated that drivers and conductors were not to converse with each other when a vehicle was in motion unless it was necessary to do so on the grounds of safety. This was one of the most frequently broken rules and now I am beyond recrimination from London Transport I confess to having broken it on a daily basis! This picture was taken in 1961 as the bus stop flag contains a plate for route 17 which could only be seen alongside a 621 route trolleybus that year. The question is though, where are the plates for the 521/621? *Ron Kingdon.*

STAFF SHENANIGANS

In most workplaces, there are staff who want to make a bob or two and others who want to take short-cuts. There are also those who want to pit their wits against supervisors; all this occurred in trolleybus work. It was a mind game but never nasty. This chapter details some of the characters who performed a 'service' for their colleagues and some of the dodges and activities that others got up to.

The refreshment hut at Tally Ho was where information was given and sought. Facts about passengers, good and bad, were exchanged and staff's indiscretions, both on and off the job, were bandied about. Rumours, often good-natured, were spread about but I didn't take much notice of these as they were usually embellished. On the matter of rumours, one thing I learned about London Transport was that I never believed anything until it took place. The hut was used by trolleybus staff from Colindale, Finchley, Highgate and Stonebridge depots. It was here that details of incidents were passed either by word of mouth or secondhand; they tended to be true with little exaggeration.

Starting with Highgate, one of their drivers was nick-named "Marks & Spencer" on account that he could often be seen in the refreshment hut with a large suitcase selling all kinds of wares. If it was his day off on a Friday, he would be there for most of the day as it was pay day when staff had plenty of money in their pockets. He carried the suitcase in the trolleybus cab and even during his stand time at North Finchley would lug it between there and the hut. If he was working a spreadover duty he would also turn up for a couple of hours. Pens, screwdrivers, children's paints could be bought; anything he could lay his hands on. I bought two sets of saws from him, one of which I still have; I also bought a leather holder to keep my trolleybus driver's badge in.

All depots had staff who could turn their hands to various trades and, at Colindale, Cyril Bulman was the barber. If someone wanted a haircut they came to an arrangement to meet in the canteen at a set time where the shearing took place. Another source of income came when Edgware garage's route 52A commenced. It terminated on the depot forecourt, and their male staff soon found that they could get a cheaper deal with him than at their regular barber's. As there was not enough time for him to deal with them at CE, he arranged 'home visits' where he would not only cut their hair but their sons' as well. I don't know whether any of the supervisors availed themselves of Bulman's expertise, but knowing what depot life is like, I expect they did. All in all, a 'nice little earner' for Bulman who presumably did not declare his earnings to the taxman!

Friday in the Finchley ouput was a hive of activity. As well as staff on duty, many of those who were resting, or who were on late turn that day, came up for their pay in their civvies. They wanted to get their wages as soon as possible so they could give their wives some housekeeping money. This was also the day that staff paid their weekly union dues to the TGWU rep. Activities designed to persuade staff to part with their hard-earned cash proliferated; raffles were held, money was collected for the Christmas Club, and many items changed hands. Boxing and wrestling match tickets were available from driver 'Covvy' Covington who was obviously making money for himself; I availed myself of some for Rose and me from time to time. Johnny Bull bred rabbits for eating, and some Fridays he had two or three for sale. They would hang, head downwards, from a meathook which was attached to a drainpipe bracket on the depot wall. When sold, he wrapped them in newspaper. Presumably those who bought them while they were on duty, kept them at the depot somewhere. With life being what it is though, and drivers being able to go home once they had finished work at the bus station, there may have been instances of the deceased animals being carried in trolleybus cabs. The clubroom was upstairs, and the number of people playing cards and snooker there on this day of the week was swollen. For those who had come up for their pay and weren't working that day, many went to the Moss Hall pub (in Ballards Lane, virtually opposite the depot) where they would down a few pints of Ben Truman ale.

By sharing route 645 with Colindale depot, we got to know some of their staff quite well and chat with some of their crews at Barnet and Canons Park. A name that became familiar to both depots' staff was Jim Drewett, a newly appointed bus inspector. When he was first promoted to this grade he had to cover for regular inspectors who were on holiday, and he was doing this when he came to Tally Ho for a short time in 1957. He wanted to make a name for himself and was booking staff for minor indiscretions, but we knew he'd come a cropper one day, so weren't really bothered by him. In fact, we could have made things nasty for him with the police, for somehow he had picked up how to drive trolleybuses and when the stand became too full (no crews for them) he would drive them round to the depot. We knew this was against the law as he only had a licence for motorbuses.

Drewett met his match with Colindale driver Charlie Beart. Having been given a permanent position at Edgware bus station, it was part of Drewett's duties to check on the nearby trolleybus terminus from time to time. On the first

On route 666, Stonebridge's 1625 is about to turn from the northbound carriageway onto the southbound one in Edgware High Street. Although the 645 was not one of my main routes, I often found myself on there when I did some overtime or worked my day off; therefore I had to be well-versed with what was required on the overhead layouts. At Edgware, northbound 645 conductors had to pull for Canons Park; this was unusual as, over the whole system, frogs were normally set for the 'straight'. Power priority was given on the facing frog to 'buses turning, so if I was going to Canons Park, once my conductor had pulled the frog handle I would give the trolleybus a couple of notches of power to allow me to coast through the pointwork and then wait until he or she was back on board. It was at this location that inspector Jim Drewett boarded Charlie Beart's 666 one night and despite rapid ringing of the bell cord was carried all the way to Colindale depot.

night of one of Beart's seven day late shifts, Drewett saw him drive a 666 straight 'in and out' of Edgware. The 666 was only going back to the depot and was not the last of the night, so it wasn't going to inconvenience anybody and would allow Beart to get home a few minutes earlier. The next night, Drewett stood at the final alighting stop in Edgware High Street and boarded the 666 before it turned across the gap in the carriageway. He told the conductor not to ring the 'bus off as he wanted to have a word with Beart who had a good idea of what was going to be said. Before Drewett had time to walk to the front of the 'bus, Beart closed the partition between cab and saloon and drove 'in and out of Edgware' again. Drewett was furious and, despite frantic ringing of the bell, was carried all the way to Colindale depot. Beart parked the vehicle on the forecourt and got out to walk to his nearby home. Drewett confronted Beart and said "I'm booking you for leaving early from Edgware, running in ten minutes early, not maintaining headway and failing to stop at a number of compulsory stops". Beart just said "Yeah, yeah, yeah," and continued his walk home. Drewett then said to the conductor, "I'm booking you too". "What for?" was the conductor's response. Drewett said, "Assisting him to run early by pulling the frog handle at the depot". The conductor replied "He would have come in anyway and left his poles up in the air". Drewett says, "Well, you're both on". The conductor could not keep a straight face and was also booked for insolence. Drewett made his reports out there and then and left

them at the depot for the Colindale guvn'r to look at the following day. Drewett was not pleased that he had to wait for another vehicle to take him back to Edgware. The next day, when Drewett started work, he was told to report to Colindale depot as soon as possible, and believing that a pat on the back was due made haste to CE. On arrival, he was told to go and see Harry Monk, the CDI, who more or less hauled him into the office and sat him down on a chair saying, "What's your game, upsetting my staff. They work hard and if they find themselves a few minutes down, they make the effort to make up the time and not lose mileage. If they want to pinch a few minutes at night and they're not the last 'bus, that's alright by me". Monk concluded by saying "I don't want to see reports such as these again" and hurled them into a rubbish bin. Suitably chastised, Drewett slunk away. Suffice it to say that on the following nights of Beart's late turn, he went straight 'in and out' of Edgware with Drewett looking on knowing full well that he couldn't do anything about it. When Beart came in the day after his run-in with Drewett he fully expected to be called in to see Harry Monk and be carpeted. This did not happen, either then or on any of the following days, and it was not until about a month later when curiosity got the better of him that he just had to ask Monk whether he wanted to see him about anything. Monk said "If it's about you crossing Drewett's path some weeks back, I told him not to go upsetting my staff, as I know you all work hard here". That was the end of the matter. Driver 1 Inspector 0.

Drewett mellowed, for one morning later on Colindale crew Charlie Armitage and Frank Sharville (driver and conductor respectively) got booked by him for arriving six minutes early at Edgware on a 666. On their next trip, Armitage and Sharville got a right hammering as the vehicle in front was not running – despite this they really got on with it and managed to get back to Edgware on time. Drewett was aware of the gap in the service and was astounded that they had been able to maintain their scheduled time. Appreciative of their efforts he said to them, "I'll forget that earlier booking then". A good example of give and take.

Many routes had relief points at places other than outside their home depots. One of these was Craven Park where Stonebridge crews changed over on routes 628, 660, 664 and 666, the latter three changing mid-journey. Route control and crew reliefs were supervised by inspectors for whom London Transport had converted a retail shop into an office. In the years of staff shortages, inspectors had to make sure that trolleybuses for which there were no crews were either run into Stonebridge depot or were parked with booms down. A practice for staff on routes that took over mid-journey was to arrive at a relief point a few minutes early as the crew coming off would probably come up a couple of minutes sharp. This allowed for the changeover to take place, the 'bus to depart on time and gave the crews the opportunity to have a few words together – maybe the conductor telling his counterpart that a passenger needed to be put off at a certain place. If there was a minor fault with the 'bus then this fact would be relayed to the relieving driver so that he was aware of the situation.

One day, Stonebridge driver Joe McKeown arrived at Craven Park to take over a Hammersmith-bound vehicle. I will call this SE10 on the 660. As was normal practice, he and his conductor sat on a wall waiting for it to turn up; SE9 arrived but no there was no sign of its driver. An inspector came marching over to find out what was happening, and assuming SE9 was McKeown's told him firmly that he was to take it over immediately. He thought McKeown was time-wasting. Usually, there was a good working relationship between inspectors and crews but the inspector must have got out of the wrong side of the bed that morning. McKeown, sensing that the inspector was about to make a pig's ear of the situation, said "No I won't" which to the inspector was like offering a red rag to a bull. He again told McKeown to take over SE9, an instruction which was again refused. The inspector was now losing his patience and then said "If you don't take over this 'bus right now you'll be suspended.", to which McKeown replied "I'll not be taking over this trolley-bus". Normally inspectors cannot suspend staff, but the inspector thought that McKeown was deliberately disobeying an order and considered it to be within his scope to do this. He told McKeown that he was suspended and without a word McKeown went home leaving the inspector with SE9. Of course, as soon as McKeown left, SE10 turned up and the inspector now had two consecutive 660s with no drivers and two conductors. Both had to be taken out of service and disgruntled passengers mobbed the inspector who had to make arrangements for drivers to run the trolleybuses back

light to Stonebridge depot for which they would have to be paid as it was not part of their duty. McKeown was not on the telephone and bearing in mind that suspensions are normally for a few days, thought he would take advantage of the situation. No sooner had he got home than he told his wife that they were going off to the seaside for a few days, which they did. When McKeown returned he found that the Stonebridge CDI had arranged for a letter to be put through his letterbox asking him to report to the depot as soon as possible. As McKeown had no quarrel with the CDI he went to the depot the same day, where the CDI told him that the inspector had been severely reprimanded for his actions and asked if it would be possible for him to work that day. McKeown said that he would, providing he was paid for his time off. The CDI said that he was going to do this anyway as he was the victim and not the transgressor. Driver 2 Inspector 0.

Colindale driver Peter Power was a bit of a 'Jack the lad'. I need to say now that if an Inspector wanted to report a member of staff for any offence, he had to tell them there and then what it was. Bob Hatton, one of the two regular inspectors at Colindale depot, wanted to 'stick him on' one day for running a 'bus into the depot early. To avoid the 'booking' Power tried to give Hatton the slip and there was a bit of a chase between trolleybuses parked in the depot. Eventually, and amazingly, the stoutly built Hatton was able to contain the situation to just one 'bus, with him at the front and the younger and fitter Power at the back, or Hatton on the near-side and Power on the offside. Anyway, there was all this ducking and diving, bobbing and weaving, and eventually Hatton got the upper hand and they were both going round in the same direction. To win the tussle, Power resorted to a marvellous piece of trolleybus initiative and when it was his turn to run round the back of the 'bus he pulled the bamboo pole out a few feet. Hatton comes charging round, sees the bamboo ready to trip him up, and performs a number of hops, skips and jumps to avoid the pole and its hook. He kept his balance but in the meantime Power had run out the depot and up the Edgware Road – no report! On another occasion, Sid Turner the other inspector at Colindale, was able to book Power. Power had been instructed to run a 645 into the depot from Canons Park as there was no relieving crew. It must have been a quiet time when headways were wide, such as a Sunday morning, for Power ran the 'bus into Colindale depot about thirty-five minutes early. It went like this. Sensing he could come off well before his scheduled time, Power left Barnet and went like a rocket all the way to Canons Park. When he got there he went without his stand time, jumped the 645 in front by getting its crew to pull their poles down, and flew back to the depot. When he arrived there, Turner – having seen him from the canteen window on the way north – was waiting for him. Not only did he get booked for arriving at the depot excessively early but was also booked for running early on his way to Canons Park – a case of being booked 'on the down' before he was due to go by 'on the up'! Power had the last laugh though, for on the final night of trolleybuses he was again told to run his 645 in from Canons Park due to the fact that there was no relieving crew. Seeing that Bob Hatton was not out on the roadway due to the extreme cold (he was probably in the canteen with the revellers) and there were no passengers on board, he got his conductor to pull the frog handle and they went straight into the depot to join the party. The appeal of that was stronger than a last drive to Canons Park in a trolleybus.

A spectacular incident concerning Power occurred when he was driving the staff trolleybus one night. He was scheduled to leave Barnet at 12.17am, arriving back at the depot at 1.09am – this was the first part of a night duty. It was general practice to leave a few minutes late and go like the clappers back to the depot, enjoying the drive at the same time. However, coming through Whetstone he failed to observe the boards and red warning lamps of some roadworks. Seeing them at the last minute he swerved and avoided them but the unexpected in-swing of the booms caused them to leave the overhead. Peter went round to the back of the trolleybus but found that there was no bamboo stowed beneath. He had two alternatives: one was to walk to North Finchley where he would have got one in either the bus station or the depot, or he could get on the roof and bring the booms down by hand. He opted for the latter, first of all battering the vehicle so that the booms were brought down lower by dragging them under a span wire. The booms were still outstretched though, so Power and his conductor, accompanied by the sole passenger on board, then clambered out of the emergency exit and onto the roof. The passenger had been persuaded to help by being told that he would get home quicker if he assisted. Grabbing hold of the booms one by one they moved their hands along the booms' length and drew them down and across until they were level with the traction wires. They were able to successfully re-wire the 645. Despite the dewirement, Power went hell for leather back to the depot. It was the only time that,

when arriving back at the depot late, he did not claim an overtime docket. Without knowing it, they had carried out conductor rule 105, which is illustrated. This implies that staff should go on the roof of a trolleybus, a practice that would definitely not be countenanced today by the trade unions or the Health and Safety Executive. There was a two hour break on this duty, during which time some crews slept on the snooker table in their clubroom.

Another escapade with Power occurred on the TD type staff bus which ran out of Edgware garage. The morning pick-up saw a number of Colindale staff board between Cricklewood and Colindale, and there was usually an element of larking around even at 4.30am. Drivers Bill Aherne and Peter Power were two of the participants in some tomfoolery one morning which ended up with Power's uniform trousers being split from front to back. Action needed to be taken as he didn't want to drive a trolleybus in such a state and on arrival at the depot the two of them were somehow able to procure a needle and thread. The mind boggles as to why they went to the ladies' toilets rather than the gents' to sew them up, but to the ladies' toilets they went. The two of them were in a cubicle just starting to mend the trousers when in walks conductress Doris who uses the next cubicle. Being aware of her presence and trying to sew up the trousers became too much for the pair of them; unable to contain their laughter, they ran out of the cubicle and down the stairs, after which Power put his trousers back on. Shortly afterwards Doris comes storming into the output shouting "Which of you men have been in the ladies' toilets?". There was no reply. The upshot of it all was that Power had to carry out the first part of his duty in his split trousers – he was able to get them stitched up during his meal relief.

This was the kind of view I saw when I took the training trolleybus into Colindale depot. At the time this picture was taken, CE had some of the lowest numbered trolleybuses in the fleet as shown by 301, 218, 323 and 347 which have been working on routes 645 and 664. Withdrawn 212 has its back to the camera while RT 3340 is on the forecourt waiting out time for its next trip on route 52A. *Fred Ivey.*

A visit to the 'House of Lords' was a useful way of losing a couple of minutes. Sometimes crews just could not help running a little bit early if there were few passengers and little traffic about. Needing to lose a bit of time one day, Colindale's Fred Collins decided to use the facilities near the working men's club at West Hendon on the way to Edgware, leaving his trolleybus parked at a bus stop. While he was away, a motorbus parked up behind to take some passengers on board. Haring down the road, northbound, was another trolleybus whose driver failed to notice Collins's trolleybus parked in front of the motorbus. He went careering past at great speed, knocking Collins's poles off the wires; the culprit's poles stayed on. When Collins came out of the lavatory he was amazed to see trolleybooms waving around in the air and only knew the reason when his conductor told him what had happened. There was no damage to the booms of Collins's trolleybus and he never found out who the guilty party was. Presumably the offender was aware of what had happened but kept his head down for the rest of the day.

At my home depot, there were many characters who had developed their own distinguishing traits. Starting with the conductors; there was a Miss Cross who was Cross by name and cross by nature – she often had problems with her regular driver and sometimes lost her temper with him. I remember two occasions when she got upset, grabbed hold of a metal paying-in tray and hurled it across the output like a discus thrower – if it had hit someone, it would have injured them. Ann Briers was known as 'ding-ding' as when she was 'under the hammer' (being very busy) she would call out "ding-ding" rather than reach for the bell cord when she was in the lower deck.

One of our conductors was known as 'Lamumba' as at the time he resembled the leader of the Belgian Congo. He was a most peculiar man but very good at his work. He had some unusual idiosyncrasies, for even in the height of summer he would always wear a rubber macintosh and London Transport cap. The oddest thing about him was that he wore goggles over his glasses. When running into the depot, trolleybuses used an overhead road that took it over an inspection pit. By this time most conductors would have got off but Lamumba did not do this on one occasion. He could not have realised that the trolleybus was going over the pit and he stepped off the platform backwards falling down the hole. His driver and the cleaners went to his assistance and helped him out of his predicament; he wasn't injured, just slightly shaken up.

We had one clippie who was on a very early turn one winter's day and when she had finished work went home and put her head down for a few hours sleep. When she woke up, her clock said 4.30, the time she had been getting up for her duty that week. She had her breakfast and started the trek to work, but as her way to the depot was by side roads she did not see any evening peak traffic. It was only when she got to the output that someone told her that it was now the evening of the same day.

It was well known that one of our conductors used to visit a 'lady' in the vicinity of the Leather Bottle pub in Stonegrove, on route 645, from time to time (I will not quote the name of the block of flats, as it still exists). As I usually worked on the City services I didn't have any first-hand experience of his escapades until one evening when I was teamed up with him on a late turn – I was working my day off. Whenever he visited 'Leather Bottle Annie' as she was known, he somehow got the 'all clear' from her, and would alight at the Leather Bottle pub which was two stops before Canons Park terminus. He would stash his ticket machine and cash bag in the conductor's locker once the trolleybus approached the Leather Bottle – it was unlikely that anyone would board from there. Drivers had to take the 645 up to Canons Park by themselves which meant serving various bus stops and leaving the terminus without any bell signals. I wasn't happy about having no conductor on board but it was his road and his way of doing things so I couldn't really argue with it. Whatever any passengers thought about his goings-on would be interesting to know. Allowing for the fact that the 'bus might go up a couple of minutes early and that there was often eight minutes stand time at Canons Park meant that he had about fifteen minutes with her! On the same theme, there were two 'working girls' who regularly travelled on the 521/609/621 routes. One was known as 'Scotch Annie' as she came from Scotland; the other one was known as 'Beaconsfield Kate' as she lived in Beaconsfield Road, New Southgate. Early one Sunday morning one of our conductors had an encounter with 'Scotch Annie'. She got off the tube at East Finchley and boarded a 609 going towards North Finchley. Having had an unsuccessful night, she said to the conductor (who to retain his marital reputation had better stay nameless) "I've got no money for my fare – how about me showing you my bazookers instead?". This he readily agreed to and the 'transaction' took place beneath the staircase – he was full of it afterwards and London Transport were a few coppers short that day.

There was one conductor who was 'over the top' when it came to calling out place names. At East Finchley he would call out "East Finchley Station", "Bald Faced Stag", "Rex Cinema", "Change here for route 102 for Golders Green or Chingford, and route 143 to Hendon Central". When he came to places such as Manor House and Nags Head he had so many announcements to make that it could not all be done before it was time to go. He was a mine of information and no doubt of great help to many people. He was like this over the whole route and on whichever service he was working. Doubtless his driver kept the window between the cab and saloon permanently closed to give him a bit of peace and quiet! After the trolleybuses had finished he transferred to Muswell Hill (MH) garage and one day my daughter Belinda and her friend were so transfixed by his performance on a route 134 bus that her friend forgot her stop and had to get off further along the route. Mentioning this extrovert brings to mind a conductor from Palmers Green garage who was so smart in his appearance that he would not come into contact with any passengers lest they leave a piece of fluff on his immaculate uniform. If he was standing on the platform or moving past people in the gangway he would put his right arm across his waist, simultaneously moving backwards to avoid contact. He had a razor sharp crease in his trousers and shiny shoes as if he had been a tailor's dummy that had come out of a window at Harrods.

Now the drivers. Some of them had their own quirks and word got to me that one would hold a conversation with himself in a foreign language while he was driving. This seemed odd to me, but one day I worked with him and when I was collecting the fares near the front of the 'bus I found it was true when I overheard him doing this. Another, Harry Cheek, always carried an empty gas mask case which he used to put nuts and bolts and bits of metal in – he would pick these up if he was walking in the street. If he saw something worth his while when driving he would get out of his cab and retrieve it. Few members of staff had nicknames but one clippie was known as 'Lady Hamilton' because she was so well-spoken, with her driver being known as 'Christmas cake'. On Christmas Eve one year he was given a Christmas cake which, apart from when he was driving, he carried under his arm all day so as not to lose it.

One driver who was very distinctive in hot weather was Fred Cox who had been on the job for many years before I started. He had retained a white dustcoat that had been issued to him early on in his driving career and wore it during the summer. He kept it very clean and was the only driver in the depot who wore one of these old style dustcoats. In the past, tram and trolleybus staff had red piping on their uniform but with the amalgamation of all road services into Central Buses in July 1950, it was replaced by a uniform with blue piping. Consequently the red piping was seen less and less. However, a younger driver, Les Strutt, had acquired some that still had red piping. It had been given to him in his conducting days by his driver who had been on trams. He obtained it as he wanted to take the rise out of some of the former tramwaymen, like Charlie Bonner, and did this by pointing to the red piping on his 'tram trousers', as he called them. He would say something like "You'll need to operate the sand pedal today" (tram drivers used sand for adhesion on wet rails). By saying this he implied that he had worked on trams. He used this uniform until it wore out, and he was the only member of staff in the depot with it. There was always an element of banter in the depot. Vic Collins, tended to be a bit heavy on the brake and Charlie Bonner used to have a friendly dig at him from time to time by saying, "I see you've got your diver's boots on again Vic" (diver's boots were cumbersome things and made the wearer heavy-footed). This teasing was all lighthearted, good fun. It was part of the friendship and camaraderie that was prevalent at Finchley depot.

On the subject of uniform, there was driver Wilson. He was a really nice bloke and started at Finchley a couple of years after me. He was always on the lookout to make a fast buck and was forever claiming he was short of money. He could certainly spin a yarn and he told us in the canteen that he had been a pilot in the Indian Air Force – I don't know if this was true. He was always up to some fiddle or dodge. Sometimes, I would give him a lift home on my motorcycle and as I had helped him, he one day offered me his new driver's overcoat for ten shillings, stating that he had another one. I took this up and it certainly came in handy for me going to work on my motorcycle on cold mornings. I'm sure he thought he was doing me a favour but of course he was

lining his own pocket. I was a conductor at the time and when I got to work I stowed the overcoat in my locker. If I put it on to walk to the relief point at Tally Ho I would place it in the driver's cab once on board. There were a large number of elderly staff who worked at the depot. A few of them, such as Bill Petch and Lofty Nash, had back problems and carried their own personal cushions to support their backs.

In the late fifties and early sixties some of our crews kept up with the fashion trends of the day. We had a few teddy boy types who got their ladies to alter their trousers so that they were in drainpipe style. With their quiffed hair they gave a bit of colour to depot life. A few of the younger men got their wives/girlfriends to cut their overcoats down so that they were 'shorties'. Some were a bit too generous in their modifications, with the result that they were too short. We also had a few 'wide boys' who peaked their caps and one of the men always wore a cravat that made him look rather dapper. Some of the female staff were only teenagers or women in their early twenties, many of them colleens from Ireland. Some wore white bobby-sox and slacks as, unless they adapted them, the standard issue skirts were too long for their liking. Combined with their agility to run and pull frog handles they brought a breath of fresh air to the job – mind you some of the more robust and well-upholstered women surprised us with their agility when they ran for their frog pulls. Some of the younger clippies used scissors, needle and cotton to alter their Gibson machine webbing into a belt to nip in their waistline, giving a touch of femininity to the male-dominated industry. Most of the women did not wear the uniform berets but some wore scarves.

Some conductors used the front lower saloon window to get into the cab so that they could have a chat with their drivers. Driver Peter Crisp and conductor Michael Norris did this on the last Finsbury Park one night; however, they overstayed departure time and left eight minutes late. Tearing up Seven Sisters Road, Peter saw the green of the traffic light signal but forgot that the frog handle needed to be pulled. The result was buckled booms with the repair wagon crew being very unhappy about being called out at midnight. The CDI had some terse words for Peter, saying, "I'll be watching your dewirements in future". The same crew were on a 521/621 going down The Cally when a postman put his leg up to stop the 'bus; he had to make this signal as his hands were full with parcels. He safely boarded but as he went up the stairs, lost his balance and fell head over heels into the roadway, parcels and all. He said he was not hurt but the crew decided to obtain the assistance of an official. The postman said it was not the crew's fault. Just before the official left, Michael said to him, "Will I get into trouble?". The inspector said, "What for?" to which the reply was "I didn't collect his fare!".

In all workplaces there are people claiming they'd been there, seen this, done that, when in fact it was just a load of hot air. One driver on an ego trip was Cyril George who claimed that he had been a tram driver at Holloway depot. In fact Cyril had been a bus driver at Hendon garage and had managed to arrange a transfer to Finchley depot where he became a trolleybus driver. Being of flamboyant nature he wore both his MSC and PSV badges. We tended to humour him when he told us make-believe stories about his tram days. We knew he hadn't worked on trams as one of the drivers asked the CDI to look at his staff record. There was no reference to him being a tram driver, and we put it down to him having a vivid imagination. It was rare for transfers to take place between motorbus and trolleybus staff and normally only occurred on residential grounds. A clashing of swords between two members of staff saw transfers take place and, at Hanwell depot, one driver had such a blazing row with his CDI that it resulted in the trolleybus driver being transferred to a nearby bus garage. Of course he had to undergo a bus driver course beforehand. It was not deemed wise to transfer motorbus drivers to trolleybus depots as there was the likelihood of them forgetting that they were driving a vehicle with poles on the top.

If there is one episode that takes the biscuit then it is the time when one of our drivers started to take a trolleybus home – he must have been day-dreaming. At the time of the incident there were only two drivers at the depot who had cars; one was driver King who lived in Totteridge Lane and who stars in this episode. On the second part of his duty, when he got to the junction of Whetstone High Road and Totteridge Lane he started to turn left down Totteridge Lane, which at this point is on a slope. Presumably he thought he had finished work and was going home. Of course the booms left the wires – this signalled his mistake, but fortunately the trolleybus had not gone past the point of no return. He brought the vehicle to a halt, stowed the booms and using the traction batteries was able to reverse back onto the High Road. The other driver who had a car was Stan Wakefield – he was of genial nature and on his late turns would fill his car with staff who were going his way. He was known as 'The Vicar', not through any religious persuasions but after the book, 'The Vicar of Wakefield'. If a crew was following him on the road, one would say to the other, "We're following the vicar today".

Staff would do favours for each other and a driver or conductor would do 'an end' for one of their colleagues. If a driver on a Colindale-based 645 wanted to get off early he would make an arrangement with another CE driver to change over mid-route. As an example, if driver A (who wanted to finish early) was going to Barnet, he would switch with driver B at, say, Childs Hill or anywhere where an inspector was not present. The result was that driver A would now finish at Colindale depot, with driver B going back to Barnet; conductors would not insert the 'new driver' on the log sheet or waybill. On another day, the favour would be returned. On the subject of entering details on log sheets, conductors were supposed to enter the *actual* time that vehicles arrived at a terminal point. This always occurred when running late, but never when running early! Crews wouldn't want to give London Transport the opportunity to consider a reduction in running times. Neither would staff want to give Mr Irons the chance to haul them into his office to explain an arrival at the depot eight minutes early on a late turn.

Covering for another member of staff occurred where gambling was concerned and it needs to be borne in mind that people in all walks of life – whether they be roadsweepers, shopworkers, even politicians – like to have a flutter on the horses. The Finchley trolleybusmen were no exception but London Transport took a dim view of gambling and placed posters in prominent places such as canteens and outputs prohibiting it. The notices stated that offenders would be dismissed. Some games were only for fun and no money was involved. Sometimes however, staff did play for money and would became frustrated when they found that it was time to take over their vehicle when they had a good hand of cards. If someone felt that they had a really good chance of winning a lot of money they would ask a colleague to carry out part of their duty, and I was once paid thirty shillings to do 'a Canons Park end' for Ken Norman who was in such a position. Again, conductors would enter the booked driver's name and badge number on the log sheet despite him being elsewhere! The only possibility of this practice coming to light would have been if someone had a dewirement which had to be reported – nobody was ever caught out in this way at Finchley.

Some of life's activities tend to get driven underground when they are discouraged and one of these is gambling. At Finchley, there was a thriving betting culture run by driver Ken Norman who had taken over from Frederick Bevan. If anyone fancied a horse in a race, they wrote their name, the bet and stake on a piece of paper (possibly a bit of ticket roll), went into the men's toilets where above the urinals there was a missing brick in which they placed their piece of paper in a tobacco tin in the cavity. As Ken was often out driving, he 'employed' Jim Constable as his 'bookie's runner'. He was the steward employed by the Sports and Social side of the depot to run errands and look after the clubroom which he kept clean – he also looked after the two snooker tables. Jim surreptitiously retrieved the pieces of paper before the day's racing commenced and gave them to his 'employer' who made it worth his while. Ken retained the bets and placed the details in a notebook. Most people bet on horses but he also took bets on dog racing and the boat race. Ken would settle up on Fridays and there was never any question of him not doing so. Most paid up their debts but there were a few sad souls who would renege and try to pay less than what they owed. They would threaten to blow the whistle on him but pressure from other staff saw them change their plans. Ken was not afraid about any whistle-blowing as the depot inspectors bet with him too! Even Mr Irons was known to put two shillings on a horse. In fact, Mr Nicholson said to Ken one day, "I don't mind you taking bets off the staff as long as I don't know about it!" – then promptly put a bet on with him! If Mr Nicholson was aware that one of the bigwigs was around he would warn Ken of their presence and suggest that he make himself scarce for a while. Mr Nicholson was an understanding man and was affectionately known as 'Old Nick'.

From time to time I had bets with Ken Norman. A good win I had with him was on 'Mr What' who won the 1958 Grand National at odds of 18/1. I picked this horse due to its similarity with my surname. I knew it was a very good Irish horse and had 10/- each way, a big bet for me in those days. I won eleven pounds, five shillings, which was more than a week's wages. I heard the race on the radio while having my dinner. What with the excitement of it all I couldn't finish my meal. Betting continued all the time I was at Finchley and it seemed to serve a useful purpose as open betting was illegal. Betting shops were not legally permitted until 1961 and gradually Ken Norman's sideline disappeared.

Continuing with Ken Norman, male conductors tended to pick up the technique of trolleybus driving by watching their drivers through the window that separated the cab from the saloon. Ken's conductor was Arnold Cox, and one evening they decided to change roles for pure devilment. Cox had been in the USA at some stage and had come back with a flash car so he had road sense; Norman had previously been a conductor so knew what to do. At Canons Park, Cox got into the cab and drove while Norman donned the conductor's equipment. At Golders Green, inspector Jim Beckford boarded the 645 – just what they wanted! Jim had been a driver at our depot and knew that Ken had been upgraded from conductor to driver many years before, and guessed what was going on. Ken thought to himself, "This is it", but Beckford didn't say a dickie bird. He did a quick check of the tickets, got Ken to sign his sheet and cleared off (I wonder whose name was signed on Beckford's sheet). Fortunately for the reprobates, Beckford didn't want to know. Arnold was only about five foot one, a dwarf in comparison to most drivers. Apparently he was only just above the steering wheel and so probably wouldn't have been accepted in this grade. Ken said that Arnold made a good job of it and he got to the approaches of North Finchley without incident. They changed back to their proper places before they got to Tally Ho as they didn't want to push their luck; there were always inspectors there.

Ken Norman didn't like finishing late and at the end of one evening peak he was a bit tight for time near the end of his duty on route 645. Those that ran into Finchley depot from the Cricklewood direction had to go via Tally Ho bus station as there was no wiring link between Ballards Lane and Woodberry Grove. Being aware that there were likely to be a number of 'buses on the stand, Ken told his conductor to pull the poles down in Ballards Lane and he batteried the 'bus into Woodberry Grove and the depot. Unfortunately, the District Superintendent was nearby and saw this unauthorised movement. He phoned Mr Patterson, one of the depot inspectors, and told him that the driver was to be instantly dismissed. However, the union fought his case and appealed against the decision; he was reinstated on humanitarian grounds. The TGWU argued he was a good chap really and such a small indiscretion didn't justify dismissal – all Ken got was a rap on the knuckles. The incident with the D.S. did not deter him from ensuring that he finished on time, so if there was no inspector on duty at Colindale depot when he was running late, he would curtail himself there. Every time he did, he got away with it. On another occasion when he was working on the 521s/621s he was told to curtail at the Nags Head due to late running. When he arrived there he was still late, so told his conductor to wind up 609 all round and they returned via that route which was quicker than going back through Wood Green. They were professional in their fiddling though, as the conductor wound back 521 or 621 when they got close to North Finchley.

When working on the 521/621, there was always a few minutes stand time at North Finchley – we usually went into the refreshment hut for a drink. Tea was served in china cups but as there was often not enough time to consume it, we would (a) 'saucer it' – pour it into the saucer to cool it down before returning it to the cup to drink or (b) take it out to the 'bus. No problem for conductors but drivers had to make sure they put the cups on the cab floor where the contents wouldn't be spilt. It wasn't wise to put them on the battery box because if they suddenly had to pull up, drivers would be hard pushed to find an explanation for liquid being found in the battery compartment!

There were a few crews who carried out practical jokes, like making passengers all sit on one side, stating that there was a problem with the spring, or that they needed to do this to even out the weight. Larking about manifested itself in a number of ways. We'd come out of the refreshment hut at Tally Ho and find that the crew of the 'bus behind had done one or some of the following things: (a) altered the route numbers and destination blinds, (b) the booms had been taken down, (c) the controller key had been put under the driver's seat, (d) the running number plates on the side of the vehicle had been slung under the staircase. The only way staff would recognise their own vehicle would be by looking for the timecard in the driver's cab. If the fleet number had been recalled (which was unlikely) then they'd know which was their 'bus. Messing about like this was just a means of entertainment amongst ourselves and was nothing more than a bit of skylarking going on – men acting as boys. All this was lighthearted and although these tactics would delay the 'bus in front, 'offenders' could be sure that the same thing would happen to them in due course. All staff had to do was to bide their time and do the same to them, but to add in something else for good measure to delay them even further. This could be done by hiding their meals under seats or putting salt in their cups of tea. However, revenge was carried out on one crew who found their bicycles locked together when they finished work.

Although drivers and conductors could change their rota lines mutually, there was a formal way of 'dumping' a partner if a crew didn't get on. This was achieved by one of them submitting their name on a piece of paper which was put in a hat. A depot inspector made a draw about every three months (rota lines became available as staff left or retired). As people's names were drawn out of the hat they were placed on a different rota line. Most times this worked out satisfactorily but again a conductor might get teamed up with a driver they didn't get on with and they'd have to go through the process again. When no-one applied to be 'put in the hat' then the open rota was taken up by whoever wanted it, or by the most senior member of the spare staff. With all the different ways people wanted to work and the diverse personalities that abounded in the depot, there were bound to be clashes, and a parting of the ways was the best way to resolve matters.

WORKSHY STAFF

With the aim of carrying as few passengers as possible, a small number of crews embarked upon all manner of ploys to achieve this; some were notorious and made a fine art of it. For example, a 660's timecard could be marked in pencil or biro at the Cricklewood timing point 'CE28, three minutes in front', indicating its position in the service and that staff should make sure it went ahead of them. Brand new time-cards would become 'graffitied' within days. I found that as a driver there could be drawbacks working with conductors other than my regular mate. They might say, "I don't want too many passengers", "Do this, do that", "Put your toe down", "Hang on here, let him go round the corner", "Leave a bit early", "Run a bit early", etc. All this was just so that they would have a smaller number of fares to collect. I would firmly but politely say, "You conduct, I'll drive".

Sometimes staff would do 'crew overtime' whereby a regular crew worked some extra hours together. Usually though, when overtime was worked, it was with someone other than their own mate. This meant that staff could find themselves paired up with someone who didn't work in their accustomed manner and both had to give and take a bit. Some conductors wanted to leave bang on the mark even at quiet periods; they considered that they should only take their allotted load at all times. Conversely, at slack times, many drivers wanted to leave a few minutes late so that they could drive at a good speed. Commonsense would prevail and there were few flare-ups.

There were the skivers who would sit out some time in the depot and would lose a 'Barnet end' or a 'Wood Green short'. This was done in the following way. A 'bus may have been run in for attention and the crew told to sit in the canteen while it was being dealt with. When the work had been completed a fitter would say to them, "You can take your 'bus – it's ready now", but the crew would remain in the canteen ten minutes longer. Staff were taking a bit of a chance of being detected by an inspector, and officials 'on the ball' would check with the depot to see if the 'bus was ready. If an inspector found somebody 'swinging the lead' he would soon get the offending crew out of the canteen and onto the road.

Most staff could just not be bothered about playing these games as it was more trouble than it was worth, but there were times when the bandits had to be dealt with. If I was on a 521 going to Holborn and the crew on the 621 behind were too close and having an easy time, I knew that when I came out of Holborn they'd soon be behind me again. Knowing that 521s/621s alternate around the Holborn Loop, I'd deliberately lose a few minutes when leaving Charterhouse Street – when I reached the bottom of Caledonian Road at Kings Cross, I'd see the back of them going north. Eventually they'd twig what was going on, but probably not until the Nags Head where they'd drop their poles and I'd go in front. Laziness was only practised by a few and they had to be dealt with.

Some drivers or conductors, through no fault of their own, could become unpopular just through the way they worked; 'Scratcher' Frank Jones was an example. He always took his time but gave a good and steady ride, though conductors working with him had a busy time. Consequently he got more

than his fair share of curtailments but it was not deliberate. 'Scratcher' was a name given to drivers who took their time, waited too long at bus stops, deliberately got themselves held at traffic lights, and who drove at an unnecessarily slow speed; this was known as 'dragging the road'. As they held up the services, inspectors would have no alternative but to curtail them short of their intended destination so as to free up the overhead line and get the services going. My regular driver, Harry Franks, was a steady plodder and another crew, knowing they were following us, might say to others, "We'll soon catch those two up." They often did and I was busier with him than with Dennis and Vic. A few drivers were notorious for 'scratching'. One day a Colindale crew had enough of the one in front messing about and holding them up. The conductor on the second vehicle went to the back of the leading vehicle at a bus stop, pulled out its bamboo pole and lowered its booms. This enabled the second 'bus to get away and the offenders had to go through the rigmarole of rewiring their 'bus. They now had to get on with it as they would be struggling for an excuse for late running if an inspector approached them as to why they were out of turn.

'Close-poling' is trolleybusman's terminology for keeping just the right amount of space away from the 'bus in front. It is not as one might think a reference to the poles of the trolleybus, but the distance between two traction standards. Other terms for closely following another trolleybus were 'being up his staircase', 'punching him up' or 'push him all the way'. At the start of the day some crews would plan their tactics, so that they wouldn't pick up too many passengers; such practices caused resentment and some staff made counter-manoeuvres a hobby. A conversation on a 521/621 might be "Went round Manor House today and a 659 punched us all the way to Holborn – we found that we had jumped him when the Holborn inspector told us we were out of sequence. They've done this two days' running now, so tomorrow we'll come up late, pole him down the road and let him do all the work". The Edmonton crew is probably thinking, "They'll come up late tomorrow so we'll go down early", and when the Finchley crew arrive at Manor House on the day in question, they find that they have got a large number of people to carry between there and Holborn because the 659 had long gone. The Finchley crew would keep an image of the EM crew in their mind's eye and eventually revenge would be exacted. Similar strategies manifested themselves throughout the system.

Stonebridge driver Stan Berry, would leave sharp from Hammersmith on a 660/666 and get a bit of a move on in the knowledge that by keeping up a good speed he might arrive at Jubilee Clock a few minutes early – thus avoiding picking up too many passengers. Sometimes when he got there well before he should have done, he would take the left turn into Harlesden High Street a bit too fast and dewire – the delay prevented him from going past the Craven Park inspectors ahead of his scheduled time. Stan was normally paired with a conductress and could do this in the knowledge that he would have to rewire the 'bus and could take his time doing it – he'd arrive at Craven Park as scheduled. One day he was working with a male conductor who as soon as he knew the poles were off was out the back and had the vehicle re-wired before Stan had a chance to do the necessary. Further delaying tactics in the form of holding the 'bus at each stop between Jubilee Clock and Craven Park were employed to avoid arriving there early.

With all the wear and tear they received, bell cords frayed and sometimes broke. When this happened we wouldn't take a 'bus out of service but would carry on as best we could, just using the push-button bells. If a break occurred, a long loop hung down – the lack of tautness indicated to passengers that it was not working. Eventually we would see an official who would arrange for a substitute to be brought out. Colindale conductor Ron Smith didn't like carrying too many passengers; he could get in such a mood when he had a full load that he would hit the cord with such force that it would whack against the ceiling. Needless to say, he was responsible for breaking many bell cords. His desire to get away from a stop quickly was shown by him calling out "both sides on" when there were just two passengers to pick up – this indicated that he wanted them to get on either side of the platform handrail. When he did pick up a full load he would sometimes vent his feelings by kicking the side of the trolleybus when he re-boarded after a frog pull. He would encourage drivers to have a dewirement which would require attention from a breakdown crew. Drivers would not agree to his ploy but he could not let a frog handle go too quickly as he would get in trouble for negligence. Despite all this, he was a very efficient conductor.

A minority of staff played up. There was an Irish conductor who bought a bottle of 'Liquafruta' (a foul smelling cough medicine) from the chemist on the corner of Nether Street. He broke the bottle on the stairs and threw the contents around the place stinking the 'bus out. It had to be run into the depot to be cleaned – all of this to get a curtailment. Okay, he'd fooled the inspector on this occasion but most staff didn't approve of such actions because somebody else had to do their work. A few conductors, finding that their trolleybus was minus a number of interior lightbulbs, would consider this to be a defect – they'd say that they couldn't see to do the job properly. This was used as a ruse to run the vehicle into the depot and thus lose part of a journey. A driver might allege that he had spongy brakes when this was not so. Maintenance staff would never argue with such an allegation for if they refused to change a 'bus over and the brakes turned out to be suspect later on, then the finger would be pointed at them. Most staff only changed a 'bus over if it was really necessary as they knew that carrying passengers was their bread and butter.

There would be the odd crew that would persistently run early or delay departure time by taking too long to drink their tea in the hut at Tally Ho. Close-poling would see two 521s/621s come along together in Friern Barnet during slack times – this made a mockery of the efforts made by staff who were trying their best to keep a regular service going. These work-shy individuals gave a bad impression to the travelling public. Unfortunately they often 'got away with it', until such time as they fell foul of an inspector who would take firm action and report them to the CDI who would give them a

warning. On the other hand, there were some crews who really wanted to be spot-on with their timekeeping. If conductors were aware that they were running even a couple of minutes ahead of time, they would refrain from ringing a 'bus off from a stop. They knew that trolleybuses were for passengers to ride on and not there to give staff an easy time. Most crews played the game and kept a reasonable distance from the one in front. During driver training it had been drummed into us that whenever possible we should not get too close to another trolleybus as we could be reducing his power input.

Although trolleybus work had a semblance of friendly competition, it was another story when it came to motor-buses. There was intense rivalry between the two sides, virtually all-out war – definitely 'them' and 'us'. This state of affairs is illustrated by bus route 43 and trolleybus route 609 which paralleled each other between 'The Woodman' public house by Highgate Station and Moorgate. Some drivers on route 43 would wait at the last stop in Muswell Hill Road and look for trolleybooms with white socks on the end of them, as opposed to Highgate's trolleybuses on routes 517/617 which did not have them. The white socks signified 609s, for our maintenance staff painted the ends of the booms white to assist us re-wiring in the dark. As soon as they saw our booms they would tuck in behind us and we would have to do most of the work to Moorgate. If they were in front of us at Highgate they had a trick up their sleeve, for they could go round the roundabout at Highbury Corner twice and come up behind us – this was something we couldn't do. There were some 43 crews who would play the game and we would 'work the road' together – they would take a couple of stops and we would do likewise all the way to Moorgate.

A ploy used by a few drivers from Edgware garage working on route 142 was to wait outside 'The Crown' public house in Cricklewood Broadway and wait for a 645, 664 or 666 to turn into the Edgware Road where they would follow it all the way to Edgware. They had the advantage, as trolleybus drivers could not wait for a 142 – if they did there would be a queue of vehicles banking up. Sometimes the 142s just had to go but if at the last minute they saw the nose of a trolleybus at the top of Chichele Road or the bottom of Cricklewood Lane, the brakes would go on and they would stop, literally straddling the junction. On one occasion a 142 driver had actually gone past the point of no return when he saw an Edgware-bound trolleybus ready to turn into the Edgware Road. He was that determined not to pick up any passengers that he stopped well over the STOP line. The policeman on point duty waved him on but quick-thinkingly the driver pulled up the accelerator pedal with his foot – this cut the engine out. He continued to place his foot beneath the accelerator at the same time that he pulled the starter switch – this gave the impression that the bus had a fuel feed problem and could not be re-started. The policeman was fooled and the crew had got their way as the trolleybus was now in front; 'strangely' the 142 was able to go after the trolleybus had passed through, with the driver saying to the policeman "Got it going".

Worth mentioning are a few of the short cuts that went on. Crew reliefs on 609s going to Barnet came off in Ballards

Lane just beyond the bus station. Some conductors would pull the frog in Kingsway and walk straight to the depot rather than reboard the 'bus and go to the changeover point – for about eighty yards there would be no conductor on board. As far as I can recall nobody ever got booked for this nor did any platform accident occur. Inspectors knew about this but normally turned a blind eye. Another shortcut also involved Kingsway, and Vic Collins again! 521s/621s that ran into the depot had to go via the bus station using the 660 terminal wires in the process. One evening he noticed a string of 660s banked up in Ballards Lane. The tailback was probably due to 660 drivers not moving their 'buses up on the stand – they were probably in the refreshment hut having a cup of tea! Often inspectors would move trolleybuses up themselves or ask a nearby driver to do it, but this had not happened on this occasion. Knowing that if he tucked in behind the 660s, we would be late finishing, he stopped the 'bus in the middle of Kingsway, climbed out of the cab and got our bamboo pole out. He changed the booms from the inbound 521/621 wires onto the outbound 645/660 wires and we went straight to the depot without inspectors being any the wiser. We couldn't have been missed as Vic wasn't hauled into the office with a report staring him in the face. I don't expect we were the only ones to do this, but it could only be done if there were no passengers on board. While mentioning the bus station, to give space there I often participated in the pastime of free-wheeling trolleybuses down the slope! As the bus station was on an incline, scotches were provided. They were kept adjacent to the inspector's box, but were only occasionally used.

And then there was Hilary . . . Hilary was eighteen years old when she came on the scene in 1960; she was a very friendly young lady and liked trolleybusmen in uniform! She travelled from Finchley to Chancery Lane on a '17 each morning; on the return trip she would get on a '21 if she knew the crew. Although it took longer, she wasn't pressed for time and the ride gave her the opportunity to find out more about us. We got to know her as she was always hanging around the trolleybuses and the inspectors' box at Tally Ho. By being in close contact with the inspectors, she had access to the duty schedules that were positioned in the box. She became very pally with one of our conductresses – they would go up to the depot together and Hilary, by looking at the rota lines, could find any of the staff she wanted to see. She was on first name terms with many of the Finchley trolleybus crews, and could tell them when she would next see them and what duty they would be on the following week. This unique lady was more knowledgeable about trolleybus operation than some of London Transport's employees! An interesting anecdote that was told to me involved Hilary and a conductress friend from Highgate depot who worked on the 517s/617s. If this clippie wanted to go out with her boyfriend when she was on a late turn and unable to change her duty, Hilary would do the second part of the shift for her! The two of them met up during the conductress's meal break and Hilary would be given either the summer dustcoat or winter overcoat, MSC badge, ticket equipment and cash, and would take over the trolleybus at the appointed time at Archway relief point. Knowing the 'ins and outs' of trolleybus conducting, she knew where she had to get out and pull frog handles and made a far better job of things than some of the regular conductors. At the end of the shift, the real conductress would meet Hilary as they approached Highgate depot, and take everything back and pay in. Her driver knew what was going on but wasn't the slightest bit bothered about it, and London Transport was never the wiser about an eighteen year old girl conducting one of their trolleybuses. The Tally Ho inspectors knew what was happening too, but they turned a blind eye. This chapter started with staff from Highgate depot and as Hilary 'worked' there she fittingly closes it.

To some Finchley crews, a 659 route trolleybus was like a red rag to a bull for they covered the same roads as the 521s/621s between Manor House and Holborn Circus. Crossing Manor House junction is Edmonton's 1715 and although it is only going as far as Kings Cross, some of our staff would be happy to follow it as it would give them an easy time as far as 'the cross'. *Peter Moore.*

Below 1512 is seen at North Acton but is going only as far as BROMYARD AVE ACTON VALE (the blind display can be compared with that of 1458 on page 30). Heavy traffic and passenger loadings are probably the cause for the late running – passengers for Hammersmith will have to board the Stonebridge 660 behind. *Fred Ivey.*

Opposite 660s leaving the depot for Hammersmith were given a total 74 minutes for the trip. There are a lot of trolleybuses in Finchley depot on Saturday 29th July 1961. The time when it was supposed to be at its emptiest was during Mondays to Fridays in the last two and a half years of operation when there was only ten minutes between the last peak hour vehicle leaving (a 521 departing at 5.16pm) and the first one coming back in (a 521 at 5.26pm). Over the years, various support vehicles were kept on the premises: AEC tower wagons, Albion and Leyland Cub trolleybus rescue trucks. A Regent breakdown tender came from Hammersmith in August 1960 and stayed until January 1962. It was here that some of the skivers would sit out half of a journey. *Brian Speller.*

INTO THE LION'S DEN

Apart from a section on one of our routes, I considered that the services operated out of Finchley depot were good ones. Working regularly as a conductor on the 521/609/621 rota meant that I got to know all the fares on these routes off by heart, who the regular passengers were, when I had to be on the platform for a frog pull and so on. As a driver, it meant I got to know the overhead as if it was the back of my hand. Working a day off or overtime on the 645 to Canons Park made a nice change despite heavy passenger loadings on the Edgware Road, but the section that could be problematical for me was the 660 between Cricklewood and Hammersmith. The regular 660 staff were forever relating problems they had on the route. There was the possibility, in heavy rain, of flooding under North Acton railway bridge where there was a deep dip, and trolleybuses would be stuck either side if it was not for the resourcefulness of the supervisory staff. The turning circle at Wales Farm Road (North Acton Station) was

well-located for turning 'buses back to Acton at these times, and on the Harlesden side of the bridge a convenient side road was used. The road under the bridge at Cricklewood Lane also suffered in this way and those trolleybuses stuck south of the Broadway were turned round at St Gabriels Church. Those on the north side were stuck until the water had subsided or could be pumped away. There was also a lot of late running on the 660s, bunching of vehicles and trolleybuses in the wrong order with the whole situation being compounded by Colindale, Finchley and Stonebridge staff trying to outdo each other with regard to the taking or not taking of passengers on the section between Cricklewood and Hammersmith. Finchley depot played a minor role only on the 660 and, as I was on the 'City' rota, I only worked on that route from time to time so was not familiar with the way that the regular staff 'worked the road'. Some of the difficulties that I experienced are related in the following text.

As a conductor, I was unfamiliar with the locality and place names and although a full size fare chart was exhibited in the lower saloon I used a miniature one. Between Cricklewood and Hammersmith, there were a lot of short distance riders, always people jumping on and off, and I had to be 'on the ball' to get all the fares in. It really was so busy – too much really, and I could only do my best for there could be up to seventy seated passengers and five standing on board – not an easy task. Most were only short or medium distance travellers, so as soon as they got off others took their place. There were times when money was thrown into my hands and I had to count how much it was and punch off tickets for the corresponding amount. People would ask for places that I'd never heard of, so I had to ask where that particular location was near to; their reply would be something like "Two stops after Craven Park". There was one place that I was quite often asked for, but never found out where it was. This was 'Electric House', and those wanting it got off by Willesden police station. Therefore, when I was asked for this place I just gave them a ticket for the appropriate fare stage, but to this day I have no idea what Electric House was. Most people knew their fare and would say "tuppenny or threepenny", but as with all routes there were those who asked for a lower fare than they should have paid – I 'collared' as many of these as I could though.

One day, when I was working with Charlie Bonner on the 660, I was so engrossed in fare collection that I didn't realise that the 'bus had stopped for me to operate the frog in Acton High Street where we turned right into Market Place. Oblivious to the flashing of saloon lights and the banging of

the timecard on the cab ceiling, I carried on dealing with passengers upstairs. Eventually, Charlie got out of the cab and pressed the push button himself, telling me later what he had done. This was the only time I delayed a trolleybus in this manner. Years later, as a driver, I got out and pulled semi-automatic frog handles when my conductor had forgotten where they were – at the Angel towards Moorgate and the Nags Head towards Archway (an advantage of conductors becoming drivers was that they were more understanding of such oversights).

It was in 1955, during my time as a conductor, that I experienced my one and only turn at Holly Park. I must have been working my day off and although I cannot remember the particular driver who I was with, he was one of the regular 645/660 men. We left Hammersmith on our first journey back to North Finchley alright and were coming back through Acton Vale when we pulled up behind some other trolleybuses parked in the side of the road west of Bromyard Avenue – they were immobilised by a power failure. The first vehicle had just passed an overhead breaker and found that 'the juice' was off, so everybody else had no alternative but to bank up behind. It took about twenty minutes for power to be restored and there must have been about fifteen trolleybuses parked up, all 607s and 660s. The inspector at Acton Market Place had come down to the scene of the hold up which must have been at about 3.40pm. Once the power was restored he ensured that 'buses departed singly for if they had tried to get away together then the power would have gone off again. He said that his colleagues at Craven Park would sort the service out.

I am going to have to use a little bit of journalistic licence here to describe how the inspectors rectified matters but as I acted in this capacity in later years, that which is related below is probably not far out from what actually happened that day.

Checking the relevant time schedule shows the running numbers involved, the order of sequence being SE18, FY104, SE39, SE32, SE16, SE34. The 660 was working on a 4/5 minute headway with each one going to North Finchley (this is assuming they were all running). We went up Horn Lane and past Gypsy Corner and came across a number of 660s which had been turned at Wales Farm Road (the turn at North Acton) to keep them away from the affected area. They would pick up their time there. At Craven Park, an inspector came over to deal with the convoy, which it had now become, approaching SE18 and saying to its crew "North Finchley so as to give me a through 'bus, then Acton Market when you come back and that should put you right". As he came past the back of our trolleybus, he bent down and pulled the bamboo pole out a few inches before shoving it back in its holder (he just wanted to make sure we were carrying one). He said to my driver "Holly Park, don't hang around there, come straight back". To the crew of SE39 "North Finchley, then Bromyard on return", telling SE32's crew to turn at Holly Park and instructing them to leave there on their time. SE16's crew would have been told "North Finchley and through to Hammersmith to cater for any passengers who want to make the full journey but if you're still late when you pass me coming back I'll sort you out then." The last one in line, SE34, was probably on time anyway. At the front of the

Acton Market inspector's mind was the urgency of trolleybuses running again between Acton and Hammersmith as it was an important passenger link. At this time of day the 660 was the only route that people could use to get between these two locations and it was considered to be a crisis if the connection was broken. As 660s had been curtailed at North Acton, there would have been nothing coming through from the Harlesden direction, so once power had been restored the Acton inspector would have grabbed a couple of northbound 660s that were not going into crew reliefs and put them on 'Acton swings' – shuttling forth between Acton Market and Hammersmith, reinstating the link until normal service could be resumed. The 'grabbed' vehicles would have been returned to their correct timings later on. Finally, those southbound 'buses trapped in Acton Vale would have been swung round in Bromyard Avenue.

I had never turned at Holly Park before so I asked my driver what to show on the destination blinds as we had one of the C class or lower numbered J's which required conductors to change both blinds. He told me to put up GOLDERS GREEN, which I did and said I was to tell passengers that we were going to Holly Park which was further than Golders Green. As most of them would not know where this was, I should tell them that Henlys Corner was the nearest familiar location. I had no idea about the turn there so my driver told me what I had to do. When we got to Holly Park, he parked the trolleybus quite a few feet away from the kerb so that he had plenty of room to reverse back on battery into Fitzalan Road. I got the poles down quickly for we were to go straight back. There was a 645 behind us which had got caught up in

Saturday 5th November 1960 and trolleybus 740 passes through Askew Arms junction on its way to Uxbridge. The 607 was a very busy route and, at times, trolleybuses were operating to a one minute headway on its busiest sections – working on this route was not for the faint-hearted. 740 spent its whole working life at Hanwell, another depot that kept its vehicles in fine fettle. *Jack Gready.*

the rest of the 660s and by the time I had lowered the first boom, it was moving slowly forwards. As soon as I put the grappling hook of the bamboo pole around the second boom, the 645 driver prepared to move past us as the road was very wide here. No sooner had I drawn the boom away from the wire than he was away – obviously a man of experience. I then placed the bamboo pole into the lower saloon and beckoned my driver back into Fitzalan Road making sure that he didn't land in the drain cover here, for if a trolleybus had low battery power it wouldn't be able to get itself out without assistance. He then pulled forward onto the other side of Regents Park Road and I reconnected the trolley arms onto the overhead, following which I changed the blinds to HAMMERSMITH. We set off straightaway as instructed and made Hammersmith and Finchley depot on time.

When I was driving on the 660s I sometimes found that I was getting the rough end of the stick from some of the Colindale and Stonebridge crews, for the regular staff on the

660 and 666 had the 'Hammersmith road' well worked out. Consequently any staff like myself who only worked on the 660 occasionally could find ourselves struggling. From North Finchley to Cricklewood everything would be alright as it was a straight run all the way apart from the right turn at Childs Hill from Finchley Road and it was likely that there would be a 645 not too far in front. Once I crossed Cricklewood Broadway and came to the stop at the top of Chichele Road it was like going into the lion's den for it was there that problems really started. The 666, which I should be following all the way to Hammersmith, had probably nipped down a couple of minutes early, whereas I would have gone across the junction just about on time. This meant that we were picking up more passengers than we should have done all the way to Hammersmith and I would lose seconds here and there due to being cautious on the twists and turns of the overhead line through Willesden, Harlesden and Acton. I was having to contend with what was, to me, fairly unfamiliar overhead.

The overhead had to conform to the many types of road layout that existed in London; the one at 'Seven Stars' was to an unusual configuration – it was not a straight crossover. 1651 is on the 666, crossing the 657 route on 1st January 1962; prominent are the fairy lights that assist westbound Isleworth drivers. For my part I had to remember that when going to Hammersmith it was 'dead' on the first crossover and 'power' on the second, but when coming back I could power all the way through. *John Gillham.*

The regular drivers knew where they could take liberties with the overhead so all the time would gain on those of us who were irregular Finchley 660 men. At the main junctions such as Craven Park, Jubilee Clock and Seven Stars I would have to be particularly careful as these were always prime locations for dewirements which would knock me back another couple of minutes if I came to grief and had to sort things out. By the time I got to Hammersmith, which was a 69 minute run, it often had to be 'straight in, straight out' – that is forgoing the layover time. This gave me a chance to get away from any other trolleybuses that had been close-poling us on our southbound trip. To have even contemplated having a cup of tea was unthinkable as it would only further delay us and give us an even heavier load of passengers, not to mention any inspector who would expect us to keep going anyway for the sake of the service. As it was, there was no point in hanging around as most periods of duty would just be a trip to Hammersmith and back; only a few spells did two Hammersmiths. On the way back to North Finchley those of us not working on the 660 regularly might get a bit more confident with the overhead, but it was no good being complacent because we could go round the Jubilee Clock and lose a pole. By the time the boom was back on the wire it was quite likely that the pack would be baying at our heels and the staff of a couple of trolleybuses behind would be having a wry smile at our predicament. Running late would make us unpopular with our conductor who was probably a regular on the 660s and it would not be until we reached the other side of Cricklewood Broadway and were on familiar roads and easier overhead that things got back to normal. With a bit of luck we would get back to North Finchley not too late or on time. Any conductor who was a bit slow on the bell or a driver who was hesitant would be punished on the Hammersmith road by the regular staff. They would soon sense a weakness and take advantage of the situation by 'close-poling' a slow-coach.

I had only been driving for a short while when I was given a piece of overtime with Joan Thomas on the 660s; it took over at 5.43pm, left at 5.54 and finished at 9.22. We had to do 'one and a Craven' – North Finchley/Hammersmith/Craven Park Circle/Hammersmith/North Finchley. In the mid-1950s there were still heavy loadings at eight and nine o'clock in the evening and we got a real bashing on all these journeys. When we got to Hammersmith on our first trip there were a couple of other trolleybuses behind us. We went straight out of Hammersmith to Craven Park, this being the only time I turned on the circle there. Fortunately there was not a 628 on the siding so we departed immediately, but despite that when we got back to Hammersmith we were still a few minutes late. It was on the return that I met Arthur Askey's lookalike for the first time; he was a timekeeping inspector at Golders Green. He approached the 'bus from across the road, asking me for the timecard which was on a ledge next to the switches that controlled the wipers and lights. Shortly before this I had lit a cigarette which was resting in front of the timecard; I had to pick up the cigarette and put it in my mouth so that I could give him the timecard through the window. I don't know why he wanted it as inspectors had their own time-sheets to consult. He looked at me and said "You're smoking, driver"; I replied "Yes" (there was no point saying that I wasn't). He asked, "How long have you been driving" and I answered, "Six weeks". He replied, "Hasn't anyone ever told you that you can't smoke in the cab"; I said "No, first I've heard of it". He said "Well you can't and I should report you, but I know that the pair of you've had a right hammering. Don't let me catch you at it again". Drivers smoking in cabs was a rule that was always broken and I knew about the rule all the time. When we got back to North Finchley it was past the time for the vehicle to go out again (9.30pm). Scarcely had I got out of the cab than the relieving driver was in it and away – we were now on what was known as 'overtime on overtime'. This meant that not only did we get paid for the overtime that we were booked to work, but the extra minutes after 9.22pm were also paid at overtime rate.

A new turning circle was commissioned in Paddenswick Road in November 1955, being just a few minutes short of Hammersmith terminus. Prior to this, inspectors were having to give generous curtailments on the 660/666 services by turning them into Bromyard Avenue when they were just a few minutes late. To obviate this and to give a better service, London Transport's overhead line staff erected a new turning circle in Paddenswick Road by the Thatched House pub (until this time it had been a battery turning point). 'Paddenswick' was not fully wired-up – there was not a facing frog so trolley arms had to be swung from the main line to a set of dead-end wires. Adjacent to the 'dead-ender' there was a traction standard on which was sometimes placed a spare bamboo pole. Providing one here obviated the need for staff to bend down to get their own. It also got them out of a predicament if, on arrival, they found they were not carrying one on their bus; if this was the case then the bamboo would be retained, and mysteriously a replacement would materialise in due course.

The overhead junctions encountered between Cricklewood and Hammersmith were not of the same magnitude as on the City routes, so it was just a point of being cautious. No doubt there were occasions when I have caused arcing on the overhead through taking power where I shouldn't have done, particularly when it was dark. As a driver I turned at Acton Market Place and Bromyard Avenue, Acton Vale, but never at North Acton or Paddenswick Road loop. On one occasion, as a conductor, we had lost so much time due to a traffic hold-up that we turned at Craven Park from the Finchley direction. This was a bit of a performance as we had to use the Stonebridge depot-bound wires for part of the manoeuvre. Turning right onto the Harrow Road we were only able to go so far on the wires before I pulled the poles down. The rest of the turn was carried out by a combination of battery and gravity power down the slight incline back into Craven Park. We left the trolley booms stowed until it was time to go. I also went into the Golders Green short working during my time on the platform. It was frustrating for drivers waiting to get out of the loop onto the Finchley Road here, for the traffic lights only worked intermittently in favour of motorbuses and trolleybuses.

One day I had an element of ease, for an inspector at Craven Park told me that there was a problem south of Harlesden and that trolleybuses could not proceed towards Acton. He instructed me to turn left at Jubilee Clock, run along the Harrow Road and turn into College Park loop. I had not used the wires along the Harrow Road before but as we were running without passengers it gave me time to find out where to go and what to do. This was achieved by flagging down a 662 and asking its driver what needed to be done. He told me to turn right into Scrubs Lane after which I should turn left into Waldo Road and then left again into Letchford Gardens which was the northern terminus of the 630 route. In Letchford Gardens there were a number of other trolleybuses parked up due to the problem beyond Jubilee Clock, so I lowered the poles as I knew that we would be there for quite a time (due to the large number of trolleybuses affected, I expect others waited in Scrubs Lane). I reckon we must have been in there for about three quarters of an hour during which time my conductor and I put our feet up. I estimated the number of minutes it would take to get to Craven Park and departed accordingly. When I got to the top of Letchford Gardens I had to turn left onto the Harrow Road. My conductor and I had to have a good look at the overhead arrangements to see what we needed to do – he had to pull a frog handle to take us onto the Harrow Road wires. I used these as far as the Jubilee clock where I turned right to regain the 660 route.

While referring to College Park, it is opportune to mention that there was no short working facility between there and Paddington on route 662. Although there was an approved curtailment point at Royal Oak, it was not a practical proposition and inspectors had no choice when vehicles were running maybe just ten minutes late but to turn them into College Park where they might have as much as thirty minutes layover. This was wasteful as far as inspectors were concerned but for the crews it was an opportunity for a

This is what the 'he-men' of the trolleybus staff could do (and that included myself!) – manipulate two trolley arms at the same time. In Letchford Gardens (where I once turned) 1604, which is on a football EXTRA to Wembley, passes 1665 whose driver or conductor is on the pavement carrying out this heavy work. *Peter Moore.*

welcome break. I only ran with the 662 between Craven Park and Jubilee Clock, but on a couple of occasions saw some Stonebridge EXTRAs on that section. These were trolleybuses that were taking people to and from major football matches at Wembley Stadium. On the same theme, I once saw one of the Paddington to Acton Vale journeys that SE operated in Monday to Friday morning peak hours. There were some unusual journeys that operated throughout the trolleybus network, and these were amongst the last to run.

This chapter is concluded by two experiences of colleague Peter Crisp, when he was still new to trolleybus driving. Like me, he had previously been a conductor on the City routes, so the 660 was unfamiliar to him. On both occasions he was doing some overtime, which comprised a North Finchley/ Hammersmith/North Finchley rounder. On the first time he was paired with a new conductor, so both were strangers on the route. As they were coming through Acton Vale westbound an inspector came across to Peter and told him to change his blind to show NTH FINCHLEY. Peter said that they hadn't reached Hammersmith yet, but the inspector said that they had. What Peter didn't realise was that they had already reached Hammersmith and he had continued to follow the wires, not realising that they were now going through Acton Vale for a second time and were on the way back to Tally Ho. On the trip related above he had followed a 'treble six' so had found his way to Hammersmith alright but on the second occasion there was not a 666 in front of him. On arriving at Jubilee Clock southbound, he noted that the Y frog signal was illuminated for the left lane and assuming that he had frog priority followed what in fact were the 628/662/664 wires. This was an understandable mistake as the frog apparatus here was the opposite way round to the accepted practice of conductors pulling frog handles for near-side lanes and in this instance required conductors to pull for Hammersmith. As Peter was going down the Harrow Road,

662 drivers coming the other way were flashing their head-lights at him in an attempt to stop him going all the way to Paddington. Eventually he worked out that he was on the wrong wires so turned at College Park and ran via the 626 link wire at Jubilee Clock to get to Hammersmith. This delayed him somewhat and he finished late, which was a common feature for those of us who did not regularly work on the 660s.

As dawn breaks, 1603 uses the '626 wire' at Jubilee Clock, Harlesden; a few journeys in one direction only in Monday to Friday morning peak hours ran from Paddington to Acton. There was a lot of variance as to what would be shown in the route aperture box; 1603's conductor has elected to use a blank display. *Hugh Taylor.*

Carrimore, who specialised in six-wheel trucks, was a notable firm in Finchley High Road. There have never been many six-wheeled vehicles on the road, but most London trolleybuses were, as exemplified by 1582 which is operating on route 645 to Canons Park. Despite not having been repainted for a number of years, the Colindale cleaning staff have presented the vehicle well. At this compulsory stop the driver acts professionally for he has his handbrake on. *Don Thompson.*

NO EFFORT SPARED

HIGH DAYS AND HOLIDAYS

It was always busy in the run up to Christmas. It was impossible to keep to time with the number of passengers and road traffic about, so there was a lot of late running and curtailments. On Christmas Day, loadings were changeable. Part of the day was quiet while at other times there were quite a few passengers on board. The really early shifts seemed unnecessary to me, but not to London Transport who were aware that some people needed to be in the City areas very early on Christmas Day morning.

I had to work on a number of Christmas Days. As a conductor I worked on one of them with 'Darkie' Stevens on the 645 – it was very quiet and London Transport must have made a loss on us ('Darkie' was to be the driver of the last Finchley depot trolleybus – this was in the early hours of 3rd January 1962).

To accommodate the early risers, a few trolleybus routes had very early starts with the 521 being one of them; following tramway practice, many 'trolley roads' had an earlier start than motorbus routes. The first one left the shed at 3.42am for Holborn Circus where it arrived at 4.39. It immediately departed for Turnpike Lane Station where it made our one scheduled turn of the year there – it arrived at 5.11am and left two minutes later for Holborn again. This was a long duty because after going back to North Finchley, it made another trip to Holborn and did not finish until 8.25 at Tally Ho. By the time the conductor had walked to the depot and paid in a meagre amount for an 8.41 sign-off, he could have felt hard done by as he had started at 3.32am. The 4.39 arrival at Holborn was the fourth to arrive as two 513s and a 643 got there before it – again, passenger needs. The first 513 left Highgate depot at 3.26am with the crew finishing at 6.17 at Kentish Town – from there they were given twenty minutes walking time to get back to the depot as there were no bus services running that early.

Most Christmas Day duties were straight-through shifts without a break – there were a few 'two bus jobs', but they too were short duties. Those allocated to the very early turns could be finished and back home before the rest of their household were up. Staff on the later shifts could be even better off – one 609 duty left the depot at 1.20pm and arrived back at 3.32, working just Depot/Barnet/Moorgate/Depot. Other duties just did a single trip to Holborn and back. The longest turns were about five hours in length which would be a couple of rounders.

Until Christmas 1959, a ten minute service operated for much of the day on the 521 and 621, giving a five minute headway between North Finchley and Holborn Circus (service reductions on all routes saw the 1960 service interval reduced by fifty per cent). The 609s started before 6am as, again, people were wanting to get into the inner areas. 645s up to rural Canons Park did not start running until about 10.30am. London Transport offered very generous levels of services on these days during the time that I worked on the trolleys but it was unprofitable as little money was paid in and staff were paid double time. It was a nice day for drivers as there was little road traffic about.

All vehicles had to be in the depot by 4pm on Christmas Day; to achieve this the last few trolleybuses on most routes only went part way. On the 521s/621s, after the last Holborn had left Tally Ho at 2.05pm, the service was cut back firstly to Kings Cross, then Finsbury Park and finally Wood Green. The schedule compilers attempted to split the returning 'buses as best they could but, even so, Woodhouse Road saw a more frequent level of service on Christmas Days than at any other time of the year for in the last half hour, trolleybuses were coming back to North Finchley at one or two minute intervals. This meant that vehicles bunched and in Tally Ho bus station any passengers hoping to go south (and there would always be a few) were met by a continual procession of trolleybuses clicking their way through the overhead points as their crews made their way to the depot and home to their Christmas dinners.

The last half hour of trolleybus operation in the vicinity of Finchley depot was hectic and the cleaners and shunters couldn't work fast enough to clear the returning vehicles. To give an idea of the turmoil, forty-one trolleybuses ran into the shed between 3 and 4pm; they banked up in Woodberry Grove and out into Ballards Lane, even beyond the frog for the depot. Crews abandoned their vehicles, leaving them with their poles on the wires, but it was safe to do this as there wouldn't be any more 645s or 660s going south. Three or four trolleybuses could arrive at Woodberry Grove together, so the conductor on the last in the convoy would often pull the handle for them all – this meant a speedier access to the depot. The cleaners and shunters came in at about 2pm in lieu of their night shift – this allowed all the vehicles to be put to bed shortly after 4pm. The foreman, who was not without his share of Christmas spirit, would then send them home. He and a skeleton staff remained, their main work being to allocate 'buses for service for Boxing Day. We were quite busy on Boxing Day as many people wanted to visit relatives and some people were back at work. There was no such thing as a two week break over Christmas then.

As TGWU rep at Holloway, it looks as if Tom Fitzpatrick has wangled an easy number. The last trams had entered Holloway depot in the first few minutes of Sunday 6th April 1952; they then had to be driven south through the Kingsway Subway where they were handed over to New Cross crews in Addington Street on the south side of the River Thames. Tom presumably has arranged to drive the last tram through the subway, either on over-time or as part of his day's work. Although it is spring he is wearing a raincoat to which is fixed his Metropolitan Stage Carriage Licence badge, he and his colleague are wearing red cap badges, indicative of tram and trolleybus staff. 184's route plate has gone as has its destination blind – the blind box flap hangs down revealing three light bulbs which illuminated the blind and the 'via KINGSWAY SUBWAY' plate. Surely there are too many London Transport officials to see 184 pass through, but they probably want to see the last tram run through the subway. Once 184 has passed, the gates will be secured although it seems this will only be with string.
London Transport Museum U53081.

By 1940, apart from three routes which ran through the Kingsway subway, trams had been annihilated from north, east and west London. The war prevented the conversion of the south London tram routes to trolleybuses and it was not until 1950 that they started to be replaced – this time by motorbuses. The first stage of the conversion took place in October 1950; one of the subway routes (31) was withdrawn at this time. The 33 and 35 were due to be replaced by motor-buses in July 1951 but the lack of progress in providing bus garages in south London earned them a reprieve. The revised date for the conversion of the final tram routes through the subway (33 and 35) was Saturday 5th April 1952. Despite the carnage of the 1930s, they had amazingly survived until within three months of the final closure of the tram system.

I rubbed shoulders with the 35 route trams between Archway and Islington; they were also to be seen in Islington on route 33. I was at work on the last day that trams worked in north London. It was a wet and dull day, but to all intents and purposes it was like any other. The trams were carrying passengers just as they had done for so many years before, but there were not crowds of people going out for last rides and taking photographs. Word had got around that 'the trams are coming off today' and there was a general conver-sation between staff and passengers about it all. I was always aware of working alongside trams because of the noise they made, particularly over crossovers. When the last trams ran into Holloway depot that night they were given a boisterous send-off.

Between Archway and Islington, tram route 35 paralleled a number of trolleybus services; two of these were the 517 and 679. Just south of the Nags Head, E3 class tram 1980 is flanked by Edmonton's 1181 on route 679 and Highgate's 1033 on route 517. It would appear that 1181 has both of its booms painted white. *Clarence Carter.*

Despite big events taking place at Harringay stadium, no extras were run for them so there were usually inspectors supervising loadings as hordes of people could flock out in a short space of time. Greyhound racing, stock car racing and speedway took place there along with the Billy Graham Christian mission in 1953. In the adjacent arena there was boxing, wrestling, speed skating and roller speedway.

London Transport would pull out all the stops to provide public transport for one-off special occasions. One such event was Coronation Day, Tuesday 2nd June 1953, when Queen Elizabeth the Second was crowned. To move the expected crowds, a massive plan was put into operation. Various levels of services operated over the trolleybus network and, at FY, extra early morning and late night journeys ran between North Finchley and Holborn Circus on the 521s/621s, and between Barnet and Golders Green on the 645s. The 645 journeys were to accommodate well-wishers wanting to use the Underground at Golders Green – stations opened at 3am and had a later finish than usual. The TGWU and London Transport had a special scheduling agreement that day, in that the first duties could sign on at 2.01am (departing from depot and garages at 2.11). Vehicles did not have to be back in until 2.49 the next morning, meaning that the the last duties need not sign off until 2.59am.

There were a few routes that were 'on the road' for just over twenty four and a half hours – our 645 was one of them. The first left the depot at 2.11am for Barnet with the last not returning from there until 2.45 the next day. London Transport was over-ambitious, and rain on the day led to poor loadings for much of the time. The very early and very late journeys ran around almost empty, and I only paid in a small amount of money. Our normal Monday to Friday run-out at this time was for seventy-nine vehicles, but on Coronation Day it was seventy-five required so our depot was able to cover all of its allocated work. Quite a lot of it was covered by staff working their day off. On the few days preceding and following the Coronation, the very early and very late journeys that operated on Coronation Day on routes 521, 621 and 645 also ran but, again, were lightly loaded. Stretching over more than twenty-four hours, there may have been some duplicate timecards issued as some running numbers may have departed from the depot before their contemporary number had run in.

Barnet Fair was held near Barnet bridge in pre-war years; in later times it was held in the Mays Lane area. During my time at Finchley, no extra vehicles were laid on for this event but we carried heavy loadings to and from it.

A two minute silence was observed at 11am on the Sunday nearest to Remembrance Day. I dismounted from my cab outside Pentonville Prison in 1955 on the way to Holborn Circus and I and my conductor stood beside our trolleybus. A notice in the depot instructed drivers to position their vehicles in the nearside of the road at these times and that staff were to observe the two minute silence. The overhead line was not overloaded by a number of trolleybuses all trying to pull away in the same section simultaneously at 11.02 for service intervals were quite wide at that time of day.

Another holiday of sorts was courtesy of the Territorial Army. After being de-mobbed from National Service, I had to do a compulsory three and a half years part time service with them, reporting to the Duke Of York's Barracks in King's Road, Chelsea. As I had been a despatch rider, I had to ride motorcycles and drive fifteen-hundred weight Bedford lorries. This kept my hand in with army matters. Sometimes it was just one day a week, while on other occasions it meant the full weekend. London Transport was compelled to make staff available and pay rostered earnings. Each year I did two weeks on manoeuvres. In 1952 it was at Hawick in Scotland, in 1953 at Buckingham Tofts near Thetford, Norfolk and in 1954 at Shornecliff near Folkestone, Kent.

DELAYS AND DISRUPTIONS

Throughout the country, whether it was trams, trolleybuses or motorbuses that were run, there were many external factors that prevented operators from running their services smoothly. Disruptions came in many forms: heavy traffic, burst water mains, gas leaks, roadworks, the occasional power failure or overhead wiring problem, a passenger being taken ill, foggy weather, icy roads, etc. When delays occurred, most crews would assist officials who would show their mettle with on-the-spot decisions, and no effort was spared to keep as regular a service as possible going whatever the circumstance. Commonsense, initiative and experience, rather than working agreements and adherence to the rule book, was the way to do things. Often we didn't need inspectors' guidance – we found our own solutions, and just got on with things. To get a service of sorts going in the opposite direction to where there was a snarl-up, some crews would turn their vehicles round in side streets with the aid of battery power. Inspectors would not reprimand them for curtailing themselves, but would probably commend them for initiative.

Petrol was de-rationed in May 1950, but initially had little effect on the volume of traffic on Britain's roads as most people could not afford to purchase a car. Within a few years, though, traffic conditions were causing problems as people were buying their own cars. Curtailments became a regular feature on weekdays, especially on the 609 route which used the A1 road out of London. London Transport could have counteracted much of this by giving more running time; they were loathe to do this and seemed to prefer lost mileage. The lack of sufficient running time meant that there were many occasions when crews really had to show their worth when trying to provide a good service. The following paragraph illustrates this.

The first part of an early turn would often be two trips from North Finchley to Holborn and back on the 521s/621s but, what with the morning peak traffic, we would regularly get into Charterhouse Street late on the second journey. It was in our interest to get back to North Finchley on time so we could have a full meal relief, and experienced trolleybus staff were often able to achieve this with a speedy run back. There was not a lot of traffic leaving the City between nine and ten o'clock in the morning (most of it was going the other way) so if we were eight or ten minutes down arriving at

Charterhouse Street on a 521, it would be 'straight in, straight out'. With a quick run up Farringdon Road we soon reached its junction with Clerkenwell Road where the 543 had frog priority for its right turn; as with all junctions it was approached at low speed. For the first few years of my trolleybus career, the frog handle was one of the cumbersome long heavy types, but in the mid-1950s an easier to use short-handled one was installed. This was beneficial for when we needed to pick up a bit of time an agile conductor, standing on the platform of a slowing-down trolleybus, would stretch out his left arm, grab the handle and pull it down as soon as it was in their grasp. Drivers would notice the light in the signal box change in their favour and, providing the traffic lights were too, would pass through at slow speed without stopping, thus saving a few seconds. If we were lucky we might just get in front of a 617/621/659 at Kings Cross which had come round the Holborn Loop the other way and be able to get a bit of a gallop on up 'the Cally' before we reached Holloway Road. At the Nags Head we had to slow up for the junction but we might get in front of a couple of trolleybuses from Tottenham Court Road that were waiting at the traffic lights in Parkhurst Road. It would be unlikely that we would have a clear run up Seven Sisters Road to 'The Manor' due to the many other trolleybus services on this road, though hopefully our progress wouldn't be impeded too much. At Manor House the 641 came up from Moorgate and again if we were fortunate we might pip one waiting at the lights in Green Lanes. The section from here to Wood Green would normally be free of traffic at that time of the morning and after we had taken the frog at Jolly Butchers Hill we were on our own to North Finchley. Not all these factors might work in our favour, but if most of them did we might get back to North Finchley on time for our relief. However, if things went against us we could arrive back at Tally Ho more behind schedule than we had left Holborn. At Tally Ho, some 'buses ran into the depot after the morning peak and when they did, we had to use the 660s' terminal wires in the trolleybus station. Normally we'd lower our own poles and battery past any 660s occupying the stand, but there'd always be one or two crews who were not so minded and they would drop a standing 660's poles enabling themselves to have a free run through the station. Stonebridge staff were not pleased to come out of the refreshment hut and find that their poles had been 'roofed'. Sometimes, an SE crew would see that we wanted to get past them, and would 'dip their sticks'.

The evening peak hour could also be challenging and in the early 1950s, motorbuses and trolleybuses leaving the City areas departed with full loads at the height of the evening peak hour. 609s were operating to a three minute headway and often left Moorgate nearly full. It would virtually be 'three bells all the way', signifying that we could only take on new passengers as others got off. In fact, when leaving Moorgate, if a route 43 bus had not come by, we might not be able to allow any more on until we got near to the Angel Islington and even then it might be just 'one off, one on', and then 'ding, ding, ding' on the bell. The three bell signal indicated to drivers that the 'bus was full. On arrival at the Nags Head, there might be twenty-five people waiting and we were

It looks as if a Finchley trolleybus has run into the depot and by-passed Stonebridge's 1658 which is having some stand time in Tally Ho bus station. The Finchley conductor or driver has used 1658's bamboo pole and left the trolleys resting on a span wire. 1658's crew are no doubt in the refreshment hut; when they return to their vehicle they will know what has happened and re-wire 1658. *Mike Abbott.*

only able to take all these on if an equivalent number alighted. Again it would be a three bell signal. The advantage of all this was that conductors, once they had collected all their fares, were able to stand on the platform for much of the way. At Archway, we might pick up 'a load of rabbits'; this was trolleybusmen's terminology for those who were hopping on and hopping off – short-riders. At East Finchley as many boarded as got off and it wouldn't be until we approached North Finchley that the 'bus started to empty. Because we weren't stopping at all the stops we could keep to time and reach Barnet in the allotted fifty-nine minutes. Vic preferred to keep going, and if we had worked a trip like this he might say to me at Barnet, "We did well there, that was a good run."

Gillingham Road is being fully utilised on 23rd December 1961 – a power failure in West Hendon caused delays and many 666s were curtailed there. This turn was made on battery and 1597 is in mid-manoeuvre; 1558's crew will be 'getting their sticks down' soon and follow suit. The driver has been winding through 1597's destination blind but is having a problem finding the correct display as a Finchley blind is fitted; Stonebridge have run out of theirs and the maintenance staff have either got one from our depot or have removed one from a Finchley trolleybus that had been dumped there.
Peter Moore.

Although the 666 service was in disarray following the power cut in West Hendon, 660s were not affected and our 1461 passes Stonebridge's 1558 and 1597 which are using battery power at Gillingham Road.
Peter Moore.

We would normally only lag behind time on wet and dark evenings when traffic tended to move slower. Some evening journeys were notorious and if we met the crew who were one week in front of us on the rota, they might say, "You don't want to do duty 138 next week as you'll get a right hammering on the 5.11 from Moorgate." Of course this was only general banter and crews just did their duties as they came up. The evening peaks were more frenetic than the mornings because everybody left work at about the same time, five o'clock. The mornings could be very busy too, but the load was spread as there was a greater degree of variance in the times that people left for work and started their jobs.

To counteract traffic problems that manifested themselves in the mid-1950s, London Transport entered into a local agreement with the TGWU at Colindale, Finchley and Stonebridge depots to turn vehicles short at Cricklewood from the Harlesden direction. Until then there had been no alternative but to curtail late running 'buses at Craven Park – very wasteful as about half a journey was lost. The new curtailment point involved reversing trolleybuses on battery power into Gillingham Road which was just north of Cricklewood Lane railway bridge, and on one occasion I was held up for a short time by a Stonebridge trolleybus doing this. Staff from SE were the most regular performers here as three of their services (660, 664 and 666) used this facility. It was agreed that an inspector would supervise these movements but due to its frequent use this became impractical and crews did it themselves with conductors beckoning their drivers back with hand signals. I never carried out this manoeuvre and am not aware of any other Finchley crew doing this as inspectors always felt it best to have the Finchley 'buses back at their end of the route. This agreement meant that much useful mileage was obtained between Craven Park and Cricklewood. Some staff were a bit sneaky and turned on battery at St Gabriels Church, which was the destination blind display used for the Gillingham Road turn. This meant that they didn't pick up passengers at the two main loading points in the Broadway.

Holly Park was extensively used as a curtailment point in the later years of trolleybus operation; quite a lot of destination blinds were not fitted with a HOLLY PARK display but 1624 has one. This would have been the scene when I turned here in 1955 though I put up GOLDERS GREEN on both blinds. *Peter Moore.*

The photographer had never seen anything like it – a trolleybus being turned ninety degrees on the overhead. Due to the busyness of Friday evenings, it was common for 660s to be curtailed at Holly Park at these times. The driver is a master of his profession and prefers to work in this way rather than use the batteries – which were in good condition as he used them in the final part of his manoeuvre. *Hugh Taylor.*

Another place that started to be used regularly in the mid-1950s was the battery turn at Holly Park. This was a side street off Regents Park Road, opposite the Express Dairy College farm – just north of Henlys Corner. Sometimes in my driving days, when I was working my day off or doing a piece of overtime on the 645s or 660s I would find myself behind a Stonebridge 660 whose crew had been instructed to turn there. On the way I might see its conductor wind up and down the rear destination blind looking for HOLLY PARK. The reason for this was that some vehicles had this display at the top of the blinds, others at the bottom, while others didn't have it at all and had to show GOLDERS GREEN STATION. Due to its upgrading, HOLLY PARK was included on destination blinds issued to Colindale, Finchley and Stonebridge depots from April 1960 – new blinds incorporating this display were only fitted when old ones wore out. From time to time I would come across a Stonebridge conductor slamming his poles down at Holly Park. With the first part of the bamboo work done, the conductor would wave his driver back into Fitzalan Road and they'd be out on the main road and the poles up again with the bamboo slid

beneath the vehicle all within two or three minutes. Very professional, and come rain or sun, there were no whines about the method of turning here. The Stonebridge staff had tuned it to a fine art and some of their drivers were so skilful that, as shown in the accompanying photo, they turned their trolleybuses round by mainly using the overhead.

To prevent ourselves from running early, such as Sunday mornings when the running time was a bit loose, we would leave a terminus a few minutes late. This enabled drivers to move at a reasonable speed rather than dawdle around; however, we could still find ourselves ahead of time and we would wait at a bus stop for a minute or two or catch a set of traffic lights. When the running time was tight, mainly in rush hours, we could often have a problem keeping to time – if it was raining, no chance. Some staff would counteract the tight running time by leaving a terminus early, but this was not in the spirit of buswork and was only done for their own benefit. I would not participate in this practice nor would most of my colleagues. Running to schedule required skill and judgement by drivers.

If two 'buses were running one behind the other then,

depending on the crew, we would 'work the road' together. This was achieved by the first 'bus going straight past a few bus stops, allowing it to pick up a bit of time. The second 'bus picked up the passengers at stops missed by the first one. Crews understood the situation and were doing this in the service's best interests, not our own.

Problems arose when a crew member failed to report for work on time, particularly if the duty took over 'on the road'; if this happened, quick action had to be taken as trolleybuses could not be left on the streets. The point inspector watching 609/645 reliefs at Tally Ho now had a situation on his hands and the last thing he wanted was to be left with a fully laden trolleybus and no-one to drive or conduct it, particularly if the one behind wasn't running. If he was on good terms with the crews, he would ask the driver or the conductor if they would stay on the 'bus until it came back to North Finchley the other way. Hopefully the latecomer would materialise or someone would be found to take over when the 'bus got back to Tally Ho. (I've known some drivers take a trolleybus all the way to Canons Park or Moorgate: I drove a 609 to Barnet one day when I wasn't relieved). There was also a time when an inspector acted as conductor for me; my mate had 'blown out' and he acted as guard. He let people alight and stopped further intending passengers from boarding. I showed PRIVATE on the front destination blind to signify that the 'bus was not in service with the same applying for the return trip to Tally Ho. The inspector alighted at the bus station and I ran the 'bus into the depot. Without a conductor on board to pull the frog handle at the top of Woodberry Grove, I had to move the trolley poles onto the depot-bound wires. This was a regular occurrence, drivers and inspectors running trolleybuses into the depot by themselves. Generous overtime dockets were freely given to those assisting operations and most staff would help out. If we had finished our day's work it was easy to accommodate an inspector's request, but if we were on a short relief then we would have to take over our second 'bus late.

There was never a point inspector at Woodberry Grove relief point, so we had to make ad-hoc arrangments when a member of staff failed to arrive. If someone didn't turn up for a 660, the poles would be dropped and passengers would be told that they would have to walk up the road to the bus station. If this happened to a 645, the passengers would be transferred to another 645 and a crew member would go to the bus station and ask an inspector what he wanted done. Passengers could be transferred from trolleybuses to Central Buses and Country Buses and vice versa where both forms of transport were using the same roads; they could not be put onto Green Line buses.

Sometimes, inspectors had a conflict of interests. Divided loyalties meant that on the one hand they wanted staff to finish work on time particularly those on twelve hour spread-overs, while on the other hand they wanted to maintain as regular a service as possible. Inspectors had worked 'on the road' themselves in the past so they knew that staff wanted to finish their day on time. It didn't matter if a crew were late coming off on their first half of duty as they could be adjusted later. Crew reliefs and finishes were marked on their time-sheets. The following occurred on a number of occasions. I was working a spreadover duty with the last part of the shift being from Barnet to Moorgate and back to the depot on a 609. Arriving at Tally Ho from Barnet I would find myself a few minutes down due to passenger loadings and traffic. An inspector would come up to me and say, "Bill, I know you're running late and on a spread and want to finish on time, but you've got a 'double road', and if I turn you at Windsor Terrace or Islington Green, there'll be a big gap from Moorgate. Do me a favour and go through and I'll double the amount of time that you finish late". I would call through to Sid, Jean, Gladys or whoever I was working with, and say what the inspector wanted – we would comply if possible as we knew the favour would be returned another time.

The terminology 'double road' meant that the 'bus in front was missing. Very occasionally, a 'treble road' would occur. Inspectors who were 'on the ball' would have seen what was on the horizon and would take steps to avoid such a big gap in the service. They would try and collar the crew of the 'bus that had two out behind it, and ask if they would mind holding back a headway; a financial incentive might be offered, or a previous favour called in. If a crew wouldn't hold back, and it should be remembered that staff had other things in their lives than work, then the crew who were going into a treble road would be pushed out a few minutes early. An inspector would say "Don't bother about the timecard, just keep going". In trolleybus parlance this would be "toe down all the way".

RUNNING INTO STAFF CUTS
Staff shortages meant that trolleybuses were off the road when they should have been carrying passengers, and arrangements had to be made to get 'buses into and out of the depot when 'staff cuts' occurred. It was necessary for forward planning to take place so that passengers would be aware of 609s and 645s being taken out of the service at North Finchley. If it was apparent, before we started work, that a 'bus movement' (as they were known) was required we would be given an instruction to run the 'bus in or out of the depot at the appropriate time. However, if the need for a bus movement only arose during our duty, there would have to be quick action by an inspector who would say "Show NORTH FINCHLEY and run it in". Drivers and conductors each received a quarter of an hour overtime for these movements. If we had to take a 'bus in, it was fair recompense; when running a 'bus out we got something for nothing as it saved us walking to the bus station.

Any 609 going to Barnet, which ran into a staff cut would not be driven to the relief point in the High Road but would go through the bus station to gain the depot. Southbound 609s would set down passengers at the stop outside the bus station and run it in light from there. 645s and 660s which had no relieving crew in Ballards Lane northbound, would run the 'bus into the depot via the bus station. Southbound 645s running into a staff cut tipped passengers out at Woodberry Grove before running in. 521s/621s with no crews could be left on Tally Ho stand although they might have to be shunted into the depot if the area became too cluttered.

When a crew member did not turn up for work it was sometimes necessary for trolleybuses, which should have gone to Barnet, to be turned outside the Tally Ho pub on battery power as shown by 1465. In fact the 609 is having a bad day for not only is 1465 being taken out of service, but another 609 is a victim of a staff cut; showing NORTH FINCHLEY, it means that the crew have been instructed to run it into the depot. *Don Thompson.*

TAKING UP AFTER STAFF CUTS

609s/645s going to Barnet picked up at their different relief points in Ballards Lane; 660s did not bother picking anyone up at the top of Woodberry Grove and would start work in the bus station. 609s going to Moorgate were unable to pick up in the High Road so they too started from the bus station. 645s towards Canons Park employed the little-used section of wire that turned left out of Woodberry Grove into Ballards Lane. By doing this, the bus stop which embraced the relief point was missed but, if people were waiting there, crews would beckon them over. It was no hardship to do this – we were there for the public and it avoided complaints.

Sometimes I would take over a 609 or 645 having found it abandoned at one of the relief points – the crew had come up a bit early and cleared off. This was not my way of doing things and I always waited for my relief to turn up – sometimes even five or ten minutes due to the fact that they had come off late on their first spell of duty and were taking up late on their second half.

There were occasions when I was not informed about a bus movement and would come down from Barnet and find that there was no relieving crew. Eventually an inspector would come over to find out what was going on and would say "Weren't you told to take it in?". On ascertaining that I hadn't, the passengers had to be transferred to the next 609 and ours run in. If I was lucky, he would say "Leave it with me, I'll deal with it, you can get off". Conversely we could be waiting for a 609 going to Moorgate and it wouldn't materialise. After a few minutes I would ask an inspector if it was running late and he would say, "Weren't you told to take it out?". When I replied that I wasn't, we would have to go to the depot and get hold of, say, FY43. When we got back, we

would be instructed to turn short, probably at Islington Green. The entry on the paperwork was put down to 'staff' when it should have been 'foul-up by depot inspectors!'

THREE-BUS JOBS

The way that duties were compiled sometimes led to difficulties on the road. 'Three-bus jobs' fell into this category. They were unpopular as one of the two spells involved working on two vehicles. A minimum of six minutes 'joining up' time was given if the next 'bus was taken over in the same direction, twelve if it was going the other way. There was a maximum of thirty minutes between leaving one 'bus and taking over another with these duties. However, if a crew came off so late that they were not able to have their six minutes, most would go straight from one 'bus to another as it saved a lot of inconvenience all round.

Occasionally on a three-bus job, when there was just the minimum time between coming off one 'bus and taking over another, a bus movement was required. This could delay the next vehicle being taken over on time, but as inspectors had a full picture of what was going on, they might say to the crew concerned, "Leave it on the stand – I'll get it run in later". Another driver might welcome this as it would save him the walk to the depot. On the other hand, we might have to take one out of the depot on one of these duties; a good inspector would arrange for it to be brought out for us if he could see we weren't coming off on time.

With three-bus jobs, some of the portions of work were very small. If we had come off a 609 from Barnet at North Finchley we could find that we took another 609 up to Barnet about twenty minutes later and come off at Tally Ho again on the way back – we just did a 'Barnet end'. The second 609

1486 on route 621 turns from Ballards Lane into Woodberry Grove while 1493 on the 609 moves in the opposite direction. Being a daytime view, this indicates the possibility of the vehicles running into or leaving a 'staff cut'. *Don Thompson.*

The left hand overhead wire from Woodberry Grove into Ballards Lane was rarely used; resuming service on route 645 to Canons Park after a staff cut, 1504 of necessity utilises this facility. 1504's conductor has just let go of the frog handle allowing 1540, behind, to start its trip to Holborn Circus. *London Trolleybus Preservation Society.*

might be running twenty minutes late, and although we knew that we would probably not be expected to take it to Barnet, we had to stay on the scene as the departing crew may not have been instructed to put the late running 'bus into the bus station. We might have to turn it round on battery at the Tally Ho pub so that it was facing the right direction for the next crew. Staff thought that three-bus jobs were an unnecessary lengthening of the day and considered them particularly arduous if they occurred on spreadovers. To the schedule compilers they were a useful facility, though in practice they could lead to operational problems.

OTHER ITEMS
If a conductor went sick on duty, they would tell an official who would make contact with the depot in the hope that they would have enough time to arrange for another conductor to take over at North Finchley. In the meantime, the crew would wind up PRIVATE on the blinds and run back out of service to Tally Ho. At the depot all efforts would have been made to find a replacement, but if it was not possible then the 'bus would have to be run in. If a driver went sick on duty, the booms were placed under the retaining hooks and the crew would travel back to Finchley on a service 'bus. Someone

qualified to drive a trolleybus would be sent to where the vehicle was parked. Those able to do this could be an inspector licensed to drive a trolleybus, a member of the depot mainte- nance staff who was similarly qualified, or another driver. One day I was on standby and had to fetch one of our 'buses from Wood Green when the driver felt unwell – that was all I had to do for my day's work.

Connections had to be made with other trolleybuses and some timecards indicated this. These were strictly adhered to and crews might have to wait a minute or two for the other one to turn up. When I started on the job, trams were still running. There was a note on the timecard of FY4 on the 521/621, which left the depot at 4.23am for Finsbury Park, that it was to connect with a route 33 tram at Manor House at 4.56am – the tram left at 4.58am. This gave people two minutes to get across from one side of Green Lanes to the other. Even the staff buses had time connections; the 521 had to meet the last 679 to Ponders End at Manor House at 1.12am – this enabled anybody wanting to travel from Wood Green/Turnpike Lane to get to Tottenham/Edmonton. Similarly the 521 staff bus had to meet Colindale's 666 staff bus from Craven Park to Edgware at Cricklewood Broadway at 4.07am.

172

It was imperative that all timed connections were maintained – these links and facilities were often made at the public's request and London Transport was very accommodating in this way. One example concerned a Sunday morning 625 from Woodford, whose passengers kept missing one of our northbound 521s/621s at Wood Green. The problem was resolved by a footnote being written on the relevant timecards stating that the connecting times should be maintained. A second example involved staff at factories in North Acton who only had an hour to get from their workplaces to Acton Market for a meal and their shopping, and back again. To make sure that FY104 on the 660s, which left Craven Park at 12.25pm, picked them up, an inked note (written in the form of a star) was made on its timecard stating that a time of 12.38 had to be maintained at North Acton. The Craven Park inspectors would specifically watch FY104, so that crews picked up their allotted load. It was in staff's interest to follow these instructions; if they didn't, a public complaint would be likely to follow.

STAFF TROLLEYBUSES
Until the start of the Second World War, London Transport made little provision to get their staff to and from work in the early hours when no other form of transport was available. Drivers and conductors had to make their own arrangements, often walking long distances at unearthly hours in all weathers, and it was not until difficulties were being experienced during wartime that more facilities were laid on. Staff motorbuses just carried a driver but trams and trolleybuses needed a second person on board as someone had to either operate point levers or pull frog handles. As a conductor was now being carried, London Transport allowed members of the public to use the staff trams and trolleybuses as they might as well have any casual revenue that could be taken. Although few journeys were advertised, word spread and a number of people became regular passengers – some journeys were very well patronised, particularly on Friday and Saturday nights. The profile for staff transport was high enough to warrant, from time to time, an official listing of all staff journeys on the tram and trolleybus network and the one for Finchley depot is illustrated. Armed with this paperwork, people could travel round much of the trolleybus system during the night. Those depots operating staff trolleybuses usually used one or two vehicles. Edmonton held the record by putting out six vehicles on Saturday nights (four concurrently). The maximum number running at Finchley was five (this was Saturday nights, when three ran simultaneously). Staff bus drivers had to be very alert for some boroughs extinguished street lighting at 1am. In winter, illumination did not come on until 6am, in time for the morning peak. Some places were pitch black so headlights were an absolute necessity.

When I started there were two night duties; they were on my rota and I worked both of them with Vic. The shunters positioned the two 'buses one behind the other, at the front of road five. Once the crews reported for work, the drivers went out and prepared them for the night's work. Satisfied all was well, they would draw the 'buses forward until they were adjacent to the traffic office where their conductors boarded. Before they left the depot, most crews made sure that a bamboo pole was stowed beneath the 'bus as the last thing anyone wanted was a dewirement at night a long way from home with no bamboo to retrieve the situation – I cannot recall anybody being caught out in this way. It was a good job that Vic or I checked, as on one occasion we came across overhead work being carried out at Nags Head junction. A number of tower wagons were positioned there, and as the power had been switched off we had to battery through.

The night duties became non-rotational before I started driving so I never worked one in this capacity. Working to a six-day week, two crews operated them week in, week out with cover being supplied for the seventh day. This was done by the night crews working one of their days off or by other staff operating the duties (with the eleven day fortnight, cover had to be supplied in the same way for three days). When the regular night men were on holiday there were others who were always ready to step in as these shifts were 'nice little numbers' when compared to the ardours of day work.

As there was a degree of ease on these shifts, those that operated them were the senior and therefore the more elderly members of the Finchley establishment. The night staff had their own small rota which comprised of twenty-one night duties, a 'buckshee' duty and six rest days over a four-week period. The buckshee shift saw the crews being given an early or late turn, whichever suited them best. Although Friday was pay day, the night crews' wages were waiting for them when they came in on Thursday nights. They were paid time and a quarter on top of the prevailing rate – this also applied at weekends and on bank holidays.

At some depots (including Finchley) the staff journeys were at the start or finish of an ordinary duty, but at others the whole shift embraced staff work only. The duties were known as 'nighters' as were the publicised all-night trolleybuses (a separate operation on a few routes). An anomaly was that on most trips, the running time for the staff bus journeys was the same as in peak hours. It was not possible to leave a few minutes late from the terminus and have a fast drive as people knew what time the staff bus was due – they expected them to be there at the correct time – particularly if they connected with another bus. Therefore, the staff journeys were a real 'scratch' at times.

Our first staff trolleybus of the night (and of the system in fact) was the 11.34pm 521 daily departure from North Finchley to Wood Green and back. Why it was classified as a staff journey is mysterious as it was the last journey of the day to Wood Green and part of a late shift. It was the only trip to Gladstone Avenue which had two minutes stand time, every other journey being given only one.

The second staff bus was duty one, which on weekdays signed-on at 12.19am and left the depot at 12.29 for Barnet. It then went to the Nags Head as a 609, and on the way picked up the late finishers from Finchley depot who were waiting at Tally Ho. When it arrived at East Finchley station, and the bus stop at Highgate Woods Underground sidings, there might be one or two of their staff there. All trolleybuses terminating at the Nags Head stood in Warlters Road, and this street was used four times each weekday night by our staff 'buses. Two vehicles could be seen together briefly – one was scheduled to leave at 1.25am, the other timed to arrive at 1.27am. Staff were always considerate in being totally quiet here and the motor generator sets were turned off so as not to disturb the residents in the houses and the block of flats in this street.

Leaving the Nags Head, it went back to North Finchley for 1.55am where it had a twenty minute layover (arriving a few minutes early, there was just enough time to nip up to the depot to get refreshments from the canteen). The blinds were changed to show 521 and it then worked to Nags Head and back to Tally Ho for 3.32. Virtually nobody was picked up there and back on this journey. Then a trip at 3.37am to 'Gabriels' – again maybe just the odd casual passenger might board. I considered that sauntering through north-west London at this unearthly hour with no-one on was a waste of time – still, that was what London Transport wanted. It was so quiet that I sat on the front nearside seat and on one occasion nodded off. I recall the 'bus turning right from Finchley Road into Childs Hill, but remember nothing after that until Vic woke me up at Cricklewood Broadway where a frog handle needed to be pulled. However, I was wide awake (and had to be) on the return trip to Finchley as a few people got on. St Gabriels Church loop was an obscure place to turn in the middle of the night. It must have looked strange to see a 521 showing CRICKLEWOOD ST GABRIELS CHURCH going through Golders Green at 3.52am, but it was standard practice to keep 521 up for this trip. From Tally Ho the 'bus went to Kings Cross as a 521 with a 6.12am finish at North Finchley. Six minutes 'walking time' back to the depot was allowed and, along with ten minutes paying-in time, a 6.28 sign-off was achieved. Duty one on Sundays carried out the same work as on weekdays until relief at 2.05am.

The third staff bus was duty two which, on weekdays commenced at 12.29am. Leaving the depot ten minutes later it worked as a 521 to Nags Head and back to Finchley depot where it was supposed to run in at 2.05am. On the occasion that I worked this duty we left the 'bus, with the lights off, on the stand at Tally Ho and walked along the deserted and silent Ballards Lane to the depot to get something to eat and drink in the canteen. I took the punch and rack with me for safety's sake as there was always the possibility of somebody stealing them from the locker in the 'bus. When we came back, there were always a few passengers waiting in the shelter, protocol of the day being that they would not board until the lights were switched back on. Some staff took the 'bus back to the depot where it was turned round on its batteries and re-poled, ready to go out at 2.56am for Holborn Circus. If it was raining, the 'bus was almost certainly going back to the depot.

During the winter-time when I was on the 2.43am start, I would sometimes see this 'bus parked with its lights ablaze, illuminating the depot forecourt. All the windows would be closed so that staff and passengers would have an element of warmth on its 3.01am trip from Tally Ho. Not only was this the first 521 to Holborn but also the earliest journey on the whole of Central Road Services, so this trip kick-started London Transport's traffic day. When it approached the City end of the route the 'bus was almost full with charladies, Smithfield market workers, postal workers for Mount Pleasant sorting office, and printers for Fleet Street (which wasn't far away from Holborn). The 'bus returned to North Finchley after which there was a trip to Kings Cross with a finish at Tally Ho at 6.38am – the duty signed off at 6.54. As duty one was a straight-through shift without a relief, it was the better of the two night duties. The crew on duty two were due to leave the depot three minutes after the 609 staff bus to Nags Head, meaning that the 2.53am and 2.56am followed each other out of the depot at that unearthly time of the morning. It was these first murmurings that got Finchley's show on the road each weekday. In the extremes of winter with snow on the ground, it was some sight seeing these two trolleybuses moving together along Ballards Lane with both vehicles' trolley heads flashing on the frosty wires.

Duty two on Sundays started fifteen minutes later than on weekdays but the first half was still Barnet/Nags Head/North Finchley. Arriving at the depot at 2.16am there was no alternative but to give the crew a long relief as no other work could be found for them at that time of the morning. The 'bus did not depart until 3.47 on a very odd journey. It went to Holborn Circus via the 609 route; it also returned via Archway, meaning that when it left Holborn it showed 521 BARNET. This trip picked up a few members of staff and when the vehicle came back from Barnet it only went as far as North Finchley. The trolley arms had to be swung in Kingsway for a return to Barnet, this being the only scheduled trip to make such a manoeuvre.

Duty three was the first 'day duty' to start. It commenced at 2.43am on Mondays to Saturdays, leaving the depot ten minutes later as a staff bus to Nags Head. This, the fourth staff bus of the night, picked up a few Highgate depot staff on the way down as they had some duties that started just after 3am. It did not pick up any motorbus staff for Holloway bus garage as they had their own staff bus and, generally speaking, motorbuses had a later start than trolleybuses – this reflected the early starting times of the trams. The return trip was to Barnet and on the way north it took on a few Finchley staff going into work. The staff bus element of the duty concluded when it came back to North Finchley.

As the 1950s progressed the reliability of staff decreased, and problems were experienced in that either a conductor or a driver would not turn up at 2.43am to man the staff bus, meaning that others were unable to get in for work. There was no question of moving up whoever was on duty four as that did not sign on until nearly 4am by which time the staff 609 should have almost done its trip to the Nags Head and back. On the occasions when a conductor did not turn up for this duty, the night depot inspector locked up the output and went with the driver as frog handles had to be pulled – any passengers got a free ride. This meant that the output was unmanned for about an hour but as no duties signed on until about the time the 'bus was brought back to the depot, it was considered to be the lesser of two evils. If the driver did not turn in then the journey was cancelled.

Bearing in mind that a 2.43am start had to be managed for six consecutive days it was not surprising that staff didn't turn in and eventually measures were taken to eradicate these difficulties. An agreement was reached between the management and the union for a third night duty. Fortunately there was an easy way to do this for, on 7th January 1959, we had been allocated a later journey on the 645 which did not run into the depot until 1.24am. With another regular crew, this new duty commenced on 4th March 1959 and from then on was known as duty one. It signed on at 11.31pm and took over in Ballards Lane at 11.43 for Edgware on Mondays to Saturdays (four minutes later on Sundays). It worked in service as a 645 as far as Colindale depot from where it became a staff bus at 12.19am – passengers could stay on despite the mid-journey change of operation. Essentially covering for Colindale staff, it returned to Finchley depot an hour after all other trolleybuses had run in. The cleaners would anxiously await its return and descended on it like bees round a honey pot in the knowledge that as soon as it had been dealt with, their night's work was over. By combining this piece of work with the 2.53am departure to Nags Head, reliability was achieved. It was a bit of a novelty for some time as it meant that the crews who, apart from the Cricklewood journey, only worked on the 'City routes' during the night had a change of scenery. I can still visualise conductor Harry Rawlings with his ticket box under his arm walking up Woodberry Grove into Ballards Lane to take over. Ted Rees was another of the night conductors and the unusually named Mr Smallbones was one of the day conductors who covered for the regular night men when they were on holiday. The first 'day duty' did not now sign on until the amenable time of 3.46am!

Unknown to him, one of our conductors was nicknamed Bonar Colleano Junior because he looked like an American actor in British films in the early 1950s. Shortly before his wedding, he and his fiancée agreed that once they were married, they would live in Holloway. She lived at Barnet and being a resourceful man he came up with the idea of using London Transport as a removal firm! This was when the staff bus duties were on the main rota and 'moving house by trolleybus' was going to be achieved when he was working duty one. He had it all mapped out. It was the custom for those who had finished work before the staff bus left the depot, and who wanted to travel towards East Finchley and beyond, to travel with it up to Barnet and back. It was better to chat with your colleagues than hang around in the depot for a time. This particular week, those planning to travel on the staff bus were unaware that they were going to be roped in as removal men. 'Bonar Colleano' made arrangements that the items to be transported were brought to Barnet terminus each night. The 'bus was in at 12.48am and out at 12.49 so there was only a minute loading time. Even though the staff on board helped, it took longer than a minute and the 'bus left late. Who was to know? – there weren't going to be any inspectors about at that time of the morning. Meanwhile, down at Holloway, the other members of the plot were waiting, and along with the remaining members of staff on board, unloaded the items. This all took some nights to complete as

only the downstairs of the trolleybus could be used – carpets, chairs, a bed and various domestic items were transported. 'Bonar Colleano' left his 'jewel in the crown' until last and when the staff bus turned up at Barnet on the final night of his seven day shift, there was a wardrobe waiting to be loaded. The crew, two members of staff and Bonar Colleano all attempted to get it into the lower saloon, but try as they might it would not go in and they were left with no choice but to stand it on the platform. This was precarious and to ensure that London Transport wouldn't have to investigate a wardrobe falling off a trolleybus travelling down Barnet Hill at 1 o' clock in the morning, three of those on board had to hold on to it to ensure that it did not fall off. Whatever the couple of regular passengers thought of these carryings-on beggars belief. Anyway, the whole esapade was carried out successfully without London Transport having the faintest idea of what was going on and it was the talk of the depot for a few days. The night depot inspector knew something was afoot, due to all the sniggering and whispering that was going on in the output at about midnight and it wasn't until after it all happened that the cat was let out of the bag. Bonar Colleano was always grateful for London Transport acting as a removal firm for him.

At 12.19am on 8th November 1961, the staff trolleybus era at Finchley concluded with the arrival back at the depot of trolleybus 1460 which had operated the aforementioned Wood Green trip. The night crews now had to resume a day shift pattern which was a culture shock for them; they had been living the life of Riley for years, but now had to get back into shift work routine and front-line bus work. The 11.43pm start in Ballards Lane was eradicated and the vehicle now ran into the depot. On the night of 7th/8th November one of our drivers got out of his trolleybus cab and a short while later got into the cab of a Routemaster. From now on a motorbus, with only a driver, would take staff home at night and bring them in in the morning. Members of the public who had used our staff trolleybuses now had to find alternative means to travel.

There has been a contretemps between some vehicles on the northbound carriageway under the railway bridge at East Finchley. The incident has delayed the 517/609/617 routes and, unable to proceed, a couple of trolleybuses have been parked up in the distance. Help has arrived and inspectors have instituted wrong line running to get the trolleybus services going again; fortunately the road is wide enough to accommodate northbound traffic as well as southbound movements. An inspector, armed with a bamboo pole, will soon be swinging 929's trolley booms onto the correct set of wires. Passing the other way in this early 1950s view is one of Birch Brother's double-deck buses on route 203. I only turned at East Finchley station once, and that was from the north – a very unusual manoeuvre. To have been curtailed there meant that I must have been running extremely late. There was no overhead link from the north, so I got the poles down and coasted into the station forecourt by a combination of battery and gravity. Once there, I put the booms on the overhead as there was a link wire to take me back towards Barnet; my conductor pulled the frog handle and off we went. In my offside driving mirror, I saw flashing and sparking from the little-used overhead – I also heard electrical crackling noises. *E J Smith.*

THE INSPECTORS

London Transport employed four types of bus inspector – (1) Undercover agents, (2) Timing inspectors, (3) Revenue men who checked tickets and fares, (4) Road officials who regulated services at strategic places on each route or at a terminus.

The undercover agents were plain clothes officials (PCOs). They were known as 'spots', and some of them stood out a mile. They were the lepers of the job, the lowest of the low and rightly despised by all. Alright they had a job to do but they were nasty, mean-minded people who suspected every single conductor, and wouldn't think twice about reporting someone with whom they had worked with as a driver or conductor. If they saw any member of staff deviate slightly from any rule, they would make a note of it and an unsuspecting member of staff would be pulled into the office where a report would be read out for some minor indiscretion. The spots normally operated in different areas to where they had formerly worked, thus preventing them from being detected. However, the PCOs didn't always get things right. One of our conductors had to attend Dollis Hill Divisional Office on a charge that he had put a penny ha'penny into his cash bag and not issued a ticket. It was a well known fact that this conductor used his pockets for keeping the cash he took, and he got away with it on the basis that the spot had made a basic written error, stating that he had put the money into his cashbag.

The spots often worked in pairs as any charge had to be substantiated by a third party; otherwise it was just one person's word against another's. Investigations often centred around re-sold tickets but these had to be retrieved before they reached the floor. The spots could be seen leaping around, like cricket fielders, trying to catch the tickets before they hit the deck! There were cases of conductors realising they were being watched, gathering 'bad' tickets from passengers and then issuing correct ones, after which they would throw away the 'duds'. Dishonest conductors were few and far between and a good half of the PCO's time was spent chasing fare evaders who had been reported by conductors.

The job of timing inspectors was to ensure that adequate running time was given for each journey and they would be told which routes they had to deal with. They would ride over the route at different times of the day and week. Boarding at a terminus they would inform a driver that they would be timing his journey; they used a stop-watch to record when the vehicle was moving and when it was stationary. Their information was passed on to the schedules department for any adjustments. Some of their work was routine but if the TGWU complained that running time was inadequate, or if

London Transport instigated a check as there had been a lot of early running, then these men would be sent out. There was never more than two or three minutes added or deducted from trips.

Revenue inspectors were known as 'jumpers', and they checked tickets on trams, trolleybuses and motorbuses and could board all three types of vehicle in their day's work. They normally worked in easy reach of their homes so a man living in Barnet wouldn't check buses at Croydon; neither would someone living in Uxbridge be seen at Upminster. By keeping a man on his own patch, he became familiar with all the dodges and wheezes of staff and passengers in particular areas and only had to focus on them rather than embrace the whole network. Only if there were specific requirements would a man work away from his normal sphere of operations.

At peak times, trolleybus conductors had their work cut out to get all their fares in – they could get a real pasting as many of the passengers only travelled short distances. They couldn't afford to be slack as there was always the possibility of a 'jumper' boarding; most had been conductors themselves and made allowances. If one boarded when we had a full standing load and he came across a passenger who had been missed he might say, "There's one upstairs, right-hand side, third seat from the front." Having obtained the relevant fare the inspector would give the conductor his board to sign (to signify that he had checked the bus). If he had marked it CORRECT then the conductor would breathe a sigh of relief. Inspectors were aware of fare dodgers and knew it was impossible for conductors to know where everyone was boarding and alighting. As far as I can recollect I was never booked by an inspector for any uncollected fare or ticket irregularity. There were some passengers who could fool the best of conductors when it came to evading their fare and if a strict revenue inspector caught such a passenger, then he would still report the conductor for breaching rule 107 which stated that all fares must be collected.

Road inspectors played a crucial role in day-to-day operations, and it fell upon their shoulders to regulate the services as best they could. They were given protection from the elements by a specially constructed hut; spartan inside, there was a telephone and possibly a stool and small step-ladder. No more than two could fit inside at a time. By using the internal telephone system they could communicate with their colleagues about the routes they were supervising. They would discuss delays, curtailments, crew reliefs and associated service matters, thus enabling them to collectively decide how to best adjust the services.

Road inspectors were to be seen at:

5/621 Tally Ho, Wood Green, Manor House, Nags Head, Holborn Circus.

609 Barnet, Tally Ho, Archway, Nags Head, sometimes Islington, Moorgate.

645 Barnet, Tally Ho, Golders Green, Cricklewood, Colindale Depot, Edgware.

660 Tally Ho, Golders Green, Willesden Garage, Craven Park, Acton Market, Hammersmith.

There needed to be good teamwork between road officials and crews and it was in everyone's interest to work together – on trolleybuses there was always good co-operation. It was counter-productive for inspectors to go round booking staff for trivial indiscretions, such as taking over a 'bus a couple of minutes late; it was not in their interest to book those who inadvertently went to the depot to take over a 'bus when all the time it was on Tally Ho stand. When this did happen and the crew realised their mistake there was a mad rush back to Tally Ho, an apology to the inspector, then get in the 'bus and drive like the clappers to pick up time. By now one or two 'buses were in front that should be behind, so boom lowering procedures had to be activated. Similarly, a crew might think that they took their 'bus over in the bus station when it was in the depot; they might say to the inspector, "Seen 23?" to which he would reply "It's in the depot". They would literally run to the depot, get hold of the 'bus in double quick time and get back to Tally Ho where the inspector would say, "Come on, get on with it – make the time up". Drivers (including myself) would fly down the road and again get round 'buses which should have been behind. As long as the mileage was done there would be no report. If the time could not be made up, some inspectors would report the matter while others would let the matter drop and put any lost mileage down to 'traffic'. Inspectors would call in their favours when they needed something done for them.

Due to the continuing staff shortage, this good working spirit was particularly necessary in the last few years of trolleybus operation, and inspectors juggled 'buses and crews around as necessary. Most inspectors were happy for staff to work to the spirit of the rule book rather than to the letter of it. Inspectors who quoted chapter and verse and reported staff for minor matters, just so that they could get their name on a report, were not helped.

Despite crews' best endeavours they could find themselves running behind time and it was not always possible to make it up, particularly on wet mornings and during Saturday shopping hours. To correct late running, inspectors would instruct staff to turn short of their intended destination. When sorting out late running trolleybuses, inspectors usually erred on the side of caution and would give generous curtailments. Those who gave 'tight' curtailments often found the 'bus came up late again and a second curtailment would ensue. In fact a tight curtailment was enough to trigger some staff to think "we'll show him" and they would really 'drag the road'. Inspectors became frustrated sometimes: they may have told passengers not to board a 521/621 on Tally Ho stand as there was one due out of the depot. When

the expected 'bus did not materialise the inspector was not popular with passengers, having to take their flak through no fault of his own.

At the start of their duty, the inspectors at Tally Ho found out what the staff cuts for the day were. They might find that two or even three successive vehicles wouldn't be running, thus creating an unacceptable gap in the service. There would, though, be many consecutively running 'buses, and gaps could be reduced by repositioning vehicles. The inspector on duty would approach a crew and explain the state of affairs, asking them to do him a favour. He would write his instructions down on paper, place his initials and number on their log sheet, which was filled in with his timings, and send them on their way. A crew might be asked to leave and run about ten minutes late for a whole round journey as there was a gap in the service behind them. The crew would probably agree to this and in return the inspector would not only give them an overtime docket but would say that if they were running into the depot when they finished later on, that he'd be looking towards Barnet if they wanted to run in a bit early on their last trip. Alternatively the crew would say "we'll swing the poles in Kingsway and not bother coming into the bus station".

Now and again, an inspector would ask us to leave early; he would do this if there was a gap in the service immediately in front of us. He would mark the log card with something like 'advanced six minutes' so that if another inspector said we were running early, we could exonerate ourselves.

If there were casualties on the day (staff not turning up or going sick at the last moment) all the inspectors' well-laid plans would go awry and they would have to re-adjust accordingly. Generally speaking, good anticipation and resourcefulness by inspectors helped make good situations out of bad which, left unchecked, would have affected the regularity of the service for up to two or three hours later. Sometimes the staff shortage and general traffic conditions beat the inspectors and, despite their best efforts, they could find themselves between the devil and the deep blue sea. Whatever course they took, they found themselves in a no-win situation and chaos reigned. They could find that one end of the route was starved of vehicles while the other had too many, and if the District Superintendent turned up at a time like this, the poor inspector could not give an answer that was acceptable. Having got the service back to normal, a lorry might then shed its load and the scenario would be repeated.

The section between North Finchley and Wood Green was only served by the 521s/621s with no other route being able to assist. Inspectors became almost paranoid about ensuring a good service on this part of the route. Making this section a priority, they would cover a gap by getting a 'bus to do a 'Wood Green short' or might resort to nabbing a 609 to act as a 521 or 621. The problem often occurred on Saturday afternoons and an inspector might say "Do two Parks instead of two Swinton Streets" (this meant do two trips to Finsbury Park instead of two to Kings Cross). Inspectors would put the cards on the table, though, and say that we might get a bit of a bashing (loads of passengers) but that we would finish about half an hour earlier. There were times when they might ask us to go further than our original destination, say Finsbury Park, and run the 'bus down to Holborn Circus. This would mean a late finish but he would give us an overtime docket far in excess of our extra time.

Other routes were dealt with in similar fashion. If there was a gap to Barnet through a lack of 609s/645s, an inspector might meet a 521/621 at the top of Woodhouse Road and ask the crew to show '609 Barnet'. To compensate for going to Barnet the 'bus would be curtailed on its next journey – Nags Head probably. Sometimes a 521/621 would be commandeered to run as a 645 down to St Gabriels. Requests to assist in this manner were not instructions to be obeyed and inspectors could not insist that a crew perform anything else than what was on their timecard. There would be the odd crew who wouldn't help and although it wouldn't be held against them, the next time they were running late and hoping for a curtailment, the inspector might not give them one. Even the most co-operative crews could not give a hand every time because there were occasions when if they finished late it would upset their domestic arrangements.

Other depots were also susceptible to staff shortages and crews on Colindale's 645s would sometimes find themselves doing a couple of Canons Park/St Gabriels Church runs instead of a trip to Hammersmith if gaps to Canons Park were anticipated. Given the opportunity, crews would jump at the chance to do this as they would have a far easier time going twice to Canons Park than once to Hammersmith. Another option to cover a gap to Canons Park would be to extend a 664 or a 666 if a gap beyond Edgware was foreseen. In the most desperate of situations a Wood Green inspector would get a Wood Green crew to run a 629 or 641 up to North Finchley; they showed EXTRA on their route blind with a NORTH FINCHLEY destination. On their next southbound trip they would be curtailed.

Trolleybus conductors used paper log sheets and it was on them that variations from scheduled journeys were recorded by inspectors. Motorbus staff were issued with log cards of a much thicker texture; conductors inserted them into a roadside recording clock, pulled a handle forwards, and a purple stamp was marked on the log card. This indicated the time vehicles passed, allowing supervisory staff to check the regularity of the services. However, in the latter days of trolleybus operation, motorbus log cards were used by Colindale and Stonebridge staff – probably due to crews from these depots trying to outdo each other between Cricklewood and Edgware. The CE and SE conductors were instructed to insert these cards into the roadside clock outside Cricklewood bus garage. However, despite London Transport's best efforts, the resourcefulness of Colindale staff has to be admired. Some would omit clocking at Cricklewood and would stop at the Red Lion, West Hendon where conductors would run round to the machine for bus routes 83 and 183 in Kingsbury Road, and clock there. The recording in Kingsbury Road implied that vehicles were on time at Cricklewood garage. Although each clock had a number on it, the LT hierarchy never seemed to fathom that a false reading was being recorded.

Inspectors would sometimes curtail a 'bus into Windsor Terrace, City Road even if it was on time or just a few minutes late at North Finchley. This was done for one of two reasons. First, to ensure that a crew would be off on time and secondly so that a particular running number which was regularly being delayed in the City area would be back on schedule at North Finchley. If we were working on, say, FY45 on route 609 and arrived at North Finchley from Barnet about four minutes late on a rainy day, it was likely that one of them would approach us and say, "Put it into the Terrace" (he only wanted us to go as far as Windsor Terrace, City Road). The Finchley inspector would phone his colleague at Moorgate and tell him what he had done so that he was aware of the situation. This would mean that when FY46 got to Moorgate that there would be a gap in the service and, what with the

1509 has been curtailed in Windsor Terrace but inconsiderate parking has created difficulties for one of my colleagues. Its rear offside wheels have mounted the pavement and there is only just enough room for it to squeeze between the parked cars and a pillar. When pronouncing a vehicle number, it was 'fifteen-o-nine'. *Fred Ivey.*

rain and heavy loadings, it would be certain that 46 would be leaving Moorgate late. If 46's crew were due to finish their day's work, then they would finish late and receive an overtime docket. If they were on relief and came off fourteen minutes late at Tally Ho, they were now on what was known as a 'late meal relief'. If the point inspector knew that their break was about an hour in length, he would cajole them into taking their second 'bus on time – particularly if it was a takeover 'on the road'. The inspector would give them a 'double docket' for their trouble. A 'double docket' was made up of the fourteen minutes that they had come off late plus fourteen minutes that they had lost on their break. For most crews this encouraged them to accede to the request. We were a bit cute sometimes, for we knew that fifteen minutes overtime was paid when we finished between eight and twenty-two minutes late; thirty minutes was paid if we came off between twenty-three and thirty-seven minutes late, and so on. So if we were going to be late, it was never seven minutes as we got nothing; it was always at least eight. Similarly, dockets were never for twenty-two minutes – they were always for twenty-three!

For many years, crews wrote down any lost mileage in a book that was kept in the depot output. Not all of the curtailments were being written down, due to forgetfulness, preventing a proper record from being kept. A few crews turned themselves short of their destinations without authorisation and as they did not enter their misdeeds in the book, it was difficult for supervisors to prove that they had curtailed themselves. Consequently, log sheets were introduced on which staff and vehicle details were entered and lost mileage recorded. As all curtailments had to be authorised by an inspector, it was now deemed essential that conductors obtain an inspector's signature on the log sheet.

Inspectors' powers of persuasion were usually successful; however, there would be the odd disgruntled crew who would take their full relief, as they were entitled to, even if it was four hours in length on a spreadover. We could work the double docket facility to our advantage. Crews could see that a service was running badly and often had a better idea than the inspectors of what was going on. Having come off fifteen minutes late, we would volunteer to take our next 'bus off on time in the knowledge that it would come up late anyway – the suggestion to do this was always accepted by inspectors. We knew we would be paid overtime for just standing about! When the late running 'bus eventually materialised, we would also have to be curtailed – we were winners all-round! There were times however, when our second 'bus was unexpectedly curtailed and it came up on time.

When crews had a 'short relief', say forty-four minutes, and came off late on their first half, there would be insufficient time for them to take up their second 'bus on time. An inspector at Tally Ho would ask one of his colleagues to arrange for the crew's second 'bus to be temporarily pulled out of the service. An inspector would collar the crew of the relevant 'bus and instruct them to show NORTH FINCHLEY on the destination blind and leave it, poles down, at the relief point.

Now and again an inspector might countermand a curtail-

ment that had previously been given by a colleague. For instance, a 609 crew that had been instructed to turn at Islington Green rather than go through to Moorgate. An inspector further along the route may have become aware of another factor and decided that it was best to cancel the curtailment and let it continue to Moorgate and turn it short at North Finchley on its next journey.

Rule 25 said that if a crew had been turned short of their destination, and there was not another vehicle to transfer the passengers to, they should continue their journey as if there had not been a curtailment. The only place where I have had to continue rather than curtail was at Windsor Terrace, for despite there being other trolleybus services and bus route 43 along the City Road, there were times when there was not another vehicle to put passengers on (the trouble with this turning point was that it was between bus stops). When this occurred I would disregard the instruction as we wouldn't leave anyone stranded – not even one. In fact I have had the grappling hook of a bamboo pole around the negative trolley arm ready to swing it over, at the same time looking for a 43 or another trolleybus to come along. If nothing appeared on the horizon I would say to my conductor "We'd best go through". I would replace the bamboo back beneath the vehicle, change the destination blind and carry on to Moorgate. Sometimes it would mean a late finish, though at other times I would be able to pick up the time – having a good conductor who was quick on the bell helped me to do this.

Rule 43 dealt with relief points and stated that 'Drivers and conductors must not obstruct the entrance to premises or cause inconvenience or annoyance to the general public'. This was generally adhered to, but when it was cold we stood in the shop doorway of Janes and Adams when relieving in Ballards Lane. The rule also stated that 'Drivers kits (whatever they were) and conductors' ticket boxes should not be placed on coping sills and steps, and every care must be taken to avoid litter at these points'.

Sometimes an inspector could do nothing more than call out an instruction to a conductor of a moving trolleybus; the man at Acton Market might shout "Paddenswick, and I'll sign your card on the way back". If the inspector could not be found when the 'bus returned to Acton Market, the curtailment would be entered on the log sheet stating that the Acton inspector had given this instruction. Paddenswick Road was not a popular place to turn, as staff had to transfer their passengers to the following Hammersmith-bound 'bus which might not materialise for a few minutes. The fact that the poles had to be swung onto dead-end wires and the turn had to be made slowly to avoid a dewirement meant that it was hardly worth doing. Five minutes carrying this out and the 'bus might as well have gone through. Some crews, if they could see that there was not a 'bus behind, did go to Hammersmith.

Some inspectors really made the effort to make sure curtailments were authorised and if North Finchley inspector Bill Cole, who was known as 'Sir' because of his strict time-keeping, only had enough time to call out an instruction to a southbound 609, he would make a point of meeting it, on its return, at the frog pull in Kingsway by the Gaumont Cinema. He would travel up to the relief point to sign our paperwork.

The inspectors who controlled the trolleybus services knew the restrictions of the overhead line, and routes like 660 and 666 with low headways and high passenger loadings needed particular attention. They would have no hesitation in turning 'buses short of their destinations. The inspectors at Craven Park really had to be 'on the ball' and if a trolleybus had been held up through traffic on its way to Hammersmith and was about fifteen minutes down, an inspector would hand signal the driver to slow down and would jump aboard. Consulting his time sheets he would call to the driver "put it into Bromyard" – by turning the 'bus into Bromyard Avenue, Acton Vale, the 'bus would be back at Craven Park on its time. The biblical number of the devil is 666; staff did not refer to this route in this capacity but it was known to some as 'the treble six' or 'the three sixes'

All inspectors, both road and revenue, would watch what was occurring 'on the road'; drivers would give signals to each other with regard to their whereabouts. If a driver knew there was an inspector lurking in a shop doorway or behind a tree, he would flash his headlights at an oncoming trolleybus and give a thumbs down signal to its driver. This drew attention to the situation; alternatively he would draw his finger across his throat and point backwards. Once an inspector had been spotted, the bush telegraph would spring into action and soon all the crews on the service knew where the inspector was. However, these officials had been drivers or conductors themselves and knew about these gestures, so it was a matter of inspectors and staff pitting their wits against each other!

One of the most flagrantly breached rules was number 18 which stated that staff 'must not smoke in or on a vehicle'. If an inspector caught a driver or conductor smoking on a moving 'bus, they would be advised on the first occasion. If the inspector caught out the miscreant again, they would definitely be 'stuck-on' (reported). If we wanted a fag at the terminus, we were supposed to get out of the 'bus – this was hardly ever adhered to and inspectors turned a blind eye.

Some of the Tally Ho inspectors would supervise loadings and ring the trolleybus off at busy times. This allowed conductors to start collecting their fares before it was 'time for the off'. On the assistance theme, I would often pull hand frogs and raise or lower trolleybooms when I was waiting in Tally Ho bus station. If a 'bus had to be run in to the depot because there was no conductor, and I was going there anyway, I would pull the frog handle at Woodberry Grove. When travelling 'passenger' to Friern Barnet, I would sometimes pull the handle at the junction of Finchley High Road/Woodhouse Road, thus enabling the conductor to get on with collecting his fares. Similarly, if I travelled up from East Finchley on a Barnet-bound 609 I might say to the conductor, "I'll get it" and pull the frog handle in Kingsway, North Finchley. Members of staff would stand on the platform and ring the 'bus off if the conductor was upstairs. Against the rules, it speeded things up.

Extreme measures had to be taken sometimes so that the trolleybus services ran smoothly. On the Friday and Saturday nights nearest to St Patrick's Day, the Galtymore club at Cricklewood attracted large numbers of Irish men and women who wanted to celebrate by dancing the night away. Trouble sometimes erupted during these evenings and when the crowd turned out they could spill out into the roadway. Anticipating that things could turn nasty, the local police along with London Transport inspectors would be out in force to deal with the situation. Being aware that there would be more trouble if the revellers boarded the trolleybuses than not, inspectors would position themselves at the stops prior to Cricklewood Broadway and tell each crew that they were to run non-stop past the boarding points. With an inspector and one or two policemen on the platform of each trolleybus, the angry mob would be repelled and the 'bus would speed past the melée. Eventually the rabble would disperse, having to make their own way home.

Some inspectors had nicknames. Mr Stokes, a point inspector at Cricklewood Broadway, was a stickler for time and would tell staff if they were just half a minute early. He would be near the Galtymore dance hall in the Edgware Road and would hold a 645 until the 660 that should be in front of it had crossed from Chichele Road into Cricklewood Lane. Similarly, he would hold 664s/666s until a 660 had crossed the Broadway. This ensured that trolleybuses departed in the right order and it worked fairly for everybody – he became known as 'Half a minute early Stokes'. The language in the depot could be pretty blue at times but inspector Fred Storey never swore, the worst he ever said being "Blooming well" or "Flipping well". If he was at Tally Ho at the same time as Vic Collins, Vic would say to me "Old blooming well is on today". There was an inspector at Holborn Circus who was an ex-boxer and who was known as 'Punch drunk' (presumably they all knew the names by which we called them). Sometimes staff were addressed formally, so if an inspector didn't know someone's name following an incident, he would address them as 'Driver' or 'Conductor' – and then book them.

Inspectors would usually book conductors if they were not displaying their MSC badges; they wore them the wrong way round on their jacket lapels or concealed them behind their Gibson machine straps so that their number could not be seen. A few drivers wore their badges the wrong way round too, but as they were not in inspectors' line of vision, they got away with it. All of this concealment indicated that they had something to hide. Inspectors were not happy if they spotted conductors chatting to their drivers through the window that separated the cab from the lower saloon. When they saw this happening they would point to the platform indicating that they wanted the conductor to return to their rightful position – this often occurred at Wood Green where there were a lot of inspectors about. They might also report conductors for sitting down, but in their defence it has to be said that trolleybuses carried very heavy loads and it was understandable that they wanted to rest their legs at quiet times.

I only clashed with inspectors twice in my trolleybus career. The first time was on a Sunday morning when loadings were light. I was a conductor at the time and was sitting down on the long seat at the back of a 521/621 which was passing through Wood Green on a trip to Holborn. Unknown to me, Inspector Long saw me and decided to make, what I thought, was a mountain out of a molehill. He waited there until we came back and at Jolly Butchers Hill, where I had to nip off to pull a frog handle, he boarded the 'bus, saying that he was booking me for not standing on the platform. I replied "Have you waited all this time just to book me for sitting down?". 'Longy' said that he had and didn't accept my explanation that I was tying up my shoe laces! He'd heard all the excuses before about sitting down and wasn't fooled by my story and 'stuck me on'. He travelled for a few stops during which time we had a right old argument. "Haven't you got something better to do?" I said, followed by "You could have checked six buses by now". We fell out for a short time. I had to see the CDI about the incident but he didn't make a big deal about it. Despite the booking, 'Longy' and I soon forgot about the matter and it is fair to say that we gained a mutual respect for each other – on the day in question he wanted to show that he was one step above me. Generally speaking, staff didn't hold grudges, for inspectors had jobs to do and if we got caught, then fair do's. 'Longy' ended up on light duties in the clothing store at Chiswick. I had to go there to collect some uniform one day, and there he was at the counter dishing it out.

The second occasion I crossed swords with an inspector was when Colin Williams booked me in the depot yard for leaving seven minutes late one morning. I had been a bit tight for time arriving and my conductor, Sid Game, went to the canteen to get two cups of tea. Williams jumped the gun and 'stuck me on' as he thought that we'd deliberately delayed the vehicle when this was not so. I was cheesed off with being booked for something so minor, so flew down to Finsbury Park (we were only doing 'a short'), had the stand time and came back to North Finchley eleven minutes early where he booked me again. Not many trolleybus drivers can claim to being 'booked' twice in just over an hour! The CDI accepted my explanation for leaving a bit late but gave me a right roasting for running eleven minutes early – good job that Bob Irons had moved to a higher grade by then, otherwise he'd have had me 'up the Manor' on a charge.

To sum up, I considered that the inspectors who supervised the road services did so very well but would reiterate that it was only achieved with the full assistance of the crews. In fact, co-operative drivers and conductors (quick on the power notches and the bell respectively), along with competent officials could soon make a good service out of what was looking potentially a bad one. The public had no idea of the efforts made by the trolleybus staff to keep the services running as efficiently as they did.

L3 1461 has just turned from Station Road into Friern Barnet Road at New Southgate on its way to North Finchley on route 621; in the background is the turning loop that existed here, and the distinct 'Crown' public house. A Tolly's van follows; it carries a spare tyre on its nearside passenger door. *Don Thompson.*

The mid-1950s service cuts saw a number of trolleybuses being withdrawn; many were C class vehicles which were replaced by others which were in better condition. One of the fortunate ones was 383 which was transferred westwards from Walthamstow to Colindale depot. Earlier on, this vehicle is illustrated working from Walthamstow depot on route 625. However, three trolleybus services were withdrawn after operations on 6th January 1959; one was route 654 which was operated by Colindale and Stonebridge depots. 383 was withdrawn at this time; in happier times, it is seen on route 645 rounding Stanmore Circus at Canons Park. Traction standard bases were painted black; a concrete haunch prevented water from entering them. *Don Thompson.*

PAY AND CONDITIONS

All workplaces need teamwork and discipline if they are to function well and that applied to Finchley trolleybus depot as much as it did to anywhere else. Even though drivers and conductors only spent a small amount of time in the depot, they still required supervision. Managing the depot was the CDI (he was variously known as the charge depot inspector or the chief depot inspector); he was supported by a number of depot inspectors who between them kept the depot running twenty four hours a day, seven days a week.

THE RULE BOOK

With the title 'OPERATING DEPARTMENT TRAMS AND TROLLEYBUSES Rule Book for Drivers and Conductors', this 193 page, red-covered hardback book was given to each member of staff upon completion of their training – an anomaly saw some conductors, who were upgraded to drivers, being given a second copy. It was London Transport's 'bible', and was for the 'direction, compliance and observance of all employees of the Tram and Trolleybus Operating Department'. All rules, regulations and agreements between London Transport and the Union were printed there for the benefit of both management and staff; by working 'to the book', staff covered themselves. Employees were expected to make themselves familiar with and obey all the rules, and inspectors endeavoured to make sure that staff were following its guidelines. Woe betide anyone who breached the more important ones, such as regularly paying in short, not stopping for passengers or failing to maintain service headways.

What were considered 'soft' rules were frequently ignored. Rule One was broken every day, "for employees must carry their rule book at all times when on duty and produce it when requested by anyone in authority in the service of London Transport". Rule Seven stated that staff were to wear white cap covers from 1st May to 31st October. Most, including myself, didn't bother.

The rule most frequently broken (though inadvertently) was the one that stated that drivers and conductors must report to the depot at their appointed time. Human nature being what it is meant that 'breach of rule ten' occurred virtually daily. When a driver or conductor turned up late for work, they were paid 'time worked only', which meant that they were only paid the hours they actually worked. This was harsh, for in many industries a late-comer would only lose the number of minutes they were late, if that. Some DIs didn't penalise staff in this way, particularly if no mileage was lost. Those who were not understanding and enforced 'time worked only' would be remembered and when they wanted a favour done another time, the member of staff who

had lost money wouldn't assist. If mileage was lost through somebody turning up late, an entry of 'LPTW' (late put to work) was inserted on the log sheet. If somebody did not turn up at all, they were marked 'Absent' – this harked back to schooldays!

THE PAY WEEK

In 1951, trolleybus staff worked a forty-four hour, six day week – no duty paid less than seven hours, twenty minutes even if it was only of six and a half hours duration. Crews rested on a different day each week. It worked on a rolling basis in that Monday was the day off one week, Tuesday the next and so on. As there were not so many vehicles operating on Sundays, staff might have three consecutive Sundays off. On the Sabbath theme, occasionally a duty applicable to the shift a crew were working on at the time had to be found for them because there were not enough Sunday duties to make up a full roster. The only time a 'double rest' occurred was on Tuesdays/Wednesdays – the end of one payroll week and the start of the next. Saturday rests were much prized and sought after, and an agreement between London Transport and the TGWU meant that spare staff for their first year of service 'shall have an appointed rest day on a Saturday once in every twenty-six weeks' – not popular at all, but they might get an extra Saturday off during that period. Drivers and conductors were paired up as crews, and their names were positioned against each other on the staff roster which detailed the duties to be covered. At the end of each pay week the names dropped down a line. Duties were compiled for Monday to Friday, with separate schedules for Saturday and Sunday. Special schedules were provided on Christmas Day and Boxing Day. At FY, Sunday duties operated on bank holidays.

Using the 1951 pay scale, conductors and drivers, upon appointment, were paid six pounds and five shillings. The fact that both received the same wage was an anomaly as it has always been recognised that drivers had a more responsible job. After six months, both received an increment and this was repeated six months later. By the time that each had completed twelve months' service, drivers received two shillings more per week than conductors. The rates were now six pounds fourteen shillings and six pounds twelve shillings respectively. By 1956, new conductors were paid eight pounds and twelve shillings; drivers were still only paid two shillings more. With twelve months' service there was a four shilling difference between the two grades; conductors eight pounds eighteen shillings, drivers nine pounds two shillings. At twenty-four months, when full establishment was enjoyed, conductors were paid nine pounds two shillings while drivers were paid nine pounds six shillings – this worked out at just over four shillings an hour each. A little known fact is that trolleybus staff were on a lower wage band than those on motorbuses. This anomaly was eradicated some time in the second half of the 1950s when all platform staff came onto the same pay scale. This was fairer – after all we were doing a similar job and, generally speaking, trolleybus staff worked harder as most services were trunk routes which carried more passengers.

There were some little known payments and one in particular is worth mentioning. If, upon a roster change, a crew had to work on a Saturday when they would have otherwise have rested, then both were paid a compensatory time and a half on top of the Saturday rate. The DIs tried to avoid these payments, but sometimes they just couldn't.

To encourage people to come on the job, and therefore alleviate the staff shortage, an eleven day fortnight was introduced in 1956. The maximum time on duty was now seven hours, forty minutes – it was hoped that an eleven day fortnight would clinch matters. It didn't and the staff shortage at Finchley depot continued – in fact it was always high. The pay week still commenced on a Wednesday. One rest day fell within one week, two the next – staff could now get three days off consecutively – Tuesday, Wednesday and Thursday. Two weeks annual leave was given; this had to be taken between May and September. If staff worked on any of the six bank holidays during the year, they were given a day in lieu for each one worked. These had to be taken in the winter months.

CONDITIONS OF SERVICE
Ten minutes were allowed for 'signing on'. This enabled conductors to deal with their side of things. When they were the first to take a vehicle out of the depot this ten minutes allowed drivers to examine their vehicles and prepare them for service (ten minutes was still given to drivers when a 'bus was taken over at Tally Ho). Ten minutes was given for 'signing off'. This was for conductors to cash up and pay in; generally speaking, drivers went home immediately they closed their cab doors. Five minutes 'parking time' (also referred to as stabling time) was allowed if a 'bus was scheduled to run into the depot after the first half of duty. When taking a trolleybus out of the depot on a second spell, 'parking time' applied – this was for putting the booms up (motorbus staff were only given two minutes starting time). At some locations (but not Finchley) drivers were expected to stay on board during traverser operations; when that was over they had to park it on an allotted 'road'.

On trolleybuses, there had to be a minimum of eight hours between duties (ten hours on motorbuses). This meant that staff could finish at 11pm and start again at 7am the next morning. Occasionally, a few people stayed in the depot canteen playing cards all night and then went out on an early turn. This happened when they were working their rest day the following day – it was a quick turn round which embraced the minimum number of hours off between duties. One odd condition was the fact that if a trolleybus driver wanted to

transfer to the Country Bus department and there was no vacancy for him at his nominated garage, he had to become a conductor there until such time as a driving position became available.

The 'RATES OF PAY AND CONDITIONS OF SERVICE' booklet contained all the agreements between LT and the TGWU. It was negotiated on the staff's behalf by the union who often had to 'fight' the management to get a good deal. The depot inspectors had to work by these conditions. For example, when using the 'marrying' facility (joining a conductor and driver from different duties) staff had to be paid the greater of any two duties – even if someone had been moved up from a spreadover onto an ordinary shift. Some matters were not covered by the booklet, so when the DIs were desperate to cover the last 'bus on any route, they would say "I'll give you an extra hour". For most staff that was enough encouragement. However, there were times when parts or even whole duties did not run. The DIs were constantly looking at the time sheets to ensure that crews were reporting for duty and would take steps to cover staff who didn't turn in. There was an element of give and take between us, so if a DI wanted me to cover an arduous late turn on my rest day, I would do it in the knowledge that when I wanted a change of shift or rest day on another occasion, he would oblige. The DIs tried to cover as much work as they could beforehand but problems came when a casualty arose on the day. Sometimes there was nothing the DIs could do and it almost pained them to see conductors or drivers sitting around idle.

EARLY, MIDDLE AND LATE
Finchley depot had some really early turns – in fact our 2.43am sign-on was the earliest start in the whole London Transport fleet. I had no trouble getting in for this and considered it to be essentially a late turn. The duty finished between 10 and 10.30am but, being almost eight hours in length, was not considered to be an 'easy number'. However, it had an early relief when a good breakfast could be enjoyed, and despite the very early start, everybody wanted to do it. When I got home I would have a sleep in the early afternoon and evening and would get up at about 9pm and potter about until it was time to leave. When I went to work I was as fresh as a daisy, doing this duty as both a conductor and a driver. Other staff had their own way of coping with this shift and some got up at about 2am. A number of other duties started around 4am. The really early shifts were over by midday – for those inclined, plenty of opportunity to do some overtime. After about 6am, duties were starting every few minutes – they tailed off about 8 o'clock. On the 645s there was a 'straight through' job, it was just one spell of duty with the crew finished by about 10am. If I did some overtime on the 2.43 start, I might not get home until about 4pm and would then sleep until about 11pm.

The middle turns, which were not so numerous, commenced between 10am and noon, concluding in the evening. Late turns started from about 3pm; there were a lot of these and again, staff were being ticked-in every few minutes. The really late shifts didn't start till about 4.30pm; they finished between 11.30pm and 12.30am. An oddity was the fact that duties were compiled in such a way that those starting before midday were numbered in the order in which they commenced – those that started after that were numbered in the order that they finished (this was in stark contrast to motorbus practice where all duties were in sign-on time order). I didn't write down my duties in a diary but would jot them down on the back of a threepenny bit bag, on the back of a pay advice card or on the inside of a cigarette packet. For the two years I worked with Jean, she would write my duties down for me.

THE PAY CLERK

The pay clerk was officially known as a depot assistant and had probably been a conductor or driver. He calculated the wages and informed the payroll office of the total pay-out. They arranged with the bank for notes, silver and copper to be delivered to the depot for pay day. It was no good using the takings as most of it was in silver and copper, and there would have been an uproar if we'd been paid in 'small change'. One of the depot inspectors paid the money out but he had to be 'on the ball' so that the last people coming in didn't just get coins.

Not only did the pay clerk have to be familiar with length of service rates but he also had to know all other pay variations. There was an ordinary rate for Monday to Friday and until 1pm on Saturday, after which an extra 8½d per hour was paid. Sunday and Bank Holidays were paid at time and a half with double time being paid on Christmas Day. Many of the extra payments were already prepared for him (allowances for starting up to 3.59am, up to 5.59am, finishing after 1.01am etc). However, much of his arithmetic had to be done manually so it was a good job that he had nine days to work out our wages. The pay week finished on a Tuesday and we were not paid out until the Friday week. He was also responsible for sick pay, holiday pay, National Insurance details and income tax. Holiday change requests were also in his remit. It was also his job to keep the seniority list for drivers and conductors up-to-date; these were compiled in the order of when drivers and conductors had entered those grades. The seniority factor meant that junior staff had to wait their turn to get their requests in many instances.

There was a bus strike as a result of a pay dispute in 1958; it started on Monday 4th May and continued for six weeks and six days – it involved maintenance staff and platform staff. No London Transport bus, Green Line coach or trolleybus worked in service during this period. The depot doors at Finchley were closed, though there was access through a small door for the foreman and other authorised persons. This was the only time I ever saw the depot doors closed. A colloquialism of the times referred to the strikers as being "on the stones" – this meant that staff were on hard times. When we were on picket duty we were allowed to go into the canteen to get cups of tea. Union meetings were held in the Moss Hall pub in Ballards Lane where we were kept informed about the situation. There was nothing much to do during this period so for much of the time I was kicking my heels. Rose had given up work by now as she was expecting our first child Julie. I only received about £2 a week strike pay from the TGWU, compared with my average wage packet of about thirteen pounds, so money was a bit tight. In the last week of the dispute, I went down to the labour exchange in Green Lanes, Harringay where I was given twenty-eight shillings. This was only a 'sub' as this amount was deducted from my first pay packet after the return to work. The overhead line staff were not involved in the dispute so it gave them the opportunity to alter wiring where necessary and make emergency repairs. The strike was suddenly called off and the first vehicles were back on the road very late on the evening of Saturday 20th June – surprisingly, few people threw in the towel after the strike.

DEALING WITH THE STAFF SHORTAGE

For virtually the whole time I was at Finchley, there was never enough staff to cover all the duties each day; the shortage became rife in the mid-1950s. Duties that needed covering peaked in the summer when many were on annual leave. Sometimes the situation was dire, and staff were regularly working their days off and doing spells of overtime – it was often half a duty before or after work. Although the first two hours of overtime was supposed to be paid at time and a quarter, and the rest at time and a half, all was paid at time and a half in the hope that it would encourage staff to do some extra work. This eased calculations for the pay clerk, who sent his totals to the payroll office.

Working a rest day was paid at time and a half. We were able to work our rest day every other week when we were working a six day week – this meant that we only had one day off in fourteen. DIs would often say to me "Do you want to work your day off this week". Alternatively I'd say something like "I'll work one of my days off next week – got an early one Tuesday". When the eleven day fortnight came in we could work two of those rest days – the 'overtime kings' might even do five bits of overtime too. One conductor overdid it and collapsed out of sheer exhaustion in the output when paying in one day. I worked many extra shifts without any adverse effects. I availed myself of the overtime opportunities as it enabled me to earn cash for my family – it also helped fund my motorcycle interest. My first three motorbikes had all been secondhand; the third was a 1949 Star Twin which I traded in for my first new bike. This was a 1953 A7 BSA which I had for three and a half years.

One of the perks of the job was 'bridging time'. If staff finished work at 2pm and started a piece of overtime at 5pm they were paid the three intervening hours at flat rate – hence the terminology 'bridging'. If they did 'a rounder' (say, Tally Ho to Holborn and back) it was particularly renumerative and well worth the effort – time and a half for the hours on the vehicle, the signing-on and signing-off time and the travelling time. With three hours bridging time (the maximum), about six hours was paid. Most staff preferred to have a long spell of bridging time and a short piece of work rather than half an hour bridging and three and a half hours work as the former was seen to be a better deal. Sometimes only the latter was on offer, so we had to take the rough with the smooth. I always considered 'bridging time' to be a very generous practice, getting something for nothing. It was an unofficial payment (to encourage staff to do a bit of extra work) as it did not appear in the wages agreement booklet. The bridging facility ended shortly after the trolleys finished, and after that we got paid only between sign-on and sign-off time – some staff who formerly would have done a piece of overtime would not now consider it. 'Bridging' was Finchley's terminology for overtime. At West Ham it was known as 'boots' on account that the extra money put shoes on the feet.

Having left it as late as possible to cover whole duties by asking staff to work their day off, the DIs posted the overtime for the next day at about 10am. There would be a rush to obtain the best paying bits, and staff inserted their names and payroll numbers against the spell of work on offer. Some were so keen that they would ask the DIs when the bridging list was going up. Although I normally marked up the overtime that I would do, the depot inspectors would often say to me "Do you want to do a bit of bridging today?"

UNIFORM
London Transport provided platform staff with a uniform – various items were issued yearly, two yearly or four yearly. Drivers were given a cap, trousers, winter jacket, a long dust coat for summer use, a mackintosh and an overcoat. The overcoat was a bit cumbersome, but the white cuff on the outside of the right sleeve was a useful feature. During the dark nights, motorists were able to see drivers' hand signals better as they pulled out into a stream of traffic. The long dustcoat tended to be awkward and I only used it occasionally, preferring to use my conductor's one. Those that did use the long dustcoat often kept the buttons undone. As an aside, motorbus drivers were not supplied with trousers until 1951/52 – they had to make their own arrangements about covering their legs until then!

Male conductors were given a cap, trousers, winter jacket and dust jacket (no mackintosh or overcoat was provided, which is why I bought an overcoat from driver Wilson). When conductors passed out as drivers they did not receive their additional items until the next uniform issue. Women conductors had a tunic, skirts or slacks, dust jacket, beret and an overcoat (an early case of sexual discrimination against men?). When I started, white cap covers were the regulation issue; they were replaced by a cap with a plastic white top which looked a lot better than the earlier ones. I kept one in my locker but only wore it if it was raining and I had to walk from the depot to Tally Ho. The use of caps declined over the years, and London Transport just let the feature go. Trolleybus staff wore a red cap badge – motorbus staff used a white and blue one.

Staff who didn't turn up in uniform tended to be reported. Most wore full uniform all the time – why wear your own clothes when LT provided us with plenty. Some would take a chance and say that it was at the cleaners, particularly if they were going out with their girlfriend after work. Occasionally, a member of staff would turn up in civvies because their uniform was virtually worn out. If they were lucky they might be able to wangle an extra garment from the central clothing store – generally speaking, staff were not given more uniform until the next issue. For a number of my early years

at Finchley, a few clippies wore Civil Defence uniforms – dark blue tunics and slacks, similar to those used by ambulance crews of the time. The only indication that they worked for London Transport was that the girls replaced the CD buttons with LT griffin buttons. These ladies preferred the CD style to the standard issue and the supervisors didn't object as there tended to be a shortage of uniform (later on, the style of uniform changed and the LT issue closely resembled the CD issue). One clippie, Connie Learner, wore her wartime grey uniform together with a peaked cap until the mid-fifties. She stood out, so if a new member of staff was looking for her they would be told, "She's the one in wartime uniform". To give a bit more warmth, some of the drivers wore a raincoat over their uniform in the colder months.

STAFF FACILITIES
The depot output was fitted out with all the accoutrements required for our day-to-day needs. There were some double-sided, double-seated cash desks which enabled conductors to stand or sit when preparing their ticket boxes at the start of the day's work, or for cashing up at the end of their duty. There were glass cases in which the schedules, rotas and other notices were displayed. Other items in the output were a clock, long table and a bench for general use. Also on the premises were a locker room, toilets, canteen, recreation room, bike sheds and motorcycle stands.

The depot canteen was open all night. Before I was married I sometimes stayed there until about 2.30am after my late turn, chatting and having a laugh with the night canteen steward and anybody else who was around. Les Strutt and I would sometimes have a meal there after which I'd give him a lift home. On one occasion we went to Strawberry Vale, a lane off the North Circular Road adjacent to Finchley High Road, where there was reputed to be a haunted house. This fact had been reported the previous week in the popular 'Picture Post' magazine; we wanted to see if there was any truth in it but didn't see anything. What with the all-night card schools at Finchley depot, and a conductor using the staff trolleybus to move house, there seemed to be an endless amount of activity being carried out by members of the London Transport trolleybus staff during the middle of the night – and that was just our depot!

OTHER MATTERS
On Saturday 16th February 1957, Rose and I were married. On our marriage certificate, the vicar inserted 'Trolley Bus driver' as my occupation. Not many men living today have that accolade. I moved from 54 Alexandra Gardens, Muswell Hill to 54 Coppetts Road, Muswell Hill where we occupied two rooms of Rose's parents' house. In October that year we moved to a private flat at 67 Fortis Green, East Finchley. At both addresses I was nearer to Muswell Hill bus garage, but didn't mind travelling to Finchley as I enjoyed working on trolleybuses and the routes that they were on; I also liked the people there. I had given scant thought about moving to Muswell Hill garage. As it was I was unable to transfer to motorbuses as I had the wrong licence.

In 1956, I changed the A7 BSA motorcycle for an Ariel

500cc Fieldmaster Twin. A year later, when Rose and I got our flat in East Finchley, we needed to get a gas cooker so the Ariel reluctantly had to go. Thereafter I used a 125 bus or 517/609/617 trolleybuses to get to and from work. I normally boarded last, this being a practice handed down from time immemorial. By getting on last, it gave me the opportunity to have a few words with the conductor – it was nearly always work-related. On the very late shifts I would use the staff trolleybus to get me much of the way home. If I finished at about midnight I would use a 125 for, in between the last southbound 517/617 and our staff trolleybus, they ran in off line of route to Muswell Hill garage. The last one left Tally Ho at 12.13am. I often got on it and if Eric Birchmore was still in MH garage, we might have a game of cards in the all-night canteen. Sometimes I would walk the last mile home. Alternatively I got a lift from Muswell Hill garage by using their staff rail bus – this went to many Underground stations, picking up and setting down tube staff. It went all the way to Sutton garage, and left ten minutes after the last 125 got in.

There were a number of former Metropolitan Electric Tramways staff working at Finchley when I started in 1951; a few were still there when I left in 1962. In fact, when I joined, I was surprised to see how many trolleybus staff were working beyond the retirement age of sixty-five. Some wanted the money, others liked the job. Once they had reached that age and wanted to continue, they had to have a yearly medical; performed at Manor House offices, it counted as their day's work. An agreement made upon the formation of London Transport in 1933 allowed any driver, who was fit, to continue until they were seventy years of age. There was no age limit for conductors and there were instances of staff at other depots working into their eighties. Conductors continuing to work beyond retirement age did not need a medical. Drivers and conductors with long service said that employment on the buses, trams or trolleybuses before the war was much sought after, as the job had status. If they went into a green-grocer's, the owner would bring him to the front of the queue and serve them first rather than let them wait. The pay was regular and on a par with the police. Vic said that when the war came, wages on London Transport stood still to help the war effort – he was right, and they never caught up again.

New drivers and conductors were put on six months probation. Conductors upgraded to driver did not have a probationary period as it was deemed that they had already served it – an anomaly meant that their driving was not checked by a DMI, as they were considered to be established staff. It was important that drivers were fit. Some, unfortunately, became ill and were unable to continue. They would be offered a conductor's job (at FY) or a light duty position (that could be anywhere within a few miles of their homes). There were some instances of staff returning to the job – those were known as re-engagements, and we had one driver who came back twice.

As trolleybuses could not be used for staff outings, an RT from Muswell Hill garage deputised; a few of our staff had PSV licences, one being Bill Bennett who often drove at these times. For these jaunts, London Transport made a motorbus

available to us for a nominal charge. There were outings to the coast for staff and their families, with excursions to Newmarket racecourse being particularly popular. There was a good sports and social side at the depot with inter-depot/garage snooker and darts matches being common. On one occasion a green RT from Tring garage came down to collect our staff for a darts match – they brought them back later. The Finchley trolleybus side, knowing that they would not have to drive back, returned well-oiled!

London Transport employees were issued with a staff pass which gave them free travel, both on and off duty. It was known as a 'sticky' on account that in years gone by, it incorporated a photograph of the member of staff – the picture was stuck onto the pass, hence the nickname. It was a useful facility and I often used the local trolleybus services. One week, Rose and I went to seven different cinemas, seven nights running. We liked to see speedway at Harringay, and were regular spectators as we both liked this sport. Staff were supposed to show their passes even when in uniform. If I knew somebody was on the job, I didn't bother. The only time that I used my staff pass out of my immediate area, was when some of us from the depot had an outing to Hampton Court. There were many eight foot wide Q1s down there – a class that I saw when working on the 660s.

Traffic circulars were issued fortnightly and gave details of general and local arrangements appertaining to bus and trolleybus operation. A regular item was of bus stop flags moved from one trolley standard to another (their numbers would be quoted, say TS 184 and 186). Additional to these were local notices that dealt with alterations to overhead, and the positioning of temporary bus stops. An item seen in the output from time to time was a blackboard; one notice I particularly recall seeing on it dealt with the arrangements that would be in force when the new bridge was being rolled-in in Caledonian Road in March 1959.

The TGWU showed its strength when need be. The Colindale depot rep, Jack O'Neill, threatened Mr Bates, the district superintendent, that he would take his trolleybuses off the road in the run up to Christmas over a schedule dispute. This was the worst possible time for 'buses to be in the depot so Bates gave in and O'Neill got his way. Jock Davis, our union rep was often having a conflab with Tom Fitzpatrick the Highgate rep in the refreshment hut at Tally Ho. On the few occasions where there was a work to rule, drivers wouldn't start until everybody was seated, and conductors would only ring the bell from the platform at every stop. All this had a delaying factor on the service and the ensuing chaos soon brought management and union together to resolve the dispute.

Finchley depot had a domestic GPO phone number of HILside 5265, though this did not appear in the inspectors' 'red book' (where first and last buses and trolleybuses were listed) until 1960. This was in contrast to bus garages which did. Staff would phone the depot if they were delayed, sick or could not come in for any reason. If they were unable to contact the depot they could phone the bus controller (who oversaw day-to-day operations throughout London) to pass on any message.

Finchley depot forecourt in the autumn of 1961 and 1469's driver has brought the vehicle out of the depot; it is waiting departure time on route 660 to Hammersmith. In the background, an RM bus has been used to train some of our men to drive a motorbus; its presence indicates that the end of the electric era at Finchley depot is not far away. *Fred Ivey.*

PREPARING FOR THE CHANGE-OVER

London Transport issued a monthly magazine which could be bought for two old pence. It included topical transport items (mainly to do with LT), stories about staff, retirement details and a long sports and social section. The June 1954 issue stated that the trolleybus system was to be scrapped in a programme that was to start in about three years time. This caused little chit-chat at the depot as it was seen to be something on a distant horizon. 1957 came and went without any sign of the conversion starting. Eventually the Finchley branch of the TGWU was informed that our trolleybuses were to be replaced by motorbuses in two stages. The 521/621 would go in November 1961 and the 609/645/660 in January 1962. I expect that this would have led to three separate rosters: one for the 221 bus route, one for the 609s and another for the 645s/660s. As the seniority factor always prevailed in depot life, I would have stayed on the 609s. However, route 629 which was operated by Wood Green depot was converted earlier than intended (it last ran on 25th April 1961 rather than 7th November that year). This allowed the 609 to be advanced to a changeover date of 7th/8th November 1961 – the same time as the 521/621. The 645 and 660 which were to be converted to motorbus operation on the night of 30th/31st January 1962 were pushed forward four weeks and would operate for the last time on 2nd January 1962.

During various stages of the conversion programme many frogs and crossovers were taken out; this simplified and even eradicated a number of junctions. Having such a wide oper-ating area, and being one of the later depots to change over meant that we experienced more of these changes than any other depot. We were involved with eight out of the fourteen stages. The following paragraphs detail the many alterations encountered.

At stage two, on 14th/15th April 1959, the first wiring alterations that affected our routes occurred. With route 581 being withdrawn, the Clerkenwell Road/Rosebery Avenue junction was taken out as were the crossovers at the junction of Rosebery Avenue with Farringdon Road. The 677 ran for the last time, so the special work at the City Road/Goswell Road intersection was removed. At Islington, the northbound link between Upper Street and Essex Road was taken out as were two of the connecting links between the Islington Green short working and Essex Road.

On 10th/11th November 1959, stage four occurred. Shortly after this much of the Theobalds Road/Clerkenwell Road overhead layout was removed – this made it much easier for the remaining services using Grays Inn Road.

Forty of our trolleybuses were either withdrawn or trans-ferred to other depots at this time. The sidelined vehicles were either kept in our depot or Wood Green's before being despatched for scrap. The depot engineers needed a bit of leeway with the change-over, and kept running a few of the 'buses that were supposed to be withdrawn on the night of 10th/11th November. One was 314, which was still working on Friday 13th November, and it was the last operational

The arrival of L3s from Poplar and West Ham depots saw the departure of the Cs and Js from Finchley – these older vehicles were now destined to be broken up. Sometimes, consec-utively numbered vehicles were seen alongside each other in service; unusual though, was for this to happen in Colindale scrapyard. 313 and 314 have unfortunately achieved this; either side of them, 831 and 835 are ready fo the chop. A bit of vandalism has occurred in the yard as someone has hurled an object through 313's near-side windscreen; doesn't matter really as she's going to be broken up soon. Earlier in the book there is a photo of me driving 314 in service. *Fred Ivey.*

spatted trolleybus in the fleet. Forty-one L3s moved in. Between then and 2nd February 1960, I would often have a J on my first half of duty and an L on my second, or vice versa. I had previously seen these L3s that had come over from the East End operating on the Commercial Road routes. They had crossed my path at Old Street when I was on a 609, and at Grays Inn Road when working on a 521/621.

Stage seven saw route 611 withdrawn on 19th/20th July 1960. At Highbury Corner, the junctions between Upper Street and Canonbury Road were taken out leaving plain wires for the remaining services. At Archway, the loop around Macdonald Road and the adjoining streets remained, but the 'special work' on Highgate Hill was removed.

Stage eight, on 8th/9th November 1960, saw routes 607 and 655 fall by the wayside. At this point it is worth stating that sometimes a notice would be posted in the depot stating revised overhead arrangements. On other occasions, staff would find things out only when they got to one of the places where there had been a change to the layout. Shortly after the 607 had been withdrawn, the semi-automatic frog, which

had previously been operated for 660s/666s to turn right into Askew Road, was altered in their favour and a chalked slogan was marked onto the now defunct semi-automatic frog box stating 'SET FOR ASKEW ROAD'. Later on, the frogs and crossover here were removed. In the Acton Market area, three frogs were taken out – this made life easier for the 660/666 staff.

Stage nine took place on 31st January/1st February 1961. At the Angel Islington, the overhead junctions that took vehicles down Pentonville Road were removed. The frogs between Euston Road and Grays Inn Road at Kings Cross were taken out as was a facing frog in Kings Cross Road. Also dismantled here were the east to west junctions at Euston Road/ Pentonville Road/Caledonian Road/Grays Inn Road.

At stage ten on 25th/26th April 1961, a big bite was taken out of the north London trolleybus services. The withdrawal of routes 627/629 saw the removal of the southbound wiring across the massive Nags Head junction. At nearby Warlters Road, all the special work was taken out at its junction with Parkhurst Road.

1451 is running late and is going only as far as NAGS HEAD HOLLOWAY on route 609; by now the north to south wire across the junction here has been removed. This made little effect as we still had a lot of crossings to consider. Short-working 521s/621s, and any route running down from Manor House to turn short at Nags Head, had sixteen items of special work and three section insulators to negotiate when carrying out the manoeuvre. There is a lot of traffic on the road; this regularly caused late running to London Transport's road services. *Jack Gready.*

It is July 1960 and no trolleybus routes have been replaced in the 'Nags Head' area as shown by the route number plates in the bus stop flag; however on the 20th day of the month, route 611 will be taken over by bus route 271 between Highgate Village and Moorgate. 1466 is just about to pass under the facing frog that will take it into Seven Sisters Road. In the righthand corner of the picture is a pointsman's canvas hut; attached to a traction standard, a bamboo pole is ready for anybody who needs it. *Alan Cross.*

The overhead department made life easy for Finchley crews after stage ten of the conversion programme – they installed a crossover on our approach to the Nags Head. Until this time, 609 conductors had to pull a semi-automatic frog handle here. 1462 makes yet another trip to North Finchley. Bus stop route plates for routes 17 and 271 are now ominous reminders that trolleybus operation in the area is on the wane. *Tony Belton.*

Just after stage ten had been implemented, an enormous amount of time and effort was put into a wiring alteration in Holloway Road on the approach to the Nags Head junction. The end of the 659/679 meant that only the 521/621, which turned right into Seven Sisters Road, and the 609 which had a straight run up Holloway Road, remained. The facing frog was replaced by a crossover, the trailing frog at the bottom of Camden Road was dispensed with and an additional set of wires, incorporating a new feeder, was erected from there up to the new crossover. All of this was unnecessary as for years, 609 conductors had been pulling a frog handle as a matter of course and wouldn't have been bothered about doing it for another six months. It was odd that this alteration was made at such a late stage in the conversion programme (probably done to justify work for linesmen) but it was much appreciated by the Finchley crews. Everything else was left up at the Nags Head even though the facility to turn right from Seven Sisters Road into Holloway Road, and vice-versa, could have been taken out. At the same time, the 627/659/679 wires across Manor House junction were taken out. Removed too was the St John Street/Islington High Street 'special work'. This was the third overhead change at The Angel and meant that what had been a very complex junction was now left as just a straightforward curve between the High Street and City Road. Many of these alterations were a big job for the

linesmen and had to be accomplished over a number of nights. In the interim, the overhead layout, though safe to pass through, looked untidy.

Highgate depot finished operating trolleybuses on Tuesday 25th April 1961; until this time they had five vehicles working on the 609s on a Sunday. They could not keep just five vehicles to operate on one day of a week, so a unique situation arose whereby HT garage operated five RMs on Sundays between 30th April and 5th November 1961. Only seventeen of these trips went to Barnet. By ridding Highgate of its trolleybuses at this time, the overhead department took down the special work at the junction of Pemberton Gardens and Holloway Road. It is worth saying, at this juncture, that some of the overhead revisions that took place during the conversion period could not take place in one night and stretched to two due to the work involved.

Stage eleven occurred on 18th/19th July 1961. Two junctions were removed on the Holborn loop – the remainder of the Grays Inn Road/Clerkenwell Road layout and the Farringdon Road/Clerkenwell Road arrangement. The Old Street and City Road double crossover was also removed. Apart from a single set of wires, everything around the Redvers Road loop at Wood Green was taken out – only a left-hand turn from Lordship Lane into Wood Green High Road remained.

954's life is over and she waits in Finchley depot for one last journey – to the breaker's yard at Colindale which she will reach under her own power. Behind is 1575, which has been recently transferred in from Highgate and is therefore partly responsible for 954's withdrawal. Three other vehicles can also be seen of which 1507 and 1514 are identifiable over the pits. A fair amount of litter is strewn around the depot – unusual at FY. *Denis Battams.*

Between stages ten and twelve of the conversion programme, Highgate garage operated Routemasters on route 609 on Sundays. From stage nine, busmen's banter saw the Highgate crews saying that they would show the Finchley trolleybus staff a clean pair of heels on our common sections of route. This was not to be the case as we gave them a good run for their money and kept up with them – in fact if we were in front of them, their drivers had to push it a bit to keep pace with us. Seen in Tally Ho bus station, RM 585 is parked next to trolleybus 1475; both are only travelling as far as Islington Green where much of the 609 service terminated on Sundays. *John Buckle.*

From 1st February until 7th November 1961, this kind of scene would be enacted every day. Finchley's 1498 is out of service in Tally Ho bus station but will be overtaken by Stonebridge's 1664 which will soon start its run to Hammersmith on route 660. On the stand are two other trolleybuses – only 1460 working short to Finsbury Park on the 521 is identifiable. Route 17 had replaced the 517/617 on 1st February 1961 and although the new route went to Camberwell Green on Mondays to Fridays, its southern terminus on Saturdays was Farringdon Street; this implies that this picture was taken on that day of the week. Rather than stand on the pavement, the Highgate conductress could have better used her time by going upstairs on RM 237, opening up the blind box housing and winding the intermediate display down a bit so that ELEPHANT was not shown. *Courtesy John Fozard.*

A Routemaster has fooled the Barnet light, for three vehicles are on the stand on 5th November 1961, the last day of dual trolleybus/motorbus operation on route 609. The light obviously did not pick up RM 580, and the driver of the 645 would not have known that two vehicles were already there – hence this interesting view. 1472's cab door is open, indicating that it is time to go; this is confirmed by an inspector looking on. One of the drivers is 1472's; maybe the other is a former Highgate trolleybusman having a last look at the interior of a trolleybus cab. *London County Council Tramways Trust.*

On Saturday 3rd June 1961, part of my duty was on FY3 on route 621. I took over at 1.50pm at Tally Ho and was due to come off at 5.29pm – the mileage to be covered was two trips from North Finchley to Kings Cross. It was common on Saturday afternoons for vehicles to be held up by traffic and that day was no exception. Somewhere along the route an inspector had told me that we were were to curtail our first trip at New Southgate rather than go through to North Finchley. When I arrived at New Southgate, a young lad poked his head into the cab and asked if I could leave up 'New Southgate' on the blind for a photograph; I obliged. In my offside driving mirror I noted that the new conductor I was working with for the day was having a difficult time with the trolley poles. I got out of the cab, took the bamboo pole off him and banged both booms up on the dead-ender. Getting back into the cab I swung 1540 round the circle and passed the trailing frog. As there were a few minutes to spare, and I knew that another vehicle would be in front of me, I dropped the poles. Forty-five years later the photographer showed me these pictures. The first photograph is of the conductor struggling with 1540's trolley arms; the second shows the driver coming to his aid and changing the booms onto the dead-ender. The third view was taken after 1540 had traversed the turning circle and the trolley poles were being dropped. Forty-five years later I was shown these photographs by Hugh Taylor.

Since April 1959, when stage two took place, North Finchley had been a by-way for vehicles that, under their own power, were heading for the scrapyard behind Colindale depot. Also passing through were trolleybuses being transferred from east London to west London depots. These vehicles didn't come through the bus station but had their poles swung in Kingsway. I can still visualise some of our 'native' Finchley trolleybuses being taken away to the scrapyard. For storage purposes, some of Highgate's cast-offs were dumped in our depot in 1960/61. Fulwell and Isleworth's Q1s that were heading for warmer climes in Spain, traversed the bus station on their way to Aldgate and Shoreditch in 1961.

In early 1961, the firm who were contracted to carry out the building work for Finchley to operate motorbuses moved in. Two huts were erected on the premises from where operations were directed. A major item they had to deal with was the installation of diesel and oil tanks. Until this time, trolleybuses entered the depot on roads one and two – those nearest the traffic office. At some stage, the wires and troughing on these two roads were removed and trolleybuses entered the depot a bit further along. This allowed watering and fuelling islands to be installed. Whereas we had had two roads in and three direct roads out, we now had one road in and two direct roads out. Still available, though, were many dead-end wires. After the November changeover, another 'out' road was removed, meaning that there was just one road in and one road out. Not all the of the remaining trolleybuses could fit in one road, so some had to be parked with booms down. They were now parked on the far side of the depot – that is, the greatest distance from the traffic office. Part of the traverser pit was filled with concrete during autumn 1961, with more being poured in after our first conversion. With the end of trolleybus operation at Finchley in January 1962, the remaining overhead and the traverser were removed. This allowed the traverser pit to be completely filled in.

The one hundred and twenty-five QI trolleybuses heading for a new life in Spain passed through Tally Ho bus station on various dates in 1961. On 28th April, number 1832 heads for Shoreditch where it will be hitched to a towing wagon to take it to Poplar garage before it goes to Dagenham Docks for shipment to Zaragoza; 1832 has a long life ahead of it as it will spend many years working there. This cannot be said for 1487 as it was one of the Finchley trolleybuses withdrawn in November 1961; most of our vehicles were forwarded to other depots at this, the twelfth stage of the conversion programme. *Tony Belton.*

BACK TO SCHOOL AGAIN

As the time approached for our depot to change from trolley-buses to motorbuses, arrangements were made for drivers to train for their Public Service Vehicle licences. No medical was needed for the transition as a dispensation between London Transport and the licensing authority covered this. Similarly, we didn't have to go through the rigmarole of having to be vouched for when applying for a PSV licence. There was blanket coverage for all drivers and conductors requiring new badges and licences in the trolleybus conversion programme (presumably, the application forms were rubber-stamped by the CDI).

It was vital that trolleybus services were maintained while motorbus driver training took place. To avoid them being depleted, only a few men were away at a time. My instruction commenced in the summer of 1961, and I had to report to Finchley depot one morning. Three of us met in the canteen for a cup of tea and before long an instructor identified himself to us – he had been a trolleybus driver at 'Tramway' (Edmonton depot). Leading us out onto the forecourt, the instructor showed us over a Routemaster bus that he had parked there. It had L plates attached to it; one was in the rear window; the other was positioned in the window at the front of the lower saloon. This was 'trolleybus style' and indicated that the instructors were former trolleybus drivers. There were now two driving schools running simultaneously at FY, a trolleybus one and a motorbus one. This happened at many other depots as well.

Our mentor told us all about the RM and said that we would now have to master an engine and a gearbox; the latter was automatic in that the gears changed up or down according to road speed. The lever on the gear-change column in the cab allowed the bus to be driven manually if required. If we opted for this, then we should listen to the engine and match its revs to the road speed (when I was driving RMs in service, I used this facility when wanting to get a move on with a heavy load – it was better to use manual in the lower gears).

The most important thing we had to be aware of from a driving point of view was the extra six inches' width of the Routemaster. They were eight foot wide compared to the seven foot six inches of a trolleybus. The instructor continually told us that the extra width was 'all on the nearside'. Positioned on the training bus was a vertical arm about ten inches in height fitted to the nearside front wing. It had a ball on the top, and was an aid for gauging the width of the bus. We were soon 'having a go' on what were to be our new charges and we ended the day back at Finchley depot where we met each morning after that.

Besides not having to consider the overhead wiring, there were a lot of differences between a motorbus and a trolleybus. We would only need to concentrate on the road ahead; the road above would no longer be there. Drivers' left legs were now virtually obsolete, for both the accelerator and brake pedal were operated with the right foot. Another major variation was the position of the handbrake; on a trolleybus it was to the driver's right – now it was to his left. Being right-handed I initially found this strange, and it took a while to get used to. A further item that was different, and which also took time to get acclimatised to, was the position of the Westinghouse air brake warning flag. It was now high up in front, near the top of the windscreen. When low air pressure occurred on an RM, the flag dropped – this was in great contrast to a trolleybus, as its Westinghouse flag rose when activated. Power assisted steering was a luxury, and with directional trafficators fitted there was no need for so many hand signals. In my opinion this was not a good idea. Motorbus drivers were able to keep the heel of their shoe on the floor of the cab when using the 'gas' pedal; the position of the power pedal on a trolleybus prevented drivers from doing this. The two things I welcomed about the motorbuses were a better cab heater and a larger offside driving mirror.

It had been found in the early stages of the conversion programme that a maximum of ten days was all that most men needed to get used to motorbuses. We were on an eleven day fortnight at the time, so had to come in one Saturday. On day one, the instructor related two important matters to us. First, that he wanted us to experience as many different driving conditions as possible. He took this very seriously and consequently we visited many areas of London that were unfamiliar to us. Secondly, and more importantly, that we should be disassociated from trolleybus routes for the duration of the course. Asking him why this was so, he replied, "I don't want you stopping for frog pulls, slowing up under junctions or taking your foot off the accelerator pedal at section insulators". This was good and intelligent thinking by the training department, and was a policy that was employed throughout the conversion programme. With the system now seventy-five per cent abandoned and in terminal decline, we didn't have to venture far to find areas where trolleybus wires were no longer to be seen. Abbey Wood, Chalk Farm, Romford North Street, Seven Kings and Streatham were all garages we went to for our meal reliefs. We even ventured onto the old airfield at North Weald and had a go on the skid pan at Chiswick Works.

I do not recall there being a progress check during the course – it was deemed unnecessary as we were street-wise. I passed my PSV test first time. This was in August 1961 and I received badge number N56344, this being a first time issue. Type training on an RT took place the next day – the steering was far heavier than on the RM. The RT used a pre-selector gear change system; I was unfamiliar with this type of gearbox, but soon got used to it. At this juncture I need to say that I could see more on my nearside on the RT than on a trolleybus, or an RM which had a wide bonnet. The engine on the Routemaster was only slightly quieter than the RT engine. The depot inspectors were kept in the picture as to when each driver was 'up for test'; as they anticipated that everyone would pass first time, I was back on my own trolleybus duty the day after I had received my RT type training.

When our PSV badges were issued, their numbers were in close proximity – the badges and licences were sent to the depot. Even though the conversion was taking place in two stages, most drivers and all conductors received their new badges and licences in the November changeover. The exceptions were a few recently qualified trolleybus drivers who received their training in November and December 1961.

Some staff, upon obtaining their PSV badge and licence shortly before the conversion, displayed the badge in the other lapel of their jacket. I kept mine aside and did not wear it until 8th November 1961. However, during the eight week period when motorbuses and trolleybuses were operating simultaneously at Finchley, I displayed both my N and T badges as it was possible that I might be asked to work a trolley duty. I inserted the N and T badges in the same holder so that they both showed. It was not until it became very cold, at the end of 1961, that I wore my overcoat and only displayed my PSV badge on it. I kept my MSC badge in a pocket in the overcoat – just in case it was needed. Drivers who only had a group H licence (trolley vehicle) received a bonus, for on passing their test they were given a full driving licence – at no cost to themselves. Although these men did not immedi-

ately buy their own cars, some did later. Some drivers looked upon the situation as a quick way of obtaining a PSV licence and once they had got it, left the job and used it for their own ends. None of our staff failed their PSV test, not even those who were over the retirement age of sixty-five – they took to their new job as a duck takes to water. Some of the older men, those who had been driving trolleybuses for twenty five years, now found themselves changing a second time. It had been a culture change moving from a Feltham tram to a trolleybus. The switch to motorbuses was less of a challenge as they were used to driving near to kerblines.

When the change to motorbuses occurred, trolleybus staff were given a one-off payment of three pounds, ten shillings for agreeing to work the motorbus system. Even those who stayed on trolleybuses until stage thirteen were given the one-off payment at stage twelve. The change in the working agreement was not popular with inspectors as they lost the flexibility that the trolleybus way of working offered. Until now they had been able to 'pinch' a 521 and use it as a 609, or nab a 521 and send it to Barnet. On motorbuses, the most that inspectors could do was to get a bus which was going one

way to go the other, and even then only if there was to be some benefit to the crew. We now signed on rather than being ticked in by a depot inspector. With two conversions, confusion was avoided by everybody signing on – this obviated the problem of mix-ups about who should be ticked off and who should sign on.

When there was a proposed change of schedules, copies had to be forwarded to the TGWU for their perusal. They had to receive them well before any suggested starting date so that they could study and either approve or reject them. Those for the 104s/125s/221s were sent well in advance as this was a big changeover with nine sets of schedules to look at. Our representatives needed plenty of time as they were used to looking at trolleybus schedules. Motorbus ones had different agreements, and were also in a completely different format. The direction of travel in which a bus was taken over 'on the road' was now described as either 'A' or 'B'. If a bus was taken over on a stand it was denoted by a 'C'.

'TWIXT TWELVE AND THIRTEEN

I was not looking forward to the elimination of trolleybuses at Finchley depot. Nothing can stop the march of progress though and on Tuesday 7th November 1961, the routes concerned in stage twelve of the ten and a half million pound trolleybus conversion programme, ran for the last time. These were the 641 at Wood Green depot and routes 521/609/621 at Finchley. I was on an early turn that day and when I stepped down from the cab at North Finchley at the end of my duty, I remember thinking to myself that it would be the last trolleybus I would be in charge of. Although trolleybuses would be at Finchley depot for another two months, I did not think that I would drive one again. As far as I recall, any

extra work that I did from then on was on motorbuses. However, exactly eight weeks later an unexpected opportunity arose for a final trolleybus drive, one which I grasped with both hands.

Finchley was involved in an experiment that saw longer Routemasters being used on route 104. Nineteen were required on Monday to Friday, twenty-three on Saturday. These buses were numbered RML 880–903, were thirty feet in length and had a seating capacity of seventy-two. This was two foot, six inches longer than the standard RM which had seats for sixty-four. Some of the RMLs were brought to the depot a few days before the changeover. Bringing in a few buses beforehand allowed conductors to give them a 'once over' if they wanted to. Their presence allowed them to familiarise themselves with the different features that they would be encountering. They had to know where the heater control unit was, see where the locker for equipment was positioned and find out the way that blinds were changed – they were given a 'budget' key in the shape of a T for this. Conductors now had the responsibility of putting the saloon lights on, so they had to know where the switches for them were. Other changes pertinent to conductors involved the Gibson machines – on trolleybuses the duty number only was painted onto one side of the machine box; now the duty *and* route number were marked on. Furthermore, the route number was now printed onto the ticket. Previously, 000 was shown, as many duties worked on two routes.

Some outer termini were fitted with passing loops, Barnet being one; a scene enacted regularly sees a 609 overtaking a 645. Here, 1510 goes round 1564 which was 'last away' from Barnet on 2nd January 1962. *Peter Moore.*

Some Routemasters were brought to Finchley depot a few days before stage twelve of the conversion programme. By this time part of the traverser pit had been concreted over; parked on it are RMLs 883, 880 and 882. Building work continues and the contractor's large hut can be seen in the right background. In the foreground is the trolleybus turntable/ traverser. *Don Lewis.*

7th November 1961 was a wet morning, causing late running; 1540 is well adrift of its time and has been curtailed at Wood Green rather than run through to North Finchley. It is not known why an inspector at Manor House is replacing the bamboo pole beneath the vehicle – maybe he has let another trolleybus go in front or is checking to see that 1540 is carrying one as it will be needed when it gets to Wood Green. An RTL heads for Victoria on route 29; a member of staff is not at all bothered about what mode of transport he uses on his way to work, so boards a motorbus rather than a trolleybus despite it being the last day he could 'travel by trolley'. *Terry Cooper.*

Dusk on Tuesday 7th November 1961 and two Finchley trolleybuses have left the depot for the last time. 1554's ferry driver has put up PRIVATE on the destination blind but a 609 route display still shows; when it arrived at Colindale scrapyard some weeks later, the blinds were still in the same position. Putting Haig whisky Christmas adverts on 1554 was premature as it was withdrawn that November night. RT 4734 turns into Woodberry Grove on the last day that Muswell Hill bus garage operates the route. *Tony Belton.*

Open ground at Stonebridge depot was a holding area for trolleybuses that had been withdrawn but had yet to be disposed of. A few days after stage twelve of the conversion programme a number of Finchley and Wood Green trolleybuses are dumped there. The two identifiable Wood Green vehicles are 1301 and 1351 which have had the blinds removed by their depot staff. 1476 and 1488 are trolleybuses that I had driven many times and they have had their blinds left in by our men; 1488's last trip was on route 609 while 1476's was on the 645. A souvenir hunter has been able to open up 1476's side box and remove the blind; this could be done easily by the dedicated collector – it needed a lot of dexterity to remove the rear blinds, but taken out many of them were. Perry's of Ealing are the firm contracted to convert Stonebridge trolleybus depot into a bus garage. *Fred Ivey.*

Delivery of RMLs was very slow and at the time of the conversion only thirteen were available; the shortfall was made up by RMs. A few more RMLs came before I left Finchley; the remainder, though delivered, had not been placed in service by then. Finchley was not allocated RMs in a long numerical sequence as happened at many other locations. We received them within the 876–986 range.

Because I had gone home in the daytime on 7th November, I didn't see what happened in Finchley depot that night. The following describes it. In the early evening, the motorbuses that would be working from FY the next day were driven by qualified staff from various garages to our depot. RTs mainly came from New Cross, RMs from Cricklewood, Hanwell and Highgate with the oustanding RMLs coming from Highgate. All the new buses had been mechanically checked over and road-tested to ensure they were in full working order. Simultaneously, a well-organised system saw maintenance staff arrive from various 'live' and former trolleybus depots. Their job was to ferry trolleybuses that Finchley had finished with to Colindale, Fulwell or Stonebridge depots for storage, or to Fulwell and Stonebridge for further service. Efficiency was at its peak, as it was arranged that the last trolleybuses

on all routes that night would be those that would be staying. This meant that the ferry staff would not have an excessively late finish, and that none of the fifteen trolleybuses that were remaining would have to be cleaned and looked at until 'close of play'. We were retaining the lowest numbered vehicles in the best condition; those in the 1449–1469 range.

The overhead layout at North Finchley was re-cast shortly after the November changeover, all the redundant frogs and crossovers being removed. The work took place over a few nights, and again there were times when everything looked messy. During this time it was important that 645s and 660s could pass through unimpeded. When the overhead staff had finished their remodelling, only a single track was left through the bus station and at first it looked odd. At this time a new frog was installed in Kingsway for vehicles to turn from Barnet; it could also have been used to get trolleybuses round from the bottom of the bus station to the top. This was unlikely as trolley arms could have been dropped and raised for any manoeuvres there, and it is also doubtful that a 645 would have used it to get back to Barnet. It is possible then, that this last new junction to be installed on the trolleybus system was never used.

Trolleybus route 609 was replaced by bus route 104 on which the longer Routemasters were trialled; RML 891 passes tower wagon 82Q at Finsbury Square. This photograph was taken soon after the changeover, and the overhead line staff are removing redundant electrical conduit from a traction standard. It is too heavy for 82Q to carry so it will be placed on service vehicle 953B which is a Bedford-Scammell articulated low-loading lorry. It is a bit late in the day for equipment to be salvaged as the system will only be running for another six months – maybe the conduit is needed on one of the routes operated by Fulwell or Isleworth depots. On the top of the traction standard in question is a hook on which bamboo poles were placed; near the bottom of the standard a clasp held them in place.

Bus route 104 replaced trolleybus route 609 – it followed it exactly. The successor of the 521/621 was bus route 221 which ran from North Finchley to Farringdon Street, Stonecutter Street. It ran via Farringdon Road only, and with the 521/621 being the last of the Holborn loop services, this method of terminating ended. As Stonecutter Street was near to Charterhouse Street, a route learning bus was not provided. A map showing the way to the new terminus was placed on the output blackboard for our information and perusal.

With the conversion, the opportunity was taken to match the frequency of the replacing motorbus routes with any lower passenger demand. This applied to the 104s and 221s, so wider headways meant a smaller number of duties. To compensate, Finchley took over the operation of the 125 from Muswell Hill garage, for which we were allocated twelve RTs. These were not MH's own buses as they needed them for work they were taking on at this time. Passenger loadings had shown that it was necessary to provide a more frequent

The new and old order meet at Barnet. Finchley's RM 879 is just starting its trip to Moorgate on route 104 while Colindale's 1584 waits out its time for its next trip on route 645 to Canons Park. By now, the CE driver would have passed his PSV test and would be qualified to drive a motorbus. *Tony Belton.*

level of service between Highgate and Moorgate than between Barnet and Highgate on the 104, so consequently MH found themselves with extra buses on route 43. They were also given some runnings on the 134 bus route. Eleven of the RTs came from New Cross garage who received RMs to operate on the former 641 trolleybus route – extended at its southern end from Moorgate to Grove Park as bus route 141. The musical chairs scenario involving routes, buses and garages was a common theme in the trolleybus to bus changeover.

Route learning buses were an important ingredient in the trolleybus conversion programme. They ensured that at each stage, staff were familiar with any new route that they would be operating. About four weeks before each changeover took place, a motorbus took staff out to see the new surroundings in which they would be working. The reason for such a lengthy learning period was that staff had to slot it in around their duties. These buses not only worked from trolleybus depots but also from a number of bus garages where staff would be operating over former trolleybus routes. We had to route learn the 125 which, on weekdays, ran from Golders Green to Southgate Station with some journeys extended to Winchmore Hill, Highlands Hospital. On Sundays it worked between North Finchley and Winchmore Hill, Station Road. Not only did we have to know which roads the 125 took, but also where the short working facilities were. The lesser used ones were specifically pointed out to us – Hendon 'Bell' and Woodside Park, Cissbury Ring.

An RT with a Muswell Hill driver, and an inspector who was familiar with the route, were laid on for us. It went out twice a day – once in the morning, once in the afternoon. It was deemed necessary that drivers *had* to do the route learning but it was optional for conductors; overtime was paid for performing this work. Most staff did it before or after their duty or on their day off. The crafty ones did it on a spreadover – this meant that they were being paid overtime during their working hours. If anybody was not able to fit the route learning in while the MH bus was provided, they could do it on a service bus provided that they had a route learning slip signed by a 125 conductor. It was important that those who were going on the new motorbus rota learnt it by 8th November. It was less essential for drivers staying on the trolley rota to do it by then, but they did have to route learn it as they might have to work on it sometime. Many of those who were doing the route learning on their day off would be in their civvies; staff smoked on the lower deck and with the general bus banter that went on, there was an informal atmosphere about it all. It was a bit of a 'jolly' really. It amused us that some would-be passengers hailed the RT as it came towards them – even though PRIVATE was shown in the blind apertures. When potential passengers in London see a red bus, they automatically think they can get on.

Date: Wednesday 8th November 1961. Time: 7am. Place: Finchley output. The topic of conversation was how drivers and conductors were going to get on with new buses and a new route. There was no aura of apprehension – it was the same job really. The bus rota consisted of work on route 104 which had RMLs (and a few RMs), the 125 which was worked by RTs, and the 221 which had RMs. Finchley was the only depot to receive three different types of bus at one conversion stage – RT, RM and RML. Counting the trolleybus, we simultaneously had four different types of vehicles; Finchley was the only place where this occurred. No type-training was given on the RMLs as they were thirty foot in length, the same as a trolleybus – drivers just got in the RMLs and drove them out of the shed. Most of the Finchley staff had been happy working on trolleybuses, but we accepted the conversion as a matter of course, soon got used to things and adapted to our new circumstances.

Finchley depot forecourt in the summer of 1961 and RM 254 is being used to familiarise Finchley trolleybus drivers with motorbuses; it is quite likely that this was the vehicle I trained on to obtain my PSV licence. Many trolleybuses are having a rest from their daily labours. *Alan Kenny.*

Until now, it had been all main road working. However, with the 125s we would be driving around leafy suburbs some of the time. What route was I booked up for that day? – the 125. Bridie and I went out into what was now Finchley trolleybus depot/Finchley garage and found the RT allocated to us. In motorbus style, we had a timecard each and by looking at them we observed that we had to go to Highlands Hospital first of all. After a bit of a wind through the destination blind, I found the correct display. Having got to Highlands Hospital, I got out of the cab and went round and sat in the lower saloon. I asked Bridie how she had got on with fares on our new route – she said that she had coped alright. Then it was off to Golders Green for a rush hour run. It was novel that day and we got through without encountering any problems. A new feature for conductors on the 125s was to punch a log card in the time-clocks at Golders Green and Woodside Park. Although it was expected that the 125 would be quieter than the trolleybus services we had been working on, it still had its hairy moments as there were a lot of schoolchildren to deal with. The 104s and 221s would be as busy or as quiet as their electric predecessors.

The biggest difference to me was the loud noise of the engine and the cramped cab of the RT. When compared to the almost silent trolleybus and its wide cab, it seemed to be two different worlds. Another factor that was immediately apparent was the lack of accessories. There were a lot more control switches in a trolleybus cab – in the RT and RM they were above me to the left as opposed to being down to my right on the trolleybus. There was a sliding cab door on the motorbus – on the trolleybus it opened outwards. There was also a specific place for the timecard to be positioned. A real downside of motorbus driving was the inability to converse with conductors. Now I had to tap on the window behind me to signal that I wanted them to come round to the front where we spoke through the nearside windscreen. Conductors did not like this as they had been used to sticking their heads into the cab from the saloon. The item I really missed was the interior cab mirror which gave a good view of the platform. A very unusual aspect that showed itself within a few days was that conductors did not consider the extra few inches in the gangway of the Routemasters to be of any great benefit. This was a different response to what London Transport had expected. A new concept for drivers was that we now had to top up radiators when they needed replenishing. All in all, the trolleybus was far more powerful at getting away from a standing start than a motor bus and I found the Routemasters slower at pulling away from a bus stop than a trolleybus.

Come break time, the topic of conversation in the canteen was how everybody was coping. Most staff said something like, "Went okay", "Ran a bit late on my first trip", "Seemed strange not having to wait at Jolly Butchers Hill for the frog pull", "The oddest thing was going through the Nags Head at twenty miles an hour". The 645/660 staff had their own remarks: "Like your new toy, then", "Look after it, don't scratch the paintwork", "You'll miss the wide trolleybus cab today". For the first few days, the inspectors at Tally Ho would say "How you getting on?" or "Which do you prefer, buses or trolleys?". It got a bit tiresome really but they were only making conversation. A terminology passing with the trolleybuses was 'on the down'. If we were taking over a northbound 104, we'd say "We're going to Barnet".

I was on a late turn on my first day driving an RML down to the City on the 104s – this was a few days after the conversion. Despite not having touched a Routemaster for about three months, I had no trouble familiarising myself with it. Maybe it was because I had been driving an RT for a few days. I was surprised to see that the overhead wires were still 'live'. I could tell that the power was still on as the 'Y' light at various junctions was shining brightly in the dark. It seemed totally pointless having 'the juice' on at Moorgate and Holborn when trolleybuses had last run on 7th November, but it was standard practice to keep the power on for a week after most conversion stages to allow for vehicle movements. Later on, in November, Cohen's who were responsible for dismantling the overhead, started to cut the wires down from the withdrawn routes – they started at the City end. This was a tough job, so they were only able to remove a few miles a night. In fact when I left Finchley in January 1962, some of the redundant wiring on the City routes was still aloft. London Transport staff removed the major intersections. The Nags Head junction was one such place, and a number of tower wagons would have been positioned there so as to take it all down in one night. This location looked a completely different place once the overhead had been removed – a few days later the mental picture of the junction went out of my head.

Those of us on the motorbus rota had an initial 'strange' appearance for a few days. For years drivers had their blue MSC badge, and conductors their orange MSC badge on display. Now we all had brand new red or green badges respectively and it took a few days for everybody to look 'normal'. It also took time for conductors to memorise their driver's new badge number. Those on the trolleybus rota were still displaying their MSC badges so for the next eight weeks there was a colourful combination. It was only on 3rd January 1962 that everybody was displaying PSV badges.

In the few days before changing from trolleybuses to buses, the 'stops and shelters' department were very active. Until now a lot of bus stop flags were fitted to traction standards; these were now taken down and new bus stop posts and flags fitted nearby. Some shelters had to be moved a few yards right or left so that they were adjacent to any newly positioned bus stops. On 7th November 1961 and 2nd January 1962, those responsible for fitting E plates to bus stop flags changed the trolleybus route numbers to the new bus route ones. This was too big a job to complete overnight and would-be passengers saw the new route numbers being displayed when the trolleybus routes involved were eking out their last day of life. Along the length of each route that was to be replaced, the publicity department stuck 'Buses for Trolleybuses' posters on almost every traction standard. Also available, was a booklet detailing the new or revised bus services. These were placed in conductor's Gibson machine boxes, and were given to those who asked for them.

A couple of snippets are worthy of note. First, there were a number of bamboo poles left in strategic positions after

With St Michael's church in the background, 1495 is seen in Bounds Green Road, Wood Green. The route and destination blinds are perfectly positioned. On this sunny day, only a Morris Minor car and trolleybus 1495 are seen in action. *Hugh Ramsey*.

stage twelve had taken place. They were not considered to be redundant material and in November a tower wagon went round the abandoned routes and collected them for further use. Secondly, on Boxing Day 1961, a few drivers on the motorbus rota were allocated trolleybus duties. This was due to some staff being classified as 'spare' that day. Boxing day fell on a Tuesday, so those who would normally have worked that day were given a duty that needed to be covered. Having not driven trolleybuses for seven weeks led to an air of complacency, and carelessness became apparent. Power was being taken where it shouldn't have been and Bill Henderson, who had become accustomed to a motorbus accelerator pedal, dewired when leaving Edgware loop on a scheduled short working 645. He kept his foot down on the power pedal, and dewired on the trailing frog.

The vehicle situation at Fulwell had become dire just after Christmas, and on 28th December, trolleybus 1456 was transferred a few days earlier than planned. This left Finchley with fourteen trolleybuses for fourteen runnings – the margin of one spare trolleybus was lost. The engineers had enough

faith in the electric vehicles to know that the service could be kept running without a stand-by. As far as I am aware, there was not an occasion in the remaining few days of the 645s and 660s at Finchley that full trolleybus availability did not occur.

I immediately took to the fact that when driving a Routemaster, I did not have to consider the overhead anymore – despite it still being above me. One habit that stayed with me for the next twenty-three years was that right until the last day that I drove buses, I always went a few feet beyond bus stops at a couple of places. One was at the Angel tube station in City Road, the other at Drayton Park in Holloway Road – both southbound. These were where trolleybus stops had been positioned on traction standards that had held power supply feeders, and where I had coasted past them on the 609s in order to clear the 'dead' (these had been the only two places on the former 521/609/621 routes where this occurred). I continued to drift past these two stops because it was programmed into me from my trolleybus days, and I did it automatically.

It is 2nd January 1962, the last day of route 645, and Colindale's 1586 has just left a request stop in Ballards Lane, Finchley. The heavy electric cables that feed electricity into the overhead wires stand out strongly in this winter view; note the icicles on the house across the road. This time tomorrow 1580 will be parked up in CE, its poles will have been placed beneath its retaining hooks for the last time and its MSC plate removed. All that remains is for a tow by one of Cohen's wagons round to their scrapyard behind the depot. *Andrew Forsyth.*

TWO BARNETS AND A CANONS PARK

On Sunday 31st December 1961, a heavy snowfall blanketed London and threw all its road and rail services into disarray. I was not rostered for work that day but was the next. Road conditions were appalling and on New Year's Day 1962, Bridie and I did not cover a lot of mileage. Some staff did not turn up for work during this bad weather and there was a lot of marrying of crews to get as many buses and trolleybuses on the road as possible. Even though the depot inspectors were successful in crewing up some of the uncovered work, there were still gaps to be filled. When, on Monday 1st January, the overtime for the following day was posted, I noticed that there was a second half of a trolley duty 'going spare'. I put myself down for this piece of overtime which was on route 645 from 8.43pm to 11.46pm.

On 2nd January, I was on a middle turn on the 221s. On the first half I had an RM but on the second half was given an RT; this was because the RMs weren't coping very well with the freezing conditions. The water in the top radiator was freezing up, causing the heaters to blow out cold air. At the time, saloon heaters were not fitted to RTs – better, though, to have a bus that was not blowing out cold air rather than one that was. It was uncommon for RTs to be put out on the 104s and 221s but as they had blinds for all Finchley routes it could happen if nothing else was available.

On Tuesday morning I told Rose why I wouldn't be home for an evening meal that day. After my 221 duty I had a snack in the canteen and found the conductor with whom I would be working for the rest of the evening. At the appropriate time we trudged out of the depot onto the still uncleared snowy streets and pavements to await the trolleybus that was to arrive at the relief point in Ballards Lane; 1464 came up to the stop. The departing driver asked what I, a motorbus man now really, was doing coming out on a night like this to drive a trolleybus – I said that I wanted to have a final drive (and was being paid overtime for it). To ensure that I was kitted out correctly, I took the red PSV badge off my overcoat and replaced it with my blue MSC trolleybus badge which was in its pocket. I climbed into the trolleybus cab which had been part of my working life for six years; it was quite cold, but to the right was the reassuring glow of the orange neon light which signified that power was available. The flickering of this light was an item that a trolleybus driver was often watching, and was something that I would naturally be doing with 1464. Everything seemed eerie for those first few seconds what with snow and ice all around, and there was a short period of unfamiliarity about the situation. The strangeness was caused by the quietness of the trolleybus – after all, I had heard a bus engine growling next to me for the last eight

Seen at Finsbury Park a few years after trolleybuses ceased to run in London, RT 965 is working on the 221; it was very unusual for RTs to operate on this route. On 2nd January 1962 I drove an RM and an RT on route 221 and finished my day driving a trolleybus on route 645. I don't think that any other London Transport driver worked on these three types of vehicle during a day. *Jim Blake.*

This was the view at the end of the photographer's road on the morning of Sunday 31st December 1961. Snow is still falling and covers the front of 1451 which is seen in Stonegrove, Edgware; a crew member, probably the conductor, has drawn '645' on its front panel for the benefit of intending passengers. *Hugh Taylor.*

Somebody's made a mess of things on the final afternoon of trolleybuses in north London; 1458 is being run into Finchley depot as there's no crew to take it over. Both trolley poles have left the overhead at the junction of Woodberry Grove and Ballards Lane, The driver has been forced to stay in the centre of the road because of the parked car – this means that as the booms take up the inside track, the angle is too great – and off they come. There is no doubt that this is the afternoon of 2nd January 1962 as a 260 plate has been inserted into the route number aperture of the bus stop flag which is attached to a new lighting standard (where is the compatriot plate for the 245?). All of this has attracted the attention of a number of spectators who are being entertained by a Finchley depot employee retrieving the situation with a bamboo pole for the last time in his career. *Alan Cross.*

The snowfall of Sunday 31st December 1961 threw London Transport's remaining trolleybus services into chaos. Colindale's 1570 on running number CE10 has been running so late on route 645 that it has lost more than half a journey (its destination would have been Barnet). It is seen late that evening parked on the St Gabriels Church loop at Cricklewood. *Denis Battams.*

weeks. The bell came from my conductor and we were away – to Barnet Church. Although he knew my name, the conductor didn't know my badge number. On ascertaining this, T9628 was now definitely inserted onto London trolleybus paperwork for the last time. In a single day I had driven an RM, an RT and a trolleybus in service. In doing so I accomplished a feat that I think was attained only by me in the whole of London Transport's history. Finchley was the only location where this could happen. I am almost certain that this was a one-off incident, for if it had occurred before, it would have been depot knowledge.

Two Barnets and a Canons Park was the mileage to be covered. Due to the extreme cold of the evening there were few passengers about. However, there were many trolleybuses around as the depot inspectors at CE, FY and SE had managed to cover most of the duties. They knew that people wanted a ride home on a bitterly cold night. It took about fifteen minutes to get to Barnet where inspector Jock Dow told me that due to staffing problems at Colindale, the 645 behind me was not running at present. Therefore I was driving the last ever 645 from Barnet to Canons Park. The journey was uneventful, though when I passed Colindale depot I looked onto the forecourt where I saw a few trolleybuses waiting there having made their last trips. These were some of

Colindale's own vehicles, and some of Stonebridge's which were being stored there. At Canons Park I pulled up behind another Finchley 645, and as there was fourteen minutes on the stand, I got out of the cab and went into the saloon of 1464. I cannot remember the words exchanged between myself and my conductor but no doubt the conversation would have been about the passing of the trolleybuses. The preceding 645 left and about a minute later the saloon lights brightened as it went out of section; shortly afterwards they dimmed as the final trolleybus of all to Canons Park came into section. The brightening and dimming of the saloon lights was a feature that would be passing from my environment that night as was the cutting in and out of the compressor, neither would I be seeing the green moquette of the trolleybus seats again. The hum of the motor generator set and the clicking of the contactors would also soon be a thing of the past. Not to be heard again was the rattling of the bamboo pole as it was withdrawn or replaced beneath a trolleybus. Departure time came, so I got into the cab and drove the last Finchley depot trolleybus away from Canons Park. Between Colindale and Cricklewood I noticed a few Stonebridge vehicles, saloon lights out, making their final journeys to Colindale depot for storage. Before long they would just be scrap in a yard behind the depot.

BUSES FOR TROLLEYBUSES   JANUARY 3

A new daily bus route 260 will replace trolleybus route 660. The route will be extended from North Finchley to Barnet via Whetstone.

Please ask the conductor for a leaflet giving details

When I arrived at Barnet, not only was 'Jock' Dow the point inspector there, but also a reporter and photographer from the Barnet Press newspaper – their staff had clued themselves up about the event. The 'press' were there as they wanted to feature the last trolleybus to leave Barnet in their next issue – this was the 645 behind me. I pointed out that I would be driving the last Finchley-based trolleybus to leave Barnet terminus so they photographed Jock, myself and 1464. There was only fourteen minutes running time to North Finchley with a further five from there to the depot so I left pretty well on time. We had a number of passengers on board and they took various items as souvenirs from inside the trolleybus (one of them gave me one of the clips which kept the fare chart holder in place). I don't know why they came with me as they could have travelled on the last trolleybus to run in Hertfordshire. As I went down Barnet Hill, 1564, 'the last Barnet' came up. It was an uneventful journey to North Finchley. I pulled up alongside the frog for the depot in Ballards Lane; having the cab door window slightly open, I heard in the quiet of the crisp cold night the click of the frog as my conductor pulled the handle down. I took him over the pointwork and he reboarded. I drove down Woodberry Grove and into the depot where my conductor alighted at the office block. Also getting off here were a few passengers – although we were supposed to run empty from Ballards Lane, we let them have a few more yards of trolleybus travel. I drove 1464 to the top of the depot where I was told "Leave it there". I knocked the circuit breakers out and got out of the cab. I had driven a London trolleybus for the last time.

I decided to watch the de-commissioning of 1464. As soon as I left the cab, one of the shunters got in and drove it onto the traverser. The booms were whipped down and she was spun round on the turntable one hundred and eighty degrees. The traverser moved to the left and to the road that allowed trolleybuses to exit the depot. 1464's poles were hoisted onto the overhead and it was driven forward a few yards and parked up; a ferry crew would soon take her over to Fulwell depot. I then walked up to the clubroom where, paid for by the sports and social side of the depot, there was free beer (the 'farewell trolleybus party' took place at a ballroom in Muswell Hill). Only two other trolleybuses came in behind me: a 645 which, due to late running even at that time of night, had come from Colindale depot rather than Edgware, and last of all 1468 from Hammersmith on route 660. A

Top It's about 11.40pm on Tuesday 2nd January 1962 and I am seen with Jock Dow in front of the last Finchley depot trolleybus to leave Barnet – a 645. I have already changed 1464's front blind to show NORTH FINCHLEY. Snow had fallen heavily two days earlier and it still remains on the ground. *Ron Kingdon.*

Left Although the compiler of this book could be deemed to be the culprit for the snow slogans either side of the war memorial plaque at Finchley depot, the finger cannot be pointed at him as he was riding on the last 660 into Stonebridge depot. However, he agrees with the sentiments and if the person responsible is reading this book, the compiler would like to shake his hand. *Michael Dryhurst.*

number of Finchley staff, using fog flares, formed a torchlight procession in front of 1468. This commenced in Ballards Lane, went through the bus station, back into Ballards Lane and concluded in the depot. As many as wanted to (enthusiasts, staff and the local mayor) rode on 1468 from the trolleybus station to the depot. Along with many other staff, I went onto the forecourt to see 'Darkie' Stevens drive her in. The last 125 had long gone, so a long walk home for a number of us was the only option. A two mile walk on a freezing night was the price paid for 'Two Barnets and a Canons Park'.

When I came in for work the following day there was not a trolleybus in the building. The fourteen trolleybuses that had been working on 2nd January had gone to Fulwell depot. The last to enter (1468) was the last to leave. When it headed south down Ballards Lane at about 1am the electric transport era in north London had ended.

More new Routemasters came to Finchley garage for the 3rd January 1962 conversion. All were ostensibly for new route 260 which replaced the 660 trolleybus service. The 260 was projected to Barnet, though operated in two overlapping sections, there were no through journeys from Hammersmith. I never worked on route 260 for the reason explained in the next chapter. The 645 was taken over by another new route, the 245 which ran between North Finchley and Stanmore Station – we played no part in its operation. A few days after the trolleys had finished at FY, service vehicles turned up and took away all the remaining electrical, mechanical and bodywork spares. These went back into stock, though no doubt many of the parts ended up at Fulwell where they would have been used on some of the ex-Finchley trolleybuses.

Three of the Finchley trolleybuses that went down to Fulwell at stage thirteen were fortunate enough to go straight into service there. The other eleven were parked up, trolley booms stowed. Delicensing took place immediately – in essence they were finished. However, to give Fulwell a bit of leeway with regard to vehicle availability, 1464 was reinstated. Recommissioning and relicensing occurred on 11th January. 1464 gained a celebrity reputation in London; she had been Poplar depot's last trolleybus on 11th November 1959, and the last 521 around the Holborn loop on 7th November 1961 – this meant that she was the last to operate in the City of London. It appears that she was the last to turn at Cricklewood St Gabriels Church on the evening of 2nd January 1962. As already mentioned, 1464 later operated the last 645 through journey from Barnet to Canons Park. She worked at Fulwell until the last day of operation of trolleybuses in London, 8th May 1962. There was no escape after that; she was sold to George Cohen's, the firm who broke up the trolleybuses during the conversion period.

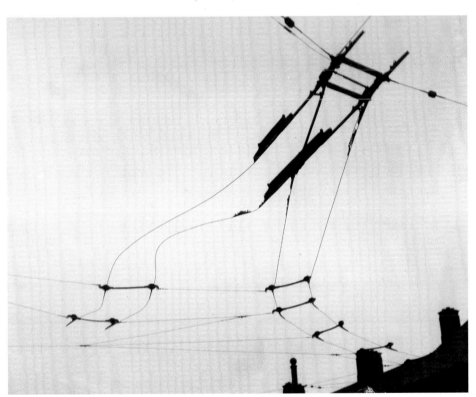

Above If fate had had its way I would have been the last man to drive 1464 in service. Fate did not have its way and after a few days in store at Fulwell depot, it was resurrected and operated there until 8th May 1962 (the last day of trolleybuses in London). 1464 has just passed Twickenham station on its way to Hammersmith Broadway on route 667. In the right foreground, a London United Tramways style information flag is fixed to a traction standard; it directs people to where they can board buses for Hammersmith and Shepherds Bush. If the sign writer was 'on the ball' he would have stated that they would be travelling by trolleybus not bus. *Fred Ivey.*

George Cohen and Son won the contract to scrap the trolleybus fleet and to remove the overhead wires and traction poles during the conversion programme. They would cut down the mainline cleanly but when it came to frogs and crossovers there tended to be a general untidiness about the situation as shown by this picture at Edgware in March 1962. *Hugh Taylor.*

Having just entered what in effect is still the trolleybus station, a guard of honour stands in front of 1468; the Mayor of Finchley (councillor F.D.Gibson) is one of a number of people carrying fog flares. Due to the posh way that he spoke, one of our drivers was nicknamed 'The Lord Mayor of Finchley'. *Finchley Times*.

LIFE AFTER FINCHLEY

After I had gained my PSV badge, I was speaking to Len Munney in the Finchley depot canteen one day – he was having a cup of tea in between journeys on route 125. Len worked at Muswell Hill garage and lived at North Finchley while I worked at Finchley and lived near Muswell Hill. I had known him for some time and in the course of conversation we wondered that now that the trolleys were going, could we transfer workplaces, and be nearer our homes? Instances of trolleybus staff transferring from motorbuses to trolleybuses and vice-versa were rare; moves between the two sections were not normally permitted. Besides, the staff shortage meant that each depot and garage wanted to hang onto what staff they had. Len and I approached the TGWU who wangled a mutual transfer for us. The move would not be permitted until after the trolleybuses had gone – this was because I was of use to Finchley until then while Len was not. Although Finchley depot had been a good place to work, personal convenience was more important now. The Finchley guvn'r called me into his office about 5th January and told me that our transfer had been approved and would take effect from 17th January 1962 – exactly two weeks after the trolleys had gone. When I walked out of the garage on 16th January, a vestige of the trolleybuses remained – the overhead was still aloft.

I turned up at Muswell Hill garage at 7.30am on 17th January and reported to Norman, one of the garage inspectors. I already knew him as years before he had been a revenue inspector. He looked at his paperwork and on seeing that I was now on MH's books, told me to go to the canteen and get a cup of tea. At about 11.30 he said that a route 43 bus was parked out of service at the southbound relief stop adjacent to Hampden Road in Colney Hatch Lane. It needed to be run into the garage; he told me to bring it in and that I could then go home.

The routes operated by MH at the time were: 43 Friern Barnet to London Bridge, 134 Pimlico, Dolphin Square to Potters Bar Station, 134A Victoria to Barnet, Chesterfield Road (Sundays), 210 Golders Green to Finsbury Park, 212 Muswell Hill Broadway to Finsbury Park, 244 Muswell Hill Broadway to Winchmore Hill, Station Road and 251 Arnos Grove to Burnt Oak. For a time, in Monday to Friday peak hours, the 212 had Express buses in addition to the stopping service (I enjoyed these as only a few stops were made between the two termini).

The 43, 134/134A, 212 and 244 were worked with RTs, while the 210 and 251 had RFs. Routes 134 and 134A were shared with other garages. Even though RFs had a pre-selector gearbox which I was now used to, I was given type

training on them, as I had to get used to the front overhang when turning around corners. I had an hour or so with an instructor to acclimatise myself.

Between 18th and 23rd January, I covered parts of duties and did my route learning. I was familiar with much of the area of Muswell Hill's routes, so it was pointless going over the parts I knew. However, a record was kept of drivers knowing the routes from the garage they worked at and was monitored by conductors signing route learning slips. I said to various conductors, "Sign this for me will you, please", which of course they did. I then made myself scarce! As the 609 had paralleled the 43 between Highgate and Moorgate, I needed to know which streets it used from there. I asked Johnny Foskett what roads to take. He told me "Straight down Moorgate, turn left at the Bank of England, along Princes Street to Mansion House, across the junction, continue up King William Street, turn right past the Monument on the left and across London Bridge. Once over the bridge, turn left into the station just past Duke Street Hill – the 43 stand is the one nearest to the station entrance". I didn't know how to get from Victoria to Pimlico on the 134, so had to go down there. I took my eldest daughter Julie with me to give her a ride. I did the Chesterfield Road part of the 134A another time.

I took up a service on route 43 on Wednesday 24th January. Two months later I changed my rota line and was paired up with conductress Pat Rowe. I already knew of her, as Jean had pointed her out to me, saying that she was her younger sister's best friend. This was when we had been working on the Archway Road five years previously (Jean and I were on the 609s and Pat on the 43s). I later found out that Bert Rowe, a driving colleague of mine at Finchley was her father. Pat and I had wanted a change of scenery in 1964 and went on the 134s (there were also some 212 duties on its rota).

At Muswell Hill I was introduced to motorbusmen's terms. One was 'Domino load' – this meant that a full load of passengers was being carried. Its origins are not known. At Finchley I had been used to overtime being called 'bridging'; now it was referred to as a 'bit of corn' – corn meant wheat which put bread on the table. Working a day off was known as 'one for the Queen' – this meant that working the extra day paid the taxman for the whole week. It was a figure of speech and came nowhere near it in reality. A common terminology used for running close to a bus in front was 'measuring him off'.

Trolleybuses and Routemasters had matching fleet and registration numbers; this was not so with RFs and RTs. I was used to glancing at the registration number of a trolleybus if I could not see its fleet number and would know which vehicle it was. I do recall, though, the first bus I drove in service on route 43; it was RT 1926. With a registration number of LUC 6, I dubbed it Lucky Six. A big difference between a bus and a trolleybus was that the latter just had the hum of the motor and MG set; motorbuses emitted a loud engine noise. There was a distinct aura of cleanliness about a trolleybus – motorbuses often smelt of oil and diesel.

I was the first of the Finchley staff to move to Muswell Hill after the trolleys came off. A few followed afterwards, Les Strutt being one of them. With the trolleybus conversion programme seeing drivers and conductors obtaining a PSV licence, there was the opportunity to transfer to a workplace that was nearer to their home. Former trolleybus staff applied for and obtained positions at bus garages across the fleet. As well as the FY/MH move-about, Colindale staff, who moved to Cricklewood to work on routes 245 and 266 when CE closed, immediately applied for, and obtained, a transfer to Edgware as a number of them lived in that vicinity.

Having been trained on Routemasters came in handy early in 1963, as one needed to be moved up at London Bridge. There was no sign of the driver and it was fast becoming an obstruction. At the time few people had been type-trained on them, so an inspector was very relieved that I was able to move it for him.

The snows of 1962/1963 were worse than the previous year and on Boxing Day 1962, Pat and I had a duty on the 210s (there was some work on this route on the 43 rota). Road conditions were so bad that there were no 134s to take us to Archway relief point. Six of us (three conductors and three drivers, including Pat and myself) walked the three miles from Muswell Hill to Archway to take over our 210s there.

I had been used to a consistency of routes on trolleybuses. At Muswell Hill there was a continual chopping and changing of services and vehicle types. The first of these occurred in February 1963, when the allocation on the 251 was replaced by extra duties on the 134. We were also given Sunday work on the 102s which ran from Golders Green to Chingford, Royal Forest Hotel. At the same time, the 210 was extended on Sundays to Leyton High Road (Hainault Road). Due to demolition in the Leyton area, it was difficult to find the way through the ever-changing roadways. Route 236 was withdrawn on this day of the week and the 210 became jointly operated by Tottenham, Leyton and Muswell Hill garages on Sundays. The 210 was cut back to Leytonstone Station in September 1968 and then to Finsbury Park in January 1970. Standing out from the rest of the buses at MH were thirteen green RFs that came to us in January 1969 – they were painted red later in the year. Just as I had seen route 609 trolleybuses as a boy and then drove them as a man, the same applied when it came to route 102. I remember seeing Guy utility buses with wooden seats on that route just after the war – now I would be driving buses on the 102.

After the trolleybuses had been replaced, London Transport embarked on a programme of replacing RTs with RMs. This commenced in December 1962 and focused on routes operating in inner London. Routes 43 and 134 came into this remit. Type training was given for the RMs but as I was already familiar with them I waived the option, as did the

other former FY drivers at Muswell Hill. The RMs started to operate at MH in June 1963. More came in 1964 and were to be seen on the other routes at weekends.

A feature of London Transport operations was the extension of a small number of bus routes on summer Saturday, Sunday and Bank Holiday afternoons and evenings to places of interest. They weren't tourist attractions as we would think of today, but places where families could spend some leisure time. One of the services coming into this category was the 102, which was projected at these times along Rangers Road and Epping New Road to High Beach, 'Kings Oak' – eleven minutes running time to and from the 'Royal Forest'. The first day that MH worked to High Beach was 12th May 1963. For just a few weeks, Muswell Hill RTs reached this location. At the start of each summer season, a route learning bus was laid on for new drivers to learn the section from Chingford to High Beach. For some reason (maybe I was on holiday) I missed this.

The 43 rota had some 102 work on it. The day came when I had to go to High Beach. I had an idea of how to get there but told the inspector at the Royal Forest that I didn't know exactly where the turning for High Beach was. He said "Carry straight on until Epping New Road comes in from your right, turn left and after about 150 yards you'll see a signpost for High Beach on your left". I saw a small signpost pointing to High Beach and took this route. It ran parallell to the main road for a couple of hundred yards and then started to climb upwards into the forest. The road became a dirt track and the trees overhanging the road were now too low for the RM. Realising that the Inspector had misdirected me and that I was on the wrong road, I got Pat to see me back between the trees to retrace my steps. A police car turned up at this point, as from the main road they had seen a bus being turned round in the middle of nowhere and came to see what was going on. When I told them what had happened they just laughed and guided me to High Beach – the terminus was in the car park at the rear of the Kings Oak pub.

The summer extension to High Beach was from May to October. At the height of the season a lot of people were carried – not enough to fill a bus but still good loadings. As the daylight hours shortened, fewer people went there so that by October we were only carrying fresh air. London Transport's way of working meant that summer schedules stayed in for a specific period, and come hell or high water, would not change until the winter schedules came in on their appointed day. The implementation of the winter schedules was extensively delayed in 1964, and led to the summer schedule continuing into November. 102s plodded up to High Beach in the fog and mist – a waste of fuel and everybody's time. What was the point of a 102 leaving High Beach at 10.52 pm on a Sunday evening in November? Engines were supposed to be switched off at a terminus, but they weren't on these late night trips for fear of not being able to start the bus again. The staff shortage led to the withdrawal of summer extensions and 1964 was the last year that the 102s ran to this point.

In January 1970, the long established route 13, which ran from Golders Green to Aldwych, came to MH; we only worked it on Mondays to Fridays. Six RMs and ten duties were put on the 43 rota, which we reverted back to in 1972. Prior to this, on 16th January 1971, route 43 changed from RM to RML; most came from Finchley garage and were from the batch supplied to FY when the trolleybuses came off in November 1961. Even though they were only two feet six inches longer than the RM, the TGWU insisted drivers had type training on them. Again, I didn't take up the opportunity to do this as I had driven them nine years previously and considered it unnecessary. Most 13s were operated by Hendon garage. MH was a long way from Golders Green and to enable the duties to come within the working hours agreement, there were times when they ran out of service to and from Golders Green. We went along the North Circular Road to Henlys Corner, and then down the Finchley Road. In service we went via the 102 route, through East Finchley and Falloden Way. If passengers wanted to, they could travel from Muswell Hill to Aldwych. Of the routes I worked on at MH, I preferred the 13. There was always something going on – a procession, hold-up, diversion, bomb scare. The RMs were upgraded to RML in October 1975. I was on the 13s on the last day that Muswell Hill operated the route – 27th October 1978. Starting in December 1973, Daimler Fleetlines worked as crew buses on routes 43 and 134. Although they were not popular, they stayed for a number of years, Routemasters ousting them from September 1982.

Pat and I stayed together as a crew until February 1984 (almost twenty-two years) when she became a counter

assistant at Finchley garage. I had to go to her assistance one day as a hefty young bloke was threatening to punch her over a fare dispute. Jumping out of the cab, I went round the back, came up behind him, grabbed him, got him down on to a seat and stopped him getting out. Pat called the police who turned up quickly. No charges were brought and no damage done.

Incidents on motorbuses were far less numerous than on trolleybuses. Nevertheless, it is worth relating a few. At London Bridge, a Ministry of Transport inspector told me one day not to drive a bus any further. He had found a major fault on a random check and slapped what was known as a PSV71 on it – that made it unfit for service. The garage was called, and two engineers arrived with a substitute bus. To prevent people boarding, a strong band with PRIVATE marked on it, was strung between the handrail on the nearside of the bus and the rail at the back. Taking the band off, it was put on the 'miscreant' which they took back to Muswell Hill. I drove the other one back in service. On another occasion when I was driving an RT on route 212, a nearside rear spring broke when travelling down Crouch Hill. They say that trouble comes in threes, so the hat trick occurred when a nearside rear tyre blew out when working on route 43 at Princes Street by the Bank of England.

Although I would pass some of my former Finchley colleagues on the 104s, this receded as some of them left the job or retired. The only other time I saw a few of them was when I went back there during my inspecting days. Such was the decline in bus operation in London that Muswell Hill closed in July 1990, and Finchley in December 1993. Both have since been demolished. I never thought I would see such mass destruction of what to me, in my boyhood, was a magnificent London Transport.

The last time I drove a London Transport bus (a Routemaster) was Saturday 24th August 1985 – duty 27 on route 134. Rest on Sunday and Bank Holiday Monday. Report to Chiswick Works on Tuesday for training as a silver badge road inspector. Having passed out in this grade, I worked in Leaside district in north London, so was reasonably familiar with its area. My main responsibility was to ensure that the routes under my control were operating regularly. This was often difficult at Tottenham and Enfield garages, Golders Green, Muswell Hill Broadway, Stamford Hill and Barnet Church, so I had to familiarise myself with the curtailment points of these routes. The job was totally different to driving, but nonetheless interesting. Due to cut-backs I was offered and accepted voluntary severance. My last day working for London Transport was 6th June 1987. I then applied for a position as a postman with the Royal Mail (formerly the GPO). They re-engaged me on 9th November 1987. The wheel had gone full circle. I retired on 7th September 1995, my sixty-fifth birthday.

It is Friday 27th October 1978, the last day that Muswell Hill garage operated on route 13. Pat Rowe and myself are photographed in front of RML 897 prior to our last trip from Golders Green to Aldwych. Note that I am displaying both my trolleybus and motorbus badges. *Charlie Wyatt junior.*

THE FINAL WORD

I drove buses for almost thirty years, from November 1955 until August 1985. If I was able to do it all over again it would be with the trolleybus, for I considered it to be the best passenger carrying vehicle. The trolley may have been old fashioned by today's standards, but used correctly it gave a much better ride than a motorbus. It was environmentally friendly and very quiet-running.

I was sorry to see the passing of the trolleybus as it had been a good friend to me. Trolleybus days were really good times. If I could go back to December 1961, see an RM, an RT and a trolleybus parked in Finchley depot and be asked which vehicle I would like to take out, I would not hesitate to climb into the cab of the trolley. In my opinion anyone could drive a bus, but it was an art to drive a trolleybus.

The J class trolleybuses were my favourites and it is painful to see this view of 927 which Jean Blackwell dubbed the 'snow bus'; I wonder what she'd have called it if she saw it in this state in Colindale scrapyard. The upper deck has been ripped off ready for the vultures to dismantle its remains; the bottom deck will soon be cut up too. If it wasn't for the fact that the registration plate hadn't been removed, 927 would have been unrecognisable. *Jim Wyndham.*

Left to right in Finchley depot on Sunday 5th November 1961 are Muswell Hill's RT 2616 which is having some stand time while working on route 125, Finchley depot's 1488, and yet-to-be christened RML 880. An enthusiasts' tour is taking place and the three vehicles have been lined up for a comparison shot. These three types of vehicle were operating simultaneously between 8th November 1961 and 2nd January 1962 at Finchley – this was the only place on the London Transport network where this occurred. *Mike Abbott.*